Ulrich Schulz · Wulf Albers
Ulrich Mueller (Eds.)

Social Dilemmas
and Cooperation

Contributors:

W. Albers, D. V. Budescu, A. Crettenden, A. Diekmann, T. Doi, I. Erev,
I. Eshel, M. Foddy, A. Franzen, R. Gardner, W. Güth, N. Hayashi, N.
Jin, D. M. Kuhlmann, B. Latané, M. Lewenstein, W. B. G. Liebrand,
R. M. Meertens, D. M. Messick, H. Ch. Micko, A. Nowack, H. Okuda,
A. Ostmann, E. Ostrom, A. Rapoport, K. Ritzberger, E. Sansone,
R. Suleiman, N. Takahashi, T. Takigawa, E. Van Dijk, P. A. M. Van
Lange, M. Van Vugt, R. Vollmeyer, J. Walker, M. Watabe, D.
Weinshall, H. Wilke, T. Yamagishi

Springer-Verlag
Berlin Heidelberg New York
London Paris Tokyo
Hong Kong Barcelona
Budapest

Professor Dr. Ulrich Schulz
Universität Bielefeld
Abteilung für Psychologie
Postfach 10 01 31
D-33501 Bielefeld, FRG

Professor Dr. Wulf Albers
Universität Bielefeld
Institut für Mathematische Wirtschaftsforschung
Postfach 10 01 31
D-33501 Bielefeld, FRG

PD Dr. Dr. Ulrich Mueller
ZUMA, Zentrum für Umfragen, Methoden und Analysen
Postfach 12 21 55
D-68072 Mannheim, FRG

With 53 Figures

ISBN 3-540-57757-2 Springer-Verlag Berlin Heidelberg New York Tokyo
ISBN 0-387-57757-2 Springer-Verlag New York Berlin Heidelberg Tokyo

© Springer-Verlag Berlin · Heidelberg 1994
Printing in Germany

42/2202-5 4 3 2 1 0 - Printed on acid-free paper

Preface

Imagine a situation with two or more players who each have the choice among at least two courses of action, not necessarily the same for all players. Suppose these courses of action or strategies have different effects on own and other's outcomes. Assume there are only two relevant types of strategies: a cooperative strategy, which gives reasonable payoffs to all players, and an individualistic or defective strategy, which gives defectors a somewhat higher payoff, but essentially lower payoffs to the others, in a way that the total sum of payoffs of the group is reduced. With other words: the solution of this game is inefficient. Such a situation is called a social dilemma.

This book poses two basic questions that are closely interlinked:

1. How is cooperation possible among rational players in a social dilemma?

Which changes in the social context of the dilemma situation are necessary in order to make it rational to choose the cooperative option? For human societies as a whole these changes can be the result of an evolution of the social structure and/or its biological basis. This raises the question, under which conditions the evolution of cooperation in social dilemma situations is possible.

2. How do real players actually behave in social dilemma situations? Do they in fact behave "rationally"? Or, conversely, what kind of reasoning, attitudes, emotions, and so forth shape the behavior of real players in social dilemmas? What kind of interventions, what kind of internal mechanisms within a real group may change players' willingness to cooperate?

The subject is not only of interest for basic research, but also of great practical importance. Here are a few examples:

- In a world of voluntary conservationists, the easiest option for me is to pollute the environment at will: The impact on the environment will be negligible;
- in a world of unconditional pacifism, I can take what I desire by force;
- if everybody uses public transportation, I can speed down the roads with my car as fast as I like;
- if everybody is vaccinated against some human-host-only virus, the safest choice for me is evading vaccination: I avoid the health risks of vaccination itself and need not be afraid of being infected with the virus.

But how, then, in the absence of a benevolent and omnipotent dictator, can it be ensured that the environment is not polluted, peace is maintained, roads are not jammed, children do not remain unprotected against measles menigitis?

What is addressed in social dilemma research is a central problem of classical Western philosophy from antiquity on: How is social order possible? How can people be brought to live and work together in peace and order, if human nature is selfish and greedy, and the resulting natural state-of-affairs among people is violence and anarchy?

There have been two types of answer to this question: The answer given by philosophers from Plato to Rousseau is: Social order is possible by the right kind of education, which enables people to overcome their evil, individualistic drives.

The other answer was given by philosophers from Hobbes to Kant: Social order is possible through the right kind of constitution, which forces people to act cooperatively despite their evil drives because of the threat of punishment if they do not.

Both answers cannot give a convincing reply to the question of how the evolution of the proposed solution from the natural state of affairs is possible: "Who educates the educators?" in the first case, and "Who shall be the guardian of the constitution?" in the second. How in a world of egoists, is an education and a constitution possible that will enforce cooperation in social dilemmas?

For a long time, the conventional answer to the question - how is the evolution of cooperation possible - was group selection: Those groups/communities/cities/nations that do not accomplish the establishment of social order, by means of appropriate education and constitution, will loose against those who do. Quite along these lines of thinking, evolutionary theory until the 1960s has argued that non-violent intraspecific competition about resources and mates, and even true cooperation among non- relatives has evolved because species who acquired these traits, were more successfull from an evolutionary point of view than those who did not.

The problem is, however, that group selection of cooperativeness necessarily requires the total population to be subdivided in subpopulations (i.e. communities), and that group selection wipes out non-cooperating communities faster than non- cooperators within communities wipe out cooperators.

After some decades of controversy, we know that despite some rare exceptions, group selection alone cannot account for the stable evolution of cooperation among humans and other higher animals (see S.A. Boorman and P.R. Levitt *The Genetics of Altruism* 1980; R.D. Alexander *The Biology of Moral Systems* 1987). The evolution of cooperativeness between non-relatives can be only the result of individual selection, and it therefore requires the concommitant evolution of suitable cognitive and emotional potentials that allow us to form groups and organize our relations within these groups in a way which makes cooperation the rational choice.

The two general questions: - when is it rational to cooperate in social dilemmas? and - how do people actually behave in social dilemma situations? mark the broad spectrum of the problem, that has been investigated in various disciplines over the last decades. These introduced many new ideas and new observations into the study of the the old question of social order in a world of born egoists. Accordingly, this volume contains contributions by biologists, sociologists, political scientists, economists, mathematicans, psychologists, philosophers.

A number of contributions deal with theoretical refinements of the choice problem itself in order to make it model real life social dilemmas more closely. What the fruitfly *Drosophila Melanogaster* is for genetics, the Prisoner's Dilemma is for the study of social dilemmas and cooperation. Starting from its most primitive version as a symmetrical one-shot Two-Person Game, it can be refined in various ways into an asymmetrical, an interated, and/or a N-Person Game. It can be replaced by other social dilemma games: the Chicken-Game, the Volunteer's Dilemma, the Battle-of-sexes Game. The two-choice scenario can be replaced by a continuous-contribution choice scenario, arriving at the public goods problem of political economy. More complicated contribution functions can be conceived of even more complicated contribution functions, and even stochastic elements into choices of players and/or outcomes of choices.

Another dimension of refinement of the basic model refers to the cognitive abilities with which the players are endowed. Will they be able to distinguish among players, actions, payoffs? What kind of insight into the rules of the game shall they have? How expensive shall the acquisition of all this information be? Shall they be payoff-maximizers or shall they be modeled as being satisfied once a certain payoff threshold has been reached?

Then how is group structure operationalized? Is communication among players allowed, and if so, communication about what? How long shall the group stay together - in terms of moves or in terms of real time? Are players allowed to have different endowments or different powers? Is bargaining allowed, and since all bargaining hinges on the enforcability of contracts - what kind of enforcement will be possible?

All these dimensions for refining the theoretical model can also be read as research design dimensions for empirical studies: How do real players behave if the game is asymmetrical versus symmetrical; iterated versus one-shot; stochastic versus deterministic; if binary versus continuous choices are available; if communication is possible versus not possible; if there is a power structure in the group or not; if the group stays together for some time or not; if defection can be hidden versus cannot be hidden, and so forth.

These questions can be approached in theoretical studies, in analytical paper-and-pencil or in computer-based simulation studies, by running experiments with real animals or real people in the laboratory, or by observing what real players do in real life situations. The reader will find examples of all these approaches in this book, which gives an impression of the state of the art of this rich and fast-evolving field.

The volume presents papers from two conferences held at Bielefeld during the summer of 1992. The first was the workshop on "Models for the Development of Cooperation: Game Theoretic, Evolutionary, and Behavioral Perspectives" held at the University of Bielefeld with the support of the Center for Interdisciplinary Research (ZiF). The second was the "Fifth International Conference on Social Dilemmas" supported by the German National Science Foundation (DFG), the Minister of Science and Research of the state of North Rhine-Westphalia, and the German Academic Exchange Service (DAAD). The subject of both conferences was cooperation in social systems from the perspectives of game theory, biology, sociology, social psychology and philosophy. As organizers of both conferences, the editors selected suitable papers for this publication. All selected papers - extended and refined versions of the original presentations - went through an anonymous review process with a least two reviewers for each paper. This volume presents the revised versions of the papers. We wish to thank the reviewers and the authors for the willingness to engage in this arduous review process.

Heike Hartwig-Jakobs and Wolfgang Haase were responsible for the enormous task of editing the texts and producing the layout of the book. We appreciate their competent and dedicated work.

Bielefeld, October 1993

Ulrich Schulz

Wulf Albers

Ulrich Mueller

Contents

Social orientation analysis of the common and individual interest problems

Toshiaki Doi[1]

Abstract

The purpose of this chapter is to show a new way to see social dilemmas and to explain people's decision making in social dilemmas. The key concept in our analysis is social orientation. We will apply the social orientation analysis, as was done for 2x2 matrix games, to an analysis of decision making by people in social dilemmas. To do so, we will present new formulations for the two types of social dilemmas: "free rider" and "tragedy of the common." Our analysis will show how our formulations are different from, interrelated with, and superior to the payoff matrix expression. Furthermore, we will also show how the two types of social dilemmas are different, how social dilemma situations are normalized, and how people's decision making can be explained using a social orientation model.

Social orientation: A model of a person

What is social orientation?

The concept of social orientation refers to how much a person cares about another person's interests (gains or losses). This concept clarifies the purpose or aim of a person who has to make a choice in an interdependent situation. For example, a cooperative orientation is supposed to lead a person to maximize the sum of his/her own and the other person's payoffs, while a competitive orientation seeks to maximize the difference between his/her own and the other's payoffs. An individualistic orientation is thought to lead a person to maximize his/her own payoff, neglecting that of the other person. Naturally, different goals lead people to different courses of action. Therefore, social orientation is considered to be an important factor in the decision making processes of people in interdependent situations.

An additive model of social orientation

The importance of social orientation in explaining the choices made by people seems to have been originally pointed out by Deutsch (1960). Attention to this concept increased considerably following work by Messick and McClintock (1968). Although many studies have been conducted on social orientation, most of them have been limited to an investigation of a few specific types of social orientation, such as the cooperative, competitive, and individualistic orientations mentioned above.

However, Griesinger, and Livingstone (1973) showed that there could be numerous different orientations, introducing the hypothesis that a person makes his/her choices so as to maximize the weighted sum of his/her own and the other person's payoffs. In their model, X represents the payoff to a particular person, and Y represents the payoff to the other person. An alternatives of choice is expressed by (x_i , y_i). The social orientation of a person is expressed by a and b, where a and b represent the weights to his/her own and the other person's payoffs, respectively. A person is supposed to make choices so as to maximize $ax_i + by_i$.

Furthermore, they showed that social orientation can be expressed geometrically in two dimensional space with coordinates X and Y , as shown in Fig.1. Any alternative of choice can be expressed by a point (x_i , y_i), and the social orientation of a person is expressed by the direction of the third axis M, in X-Y space. This direction is given by a and b. A person is supposed to choose the alternative that gives the highest m_i on M. In other words, m_i is considered to express the attractiveness (or subjective value) that a person feels for the alternative of choice (x_i , y_i).

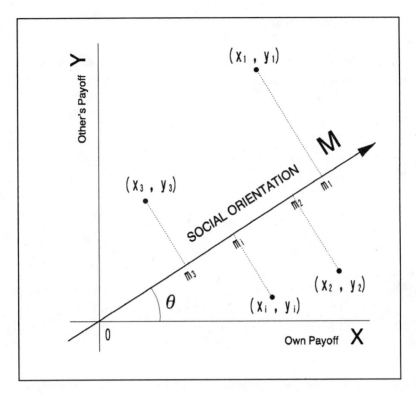

Figure 1:   Geometrical expression of social orientation.

Doi and Imai (1986) showed that m_i can be expressed by equation (1).

$$m_i = x_i \cos\theta + y_i \sin\theta \tag{1}$$

In other words, m_i is given by $ax_i + by_i$, where $a = \cos\theta$ and $b = \sin\theta$. The direction of the M axis is described by either b/a (the slope of M), or simply by θ (the angle between M and X). There are numerous pairs of a and b that give the same direction to M. However, there is only one θ that gives a particular direction to M. Therefore, θ seems to be superior to a pair of a and b in expressing the direction of M. We will use θ to express the social orientation of a person in our analysis.

A model of a person: State or trait?

Some directions of M are given the interpretations shown below, including the three examples of social orientation previously discussed.

θ	interpretation	m_i	maximizing (or minimizing)
90°	altruism	y_i	other's payoff
45°	cooperation	$\dfrac{(x_i + y_i)}{\sqrt{2}}$	sum of own and other's payoff
0°	individualism	x_i	own payoff
−45°	competition	$\dfrac{(x_i - y_i)}{\sqrt{2}}$	difference of own and other's payoff
−90°	aggression	$-y_i$	(minimizing) other's payoff

It is basically a personal matter what to maximize in a given situation. Therefore, θ is thought to describe the internal state of a person at the moment of decision making. If each person has his/her own value of θ, there will be individual differences in θ among people. Furthermore, it is very likely that the value of θ is affected by a variety of factors, such as the way the choice situations are shown to a person, whether payoffs are monetary or not, the amount of information available about the other person, the interactional experience with the other person, etc. However, we consider that every person has a basic direction of M, which is not affected by the above factors, and is relatively stable. This basic direction will form the basic choice attitude of a person in an interdependent situation. In this regard, the basic direction is considered to be a personal trait or disposition. Various factors are considered to cause fluctuation in the direction of M around the basic direction. This basic direction and the fluctuation around it form the actual internal state of a person. Therefore, we can treat social orientation θ in two different ways: as a trait of a person which is relatively stable over various situations, or as an internal state of a person at the moment of decision.

Equation (1) shows us clearly which alternative a person will choose according to his/her θ. Thus, we can regard equation (1) as a model of a person in an interdependent situation. This model indicates that we can predict how a person will make choices in a given situation, if we knew his/her value of θ. Furthermore, the expression of social orientation by θ makes it possible to deal with a variety of orientations in a single dimension, quantitatively. This quantitative nature of θ makes it possible to analyze the choice making of people in interdependent situations, intensively and systematically, as we will see in the next section.

Social orientation analysis of 2x2 matrix games

Doi and Imai (1986) applied equation (1) directly to the 2x2 symmetric matrix games shown in Fig.2.

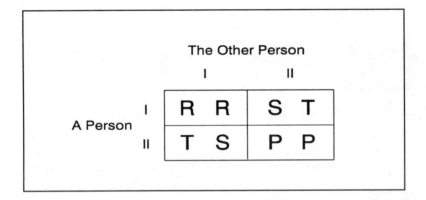

Figure 2:   2x2 symmetric payoff matrix (it is usually expressed so as to satisfiy $T > S$).

They analyzed mathematically the relative dominance of alternatives across various values of θ. In their analysis, they derived two variables which are given by equations (2a) and (2b).

$$V = \frac{R + T - S - P}{T - S} \tag{2a}$$

$$U = \frac{R - T - S + P}{T - S} \tag{2b}$$

They showed that these two variables are crucial for the characterization of 2x2 payoff matrices and the explanation of people's choice making for those matrices. The results of their analysis are summarized as follows:

(1) Payoff matrices are normalized by V and U. That is, those matrices that share the same V and U are equivalent decision making situations. Since the essential features of the given matrix can be expressed by V and U, it is possible to express any matrix by one point in the 2-dimensional space, where the two coordinates are V and U. Equivalent matrices are expressed by the same point in this V-U space. Doi & Imai called V and U characteristic values of the payoff matrices, and the V-U space, characteristic space.

Furthermore, the classification of 2x2 matrix games by Rapoport & Guyer (1966) is shown geometrically in V-U space in Fig.3. The famous games, such as "Prisoner's dilemma," "Maximizing difference," and "Chicken" will be found in one of 12 regions.

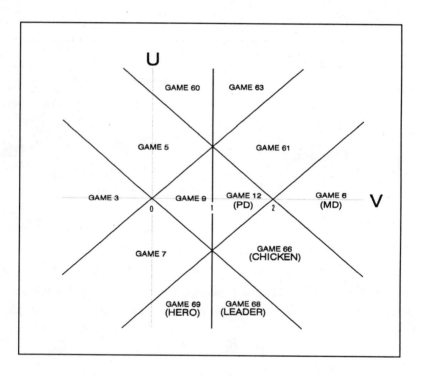

Figure 3:   12 games classified by Rapoport & Guyer (1966) in V-U space.

(2) The relative dominance of alternatives can be displayed geometrically in V-U space, as is shown in Fig.4. The whole space is divided into four regions by the two lines given in equations (3a) and (3b).

$$V + U = \frac{2\cos\theta}{\cos\theta + \sin\theta} \tag{3a}$$

$$V - U = \frac{2\cos\theta}{\cos\theta + \sin\theta} \tag{3b}$$

Alternative I dominates alternative II in region A, and II dominates I in region C. That is, a person should choose alternative I if the given matrix is in region A, and II if it is in region C. Neither alternative dominates the other in region B or D.

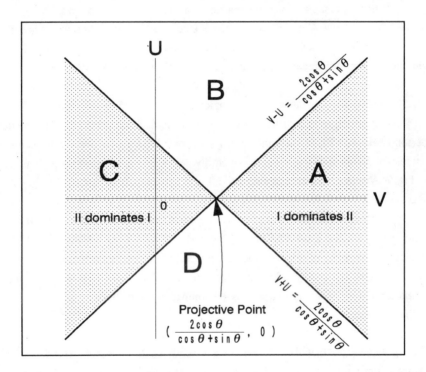

Figure 4:   Dominancy of two alternatives in 2x2 payoff matrix.

(3) The intersection of lines (3a) and (3b) in $V-U$ space is expressed by the coordinates $(\ v(\theta)\ , 0\ )$, where $v(\theta)$ is given by equation (4).

$$v(\theta) = \frac{2\cos\theta}{\cos\theta + \sin\theta} \tag{4}$$

That is, the intersecting point is uniquely determined by θ, and always stays on the V axis. $v(\theta)$ is a monotonically decreasing function of θ. For example, $v(-45°) = \infty$, $v(0°) = 2$, $v(45°) = 1$, and $v(90°) = 0$. Therefore, the division of the space by two lines moves to the right or left according to the value of θ. It appears as if the social orientation of a person is projected on the point ($v(\theta)$, 0) in $V-U$ space. Doi and Imai called this point ($v(\theta)$, 0) the projected point of θ, and $v(\theta)$ the projected value of θ.

When a person is given the matrix expressed by the projected point ($V(\theta)$, 0) in the space, the two alternatives are indifferent. Then, the two alternatives are indifferent to a cooperative person if V of the given matrix is equal to 1. Similarly, the two alternatives are indifferent to an individualistic person, when $V = 2$.

(4) There is no dominant alternative in region B or D. Therefore, a person needs some kind of decision principle to determine his/her choice. A decision principle refers to the way a person deals with uncertainty in a given situation. A particular decision principle will be expressed by an indifferent curve which divides $V-U$ space into two regions, as shown in Fig.5. A person will choose alternative I if the given matrices are in the right side of the space, and II if they are in the left side.

The indifferent curve drawn by a decision principle will stay in region B and D, passing through the projective point ($v(\theta)$, 0), if it does not violate the dominance principle. The shape of this curve is determined by the decision principle of a person, and it moves to the left or to the right according to the value of θ. That is, the choice making of a person for the given matrices is determined by both his/her social orientation and decision principle.

(5) Fig.4 indicates that the V axis always stays inside of region A and C. Therefore, choice making for various given matrices is determined only by θ if those matrices are chosen from the V axis. That is, for any matrix on V, a person should choose alternative I when

$$V > v(\theta) \tag{5a}$$

is held, and II when

$$V < v(\theta) \tag{5b}$$

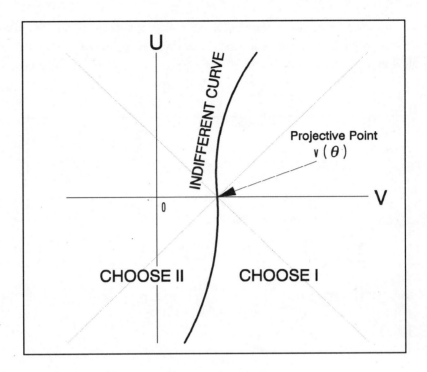

Figure 5: An example of an indifferent curve given by a decision principle which does not violate the dominance principle.

is held, if $-45° < \theta < 135°$ (the sign of the inequality should be reversed if $\theta < -45°$ or $135° < \theta$). In other words, choice making is determined by the comparison of two values: one from the given matrix, and the other from the internal state of a person.

Equation (5a) and (5b) indicate that a cooperative person will choose alternative I when $1 < V$, and II when $V < 1$. Similarly, an individualistic person will choose alternative I when $2 < V$, and II when $V < 2$. However, a competitive person will never choose alternative I, since $V(-45°) = \infty$.

(6) Social orientation is basically a personal state or trait. Therefore, if each person owns a different value of θ, we have to consider a distribution of θ for a group of people. If a series of matrices from the V axis are given to a group, our analysis allows us to predict the choice results for that group. That is, the proportion of the group choosing alternative I should be a monotonically increasing function of V, as shown in Fig.6. Doi and Imai

made clear that the choice proportion curve in Fig. 5 directly reflects the distribution of θ for people in the group. Furthermore, in their theoretical analysis, they derived the method to assess the distribution of θ for a group from the choice proportion curve in Fig.5.

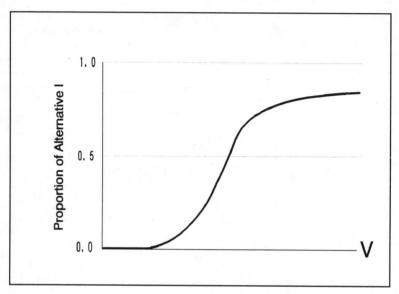

Figure 6: Proportion of alternative I of a group of people, given various matrices from V axis.

$V-U$ space happens to coincide with the 2-dimensional space discussed in Harris (1968). However, his coordinate system is different from that of $V-U$ space. If we rotate it 45 degrees, the $V-U$ coordinate system will coincide with that of Harris' space. The $V-U$ system and Harris' system are equivalent for the purpose of displaying the classification of 2x2 matrix games by Rapoport. However, it is not our purpose to express the classification of matrix games. $V-U$ space is derived from a theoretical analysis and is found to be useful for the explanation of people's decision making in matrix games--our purpose.

Summarized results of the social orientation analysis indicate that V and U are particularly convenient and effective for the characterization of payoff matrices and for explaining the decision making of people; especially since the characteristic value V of a matrix is closely related to the social orientation θ of a person. Furthermore, V and U are closely related to the expression of common and individual interest problems, as we shall see later. In this regard, the $V-U$ coordinate system is superior to Harris' system.

However, the analyses by Doi and Imai were based on the model of a person described by equation (1). Therefore, the $V-U$ coordinate system is only effective for analyses based on that equation. Then, the question is, whether equation (1) is really valid for the explanation of decision making by real people, or not. In their theoretical analysis, Doi and Imai made clear that the validity of equation (1) could be confirmed if we obtained data as shown in Fig.5. Experimental studies carefully conducted by Doi (1988, 1990) support the validity of equation (1). He also showed that it is possible to assess the distribution of θ for a group from the experimental data, utilizing the assessment method derived by Doi and Imai. Therefore, the practicality of their assessment method was also verified.

Social dilemmas of common and individual interest: Free rider and the tragedy of the common

Common or social interest is defined as any interest that, if it is given to a person in a group, no other person can be excluded or kept from sharing it (Olson, 1965). There are social dilemmas that emerges when the achievement of common and individual interests are incompatible. A number of examples of such dilemmas have been identified, and various models to describe them have been proposed. They are basically classified into two types: "free rider" and "tragedy of the common." We can regard the first type of dilemmas as decision problems in the achievement of common (or social) benefit through individual cost, and the second type as problems in the achievement of individual benefit through common (or social) cost.

Free rider (collective action): Common (social) benefit through individual cost

The most popular examples of this type can be found in a national state or a labor union, which provide collective goods to all members of a group (Olson, 1965). Labor unions are expected to strive for higher wages and better conditions, which are common benefits for all members. No one is excluded from getting such benefits, but they are expected to expend their personal resources too, such as paying annual dues to the union. Such a personal contribution can be interpreted as an individual cost to achieve a common interest. Everybody is expected to pay his/her cost in order to achieve this interest. Therefore, this type of decision situation is called a "collective action" problem (Olson, 1965).

However, those who do not pay the cost can share the benefits achieved by the union. How voluntarily then does a person participate in the union by paying the personal cost? This kind of situation will be found in any group or organization whose goal or purpose is to achieve a common interest. The crucial aspect of this type of situation is that any person can share the common interest without paying his/her individual cost, as long as other people keep paying their individual costs. Therefore, this is often called the "free rider" problem.

Tragedy of the common: Individual benefit through common (social) cost

Overpopulation and pollution are examples of this type. As Hardin (1968) explained, the rational herdsman tries to keep as many cattle as possible on the common that is open to all. If every herdsman does the same, the result is overgrazing and a shortage of pasture, which results in "the tragedy of the common."

Overgrazing happens when the number of cattle exceeds the carrying capacity of the common. Everybody has to share the damage caused by overgrazing, if it happens, regardless of the number of cattle he/she keeps on the commons. Keeping more cattle on the common is of personal benefit to the owner of the cattle. Thus, we can regard the shortage of pasture as a common (social) cost of individuals keeping more cattle.

In the case of air pollution by cars, polluted air is considered to be the social cost of driving a car. Polluted air injures everybody's health. Everybody is forced to share this cost, regardless of whether he/she uses a car or not. On the other hand, driving a car is a personal benefit to a driver.

The above examples are situations where an increase in somebody's individual interest forces everybody to share the social cost of it. How is it likely that people will hesitate to increase their own cattle? The result of people's behavior in such situations is considered to be tragic. These types of situations will be found whenever people consume natural resources that are open to all. Examples of such situations, such as the greenhouse effect from carbon dioxide, ozone holes, destruction of the rain forest, and a variety of other environmental problems are ubiquitous on this planet.

The rational person in social dilemmas

Both free rider and tragedy of the common are situations described by common (social) interest and individual interest. The first type is the situation where social interest is positive, but individual interest is negative. The second type, on the other hand, is the situation where social interest is negative and individual interest is positive. Both common and individual interests appear only when people take a particular action in either type of situation. Abstaining from taking action just maintains the status quo--no common or individual interests is produced. In either type of social dilemma, people are facing a decision of whether to take a particular action or to maintain the current situation.

The first type has the following situational feature: When everybody takes action, the resultant social interest is far more than the individual cost, even if the increase in the social interest produced by a single person's action is very small. However, a person can be better off by not taking action. This is because he/she can share the social interest produced by other people's actions. Therefore, the rational person (in an economic sense) will be reluctant to take action, particularly when the social interest produced by that person's actions is less than his/her individual cost. That is, the rational person is a "free rider." If everybody wants a free ride, they will fail to achieve the social interest.

Similarly, when all the people take the action of the second type, the resultant social cost is far more than the individual benefit, even if the social cost of one individual's personal gain is extremely small. However, an individual can be better off by taking action. Therefore, the rational person will take the action. If everybody does so, everybody has to suffer the negative consequences--the "tragedy of the common."

From the point of view of the rational person, keeping the status quo is the preferable choice in the first type of situation, while taking action is preferable in the second type. However, rational people will fail to achieve the social interest in the first type, and they will suffer tragic consequences in the second type. On the other hand, if people make their decision contrary to the rational person's view, they can achieve social interest in the first type, and avoid tragedy in the second. Therefore, it is desirable, from a social stand point, for everybody to take action to produce the social benefit in the first type, and to keep the status quo to avoid tragic consequences in the second type.

The situational features described above are exactly the same as those of the "Prisoner's dilemma" game which has frequently been used in experimental game research. Such an understanding made many researchers pay more attention to N-person dilemma games, and both types of dilemmas are called "social dilemmas" (Dawes, 1980). Nevertheless, the two types of social dilemmas have their own situational features: that is, the productiveness of taking action and the stupidity of keeping the status quo in the "free rider" situation, and the destructiveness of taking action and wisdom of keeping the status quo in the "tragedy of the common." Hamburger (1973) noticed the difference in the situational features of the two types, and named the first type "construction" and the second type "conservation." Likewise, Platt (1973) called the first type "counter traps" or "social fences" and the second type "social traps."

Formulation of 2-person situations described by common and individual interest

We will try to analyze and explain people's behavior in the two types of social dilemmas by applying the social orientation analysis based on equation (1). To do so, we will formulate 2-person situations described by common interest and individual interest, since equation (1) is a model of a person in a two-person interdependent situation. We will present two types of formulations. They are simply called Type A and Type B.

In either type, a person has to make a decision, to take a particular action or not. Taking the action affects both common and individual interests, while not taking action simply maintains the status quo. Individual interest is restricted to be negative in Type A, and positive in Type B. That is, taking the action demands that a person pay an individual cost in Type A, while in Type B it means simply the pursuit of an individual benefit.

In both Type A and Type B, the common interest can be positive or negative. If the common interest is negative in Type B, we can regard it as a social cost for the achievement of an individual benefit. "Free rider" is the case of Type A where common interest is positive, and "tragedy of the common" is the case of Type B where common interest is negative. Both Type A and Type B include non-dilemma situations--the situations where common and individual interests coincide.

Type A: Negative individual interest and common interest

Type A can be expressed by the following variables:

G_2 : common interest produced by the joint actions of two people
G_1 : common interest produced by a single person's action
C : individual cost to take the action ($C > 0$)

α : common interest given by the situation

I : common interest produced by the interactional effect of the joint actions

G_2 and G_1 are the resultant common interests that are produced by the actions of either or both of two people. The subscript denotes the number of people who took the action. G_2 and G_1 can take on any value, positive or negative, in this formulation. C is simply the individual cost that a person has to pay when he/she takes a particular action. α is the interest which is given to the two people equally by the situation, regardless of their individual decision making. In other words, we can consider α as an expression of the richness of the situation.

The interrelation among G_2, G_1, and I are described in equation (6).

$$G_2 = 2G_1 + I \tag{6}$$

If $I = 0$, then $G_2 = 2G_1$. That is, the common interest produced by the joint actions of two people is twice as much as that produced by the single person's action. In other words, common interests produced by each person are additive when $I = 0$. If $I > 0$, then $G_2 > 2G_1$. The common interest produced by the joint actions of two people is more than twice as much as that produced by a single person's action. In this case, the joint action is more productive than a single person's action, in terms of common interest. Similarly, the joint action is less productive than a single person's action when $I < 0$. Therefore, it seems reasonable to say that I describes the productivity of the joint actions of two people.

Let W_{ij} express the net payoffs to a person in Type A, where i represents the person's own decision and j the other person's decision, respectively. $i,j = 1$ when people take the action, and $i,j = 0$ when they do not. W_{ij} is given by equation (7).

$$W_{ij} = ijG_2 + (i(1-j) + j(1-i))G_1 - iC + \alpha \tag{7}$$

There are four possible net payoffs to a person. It is easy to put them into a 2x2 matrix format. There are the following correspondences between W_{ij} and the payoff matrix in Fig.2:

$$R = W_{11} = G_2 - C + \alpha \tag{8a}$$

$$T = W_{01} = G_1 + \alpha \tag{8b}$$

$$S = W_{10} = G_1 - C + \alpha \tag{8c}$$

$$P = W_{00} = \alpha \tag{8d}$$

There is a one to one correspondence between the expressions of the payoff matrix and Type A situations. Therefore, for any Type A situation, there exists a mathematically equivalent payoff matrix, which is given by equations (8a-d). Then, for any payoff matrix, it is possible to obtain the equivalent expressions of Type A, as are given by the following:

$$G_2 = R + T - S - P \tag{9a}$$

$$G_1 = T - P \tag{9b}$$

$$C = T - S \tag{9c}$$

$$\alpha = P \tag{9d}$$

$$I = R - T - S + P \tag{9e}$$

Type B: Positive individual interest and common interest

Type B can be expressed in the same way as Type A using the following variables:

H_2: common interest produced by the joint actions of two people
H_1: common interest produced by a single person's action
D: Individual benefit given to an action taker ($D > 0$)
β: common interest given by the situation
J: common interest produced by the interactional effect of the joint actions

The interrelation between H_2 and H_1 is described in equation (10).

$$H_2 = 2H_1 + J \tag{10}$$

The net payoffs of Type B, Z_{ij}, is given by equation (11).

$$Z_{ij} = ijH_2 + (\, i(1-j) + j(1-i))H_1 + iD + \beta \tag{11}$$

i and j represent the choices of the two people in the same way as Type A. There are the following correspondences between the payoff matrix and the net payoffs in Type A and Type B:

$$R = W_{11} = Z_{00} \tag{12a}$$

$$T = W_{01} = Z_{10} \tag{12b}$$

$$S = W_{10} = Z_{01} \tag{12c}$$

$$P = W_{00} = Z_{11} \tag{12d}$$

That is, there is a one to one correspondence among the expressions from the payoff matrix, Type A, and Type B. For any payoff matrix we can find equivalent expressions of Type A and Type B, and for any Type A situation we can find equivalent expressions of payoff matrix and Type B, and so on.

Further analysis of type A and type B

Geometrical expression of type A and type B

Type A and Type B can be shown geometrically in 2-dimensional space with coordinates X (a person's own payoff) and Y (the other person's payoff), as shown in Fig. 7a and Fig. 7b. They are expressed by the combinations of vectors which correspond to various interests in the given situation. The direction of a vector expresses the nature of the interest. Common interest is expressed by a vector of **45°**, and individual interest by a vector of **0°** or **90°**. The net payoffs in Type A or Type B are expressed by four points which are given by the combinations of vectors. Naturally, these four points express the payoff matrix which is equivalent to the given Type A or Type B situation. Four points form a quadrangle. Different matrices are expressed by different quadrangles, and symmetric matrices by symmetric quadrangles.

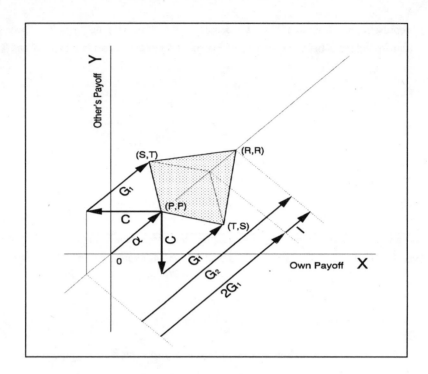

Figure 7a: Geometrical expression of Type A.

Type A can share the same quadrangle (payoff matrix) with Type B in *X-Y* space. Such Type A and Type B situations are, mathematically, equivalent decision problems. However, they are clearly different in terms of their descriptions of the given situation. Their descriptive differences can be explained as follows: In Type A or Type B a person has two alternatives--to take a particular action, or to keep the status quo by not taking it. The status quo of Type A situations corresponds to the point (*P* , *P*) in *X-Y* space. This point is given by the vector $\vec{\alpha}$ from the origin of the space. It is possible to say that two people stand on this status quo point before making their decisions. They will stay on this point if neither of them takes the action. They will move to one of the other three points if either, or both of them, take the action. They will move to the point (*R* , *R*) if both of them take the action. Similarly, the status quo of Type B is expressed by the point (*R* , *R*), which is given by vector $\vec{\beta}$. People will stay on this point or move to the other points, depending on their decisions. They will reach the point (*P* , *P*) if both of them take the action.

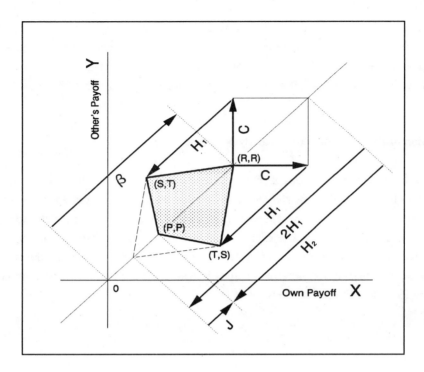

Figure 7b: Geometrical expression of Type B.

Result or process

The vector expressions of Type A and Type B situations shown in Fig.7a and Fig.7b describe the process of by which people reach the final payoffs after making their decisions. Furthermore, the two alternatives of choice in Type A and Type B contain definite meanings in terms of behavior--to take a particular action, or to keep the status quo. The payoff matrix does not show this process, or that the two alternatives contain any behavioral implication at all. The payoff matrix is merely an expression of the final results.

The status quo point and the process of how people reach the net payoff are completely different in Type A and Type B, even if they share the equivalent payoff matrices. We have formulated Type A and Type B as models of two types of social dilemmas--"free rider" and "tragedy of the common." These social dilemmas are real and ubiquitous problems which have become extremely important issues in our society. Our formulation and geometrical expression of

Type A and Type B show clearly what a decision to take action means to people, the process of by which they will obtain the final result, and how the two types of social dilemmas are different. Payoff matrices can not show this process or such difference at all. Therefore, our formulations seems to be superior to the payoff matrix in regard to describing real social dilemmas.

Application of the social orientation analysis to type A and type B

As we have seen in the previous section, there is a one to one correspondence among the expressions of Type A, Type B, and the payoff matrix. Therefore, we can apply the results of social orientation analysis to the expression of Type A or Type B, straightforwardly. We derived V and U in our social orientation analysis of 2x2 payoff matrices, and we showed how V and U are effective for the characterization of 2x2 payoff matrices and the explanation of people's choice making for the given matrix. V and U of Type A and Type B are given by equations (13a) and (13b), respectively.

$$V = \frac{R + T - S - P}{T - S} = \frac{G_2}{C} = \frac{-H_2}{D} \tag{13a}$$

$$U = \frac{R - T - S + P}{T - S} = \frac{I}{C} = \frac{J}{D} \tag{13b}$$

V and U are simply given by the ratios of common interest and individual interest. It is possible to say that the description of Type A or Type B expresses the essential feature of the given situation more directly and clearly than matrix games.

Equation (13a) and (13b) make it possible to normalize Type A and Type B situations in the same way as payoff matrices. Therefore, all situations which share the same V and U are equivalent as decision problems, regardless of whether they are given by the expressions of the payoff matrix, Type A, or Type B. Equivalent decision problems are expressed by the same point in V-U space as shown in Fig.3. They share the same shape of a quadrangle in X-Y space as shown in Fig.7a and Fig.7b. The size and location of a quadrangle in the space are not related to the values of V and U . Furthermore, all the results of the social orientation analysis, which are summarized in the second section, are effective for the explanation of choice making by a person in a situation of Type A or Type B. That is, we can explain people's decision making in Type A and Type B situations in the same way as in matrix games.

Social orientation and descriptive difference of the given situation

According to the social orientation analysis, the choice making of a person basically depends on his/her social orientation. A person will make the same decision for equivalent decision problems regardless of their descriptive differences. Then, are such descriptive differences among Type A, Type B, and the payoff matrix trivial? It is so only when the social orientation of a person is fixed for different expressions. If a person has different social orientations in Type A and Type B, he/she might make different choices. So, do people keep the same orientation for Type A, Type B, and for the payoff matrix expression?

V and U given by equations (13a) and (13b) are simply the ratios of common interest and individual interest. That is, Type A and Type B describe the essential structure of a decision problems, directly and explicitly. However, the essential structure is hidden in the expression of the payoff matrix. Therefore, people might perceive the given situations differently in matrix games and Type A or Type B situations. This difference might affect the state of their social orientation. Furthermore, descriptive differences between Type A and Type B are also likely to affect the social orientation of people. As we have seen, there are definite differences between Type A and Type B in the process by which people reach the final results after decision making, and in the meaning of the status quo and the action. These descriptive differences might affect the social orientation of a person. As a result, people may make different decisions in Type A and Type B, even if the given situations are equivalent mathematically. In this regard, Pruitt (1967) showed experimentally that different expressions of games, matrix games and decomposed games, affect people's choice making, even if the given games are mathematically equivalent.

Therefore, it is highly likely that the way the given situation is described affects the state of the social orientation of a person. If so, the descriptive difference is not a trivial matter, and it is necessary to investigate how different expressions of decision problems affect people's social orientation and choice making behavior. For example, it is not justified to apply social orientation assessed by decomposed games for the explanation of people's behavior in matrix games. We have to assess the social orientation of people from the data obtained by matrix games in order to study choice making of people in matrix games. We need the date obtained by Type A situations for the study of people's choices in Type A, and so on. In this regard, the assessment method derived by Doi and Imai (1986) is thought to be quite effective and useful. Their method can be applied to any type of description of a 2-person, 2-choice situation, as long as the net payoffs are expressed by a payoff matrix.

Final remarks

"Free rider" and "tragedy of the common" are two types of important social dilemmas. Examples of them are ubiquitous in our society. Our formulations, Type A and Type B, can express both types of social dilemmas clearly, without loosing important features of the situations. They describe the status quo, the meaning of the action, and the process by which people reach the final result after decision making. Payoff matrices can not show these features. Furthermore, these formulations are simple and clear, and thus can be used for experiments in the laboratory as easily as payoff matrices. Experimental game research using matrix games has often been criticized because the game situations lack the reality of the concrete problems in our society. Experimental results are thus considered to be irrelevant in regard to understanding people's behavior in the real world. Since the Type A and Type B formulations are more reflective of real-world social dilemmas than are the payoff matrices, they may bring an answer to this criticism.

Social dilemmas are usually understood as problems in a large group. Therefore, researchers working on social dilemmas have paid a lot of attention to N-person games. Our formulations, Type A and Type B, are restricted to 2-person situations. However, our formulations can easily be extended to N-person situations, simply by adding the common interest terms G_n , G_{n-i} , ... , G_1 in the case of Type A. Furthermore, the model of social orientation, that is, equation (1), was successfully extended to N-person situations by Doi (1990). He showed clearly how the meanings of social orientations are different according to the values of N, and how social orientations in 2-person and N-person situations can be interrelated. That is to say, we can analyze the choice making of people in N-person social dilemmas in the same way as we did for 2-person situations.

Although our analysis is heavily based on the model of social orientation, we do not consider social orientation as the only important factor working in the decision making process of a person. There may be decision situations where people's choice making is affected strongly by other factors. Nevertheless, it seems that social orientation is one of the basic factors in human decision making in interdependent situations, especially when communication among people is extremely limited. Thus, it would be worthwhile to see how far our invistigation based on social orientation can go in the research of human decision making in such situations.

Footnote

1   Faculty of Industrial Science & Technology, Science University of Tokyo, Hokkaido, Japan

References

Dawes, R.M. (1980). Social dilemmas. *Annual Review of Psychology, 31,* 169-193.

Deutsch, R.M. (1960). The effect of motivational orientations upon trust and suspicion. *Human Relations, 13,* 122-139.

Doi, T. (1990, March). *Social motivation of the individual in N-person games.* Paper presented at the Fourth International Conference on Social Dilemmas, Sapporo, Japan.

Doi, T. (1990). An experimental Investigation of the validity of the characteristic space theory and the measurement of social motivation. *The Japanese Journal of Experimental Social Psychology, 29,* 15-24.

Doi, T. (1991, September). *Assessment of social orientation in two-person two-choice interdependent situations.* Paper presented at the International Conference on Social Value Orientations in Interpersonal and Intergroup Relations, Leuven, Belgium.

Doi, T., & Imai, S. (1986). 2x2 game ni okeru sentaku koudo no tokusei kukanron to sentaku kettei katei no doukiteki-ninchiteki model [A characteristic space theory and a motivational-cognitive model of choice behavior]. *Japanese Psychological Review, 29,* 186-210.

Griesinger, D.W., & Livingstone, J.W., Jr. (1973). Toward a model of interpersonal motivation in experimental games. *Behavioral Science, 18,* 409-431.

Hamburger, H. (1973). N-person prisoner's dilemma. *Journal of Mathematical Sociology, 3,* 27-47.

Hardin, G. (1968). The tragedy of the common. *Science, 162,* 1243-1248.

Harris, R.J. (1968). A geometrical classification system for 2x2 interval-symmetric games. *Behavioral Science, 14,*138-146.

Messick, D.M., & McClintock, .C.G. (1968). Motivational bases of choice in experimental games. *Journal of Experimental Social Psychology, 4,* 1-25.

Olson, M. Jr. (1965). *The logic of collective action.* New York: Schocken.

Platt, J. (1973). Social traps. *American Psychologist, 28,* 641-651.

Pruitt, D.G. (1967). Reward structure and cooperation: The decomposed prisoner's dilemma games. *Journal of Personality and Social Psychology, 7,* 21-27.

Rapoport, A., & Guyer, M. (1966). A taxonomy of 2x2 games. *General Systems, 11,* 203-214.

Toward more locomotion in experimental games

Paul A.M. van Lange[1]

Abstract

This chapter evaluates the traditional experimental gaming approach to the study of social interdependence. In addition to outlining several strengths, it is asserted that this approach is limited in two respects: (1) it does not enable a researcher to examine the ways in which individuals express their simple motivations and simple strategies when they are provided with more varied domain of options, and (2) it neglects an important domain of social interaction, namely those situations in which individuals are able to alter the underlying interdependence structure. The chapter reviews prior research that extends the traditional experimental gaming approach by offering subjects the possibility to alter the nature of interdependence. It is concluded that the ways in which individuals express their simple motivations and strategies may be importantly shaped by the availability of other options than a cooperative and noncooperative choice. To provide more insight into these processes, we should consider a greater locomotion in the way in which we use outcome matrices in our research on social interdependence.

Interdependence and locomotion

One has to be exceptionally inventive to come up with examples of real-life situations in which individuals' behaviors do *not* impact one another's outcomes. Even the most mundane behaviors may have influence on the well-being of other individuals: Things we say or do and/or things we don't say or don't do. Undoubtedly, situations of social interdependence differ -- and are perceived to differ -- in fundamental ways. Such differences have a large impact on how we approach interdependent others, and how patterns of social interaction may develop over time. However, the psychological richness of interdependent situations we face in everyday life, and particularly the variety of ways in which we like to alter these situations, is only partially reflected in prior research on social interdependence. Indeed, in reality we often have more choices than a cooperative and a noncooperative choice. For example, rather than choosing "noncooperatively" (i.e., making a self-beneficial choice at the expense of others), we may: avoid that particular situation, delay a decision, or alter the situation in particular ways. Each of these decisions potentially has consequences for the type of interdependence we will face in the immediate or more distal future. In this context, all choices (other than simple cooperative or noncooperative choices) that affect the underlying interdependence structure is referred to as *locomotion* because such options allow individuals to move from situation to situation, thereby altering the underlying interdependence structure.

The major assumption underlying this chapter is that individuals' motivations and strategies are reflected not only in cooperative and noncooperative choices, but also in their preferences to alter interdependent situations in particular ways. Before we discuss the rationale and the implications of this assumption, we evaluate the strengths and limitations of the traditional experimental gaming paradigm, in particular the ways in which outcome matrices typically have been used as a research tool.

The outcome matrix as a research tool

In more than forty years of research, social and behavioral scientists have focused on the question of what factors influence the probability of cooperative, or conversely, the probability of noncooperative choices (e.g., Dawes, 1980; Messick & Brewer, 1983; Pruitt & Kimmel, 1977; Van Lange, Liebrand, Messick, & Wilke, 1992). Inspired by game theory (e.g., Luce & Raiffa, 1957), this line of research has used the outcome matrix as a *research tool* to find answers to the above question. It is precisely the outcome matrix -- and the ways in which it typically has been utilized -- that has led to mixed feelings of sympathy and irritation, respect and scepticism (Nemeth, 1972).

Generally, it is not surprising that the outcome matrix as a research tool has attracted many experimental social and behavioral scientists. As outlined by Pruitt and Kimmel (1977), outcome matrices allow researchers: to precisely specify the properties of interdependence one is interested in; to yield behavioral measures, as opposed to questionnaire measures; and finally, to examine constructs such as cooperation, or competition in a fairly direct and economical way -- matrices are relatively easy to employ and permit "conflict without injury." Below, we first discuss in what specific ways prior research using outcome matrices has been particularly fruitful.

First, one line of research has used outcome matrices to provide more insight into the relative impact of various *motivations* by comparing the number of pro-social choices in different outcome matrices. These motivations typically are assessed by employing so called "one-shot games" or single-trial matrices which enable a researcher to fairly unambiguously attribute behavior to underlying motives or goals, rather than to strategies used to achieve certain goals. Examples are appetitive and aversive forms of competition (e.g., Kuhlman, Camac, & Cunha, 1986; Messick & Thorngate, 1967) and greed and fear as two distinct motives underlying noncooperative choice behavior (e.g., Simmons, Dawes, & Orbell, 1984; Van Lange, Liebrand, & Kuhlman, 1990; Yamagishi & Sato, 1986). Also, single-trial matrices have been shown to be useful in demonstrating that a significant number of individuals do cooperate, even if selfish reasons could not underlie such choices (e.g., Caporeal, Dawes, Orbell, & Van de Kragt, 1989). Moreover, different single-trial outcome matrices typically elicit an understanding of subjects that matches the game theoretical principles underlying these matrices, thereby supporting the internal validity of the motivations assessed (cf. Van Lange, Liebrand, & Kuhlman, 1990). Furthermore, there is a line of research that uses games -- derived from outcome matrices -- to study individual differences in social value orientations (Messick & McClintock, 1968). Examples of more dominant social value orientations, or simple motivations are: cooperation (maximizing joint gain), individualism (maximizing own gain) and competition (maximizing relative gain over others). This research has revealed that these different motivations correspond to behavior outside the laboratory, thereby supporting the ecological validity of the game theoretical approach to study simple motivations (Bem & Lord, 1979; Kuhlman, Camac, & Cunha, 1986; McClintock & Allison, 1989).

Second, outcome matrices have also been employed in an attempt to examine strategies used to achieve certain goals -- this has been examined by using iterative "games." Typically, this line of research examines how individuals respond to others pre-programmed to follow cooperative, noncooperative, Tit for Tat (TFT), or more specific behavioral and/or verbal strategies in an attempt to study processes such as trust building, promise, threat, retaliation, or exploitation (Harford & Solomon, 1967; Lindskold, 1978; Oskamp, 1971; Pruitt & Kimmel, 1977). One very robust finding is that individuals respond more cooperatively toward TFT than toward a 100% cooperative strategy, and almost all individuals respond noncooperatively toward a 100% noncooperative strategy (e.g., Solomon, 1960). Also, research has demonstrated that, relative to the 100% cooperative strategy, TFT elicits greater levels of cooperation only from actors with individualistic motivations: the choices of cooperatively or pro-socially as well as competitively oriented subjects are not affected by the differences between these two strategies (e.g., Kuhlman & Marshello, 1975; McClintock & Liebrand, 1988). This line of research has been fruitful in providing more insight into what strategies individuals adopt in response to strategies followed by an interdependent other.

Thus, prior research on experimental games demonstrates the existence and relative importance of *simple* motivations and *simple* strategies, and how simple motivations may be reflected in simple strategies individuals adopt in response to strategies followed by the interdependent other. These motivations and strategies are simple because individuals are forced to choose between two options: cooperation versus noncooperation. Consequently, it is not clear whether such motivations or strategies may be influenced in some ways when they are provided with more options. Also, assuming that the simple motivations and strategies are relatively robust, it is not clear in what ways individuals express such simple motivations or strategies once they are provided with a broader domain of options (e.g., to withdraw from the situation, to alter the situation in particular ways). For example, it may well be that some individuals -- because of their dominant simple motivation (e.g., cooperation) -- wish to avoid particular interdependent situations (e.g., highly competitive situations), rather than making a noncompetitive choice.

Generally, we believe that the way in which outcome matrices have been used in prior research often is limited to particular domains of social interaction, and by implication is neglecting other potentially important domains of social interaction. As outlined by Kelley (1984), in the most general sense, "the limitations stem from the fact that a particular matrix describes the interdependence only at a given point in time." (p. 958). The simple fact that the outcome matrix -- that represents a particular type of interdependence -- does not change over subsequent periods of interaction limits it generalizability across domains of social interaction. Change in the type of interdependence may occur for a variety of reasons.

First, in several domains of social interaction, the most attractive solutions to interdependent situations may become more rewarding to the extent that such solutions have been obtained more frequently in the past. For example, after a series of mutually gratifying, but superficial interactions, individuals may explore more substantial domains of interaction, thereby increasing their levels of interdependence. Thus, over time, such individuals may become more interdependent. In another domain of social interactions, the reverse may be true: attractive solutions to interdependent situations may become *less* rewarding to the extent that mutually gratifying interactions have been obtained more frequently in the past. For example, in the beginning two individuals may find it exceedingly interesting to get to know each other, but after a period of time there may be a decline in how much time they want to spend together -- the most interesting pieces of information have been exchanged. Hence, through their own "successful" actions (intensifying interaction), over time these individuals may face less intense situations of interdependence: The level of interdependence has declined.

Second, interdependence structures may also change over time because of interactions that were *not* mutually gratifying. For example, one incident of exploitation may lead to lower levels of trust, and therefore lead to fewer interactions. The one who was exploited may decide to avoid the other as much as possible, thereby decreasing the level of interdependence.

There are many more ways in which the static use of the outcome matrix -- which is characteristic of prior research on social interdependence -- places constraints on the generalizability of the situation that is examined (e.g., sequential factors, for a more complete analysis, see Kelley, 1984). The above examples make clear, we hope, that research on social interdependence needs to be extended in order to capture more locomotion in the use of outcome matrices to specify change over time and the ways in which individuals can express their desires to alter interdependent situations.

The outcome matrix as a conceptual tool

The next question, of course, is: In what ways do interdependence structures alter over time, and in what ways would individuals be motivated to change the interdependence structure? A potentially fruitful way to approach this question is to systematically analyze and conceptualize the most important properties of the outcome matrix. We will do that by using the concepts underlying Kelley and Thibaut's (1978) interdependence theory. Although these concepts have broader implications, we will confine ourselves to (a) the matrix representing two interdependent individuals who are provided with two options, and (b) symmetric outcome matrices -- both individuals are provided with the identical outcome matrix.

Two general parameters can be distinguished from any outcome matrix. The first is *Grand Mean* (GM), or the average outcome in a given matrix, which presents the level of satisfaction (when GM is positive) or dissatisfaction (when GM is negative). The second general parameter is the sum of the specific control indices identified by Thibaut and Kelley (1959). This parameter may be referred to as "*Level of Importance* (LI)" (Kelley, 1922[2]; Van Lange & Veenendaal, 1992), and consists of: (1) *reflexive control* (RC), the consequences merely due to own choices, (2) *fate control* (FC), the consequences merely due to other's choices, and (3) *behavioral control* (BC), the consequences due to the combinations of own and other's choices. Table 1 presents four outcome matrices -- all of which are prisoner's dilemmas -- which differ in Grand Mean and Level of Importance. Mathematically, RC reflects the difference between the average outcome for each row (i.e., main effect for own choice); FC reflects the difference between the average outcome for each column (i.e., main effect for other's choice); and BC the variability left after subtracting RC and FC from the original matrix. (BC is zero in all outcome matrices in Table 1 because they are all specific examples of prisoner's dilemmas.) LI is the sum of RC, FC, and BC.

As LI increases, there is more "at stake" because the intensity of the consequences due to own (RC), other's (FC) as well as own and other's choices (BC) will be greater.

Table 1

Four outcome matrices (prisoner's dilemmas) differing in Grand Mean (GM) and Level of Importance (LI)

Matrix 1: Low GM and Low LI (GM = 0; RC = 2; FC = 6; BC = 0; LI = 8)

	Coop	Noncoop
Coop	+ 2 + 2	+ 4 - 4
Noncoop	- 4 + 4	- 2 - 2

Matrix 2: Low GM and High LI (GM = 0; RC = 10; FC = 30; BC = 0; LI = 40)

	Coop	Noncoop
Coop	+ 10 + 10	+ 20 - 20
Noncoop	- 20 + 20	- 10 - 10

Matrix 3: High GM and Low LI (GM = 20; RC = 2; FC = 6; BC = 0; LI = 8)

	Coop	Noncoop
Coop	+ 22 + 22	+ 24 + 16
Noncoop	+ 16 + 24	+ 18 + 18

Matrix 4: High GM and High LI (GM = 20; RC = 10; FC = 30; BC = 0; LI = 40)

	Coop	Noncoop
Coop	+ 30 + 30	+ 40 0
Noncoop	0 + 40	+ 10 + 10

As regards symmetrical outcome matrices, GM is meaningful only in light of generalized expectations and norms regarding satisfaction or dissatisfaction (*Comparison Level*, or CL) or in comparison to actual alternative interdependence situations (*Comparison Level of Alternatives*: CLalt; alternative outcome matrices). Similarly, Level of Importance is meaningful only *outside* the specified outcome matrix: LI is meaningful only by comparing it to CL (generalized expectations and norms regarding how much is at stake), and CLalt (how much is at stake relative to alternative outcome matrices). In contrast, the three components of LI are meaningful not only to CL or CLalt, but also *within* the specified matrix. At least implicitly, individuals may compare: RC to FC, RC to BC, FC to BC, or any of these specific forms of control to the general parameter of LI. For example, the amount of FC relative to LI reflects the degree to which other's actions impact the outcomes an individual receives. Accordingly, individuals should feel more dependent on the other to the extent that FC accounts for a greater proportion of LI. The well-known Prisoner's dilemma, for example, is characterized by (a) a greater FC than RC, and (b) and a relative absence of BC. In such situations, individuals will be aware that most of their outcomes are determined primarily by the other's choice -- that he/she is importantly dependent on the other.

This conceptual analysis is important because it helps to understand what property in any given outcome matrix may change -- or individuals may want to change -- over time. The first general, and obvious change individuals should wish is an increase in GM (individuals should maximize satisfaction and minimize dissatisfaction). Consequently, other things being equal, individuals should always be motivated to move to outcome matrices with greater GM. In addition, there may be relatively "unintentional" changes in GM. For example, at a certain point in time, GM may drop below zero (or, any outcome within the matrix may drop below zero) because of "boredom" or "fatigue" (Kelley, 1984). The simple fact that CL exceeds any outcome in the matrix, would imply that, if possible, individuals should want to withdraw from the outcome matrix, thereby lowering the interdependence to zero.

A second general change that may occur over time is related to Level of Importance. There is a particular domain of situations in which interdependent actors increasingly may realize the importance of outcomes associated with own and other's choices in a given situation. For example, while individuals initially may be somewhat indifferent to the possible outcomes ("it is just something minor"), over time (after successive interactions) the interdependent situation may turn into something quite important, and hence both one's own actions and the other's actions will have a major impact each other's well-being ("if we can succeed in this ..."). Thus, over time LI may increase. Similarly, for some interactions the reverse may be true: over time LI may decrease (e.g., individuals may lose interest in one another or in a joint task).

Third, the relative magnitude of the three types of control -- RC, FC, and BC -- may also change over time. For example, it may be that while LI remains essentially the same, a person becomes increasingly dependent on the other, reflected by lower levels of RC, and greater levels of FC. Conversely, as we may observe in subordinate-supervisor relationships, the subordinate may become increasingly independent, reflected by greater levels of RC, and lower levels of FC.

Prior research relevant to locomotion in experimental games

One of the first attempts to add a fundamentally different choice to the traditional dichotomous choice of cooperation versus noncooperation has been made by Miller and Holmes (1975). In their expanded Prisoner's dilemma game, they added a withdrawal choice by which subjects were enabled to avoid both behavioral assimilation and exploitation when the partner consistently chose noncooperatively. That is, a person did not need to make a noncooperative choice when he or she expected the other to choose noncooperatively. Instead, withdrawal may yield higher outcomes than a noncooperative choice. As can be seen in Table 2, the Expanded Prisoner's Dilemma (EPD) used by Miller and Holmes (1975) is fundamentally different from the simple PDG. In fact, through the withdrawal choice, a person can make sure that his/her outcome would not drop below 1, and would not be higher than 2. So, through this particular option, the person him or herself can to a large extent "control" LI as well as FC. The withdrawal choice can therefore be construed as a move toward decreasing levels of importance (because of lowering of LI) or as a move toward decreasing levels of dependence (because of lowering of FC).

Table 2

The Prisoner's dilemma (a) and Expanded Prisoner's dilemma (b) matrices used by Miller and Holmes (1975).

(a)   PDG: Level of Importance and FC are fixed, and cannot be influenced by the individual
       (GM = 0; RC = 5; FC = 15; BC = 0; LI = 20).

	Coop		Noncoop	
Coop		+5		+10
	+5		-10	
Noncoop		-10		-5
	+10		-5	

(B)   EPD: Level of Importance and FC are not fixed, and can be influenced by the individual
       through making a withdrawal choice.

	Coop		Withdr		NonCoop	
Coop		+5		+2		+10
	+5		+5		-10	
Withdr		+5		+1		+10
	+2		+1		+2	
Noncoop		-10		+2		-5
	+10		+2		-5	

One of major findings Miller and Holmes (1975) observed was that, relative to the PD, in the EPD persons with cooperative motivations were far less likely to adopt a noncooperative strategy in response to a noncooperative strategy followed by the other. Instead, they tended to opt for withdrawal. This provides a nice demonstration of the idea that simple motivations and strategies may be expressed in other ways than by making cooperative or noncooperative choices. Cooperators wish to decrease LI (and thereby lowering FC) in order to protect themselves to exploitation.

In a more recent experiment of Insko, Schopler, Hoyle, Dardis, and Graetz (1990), the withdrawal choice reflected both a move toward an Level of Importance of zero and a move toward complete independence, whereby dependence (and interdependence) are eliminated all together. That is, through a withdrawal choice a person (or group in this particular study) is able to reduce LI to zero and to end up with an outcome identical to GM. That is, when a person wishes to be independent, a person can guarantee an outcome identical to GM (48) for himself or herself (as well as for the other person), and there is no variability in these outcomes. Thus, in any submatrix that contains a withdrawal option, LI is zero, and by implication there is no FC.

Insko et al. (1990) demonstrated that relative to individuals, interdependent groups were more likely to make withdrawal choices in the PDG-alt matrix. This suggests that, at least in part, groups are more likely than individuals to eliminate LI: this may be motivated by the tendency to eliminate FC and to protect themselves from exploitation by the other group. Again, simple motivations and strategies are reflected in other choices than cooperation and noncooperation.

As noted explicitly by Insko et al. (1990), different simple motivations or specific strategies could underlie a withdrawal choice, particularly when the game takes an iterative form. Withdrawal could be tactical, especially when it follows a prior successful attempt toward exploitation (i.e., when the other cooperated, but the person himself or herself made a noncooperative choice). The withdrawal choice may also be attractive as a means to protect oneself to exploitation: when one anticipates the other to choose noncooperatively, then clearly the withdrawal option is the dominant option (unless someone is motivated "to revenge in advance").

A third study we would like to discuss is an experiment conducted by Orbell, Schwartz-Shea and Simmons (1984). Using a nine-person Prisoner's dilemma, they had subjects first make a cooperative or a noncooperative choice, followed by the option to leave (Exit) or not to leave (Not-Exit) the Prisoner's dilemma. Through this Exit option, subjects were enabled to become completely independent of others, thereby eliminating FC. There was still variability in the outcomes associated with Exit, but this was *externally* determined by means of a lottery. The expected value of the Exit option was varied: In the low-exit-incentive condition subjects could expect greater outcomes by Exiting than by a noncooperative choice if fewer than 25 percent cooperated, or by a cooperative choice if fewer than 75 cooperated; in the high-exit-incentive condition subjects could expect greater outcomes by Exiting than by a noncooperative choice if fewer than 50% cooperated, or by a cooperative choice regardless of the number of others choosing cooperatively. This study revealed that quite a number of subjects exited, the maximum being 46%

in the high-exit-incentive condition when discussion was not permitted.

Certainly, there are situations in which most individuals are inclined not to exit (e.g., when discussion is possible, and costs are associated with exit). But the important observation is that individuals do seem to consider exiting, and actually may eliminate interdependence. Orbell et al. also found that noncooperators were somewhat more prone to exit than were cooperators, and explained this finding by the idea that cooperators may find the exit option morally less acceptable than do noncooperators. Recently, Dawes and Orbell (1992) obtained a very similar finding, and offered an alternative explanation -- namely that cooperators and noncooperators differ in levels of expected utility. Cooperators are more likely not only to cooperate themselves, but also to expect others to cooperate, thereby anticipating outcomes flowing from mutual cooperation. Noncooperators, on the other hand, tend to expect noncooperative behavior from others and are inclined to choose noncooperatively, anticipating outcomes resulting from mutual noncooperation (cf. Dawes & Orbell, 1992). Because the outcomes associated with mutual cooperation are greater than those associated with mutual noncooperation, it is understandable that cooperators are less prone to exit.[3]

The experiments discussed above are consistent with the assumption that individuals' simple motivations and simple strategies are reflected not only in cooperative and noncooperative choices, but also in preferences for particular types of social interdependence: namely whether to decrease Levels of Impact underlying the interdependent situation.

Toward more locomotion in outcome matrices: A demonstration

In his transition list approach, Kelley (1984) proposes a new method for describing the ways in which individuals affect and control each other. It stresses the importance of transition lists, which specify possible shifts from one outcome matrix to the other. The primary purpose of this approach is to overcome limitations associated with the static use of outcome matrices. Inspired by this approach, Van Lange and Veenendaal (1992) have conducted research to examine transitions between matrices that differ in Level of Importance, and to study whether simple motivations described earlier would affect such transitions. Accordingly, prior to the decision task, subjects' social value orientations were assessed by a series of decomposed games (cf. Messick & McClintock, 1968), in which subjects make choices for either a pro-social option (which allows for greatest joint outcomes), an individualistic option (which allows for the greatest outcomes for self), or a competitive option (which allows for the greatest relative advantage over the other's outcomes). Consistent with prior research, subjects were classified as pro-social, individualistic, or as competitive, when they made six choices (out of a total of nine choices) consistent with one of these distributions of outcomes to self and an unknown other (for more information regarding similar assessment and classification procedures, see McClintock & Allison, 1989).

After the assessment of social value orientations, the actual decision task was explained. In this task, subjects were enabled to choose for situations that systematically differed in terms of Level of Importance (LI). As can be seen in Table 3, a subject was provided with five situations characterized by identical Grand Means (0), but differing Levels of Importance, varying from 40 in matrix 1 to 200 in matrix 5. At least two major motives may underlie preferences toward increasing LI. First, an individual may be very confident of achieving mutual cooperation, which results in greater outcomes for himself or herself, as well as for the other. Second, an individual may be confident that he/she is able to take advantage of the other's cooperation. Each of these reasons flow from the expectation that the interdependent other will cooperate. Conversely, the major motives underlying preferences toward decreasing LI may flow from the expectation that the interdependent other will not cooperate. After all, this would imply expectation of a loss regardless of the own choice. This expected loss can be reduced by moving to outcome matrices with lower LI. In addition to these major motives, more specific motivations may underlie these outcome matrix preferences, such as: (1) the tendency to avoid versus seek risk or adventure by moving toward matrices with lower versus greater LI; (2) the need to increase knowledge, and to gather information regarding the other's intentions in increasingly "diagnostic" situations -- when there is more "at stake" an individual's choice may be perceived to be more strongly related to his or her true intentions and motivations, and (3) the tendency to increase the own level of FC (to derive pleasure from exercising control over the other's outcomes).

Table 3

Prisoner's dilemmas differing in Level of Importance (Van Lange & Veenendaal, 1992)

Matrix 1: Lowest LI (GM = 0; RC = 10; FC = 30; BC = 0; LI = 40)

	Coop	Noncoop
Coop	+ 10 + 10	+ 20 - 20
Noncoop	- 20 + 20	- 10 - 10

Matrix 2: Rather Low LI (GM = 0; RC = 20; FC = 60; BC = 0; LI = 80)

	Coop	Noncoop
Coop	+ 20 + 20	+ 40 - 40
Noncoop	- 40 + 40	- 20 - 20

Matrix 3: Moderate LI (GM = 0; RC = 30; FC = 90; BC = 0; LI = 120)

	Coop	Noncoop
Coop	+ 30 + 30	+ 60 - 60
Noncoop	- 60 + 60	- 30 - 30

Matrix 4: Rather High LI (GM = 0; RC = 40; FC = 120; BC = 0; LI = 160)

	Coop	Noncoop
Coop	+ 40 + 40	+ 80 - 80
Noncoop	- 80 + 80	- 40 - 40

Matrix 5: Highest LI (GM = 0; RC = 50; FC = 150; BC = 0; LI = 200)

	Coop	Noncoop
Coop	+ 50 + 50	+ 100 - 100
Noncoop	- 100 + 100	- 50 - 50

In this study, subjects made either cooperative or noncooperative choices, and took turns regarding who was going to determine the specific matrix in which they were going to make choices. As determined by the experimenter, subjects began with matrix 3 (the "neutral" situation; see Table 3), and by means of a bogus lottery it was decided that "the other" was going to determine the outcome matrix for the second trial, the subject himself or herself the third trial, etc. In total, there were seven trials. Thus, this experiment examines subjects' choice behavior (cooperative vs. noncooperative) and his or her preferences for matrices differing in LIs as a function of subjects' social value orientation. Moreover, as a further step toward extending prior research, we manipulated a classic variable -- the other's strategy (cooperative vs. noncooperative). That is, consistent with many prior studies (cf. Oskamp, 1971), the other was preprogrammed to consistently make either cooperative or noncooperative choices.

One of the major findings was that, relative to another who consistently made cooperative choices, subjects preferred lower levels of LI when the other consistently made noncooperative choices. Moreover, this effect for other's strategy was moderated by the subjects' social value orientations. The effect for other's strategy was significant for subjects with individualistic or competitive value orientations (i.e., orientation toward maximizing own gain, or relative benefit over the other, respectively), but was not significant for those with pro-social orientations (i.e., orientation toward maximizing joint gain).

Pro-social subjects appeared to prefer rather high LIs regardless of other's strategy, and consistent with prior research (Kelley & Stahelski, 1970; Kuhlman & Marshello, 1975) they exhibited behavioral assimilation (i.e., behaved cooperatively in response to a cooperative strategy, and behaved noncooperatively in response to a noncooperative strategy). How can these findings be understood? One possible interpretation is that pro-socials want to retaliate -- at some costs to self -- which is better possible when they remain in matrices with high LI. This explanation is consistent with the so-called overassimilation effect (Kelley & Stahelski, 1970), the tendency among pro-social subjects to exhibit even more noncooperative behavior than individualists or competitors in response to a noncooperative other. Another interpretation is that pro-socials remain optimistic regarding the possibility to stimulate other's cooperative choice behavior. Apparently, individualists nor competitors wish to retaliate, or think (or wish) to be able to stimulate other's cooperative choice behavior. Although it is not clear what precise mechanisms underlie these differences between pro-socials versus individualists and competitors, the experiment does reveal that social value orientations are reflected not only in cooperative versus non-cooperative choice behavior but also in how much LI these wish in response to the strategy followed by the other. Moreover, the strong effect for other's strategy on outcome matrix preferences demonstrates that, overall, individuals want to do more than just behaving noncooperatively in response to noncooperative others: they want to move to different situations of interdependence.

Conclusions

The traditional approach to experimental games has at least two drawbacks. First, it does not enable a researcher to examine the ways in which individuals express their simple motivations and simple strategies when they are provided with a more varied domain of options. Second, it neglects an important domain of social interaction, namely those situations in which individuals are able to alter the underlying interdependence. Prior research in which subjects are able to withdraw from the situation, as well as more recent research based on Kelley's (1984) transition list approach, suggest that simple motivations and strategies relevant to interdependent situations are reflected in a more varied set of actions than just cooperative or noncooperative choices. Moreover, although not discussed in this chapter, interesting social motivations may be disclosed when a more dynamic approach is taken to the study of social interdependence. Thus, a greater locomotion in the way we use outcome matrices may enhance our understanding of simple motivations and strategies and may reveal new motivations and strategies that could not be observed in the traditional approach to experimental games.

Footnotes

1   Free University, Department of Social Psychology, Amsterdam, The Netherlands.

2   Personal (bitnet) communication, November 1992. Of course, the term "Level of Importance" is somewhat arbitrary. However, the term seems appropriate because it is relatively neutral and because it reflects "how much is at stake" or the variability in individual outcomes presented in the outcome matrix.

3   To our knowledge there is one other published study that examined the exit option. In an experiment by Yamagishi (1988) exiting coincided with the noncooperative option. Subjects were facing a free-rider problem, and were asked to make a choice between contributing to the public good and exiting. This study revealed that exiting as an individualistic solution to the free rider problem was rather powerful, ranging from 23% (when exit costs were high) to 38% (when exit costs were low) of the choices.

References

Bem, D.J., & Lord, C.G. (1979). Template matching: A proposal for probing the ecological validity of experimental settings in social psychology. *Journal of Personality and Social Psychology, 37,* 833-846.

Caporael, L.R., Dawes, R.M., Orbell, J.M., & Van de Kragt, A.J.C. (1990). Selfishness examined: Cooperation in the absence of egoistic incentives. *Behavioral and Brain Sciences, 12,* 683-699.

Dawes, R.M. (1980). Social dilemmas. *Annual Review of Psychology, 31,* 169-193.

Dawes, R.M. & Orbell, J.M. (1992). *Optimism about others as cooperators' comparative advantage.* Paper presented at the fifth international conference on social dilemmas. Bielefeld, Germany.

Harford, T.C., & Solomon, L. (1967). "Reformed sinner" and "lapsed saint" strategies in the prisoner's dilemma game. *Journal of Conflict Resolution, 11,* 104-109.

Insko, C.A., Schopler, J., Hoyle, R.H., Dardis, G.J., & Graetz, K.A. (1990). Individual-group discontinuity as a function of fear and greed. *Journal of Personality and Social Psychology, 58,* 68-79.

Kelley, H.H., & Stahelski, A.J. (1970). Social interaction basis of cooperators' and competitors' beliefs about others. *Journal of Personality and Social Psychology, 16*, 66-91.

Kelley, H.H. (1984). The theoretical description of interdependence by means of transitionlists. *Journal of Personality and Social Psychology, 47*, 956-982.

Kelley, H.H. & Thibaut, J.W. (1978). *Interpersonal relations: A theory of interdependence*. New York: Wiley.

Kuhlman, D.M., Camac, C., & Cunha, D.A. (1986). Individual differences in social orientation. In H. Wilke, D. Messick, & C. Rutte (Eds.), *Experimental Social Dilemmas* (pp. 151-176). New York: Verlag Peter Lang.

Kuhlman, D.M. & Marshello, A. (1975). Individual differences in game motivation as moderators of preprogrammed strategic effects in prisoner's dilemma. *Journal of Personality and Social Psychology, 32*, 922-931.

Lindskold, S. (1978). Trust development, the GRIT proposal, and the effects of conciliatory acts on conflict and cooperation. *Psychological Bulletin, 85*, 107-128.

Luce, R.D., & Raiffa, H. (1957). *Games and decisions: Introduction and critical survey*. London: John Wiley and sons.

McClintock, C.G., & Allison, S.T. (1989). Social value orientation and helping behavior. *Journal of Applied Social Psychology, 19*, 353-362.

McClintock, C.G., & Liebrand, W.B.G. (1988). The role of interdependence structure, individual value orientation and other's strategy in social decision making: A transformational analysis. *Journal of Personality and Social Psychology, 55*, 396-409.

Messick, D.M., & McClintock, C.G. (1968). Motivational basis of choice in experimental games. *Journal of Experimental Social Psychology, 4*, 1-25.

Messick, D.M., & Brewer, M.B. (1983). Solving social dilemmas: A review. In L. Wheeler & P. Shaver (Eds.), *Review of Personality and Social Psychology*. Beverly Hills: Sage.

Messick, D.M., & Thorngate, W. (1967). Relative gain maximization in experimental games. *Journal of Experimental Social Psychology, 3*, 85-101.

Miller, D.T., & Holmes, J.G. (1975). The role of situational restrictiveness and self-fulfilling prophecies: A theoretical and empirical extension of Kelley and Stahelski's triangle hypothesis. *Journal of Personality and Social Psychology, 31*, 661-673.

Nemeth, C. (1972). A critical analysis of research utilizing the prisoner's dilemma paradigm for the study of bargaining. In L. Berkowitz (Ed.), *Advances in Experimental Social Psychology*, *6*, 203-234.

Orbell, J.M., Schwartz-Shea, P., & Simmons, R.T. (1984). Do cooperators exit more readily than defectors? *The American Political Science Review*, *78*, 147-162.

Oskamp, S. (1971). Effects of programmed strategies on cooperation in the Prisoner's dilemma and other mixed-motive games. *Journal of Conflict Resolution*, *15*, 225-259.

Pruitt, D.G., & Kimmel, M.J. (1977). Twenty years of experimental gaming: Critique, synthesis, and suggestions for the future. *Annual Review of Psychology*, *28*, 363-392.

Simmons, R.T., Dawes, R.M. & Orbell, J.M. (1984). *Defection in social dilemmas: Is fear or is greed the problem*? Unpublished Manuscript. Department of Political Science, University of Oregon.

Solomon, L. (1960). The influence of some types of power relationships and game strategies upon the development of interpersonal trust. *Journal of Abnormal and Social Psychology*, *61*, 223-230.

Thibaut, J.W., & Kelley, H.H. (1959). *The social psychology of groups*. New York: Wiley.

Van Lange, P.A.M., Liebrand, W.B.G., & Kuhlman, D.M. (1990). Causal attribution of choice behavior in three N-person Prisoner's dilemmas. *Journal of Experimental Social Psychology*, *26*, 34-48.

Van Lange, P.A.M., Liebrand, W.B.G., Messick, D.M., & Wilke, H.A.M. (1992). Introduction and literature review. In W. B.G. Liebrand, D.M. Messick, & H.A.M. Wilke (Eds.), *Social dilemmas: Theoretical issues and research findings* (pp. 3-28). London: Pergamon Press.

Van Lange, P.A.M., & Veenendaal, A.F.M. (1992). *Seeking and avoiding interdependence: A transition list approach*. Paper presented at the fifth international conference on social dilemmas. Bielefeld, Germany.

Yamagishi, T. (1988). Exit from the group as an individualistic solution to the free-rider problem in the United States and Japan. *Journal of Experimental Social Psychology*, *24*, 530-542.

Yamagishi, T., & Sato, K. (1986). Motivational bases of the public goods problem. *Journal of Personality and Social Psychology*, *50*, 67-73.

Individual reasoning process in the participation game with period

Tetsuo Takigawa[1]

Abstract

A game with period was introduced to examine the effect of revised feedback information on increasing participation, as it related to the individual reasoning processes. Five one-shot games and a game with period were played by the same subjects in the experiment 1. The result showed that the level of participation in the game with period was lower than the one-shot games, due to the change in players' decision rule with respect to the information seeking. In the experiment 2, a persuasion procedure on reasoning was introduced to the same game with period. However, the persuasion effect on the individual reasoning process was not so evident.

Introduction

When the public TV calls for a fund-raising, the updated information of the cumulative level of donation is usually announced in real time during the campaign period. Dorsey (1992) analyzed such real-time continuous revision of voluntary contributions in different payoff situations and found the effectiveness of the real-time feedback information in increasing the contribution level under certain environmental conditions. The present paper focuses upon the subject's individual reasoning process during the discrete multi-trial period, especially upon the psychological discrepancy between an agreeable explanation of a reasonable choice and the decision not to choose at all.

The present situation may be summarized as follows. A sort of raffle is offered to the members of a group. The members are designated as the potential participants. Each potential participant can buy a raffle by paying some amount of money, say $10. The members who bought the raffle are called the participants. If the number of participants is greater than, or equal to, a required number, then the participants get $20 and the nonparticipants nothing. If the number of participants is smaller than the required number, the participants lose their money. The required number of the participants is the provision point in this situation, that is, the total gain function is step wise at this point.

There is no possibility of free riding in this situation and the amount of individual investment is limited just enough to pay for one raffle. The situation effect might change if free riding is permitted by allowing the people who did not pay also get paid, and if the amount of individual investment is made variable; however, we began with a simpler situation in the present study.

A special feature of the present situation is that the potential participants were allowed to have several trials before they decided. All potential participants were asked in each trial whether they intended to participate or not after the announcement of the cumulative number of participants in the past trials. The decision opportunity continues until cumulatively all the potential participants decided to participate, or the predetermined number of trials has elapsed. We denote the number of potential participants with N, the required number of participants with M, and the length of trials with T.

Experiment 1

The first experiment was conducted to see if the trial by trial feedback information was more effective in increasing the number of participants in comparison with the one-shot games. Two conditions were adopted to see the difference between two situations, $T=1$ (one-shot) and $T=8$ (with an 8-trial period), and both with $N=16$ and $M=8$. In each situation, the same 16 college students were asked whether they would like to participate or not under the given circumstance.

The subjects played five independent one-shot games first and then, two weeks later, played a game with period. Under the one-shot $(T=1)$ condition, the subjects' decision should be made only once on the first and last opportunity and the game result was determined by the single trial. In the game with period $(T=8)$, 16 subjects were allowed to have an 8-trial period to decide. If the number of participants reached the required number M, only the participants of the one-shot games got 5 points which were added to the seminar credit, and the participants of the game with period got 10 points. On the other hand, if the number of participants did not reach M, the one-shot game participants lost 2.5 points and 5 points in the game with period. The subjects were told that the points gained or lost in the experiments would be considered at the class's final evaluation, the class being the author's.

In each game the subjects were asked to write down his or her decision and also the reason why she did or did not participate in each trial as precisely as possible on a response sheet. Table 1 and 2 show the results of one-shot games and a game with period. It is evident that with the more number of required participants M, the smaller number of participants there was in one-shot games. In the one-shot game with M=8 and T=1, which is the counterpart of the game with period, the number of participants was 12. On the other hand, as shown in Table 2, the cumulative number of participants in the game with period with M=8 and T=8 was only 5 on the 2nd trial and there were no more participants thereafter.

Table 1

Five one-shot games (N=16, M=1, 4, 8, 12, 16).

Required No. of Participants (M)	1	4	8	12	16
No. of Participants	16	15	12	6	2

Table 2

A game with period (N=16, M=8, D=8).

Trials	1	2	3	4	5	6	7	8
No. of Participants	3	2	0	0	0	0	0	0
Cumulative No. of Participants	3	5	5	5	5	5	5	5

In Table 1, the subjects who participated in the games with a larger M participated consistently in the games with the smaller M. For example, the 2 subjects who participated in the game with M=16 also participated in all games with a smaller M. In Table 2, 2 out of 3 subjects who participated in the 1st trial were the very same subjects who participated in the one-shot game with M=16, and the 5 subjects who participated by the 2nd trial were the subjects who participated in the one-shot game with M=12.

Discussion

The results obtained under the 2 conditions were contradictory. Even though the number of participants in the one-shot game with M=8 was 12, only 5 subjects participated in the game with period with M=8.

The subjects unanimously reported that the most important information in the game with period was how many people have already invested in the past trials. However, the numbers of participants did not increase after the 2nd trial because the majority of subjects decided to wait and see how the number would vary along the trials. The 11 subjects who did not participate reported that they were disappointed with the fact that there were so few participants and, at the same time, were satisfied with their decision not to participate. On the other hand, the subjects who participated reported more or less unanimously that there were few leaders in the class and regretted that they decided to participate without checking the atmosphere of the class.

As a result, the nonparticipants (the information seekers) did not get the feedback information which they had expected in order to participate, namely the increasing number of participants. It is clear that the subjects got some information along the trials. The problem here is whether the information decreased the uncertainty or not. The uncertainty here is mainly social which comes from one's lack of knowledge about the actions of the other participants (Messick, Allison, & Samuelson, 1988). The answer should be yes. What the potential participants saw in the feedback information was that many conditional participants remained in the game including themselves. The reason why the remaining people are identified as conditional participants is that all the subjects were sure to participate if the remaining required number of participants got small enough, say 1 or 2, as shown in Table 1 in one-shot games. There were no unconditional nonparticipants in the subject group.

The decision rule adopted by most of subjects was the risk-avoiding or the mini-max strategy that is summarized as follows. At the beginning, the potential participants should hesitate to participate because the uncertainty of how many people are going to participate is at the maximum. If a certain number of people participated in the past trials and the revised required number of participants to get the profit is smaller than or equal to the number which you personally think safe to invest, then you participate.

However, if all the potential participants follow the decision rule described above, then the trials go on through the last trial (T-th trial) with the knowledge that nobody has paid so far. So, what you see in the last trial is that no one participated in the previous trials. After all, the knowledge of the number of participants in each trial, which is zero, will not help to increase the number of participants provided that all of the potential participants adopt the risk-avoiding or the mini-max strategy.

On the other hand, in reality, 3 subjects decided to participate without thinking of the uncertainty on the first decision opportunity as shown in Table 2. Their motive of participation was reported to be based on the unconditional cooperation motive or the maxi-max strategy. These 2 motives were not clearly separable from each other in the subjects' report. In addition to the first 3 participants, 2 other subjects decided to participate in the second trial. These 2 subjects reported that they expected the number of participants would increase after seeing the 3 participants in the first trial. Their decision rule was consistent with the one they adopted in the one-shot games, namely they did not participate only in the one-shot game with $M=16$ but did participate in the games with smaller M.

In spite of the fact that some subjects demonstrated the consistency of decision rule under the two different conditions, we could not see the effectiveness of introducing the feedback information in the game with period. Rather, the number of participants in the game with period with $M=8$ was smaller than in the one-shot game of the same M. Moreover, in comparison with the result that the number of participants in the one-shot game with $M=4$ was 15, nobody participated in the game with period even after the revised required number after the 2nd trial dropped to 3.

The results imply that the majority of subjects switched their decision rule of not looking for a way to decrease the uncertainty in one-shot games to the so-called "wait and see" information seeking strategy that was available in the game with period. As a result, the number of participants in the game with period did not reach the required M, which was reachable in the one-shot games.

Persuasion procedure

Now we focus upon a question whether another decision rule other than the "wait and see" strategy is effective in order to increase the number of participants in the game with period. The feature of the present situation is: that there is no dominating strategy in the games and that the optimal strategy is to participate if and only if it is certain that the number of participants reaches the required number M; Otherwise, not to participate is the best choice. On the other hand, it will never become certain along the trials as far as the majority of people adopt the "wait and see" strategy.

One of the possibilities of getting enough number of participants is to change the incentive structure so as to make the participation more attractive. However, it changes the game itself. Another possibility to be considered in the present study is to change the subjects' cognitive structure of the situation. In this section, we examine a persuasion procedure to check if some number of potential participants are persuaded to participate and not to choose the "wait and see" strategy. If a majority of the unconditional participants change their mind to participation on the earlier trials, then they make themselves a core of participants to get more number of participants.

The following explanation of a reasoning process was prepared to persuade the subjects in the game with period.

"We assume first that a substantially small number of people out of many are required in order to get provision. Let's begin with the case of $M=1$. If only one person is required to get provision, you are happy to pay \$10 to get \$20. This is a sure thing so that all the potential participants except unconditional nonparticipants invest without necessity of knowing other people's decision. And it is certain that there is no unconditional nonparticipants among you as shown in Table 1. Then, how about the case of $M=2$? If you participate on the 1st trial then the situation becomes exactly the same one with the case of M=1 for the remaining potential participants in the next trial. All other people will participate in the next trial because it is a sure thing. The same reasoning path can be used in the case of M=3. If you participate, the situation becomes exactly the same with M=2 in the next trial, and should another person participate then the situation becomes the M=1 case in the 3rd trial. Even in the situation of M=m where m is very large, M decreases to 1 in the m-trial period. The most interesting paradoxical conclusion is that only one trial is the necessary period because all of the potential participants invest on the 1st trial if they think this way."

Experiment 2

In order to see whether or not the reasoning process described above is effective in increasing the number of participants in the game with period, the same subjects as in the experiment 1 were persuaded by the experimenter, being told of the reasoning process, and then played the same game with M=8 and T=8 as they had played a couple of weeks ago. Table 3 shows the result.

Table 3
A game with period (N=16, M=8, D=8) after persuasion.

Trials	1	2	3	4	5	6	7	8
No. of Participants	3	2	1	0	0	1	3	6
Cumulative No. of Participants	3	5	6	6	6	7	10	16

Discussion

The result suggests that the persuasion be effective in getting the required number of participants. However, the number of participants did not increase linearly and the persuasion effect was found to be only partial and indirect when the analysis of the subjects' report was done. For example, the 5 participants in the 1st and 2nd trials were the same subjects in the game without persuasion (Table 2). The subjects who participated in the 3rd and 6th trials had not participated in the earlier game with period, and they played an important role in increasing the number of participants thereafter in the current game. They reported, however, that they participated not because they were persuaded by the experimenter but because they liked to see what would happen if they participated, apparently to check the validity of the experimenter's explanation. This may be described as a partial or indirect effect of persuasion.

There were 2 subjects who reported that they believed the experimenter's explanation but they were the participants in the 1st trial in the games with and without persuasion so that the persuasion did not make any explicit difference. The other 14 subjects including 3 subjects who had participated at the beginning of the two games with period reported that the reasoning process explained by the experimenter seemed to be very unnatural.

One typical argument made by subjects is summarized as follows: I cannot point out what is wrong with the reasoning explained by the experimenter but I felt that there was something questionable about it, especially concerning the ambiguity of who is the first participant. And then, who is the second, third, ... on each trial in the course of the reasoning? I participated because the revised required number became very small.

It is suggested from the present study that without any coercive assignment of the decision sequence that all potential participants have to follow, the reasoning process does not become effective. The majority of the subjects did not accept the persuasion as an agreeable framework for decision making but all subjects agreed to make the total contribution maximal if and only if a coercive assignment existed and all potential participants understood the rule. However, it is an open question whether each member could have had the controllability over one of many links of the long line of participation or not. This is a different aspect from the sequential games (Rapoport, 1992). On the other hand, the conclusion of the reasoning does not require the strict coercive assignment of the sequential order because if all potential participants consent to the validity of the reasoning, all of them would participate in the 1st trial so that the longer period is not necessary. However, most of the subjects did not agree with the conclusion even though they could not make any clear opposing argument. They adopted the "wait and see" decision rule just because it was allowed. This is a big discrepancy between the imaginary positive reasoning and the reality.

Footnote

1 Hokkaido University, Bungakubu, Sapporo, Japan

References

Dorsey, R. E. (1992). The voluntary contributions mechanism with real time revisions. *Public Choice, 73*, 261-282.

Messick, D. M., Allison, S.T., & Samuelson, C. D. (1988). Framing and communication effects on group members' responses to environmental and social uncertainty. In S. Maital (Ed.) *Applied Behavioral Economics, Vol. II.* (677-700). Brighton: Wheatsheaf.

Rapoport, A. (1992). Provision of step-level public goods: Effects of different information structures. *Paper presented at the 5th International Conference on Social Dilemmas*, Bielefeld, Germany.

The position effect:
The role of a player's serial position in a resource dilemma game

Ramzi Suleiman[1], David V. Budescu[2], and Amnon Rapoport[3]

Abstract

We consider the following single-stage resource dilemma game with both strategic and environmental uncertainty: Members of group N are required to share a common resource whose size x is not known with precision. Rather, x is sampled randomly from a probability distribution which is common knowledge. Individual players make their requests privately; their requests are granted if and only if the total group request does not exceed x.

We examine a sequential protocol of play in which individual requests are made in a prespecified order. Players are not informed about previous requests in the sequence; they are only told their serial position in the sequence.

Data from 45 subjects, in correspondence with our previous studies, show significant effects due to resource uncertainty. In addition, they reveal a significant position effect with players appearing late in the sequence making smaller requests.

Introduction

In his classical essay "The Tragedy of the Commons" Hardin (1968) described and analyzed a hypothetical situation in which a group of herdsmen jointly use a common pasturage to graze their sheep. When considering the option of increasing one's herd, each herdsman comes to the rational conclusion that his personal gain from this act exceeds the negative externality - in the form of increased grazing - carried by the rest of the herdsmen. Paradoxically, if all herdsmen behave rationally, adding more and more sheep to their herds, the ultimate result will be the destruction of the commons.

Hardin's parable was used to analyze various environmental and ecological problems such as the management of ground waters, forests, and fisheries, where the interactive decisions of rational selfish users often cause the resource level to fall sharply to hazardously low levels. It has also stimulated a considerable amount of laboratory research, carried mostly by social psychologists. In a series of experiments, Messick and his colleagues (Messick, Wilke, Brewer, Kramer, Zemke, & Lui, 1983, Samuelson, Messick, Rutte, & Wilke, 1984, Samuelson & Messick, 1986a, 1986b, Rutte, Wilke, & Messick, 1987) used a replenishable resource paradigm. On any given trial subjects independently and anonymously stated their demands, the resource was replenished (by multiplying the residual amount by a commonly known replenishment factor exceeding unity), and the result constituted the size of the pool for the next trial. The experiment terminated after a fixed number of trails, or when the resource was exhausted, whichever came first. On all trials, the exact amount in the resource was known with certainty to all players. Suleiman and Rapoport (1988), argued that the assumption of a fixed and known resource fails to capture many realistic resource management problems characterized by resource uncertainty. Groundwater reserves can not be estimated to the last barrel, nor can we estimate the exact size of Northern Seas fisheries. In such cases, as in many others, an environmental uncertainty regarding the resource size is coupled with the strategic uncertainty about others' requests from the shared resource.

To investigate the joint effect of both uncertainties, Suleiman and Rapoport (1988) proposed a simple paradigm: members of a group of size n can privately request from a shared resource whose exact size (x) is not known. Rather, x is sampled randomly from a probability distribution which is common knowledge. Each member is awarded his/her request if, and only if, the total group request does not exceed the pool size. If the group request exceeds the amount in the random pool, all the requests are denied. Rapoport, Budescu, Suleiman, and Weg (1992), and Budescu, Rapoport, and Suleiman (1990) implemented this paradigm to study the effects of different levels of environmental uncertainty (modelled by a uniform distribution with a fixed mean and varying range) on individual and group requests. Both experiments implemented a simultaneous protocol, in which subjects are instructed to make their requests simultaneously.

Erev and Rapoport (1990) have argued in favor of a sequential protocol of play under which decisions are made in a prespecified order such that 1) each player knows her position in the sequence, and 2) each player is fully and accurately informed of the requests of all the players preceding her in the sequence. Rapoport et. al (in press), reported a resource dilemma experiment under strategic and environmental uncertainty which implements the sequential protocol. Their results show significant effects of resource uncertainty with individuals requesting more as the resource uncertainty increases, and a position effect, according to which "first movers" request more than others who make their requests later in the sequence.

The simultaneous and the sequential protocols of play described above do not exhaust all the information structures that underlie resource dilemmas in real life. There are several ways in which the two properties defining the sequential protocol above may be relaxed or modified to form other, possibly more realistic protocols of play. These protocols reflect other assumptions about the information each group member has when she makes her request from the limited (and unknown) resource. For example, player j may be informed of her position in the sequence as before, but only learn the requests of the players preceding her in the sequence with uncertainty. In other words, the total request of all preceding players under this new protocol is assumed to be a random variable with a known distribution function. In a second modification of the sequential protocol, which is particularly applicable to resource dilemma situations with a large number of group members, player j may be only informed about the requests of players j-1, j-2,...,j-t, where $1 \leq t \leq j-1$. In yet another modification of the sequential protocol - the one examined in the present paper - we retain the first property of the sequential protocol but omit the second. Specifically, the *positional order protocol* is characterized by the assumption that each player j only knows her position in the sequence; she never learns the requests of the players preceding her in the sequence.

Hypotheses

The present paper tests competitively two hypotheses concerning he effects of the positional order protocol. Although the paper examines the resource dilemma game described above, it has implications to other noncooperative interactive situations (the Prisoner's Dilemma, Chicken, Battle of the Sexes games, public good experiments, etc.). The *game theoretical hypothesis,* derived from classical game theory, considers positional order information irrelevant. Consequently, it recognizes no difference between the simultaneous and positional order protocols. The alternative *positional order hypothesis* derives from Schelling's (1960) analysis of coordination games, and from recent research on the effects of different information structures on the provision of step-level public goods conducted by Rapoport and Erev (1992). It states that information about the order of play affects behavior. The strong version of the hypothesis states that each player assumes that all the group members will take advantage of their position in the sequence and assume others to do so. As a result, when it is her turn to play, each player will assume that the decisions of all the players preceding her in the sequence are known. Thus, the strong version of the positional order hypothesis recognizes no difference between the sequential and positional order protocols. The weak version of this hypothesis, supported by the study of Rapoport and Erev (1992), states that only some of the players will exploit the positional order information as described above, while the remaining subjects will ignore this information and consider it irrelevant. According to this weaker hypothesis, the positional order protocol will yield results which fall between the results obtained under the simultaneous and sequential protocols.

To illustrate the two hypotheses in a simpler and more familiar game, consider the two games in tree (extensive) form presented in figures 1(a) and 1(b). In game 1(a) player 1 has to choose between x_1 and y_1 and player 2, who is not informed of player 1's choice has to choose between x_2 and y_2. Player 2's information set is denoted by a broken ellipse. In game 1(b) the roles of the two players are reversed. In each game each player knows the entire game tree which is assumed to be common knowledge, and consequently knows when it is her turn to play. The classical abstraction of each of these two games via the notion of strategy (Luce & Raiffa, 1957) gives rise to the game of chicken which is presented in strategic normal form at the bottom of figure 1. The strategic form game does not reflect information about order of play, which varies from game 1(a) to 1(b) and the game theoretical hypothesis, applied to game 1(a) or 1(b), yields the same predictions for the two players. The strong version of the positional order hypothesis asserts that, knowing that she is the first to move and that player 2 knows it, player 1 in game 1(a) will chose y_1. Assuming that player 1 has taken advantage of her first position, player 2 will chose

x_2. If the game is presented in tree form, the positional order hypothesis predicts the outcomes (y_1, x_2) and (x_1, y_2) for games 1(a) and 1(b), respectively. Under the weak version of the hypothesis, the predictions above will be attenuated because some of the players will ignore information about order of play and "frame" the game as if it was played under the simultaneous protocol.

Method

Subjects. Fourty five psychology undergraduates at the University of Haifa participated in the experiment. Subjects volunteered to participate by listing their names in one of the prespecified time slots on a departmental bulletin board. In addition to obtaining class credit for their participation, subjects were paid contingent on their group performance as will be explained below.

Design. The study employed a three way within subject factorial design. The factors were: level of environmental uncertainty (3 levels), sequential position in the group (5 levels), and the presence/absence of postdecison questions (2 levels). The actual resource on each trial was selected randomly from one of three different uniform distributions with equal means but different upper and lower limits (and consequently, different variances), reflecting increasing levels of environmental uncertainty. These conditions were:

Condition I: Mean=500 points and Range=0 points (500-500).

Condition II: Mean=500 points and Range=500 points (250-750).

Condition III: Mean=500 points and Range=1000 points (0-1000).

At the beginning of each trial subjects where assigned different positions (first, second,...fifth), that determined the order in which they entered their requests from the random source. The experiment consisted of two blocks of 15 games (all possible combinations of the levels of resource uncertainty and the 5 sequential positions).

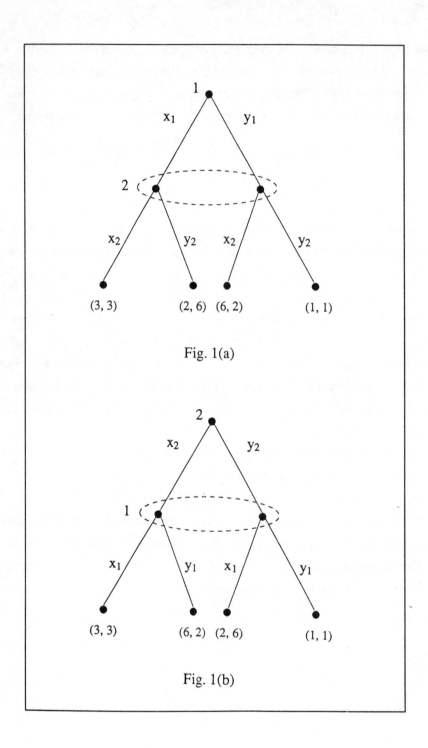

Fig. 1(a)

Fig. 1(b)

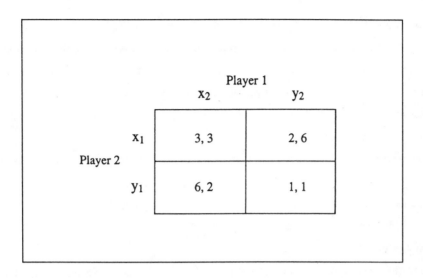

Figure 1: The game of Chicken presented in tree and strategic forms.

In the first block all games were presented in a random order. In the second block the games were repeated in a different random order, with each trial followed by a series of questions regarding the source and the expected requests of the other players. This procedure was adopted in order to minimize possible contamination of subjects requests by the postdecision questions. Subjects received no trial by trial feedback regarding the size of the source, the requests made by other players, or the group outcome for that trial.

Procedure. The experiment was controlled by a DEC PDP 11/73 computer. Upon arrival to the laboratory, subjects were randomly assigned to five private and soundproof cubicles. They were then given written descriptions of the experiment explaining the nature of the task, the various parameters, the payoff structure, and the mechanics of the experimental procedure. The descriptions stressed the following characteristics of the experiment:

1. Each group consists of five players.
2. No communication is allowed among group members.
3. The experiment consists of 30 independent trials, with no feedback between trials about requests or outcomes.
4. At the beginning of each trial subjects are provided information about the trial number, the

limits of the resource, and their assigned positions in the sequence.

5.   After the players 1 through j-1 enter their requests, each player j is instructed to key in her request, within the specified boundaries of the common resource. No information about the amounts requested by the previous players (individually or combined) is given.

6.   Requests are granted if, and only if, the joint group request does not exceed the amount available in the resource.

After each of the last 15 trials (second block) each subject was asked to answer the following:

1.   Estimate the size of the common resource (except for Condition I).

2.   Give his best estimate of the total request of all previous players (except for players in the first position).

3.   Give his best estimate of the total request of all the following players (except for players in the last position).

The subjective and private nature of the estimates was emphasized. There was no time limit for specifying the requests or answering the questions.

To motivate the players, they were informed that at the conclusion of the experiment six trials would be randomly selected, and the number of points earned on those trials would be converted to money to determine their payoffs.

The conversion rate was 20 points to 1 NIS (approximately 32 points to $1). On the average, each experimental session lasted just under 2 hours.

Results

Harvest decisions

The requests from the source were submitted to a three way within- subject ANOVA. The analysis identified significant main effects for the level of environmental uncertainty ($F(2,43) = 18.34$; $p < .01$), and position ($F(4,41) = 4.05$; $p < .01$), but no interaction between these two factors ($F(8,37) = 1.95$; $p > .01$). There was no significant difference between the two replications of the task (with and without questions), nor any significant interactions involving this factor. Table 1 presents the means and the standard deviations of the individuals requests for each position and under each condition of environmental uncertainty.

Table 1

Means (and Standard Deviations) of Individual Requests from the Resource by Condition and Position

		Position in Sequence					
Condition		1	2	3	4	5	Overall
I	M	95	92	88	81	85	441
(500-500)	SD	(64)	(56)	(42)	(35)	(61)	
II	M	139	110	106	113	102	570
(250-750)	SD	(113)	(82)	(86)	(117)	(97)	
III	M	182	164	154	117	121	735
(0-1000)	SD	(166)	(133)	(146)	(87)	(97)	
Over	M	139	122	116	103	102	580
Condition	SD	(126)	(99)	(104)	(87)	(88)	

The results in Table 1 show that the means follow a very clear and consistent pattern with subjects requesting more as the level of uncertainty increases. Similarly, subjects request more the earlier is their position in the sequence.

A similar pattern is observed for the standard deviations, reflecting a higher variability in those conditions that produced higher mean requests. The correlation between the 15 means in Table 1 and their corresponding standard deviations is an impressive 0.93. This fact lead us to re-analyze the results after submitting them to variance stabilizing transformations (e.g. Smith, 1976). A similar pattern of results was obtained: We found significant main effects for the level of environmental uncertainty ($F(2,43) = 14.79$; $p < .01$), and position ($F(4,44) = 4.05$; $p < .01$), but no interaction between these two factors ($F(8,37) = 2.53$; $p > .01$).

It is interesting to observe the within-subject consistency of requests across conditions. The correlations between the mean requests in the three uncertainty conditions (across the 5 positions) vary between 0.58 and 0.75 with a median value of 0.60. The correlations between the mean requests in the five positions (across the three levels of uncertainty) range from 0.42 to 0.76 with a median of 0.67. Thus, we observe a stable pattern of consistent differences between the various subjects.

To validate the results regarding the position effect we calculated for each subject the mean request in each position and computed the rank (Kendall) correlation between this value and the player's position in the sequence. Most correlations (65%) were negative with a median of -0.20. This indicates that the higher requests were usually registered by the first players in the sequence. Furthermore as the uncertainty about the source increased, the proportion of negative correlations increased (56%, 62% and 69% for Conditions I, II, and III respectively), and the median correlation decreased (-0.11, -0.20 and -.31, respectively).

While our major concern is with individual behavior, it is of interest at this point to investigate the effect of the resource uncertainty on group performance. We combined all requests within each group and compared the resulting sum to the mean value of the random source (500 points). This comparison served to determine whether the groups' demands on any given trial were provided. As expected, the proportion of trials on which the group's demands were provided decreased as a function of the variability of the source (83%, 51% and 27% for conditions I II and III respectively). The difference between the three levels is significant ($F(2,7) = 18.1$; $p < .01$).

Estimates of the uncertain resource

Table 2 presents the means and standard deviations of the estimates of the resource computed from the subjects' answers to the questions on trials 16-30. The ANOVA performed on these estimates failed to reveal significant effects for the level of uncertainty ($F(1,44) < 1$), the player's position ($F(4,41) < 1$), or the interaction between these two factors ($F(4,41) = 2.43$; $p > .01$).

Table 2

Means (and Standard Deviations) of the Estimates of the Random Resource by Condition and Position

		Position in Sequence					
Condition		1	2	3	4	5	Overall
II	M	506	521	511	482	530	510
(250-750)	SD	(138)	(141)	(150)	(164)	(153)	(149)
III	M	589	607	612	621	622	610
	SD	(237)	(263)	(269)	(275)	(247)	(266)
Over M		547	564	562	551	576	560
Condition	SD	(197)	(214)	(222)	(236)	(209)	

Table 2 shows that with only one exception, all mean values are above the expected value of 500. Essentially, the estimates of the resource are larger, and more heterogeneous, for the higher range of resource uncertainty (0-1000), than for the lower one (250-750). The correlation between the 10 means and their respective standard deviations is 0.94. Following a variance stabilizing transformation, a significant effect for the level of uncertainty was uncovered ($F(1,44) = 11.15$; $p < .01$).

Estimates of others' demands

Recall that in the second block of trials each subject was asked to estimate the total request of the players preceding her in the sequence (Question 2) and following her in the sequence (Question 3). We analyzed these estimates separately after dividing each by the number of previous and subsequent players respectively. The first set of estimates (Question 2) was submitted to a 3 by 4 condition by position ANOVA (clearly, position 1 was omitted). The analysis uncovered significant main effects due to condition ($F(6,39) = 1.04$, $p < .01$). The same pattern of results was obtained after submitting the estimates to a variance stabilizing transformation. The means and standard deviations of the estimates of the requests of previous players in the sequence are shown in the top part of Table 3.

Table 3

Means (and Standard Deviations) of the Estimates of Requests of the Other Players by Condition and Position

Players Preceding the Focal Player in the Sequence

Position in Sequence

Condition		2	3	4	5	Overall
I	M		120	125	103	96	111
(500-500)	SD		(75)	(155)	(37)	(32)	(90)
II	M		170	134	133	119	139
(250-750)	SD		(150)	(80)	(84)	(91)	(106)
III	M		228	163	163	131	171
(0-1000)	SD		(232)	(125)	(73)	(55)	(143)
Over M		173	141	133	115	
Condition	SD		(170)	(124)	(73)	(65)	

Players Following the Focal Player in the Sequence

Position in Sequence

Condition		1	2	3	4	Overall
I	M	101	107	98	102	102
(500-500)	SD	(37)	(38)	(36)	(42)	(38)
II	M	112	126	126	122	121
(250-750)	SD	(52)	(56)	(65)	(112)	(75)
III	M	141	142	140	152	144
(0-1000)	SD	(43)	(62)	(80)	(131)	(86)
Over M		118	125	121	125	
Condition	SD		(48)	(55)	(65)	(104)	

The second set of estimates (Question 3) was submitted to the same analysis (after adding position 1 and omitting position 5). The ANOVA revealed a significant main effect due to condition ($F(2,43) = 14.52$, $p < .01$) but not for position ($F < 1$) or the condition by position interaction ($F < 1$). As before, the variance stabilizing transformation did not change the pattern of the results. The means and standard deviations of the estimates of the requests of the following players in the sequence are presented in the bottom part of Table 3.

When compared to each other, the two parts of Table 3 show an interesting finding. Subjects expected that players preceding them in the sequence would take advantage of the position such that the earlier the subject in the sequence the higher her request. In contrast, the subjects did not expect players following them in the sequence to be affected by their position. In making their estimates, the subjects seem to focus only on the requests already made, not on requests about to be made. In both cases the subjects estimated that the requests of the other players would increase as the uncertainty of the resource increases.

Discussion

A major finding of the present study is that subjects request more as the level of resource uncertainty increases. This result is congruent with similar results obtained for symmetric and asymmetric groups of five members playing under the simultaneous protocol (Rapoport et. at, 1992, and Budescu et. al,1990, respectively); as well as for groups playing under the sequential protocol (Rapoport et. al, in press) where subjects have full information about the total request of players who preceded them in the sequence.

Two additional results replicated here are that subjects give higher estimates of the resource and expect other players to request more, as the level of resource uncertainty increases. Subjects either use these estimates in deciding about their own requests, or they make their requests and only then rationalize them by congruent beliefs regarding others' behavior and/or available shared resources.

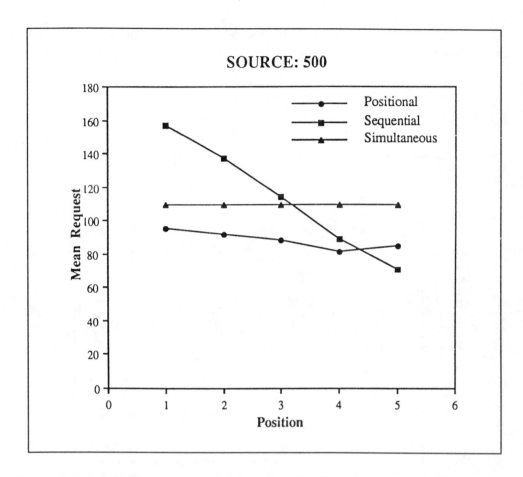

Figures 2 a: Individual requests as a function of position for each resource condition compared with results obtained under the simultaneous and under the sequential protocols.

The most intriguing finding in the present study is the emergence of the "position effect". Subjects appearing earlier in the sequence requested significantly more than those who placed their requests later. This result is strongly supportive of the positional order hypothesis and stands in contrast to the game theoretical hypothesis. To further illustrate the magnitude of the position effect obtained in the reported experiment, figures 2(a), 2(b), and 2(c) compare the mean individual requests obtained in the present study (plotted as a function of position), with results obtained under similar resource conditions in two previous studies, one implementing the simultaneous protocol (Rapoport et. al, 1992), and the other the sequential protocol (Rapoport et. al, in press).

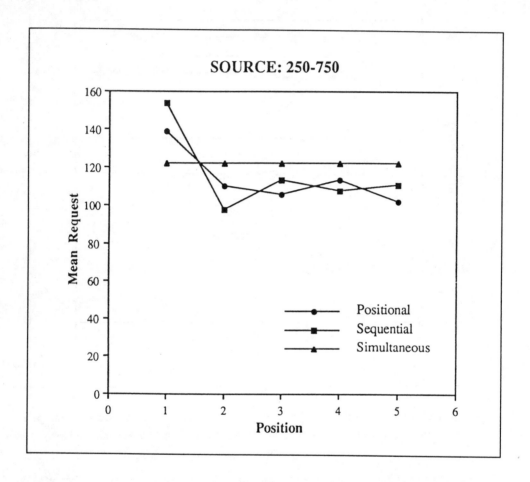

Figures 2 b: Individual requests as a function of position for each resource condition compared with results obtained under the simultaneous and under the sequential protocols.

The figures show clearly that with the increase in the resource uncertainty, the graph of requests for the positional order protocol shows higher similarity with the one from the sequential protocol. The results obtained here do not permit conclusive judgments in favor of the strong or weak version of the positional order hypothesis. Nevertheless, the high variance between subjects' requests under all resource conditions (see Table 2) together with the reported within-subject consistency across conditions suggest that different subjects might adhere to different principles while managing a shared resource.

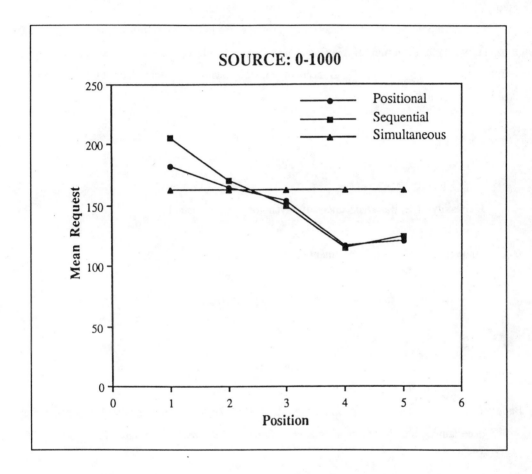

Figures 2 c: Individual requests as a function of position for each resource condition compared with results obtained under the simultaneous and under the sequential protocols.

As we noted before, game theory treats the extensive and strategic (normal) forms of the game as equivalent while considering the information about the positional order irrelevant. The results obtained in the present study, together with those reported by Rapoport and Erev (1992) for a different type of social dilemma, constitute in our opinion a challenge to classical game theory.

Our results, supported by the theoretical remarks made in the introduction, suggest that information about the order of play significantly affects players' choices. We contend that a refinement in theory is needed to account for the asymmetry introduced to the game by positional order information.

Footnotes

1   University of Haifa, Department of Psychology, Haifa, Israel

2   University of Illinois, Department of Psychology, Champaign, USA

3   University of Arizona, Department of Management, Tuscon, USA

References

Budescu, D.V., Rapoport, A., & Suleiman, R. (1990). Resource dilemmas with environmental uncertainty and asymmetric players. *European Journal of Social Psychology, 20,* 475-487.

Erev, I., Rapoport, A. (1990). Provision of step-level public goods: The sequential contribution mechanism. *Journal of Conflict Resolution, 34,* 401-425.

Hardin, G.R. (1968). The tragedy of the commons. *Science, 162,* 1243-1248.

Messick, D.M., Wilke, H., Brewer, M.B., Kramer, R.M., Zemke, P.E., & Lui, L. (1983). Individual adaptations and structural change as solutions to social dilemmas. *Journal of Personality and Social Psychology, 44,* 294-309.

Rapoport, A., & Erev, I. (1992). Provision of step-level public goods: Effects of different information structures. Unpublished manuscript.

Rapoport, A., Budescu, D.V., Suleiman, R., & Weg, E. (1992). Social dilemmas with uniformly distributed resources. In W.B.G. Liebrand, D.M. Messick, & H.A.M. Wilke (Eds.), *Social Dilemmas: Theoretical issues and research findings* (pp. 43-57). Pergamon Press.

Rutte, C.G., Wilke, H.A.M., & Messick, D.M. (1987). Scarcity or abundance caused by people or the environment as determinants of behavior in the resource dilemma. *Journal of Experimental Social Psychology, 23,* 208-216.

Samuelson, C.D., & Messick, D.M. (1986a). Alternative structural solutions to resource dilemmas. *Organizational Behavior and Human Decision Processes, 37,* 139-155.

Samuelson, C.D., & Messick, D.M. (1986b). Inequities in access to and use of shared resources in social dilemmas. *Journal of Personality and Social Psychology, 51,* 960-967.

Samuelson, C.D., Messick, D.M., Rutte, C.G., & Wilke, H. (1984). Individual and structural solutions to resource dilemmas in two cultures. *Journal of Personality and Social Psychology, 47,* 94-104.

Schelling, T. C. (1960). *The strategy of conflict.* Cambridge Mass: Harvard University Press.

Smith, J. E. K. (1976). Data transformations in analysis of variance. *Journal of Verbal Learning and Verbal Behavior, 15,* 339-346.

Suleiman, R., & Rapoport, A. (1988). Environmental and social uncertainty in single-trial resource dilemmas. *Acta Psychologica, 68,* 99-112.

Acknowledgment

This research was supported by a grant from the Basic Research Fund of the Israeli Academy of Science and by NSF grant number SES-9122686.

Positive and negative mood effects on solving a resource dilemma

Regina Vollmeyer[1]

Abstract

A resource dilemma is a situation in which maximizing individual profits contradicts the conservation of a resource. How do people solve a resource dilemma if they are in positive or negative mood? There are some models which offer different explanations and predict different outcomes: (1) the cognitive capacity explanation expects that people in negative mood are hampered in performing a cognitive task because their cognitive capacity is reduced by thinking about their emotional state; (2) the mood repair explanation assumes that people in negative mood overexploit the resource to improve their mood; (3) the motivational explanation claims two different strategies depending on mood state. The hypotheses derived from the three models were tested in two experiments. The results lend some support to the motivational explanation.

Introduction

Since the early eigthies, interest in the effects of mood on cognition has increased enormously. A large amount of empirical and theoretical work has been done on the effect of mood on memory (Blaney, 1986, for a review; Ucros, 1989, for a meta analysis) and some on problem solving (a short survey is given later). However, the influence of mood on the cognitive processes involved in social dilemmas has been addressed only in a few studies (Knapp, 1986; Knapp & Clark, 1991). Because solving social dilemmas can be characterized as problem solving, it is possible to extend our understanding of the effects of mood in social dilemma by reviewing recent findings on the effects of mood on problem solving in general. The research on problem solving focuses individuals whereas the research on social dilemma focuses on several players. A social dilemma in which only one individual takes part is called a resource dilemma (Knapp, 1990). Therefore research into resource dilemmas links problem solving with social dilemma.

Two concepts must first be defined: problem solving and mood. Problem solving means finding a way to get from a given state to a goal state when the means to get to the goal state are unknown (otherwise it is called a task). For example, if a person is losing in a game, but the goal is to win, one has to find a way to change the outcome. There are two different types of problems: well-defined problems in which the goal is concrete (e.g., "win 100 points"); and ill-defined problems in which the goal is vague (e.g., "maximize your profit"). In the latter case, knowledge and creativity are necessary to define the goal. What do problems and social dilemmas have in common? According to Dawes (1980, p. 169), social dilemmas "are defined by two simple properties: (a) each individual receives a higher payoff for a socially defecting choice (...) than for a socially cooperative choice, no matter what the other individuals in society do, but (b) all individuals are better off if all cooperate than if all defect.". Whereas in social dilemmas the individual regards herself/himself in comparison with other persons, an individual who is confronted with a problem has to reflect only on her/his own behavior. However, the cognitive processes involved in solving either are essentially the same. First, the structure of the problem task or the dilemma has to be represented, second, the goal has to be defined, and finally, the means to get to the goal state have to be generated. Despite these similarities, only Holding (1987) and Thagard (1992) have tried to conceptualize social dilemmas in terms of problem solving.

Mood must also be defined. Mood can be best understood in contrast with emotion. Morris (1989, p. 3) proposed that "... moods can be defined as affective states that are capable of influencing a broad array of potential responses, many of which seem quite unrelated to the mood-precipitating event. As compared with emotions, moods are typically less intense affective states and are thought to be involved in the instigation of self-regulatory processes.". For example, when solving a social dilemma players get angry or sad if others defect. These emotions are more intense than a mood, which is unrelated to the game. In the following experiment I wanted to test whether mood had an impact on cognitive performance as both should have the same effects.

To explain the effect of mood, several models have been put forward, of which three models are of most interest: the cognitive capacity explanation, the mood repair explanation, and the motivational explanation. First, I will present a short description of the respective models. Then I will outline a study testing hypotheses deduced from the models.

The cognitive capacity explanation. Starting out with the phenomenon that depressed people suffer an impairment in cognitive performance, Ellis and Ashbrook (1988) put forward their resource allocation model. Like Norman and Bobrow (1975), and Kahneman (1973) they assumed that working memory has a limited cognitive capacity. In their opinion, a part of that capacity is allocated for mood thus leaving less space for another cognitive task. If the task is easy or the mood is not intense, both can be processed. In a reply to Hertel and Hardin (1990), who proposed a motivational model, Ellis (1990) failed to specify the effects of reaching the limits of capacity. Does the attention drop? Or is there a loss in motivation? He stated: "... there is nothing about resource allocation explanations that place constraints on where deficits in performance might occur." (1990, p. 61).

The mood repair explanation. To the theory that mood takes up space in working memory Knapp and Clark (1991) proposed an alternative: the hypothesis of mood repair (Isen & Levin, 1972; Isen & Simmonds, 1978). The hypothesis states that people in sad mood want to improve their mood by seeking immediate gratification. Seeking short-term gains will be especially detriemental to performance in a resource dilemma (Hardin, 1968), that is, situations in which maximizing short-term profits contradicts the conservation of a common resource.

The motivational explanation. The general assumption of this theory is that positive and negative moods influence cognition in an asymmetrical way, because they lead to two styles of processing. Positive and negative mood have different cognitive effects, because each of them triggers different styles of processing (see below). Different, though not necessarily comparable models, have been proposed by the following researchers: Isen (1984, 1987), Fiedler (1988), Schwarz, Bless, and Bohner (1991), and Hertel and Hardin (1990).

Isen (1987) described the asymmetrical influence of mood on cognition, as causing change in not only the content of the representation of the material presented but also the types of strategy used: In positive mood one uses the strategy of summarizing and simplifying the decision situations. She suggested that people in a positive mood do not get involved in tedious, or effortful strategies. Fiedler (1988) named the strategy in positive mood "loosening" and the strategy in negative mood "tightening", a differentiation made by Kelly (1955). In positive mood a person makes a loosening interpretation of the situation: there is some degree of optimism leading to more free associations, more risk taking, and creative thinking. Negative mood triggers the tightening interpretation, that can be observed in processes like simplifying the structure of new thoughts. While people have a tightening interpretation strictness and error avoiding predominate. Schwarz et al. (1991) summarized the existing models and came to the conclusion they all assume that in a positive mood, people choose simplifying heuristics whereas in a negative mood, effortful, detail-oriented analyses are adopted. Scharz and others have examined in the field of attitude change where people in sad mood verbalized more thoughts about a text than people did in happy mood. Hertel and Hardin (1990) proposed the "initiation"-hypothesis also asymmetrical as it is restricted to depressed mood. They explained the poor performance in memory tasks of depressed persons as due to a deficit in cognitive initiative. In support of this model, Klauer, Siemer, and Stöber (1991) distinguished styles of processing by means of the concept of "readiness to make an effort".

Empirical results regarding the influence of mood on problem solving. As mentioned earlier, only a few studies addressing this question exist. A lot of work has been done on the impact of negative mood on cognitive performance, under the hypothesis that negative mood would induce a drop in performance. However, the results are ambiguous. Salovey and Palfai (1991) found no influence of mood on a deductive or an inductive task though there was an effect on reaction time. Slife and Weaver (1992, Exp. 1) induced positive or negative mood before presenting subjects with mathematical tasks. No influence of mood induction could be found, but when a depression inventory was used, a relationship with severe depression was demonstrated (1992, Exp. 2). However, induction of sad mood and a severe depression are not comparable, given that depression is much more intense. Using analogical problem solving (in which subjects have to transfer their knowledge about a source problem to a target problem) Hesse and Gerrards (1989) found no difference in performance between neutral and negative mood, but they observed that the strategies used differed. Subjects with a negatively induced mood described the source problem concretely but the description of the target problem remained highly abstract. In two studies, Knapp (1986; Knapp & Clark, 1991) demonstrated a deteriorated problem solving performance in negative mood, as subjects in negative mood exploited a resource dilemma, that is such subjects withdrew too much from a limited resource. Dobson and Dobson (1981) found that depressed and non-depressed students differed in their strategy which was interpreted as a problem solving deficit and a conservative style in depression. These empirical studies say something in favor of each model: changes were found in strategies (consistent with the motivational model) but sometimes also a drop in performance was observed (consistent with the capacity model) and in studies using a resource dilemma an overexploitation of the resource (consistent with the mood repair hypothesis) was observed.

The influence of positive mood on problem solving tasks has not been examined as much as that of depressed or negative mood. A review of the pertinent studies was given by Fiedler (1988). Experiments by Isen showed that more associates to a word were generated in positive mood (Isen, Daubmann, & Nowicki, 1987; Isen, Johnson, Mertz, & Robinson, 1985) and more abstract categories were generated (Isen & Daubmann, 1984). On a creative task, Abele (1990a) found that positive mood resulted in better performance than neutral mood. However, in a resource dilemma, Knapp (1986; Knapp & Clark, 1991) obtained no differences for subjects in positive and neutral mood, despite their finding of an effect of negative mood. These studies appear to demonstrate that if the task demanded creativity the people in a positive mood showed more variety in their answers. Thus it seems important what kind of task is used. In summary, there is some evidence in favor of the motivational model, because a number of studies show a change of strategy in positive mood while showing no drop in performance. No predictions can be derived from the mood repair or cognitive capacity explanation with regard to the effects of positive mood.

Before introducing the empirical question I wish to show how mood can be induced, as these methods are not well-known by social dilemma researchers. Spies, Gerrards-Hesse, and Hesse (1990) drew up a classification scheme. They formed the following categories:

(1) Free mental imagination of emotional situations

In this category falls the use of hypnosis and the use of imagination (this is explained further down).

(2) Guided mental imagination of emotional situations

With the aid of presented material (for example: music, films, stories, or emotional sentences like the Velten, 1968, statements) the subjects are instructed to feel either a positive or a negative mood.

(3) Presentation of emotional material

In contrast to the second category, the subjects are not explicitly asked to feel the mood. For

example, a method for induction of positive mood is to give presents, or let subjects find money.
(4) Presentation of situations where needs are satisfied

These are situations where subjects get positive or negative feedback in social interaction (compliments) or they get positive or negative feedback in a performance task.

Spies, Gerrards-Hesse, and Hesse (1990) also made a qualitative review of studies. By examining the efficacy of the methods they found that presenting emotional stories (category 2) was the most effective method. However, the imagination method (category 1) was just as good for inducing negative mood though less so for positive mood.

It was the aim of this study to test the competing models by applying them to a resource dilemma. Whereas the capacity model assumes subjects in both positive and negative mood, will be worse at solving the dilemma, the motivational model directs attention to the different strategies used by subjects in positive or negative mood. This perspective is more informative than the capacity model, because not only does it makes predictions regarding the result of the solving process, but also about the way in which subjects get there. To test this it is necessary to find measures for the different strategies that people may use in solving a resource dilemma while in either a happy or a sad mood.

From the models, I formulated three separate hypotheses to be explored. Under the cognitive capacity explanation I expected people in sad mood to perform worse than people in neutral mood. Under the mood repair explanation people in sad mood should exploit the resource (short-term gains, long-term losses) while people in neutral mood should make long-term gains. The motivational model predicts that people in happy mood risk and vary more while people in sad mood are more rigid.

Experiment 1

Subjects. Subjects were 66 students studying various disciplines at the Johannes Gutenberg-University of Mainz, Germany. Six students were excluded from the analysis because they did not pursue the problem as instructed. Thirty female and 30 male students (20 per experimental group) participated individually in the experiment for less than one hour (there was no time limit) and they received an average of 12 DM (US $ 8), depending on their yield. They earned more money if they withdrew a larger amount of fish.

Procedure. The subjects were told they would participate in a study on solving an ecological problem. Before solving the dilemma, one group was requested to write about a negative personal life-event, while a second group had to write about a positive life-event. This was the mood induction. Neither task was presented to the control group. A pretest had demonstrated that a neutral mood induction was equivalent to this control group. After the mood manipulation, the subjects had to solve a resource dilemma and then answer the treatment check on mood.

Mood induction. As the imagination method is an effective method to induce mood it was used in this experiment. It consists of having subjects imagine a happy or sad personal event. This procedure was first used by Brewer, Doughtie, and Lubin (1980) and is common in laboratory mood manipulation studies. The subjects had as long as they wanted to write down a story after reading the following instruction:

In the life of every person there are events, that are especially sad (happy). Even if the events happened long ago, they arouse feelings of sadness (happiness) as soon as one remembers them.

Please write down such a - present or past - event that particularly makes you feel sad (happy) and write down your thoughts.

It has been discussed, whether the influence of mood is merely an effect of "subject compliance" (Blaney, 1986). To test this hypothesis, Parrott (1991) conducted an experiment in which after the mood manipulation a cognitive task was given. One group was informed that there should be a link between the two tasks whereas the other group was given a false explanation. However, no difference between the two groups was found. Therefore, the mood manipulation task in this study was not presented to subjects as a different experiment, which would be one way to obscure the link between tasks.

Resource dilemma. Studies show that mood induction lasts only about 10 to 15 minutes (Abele, 1990b), or 20 minutes (Isen, Clark, & Schwartz, 1978). Therefore, a dilemma was needed, which could be completed in a short time period. This feature was offered by the "fishing conflict-game" by Spada and Opwis (1985), which could be solved in about 5 minutes. The same dilemma was used in studies by Knapp (1986) and Knapp and Clark (1991). A pond of fish has to be imagined, which has to be cultivated by the subjects. The subjects can manipulate the system only by withdrawing a certain amount of fish (in tons). In the beginning, the subjects were informed of the current stock of fish (95 tons), but not about the relationship between fish stock and reproduction. The goal of the dilemma was to maximize the fish yield withdrawn in 25 trials. The reproduction of fish is a curvilinear function of the current stock (see Figure 1). The maximum growth rate of fish is 45 tons per trial at a stock of 100 tons. The best way to handle the resource is to withdraw 45 tons at the stock of 145 tons. By continually doing this the subject can maximize the yield. If the stock falls under 10 tons or reaches its maximum of 152 tons, no reproduction is possible. Subjects indicate the amount they wished taken out of the pond and the experimenter reported the actual amount after reproduction.

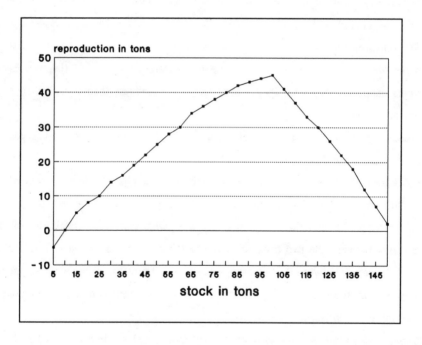

Figure 1:   Relationship between stocks and reproduction

Dependent variables. As alternative models are possible to explain the influence of mood on solving a resource dilemma and the models demand different criteria, four dependent variables were used. The hypothesis derived from the capacity model demands a measure of performance. This measure is the total fish yield withdrawn in 25 trials plus the fish stock after the last trial. This last amount is added to discourage subjects from emptying the pond on the last trial. The fish yield can range theoretical from 95 to 1125 tons.

For the mood repair hypothesis performance is relevant well. Exploiting the pond short-sightedly, leads to a low total yield. A second dependent variable is the stock amount after each trial. The stock can vary from an empty pond(0 tons) to 152 tons. In the case of overexploitation the stock should fall to near zero.

To test the motivational model, a measure of subject stability was required. Such a measure was necessary for investigating whether subjects in elated mood vary more and take more chances in their withdrawals than subjects in depressed mood. The difference between the highest and the lowest stock that a subject reached on any of the 25 trials (called "stock range") was used as such an indicator. The theoretically possible values of this measure can range from 0 to 152 tons. The higher difference indicates a willness to change. Subjects with a high variation have obviously reached more extreme amounts of stocks. This need not have a big influence on the fish yield, as yield and stock range has a low correlation ($r = -.33$, $p < .05$).

Another indicator of variation was called "withdrawal consistency". According to the motivational model, people in sad mood are more rigid, thus they withdraw nearly the same amount of fish every trial. Whereas people in happy mood should vary their withdrawals by taking different amounts. To record this behavior I calculated the absolute difference between every two consecutive withdrawals and added these 24 differences. This sum divided by the number of differences (24) would be high if the withdrawals were varied a lot. As a covariate the time for solving the dilemma was measured as a control for the effectiveness of the mood manipulation.

Treatment check. To test whether the manipulation of mood had been successful subjects rated their mood on a six-point scale. This was done after completing the dilemma task. However, they were asked to not only rate their mood now but what they thought it had been before the experiment and after writing the story. If the treatment check had been presented immediately after the manipulation it may have altered subjects' moods and affected the subsequent task.

Nevertheless, presenting the questionnaire after the dilemma may be considered problematic, as Strack, Schwarz, and Nebel (1990) demonstrated that moods described retrospectively can be biased. If your performance in the dilemma was poor one may tend to rate one's earlier mood as worse than it actually was.

Results

Effectiveness of mood induction procedure. The effectiveness of the mood induction was evaluated through three ratings. After finishing the dilemma task subjects rated their feeling before the experiment, after writing the story, and after the dilemma. The control group only answered the first and the last question. A repeated measurement MANOVA was conducted with the three ratings as dependent variables and induced mood as an independent variable. The mood by time interaction was significant, $F(2, 72) = 23.15$, $p < .001$. An ANOVA with the dependent variable "mood after writing the story" was conducted and showed a main effect for the mood induction, $F(1, 39) = 84.4$, $p < .001$. Therefore writing the stories had the expected effect on mood. As can be seen in Table 1, subjects in the control group describe themselves in a manner more similar to the subjects in the elated mood group than to those in the sad group. This confirms results found by Schwarz (1987) that people in everyday life are more likely to be in an uplifted mood.

Table 1

Means for the 3 treatment-check questions (1 = happy, 6 = sad)

	mood before experiment	after story writing	after problem solving
experimental group:			
happy mood	2.6	1.8	2.3
sad mood	3.1	4.4	2.8
control group	2.6	2.2	

Effects of mood on performance in a resource dilemma. The first dependent variable was the total fish yield withdrawn over 25 trials. According to both the mood-repair hypothesis and the resource-allocation model, it was expected that sad mood subjects should have produced a lower yield than those in the control group. To test this hypothesis the control group and the group in sad mood are compared. The time used to solve the dilemma was taken as a covariate to take into account that the mood induction may weaken over time. If the mood induction vanishes, subjects using more time would have a bigger yield. An ANOVA with the dependent variable fish yield, the independent variable mood induction (control group, sad mood, happy mood), and time as a covariate was conducted. There was no significant effect of mood induction, $F(2,56) = .71$, $p <$ .50, (see Table 2) or of the covariate, $F(1,56) = 2.76$, $p < .10$. Therefore, this result fails to support the hypotheses derived from the mood-repair hypothesis and the resource-allocation model.

Further exploration was made to test the mood-repair hypothesis. It was predicted, that subjects in sad mood overexploit the stock in the early trials, leading to low initial stocks. As no prediction is made regarding happy mood, this group was not included in the following analyses. The stock amounts over 25 trials are depicted in the Figure 2.

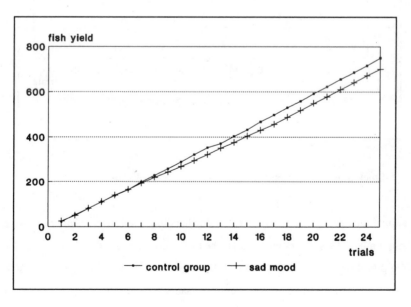

Figure 2: Cumulative fish yield by group in sad mood and control group

It is obvious that the mood induction has no influence on the stocks during the early trials. Therefore the predicted effect of exploitation could not be found.

A further exploration was undertaken to test the resource allocation model. Even if the sum of withdrawals did not differ as expected between the control group and the sad mood condition, perhaps the cumulative fish yield would demonstrate that over the course of the experiment the groups would eventually differ. However, as the Figure 3 shows, this was not the case. The subjects in sad mood do not withdraw a smaller amount over trials than the control group.

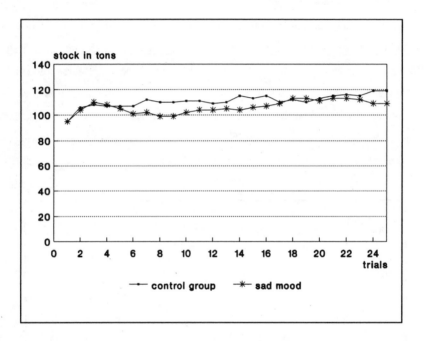

Figure 3:   Stock amount by group in sad mood and control group

The motivational model predicted different ways of handling the resource dilemma depending on mood. In happy mood the stock range, that is, the difference between the highest and lowest stock amount, should be bigger than in sad mood. This hypothesis was tested in an ANOVA with the stock range as dependent variable, mood induction (sad vs. happy mood) as independent variable and time as covariate. The means are reported in Table 2. There was indeed a significant effect of mood induction, $F(1,37) = 6.14$, $p < .02$, and a not significant effect for the covariate, $F(1,37) = 2.99$, $p < .09$.

Table 2

Means and standard deviations (in paratheses) for "fish yield" (minimum = 95, maximum = 1125) "stocks range" (minimum = 0, maximum = 152) and "withdrawals consistency" (minimum = 1, maximum = 30) for the experimental groups

	yield	range	consistency
experimental group:			
happy mood	887 (224)	71 (21)	9.3 (4.2)
sad mood	801 (226)	55 (22)	7.1 (5.2)
control group	885 (206)	61 (20)	9.8 (7.9)

The second indicator for variation, the withdrawal consistency, correlated with the stock range, $r = .42$, $p < .01$. It was analyzed with an ANOVA with mood induction (sad vs. happy mood) as the independent variable and time as a covariate. The means are again reported in Table 2. The mood effect just failed the significance level of .05, $F(1,37) = 3.28$, $p < .08$, but there was an effect of the covariate, $F(1,37) = 9.33$, $p < .005$. Time spent with solving the dilemma has negative correlation with the withdrawal consistency ($R^2 = -.25$), thus indicating that a lot of variance of this variable can be explained by duration of solving the dilemma. The longer time taken over the task the more inconsistent are withdrawals. However, this correlation could be because that sad subjects are both consistent and fast. As they do not have to think about their next withdrawal they do not need so much time.

Discussion

In the present study the influence of mood on solving a resource dilemma was tested. Three predictions derived from explanations of the effect of mood on cognitive performance were examined. The capacity model's prediction of a drop in performance especially for the subjects in negative mood, could not be confirmed. Mood repair through exploiting the resource could not be demonstrated either. According to the motivational model, it was expected that the positive and the negative mood inductions would lead to a different strategy in solving the resource dilemma. This could be demonstrated: subjects in happy mood varied more whereas subjects in sad mood were more rigid. To replicate these findings, and to examine whether these effects are present if the task is easier, another experiment was conducted.

Experiment 2

The aim of the second experiment was to examine the same hypotheses as in Experiment 1, that is, to test hypotheses derived from the three different explanations. In addition, I made the dilemma easier, as, under the assumption of the resource allocation model, people in positive or negative mood should perform better if the task is made easier. Following the results of the first experiment, I expected no drop in the performance when people were in sad mood (the prediction from resource allocation explanation). Also people should not overexploit the resource in consequence of their sad mood (the prediction from the mood repair explanation). However, in happy mood they should vary their withdrawals more thus reaching lower and higher stocks.

Subjects. Subjects were 33 female students and 27 male students from different disciplines at the Johannes Gutenberg-University of Mainz, Germany. For their 1 hour participation they received .015 DM per ton of fish withdrawn.

Procedure. Similar to Experiment 1 they were told to solve an ecological problem. Again they got the mood induction (happy story, sad story, or control) then answered the treatment check before they solved the resource dilemma. The same mood induction and treatment check was used as in Experiment 1.

Resource dilemma. Like in Experiment 1 the fishing conflict-game was used, but this time subjects started the dilemma at a stock of 120 tons. Starting at this amount makes the dilemma easier, as after the first withdrawal the player is closer by chance to the optimal stock for reproduction (100 tons). Also the risk is lower that the player produces low stocks at which the reproduction amounts are small.

Dependent variables. As the resource dilemma and the hypotheses are the same as in Experiment 1, the effect of mood was measured with the same variables: fish yield, stock amount, stock range, and the withdrawal consistency. Again the time a subject took for solving the dilemma was recorded to examine whether the mood changed over time.

Results

Effectiveness of mood induction procedure. The effectiveness of the mood induction was measured with three ratings. After completing the resource dilemma task subjects had to rate their mood before the experiment, after writing the story, and after solving the dilemma. As the control group did not write the story they made only two ratings. A repeated measurement-analysis of ratings showed a significant interaction of mood induction (sad, happy) with time, $F(2,72) = 23.2$, $p < .001$, and an effect of mood induction on ratings after writing the story, $F(1,36) = 99.1$, $p < .001$. Again the means are as expected (see Table 3).

Table 3
Means for the 3 treatment-check questions (1 = happy, 10 = sad)

	mood before experiment	after story writing	after problem solving
experimental group:			
happy mood	3.8	2.2	3.5
sad mood	3.7	6.0	4.3
control group	3.9		3.6

Effects of mood on performance in a resource dilemma. The mood repair hypothesis and resource allocation model predict that the total fish yield withdrawn over 25 trials should differ between the control group and the group in sad mood. According to the mood-repair hypothesis, sad subjects should overexploit the resource (short-term gains) but as a consequence have long-term losses. The resource allocation model predicts a bad performance from being in an induced sad mood. An ANOVA was conducted with the dependent variable fish yield, the independent variable mood induction (control group, sad mood, happy mood), and the covariate time spent solving the resource dilemma. But no significant difference could be found between the experimental groups, $F(2,56) = .82$, $p = .44$ (for means see Table 4). Also the covariate was not significant, $F(1,56) = 3.0$, $p = .09$.

Similar to Experiment 1 a further exploration examined the mood-repair hypothesis. People in sad mood should exploit the resource in the first trials to improve their mood. As Figure 4 demonstrates the group in sad mood does not differ from the control group. The sad group does not overexploit the resource, either in the beginning nor during the dilemma. This result is consistent with Experiment 1.

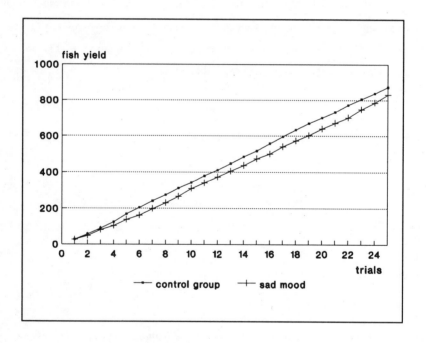

Figure 4:   Cumulative fish yield by group in sad mood and control group

Also the cumulative fish yield was analyzed. According to the resource allocation model the group in sad mood should have lower yields than the control group, because they do not have enough cognitive capacity to understand the dilemma. However, as the dilemma consists of 25 trials there was an opportunity for the group in sad mood to recover from early losses. The cumulative fish yield demonstrates that this is not the case (see Figure 5). On the average, both groups withdrew a similar amount of fish on each trial. This result also replicates Experiment 1.

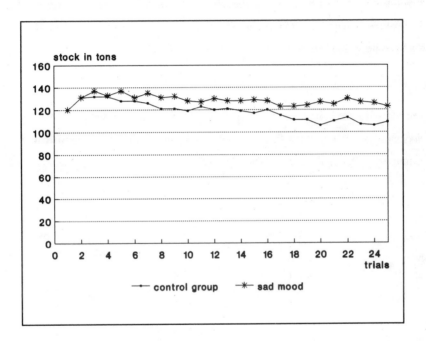

Figure 5: Stock amount by group in sad mood and control group

Following the findings of Experiment 1, it was expected that under induced moods a difference in strategy would be observed. People in happy mood should vary more in their withdrawals, thus sometimes risking a lot, and leading to low stocks, or withdrawing just a little, leading to higher stocks. This should be indicated by the dependent variable stock range, which measures the difference between the highest and lowest stock amount. Again only the two experimental groups are analyzed, but the t-test missed the 5%-level, $t(1,38) = 1.85$, $p = .07$. However, the means (see Table 4) are in the expected direction showing that people in happy mood got to lower and higher amounts of stocks. Taking into account the large variance, I calculated the effect-size (Cohen, 1969) as a medium effect (d = .68). Even if the effect is not significant, the effect-size and the fact that it replicated Experiment 1, is strong evidence for the motivational model.

The withdrawal consistency was the second indicator of variation. Both indicators (stock range and withdrawal consistency) correlated, r = .44, p < .05. In Experiment 1 the effect of mood on withdrawal consistency missed the 5% level, but in this experiment there was a clear finding that people in happy mood did not vary significantly more in their withdrawals from trial to trial than people in sad mood, t(1,38) = .22, p = .83 (see Table 4).

Table 4

Means and standard deviations (in paratheses) for "fish yield" (minimum = 95, maximum = 1125) "stocks range" (minimum = 0, maximum = 152) and "withdrawals consistency" (minimum = 1, maximum = 30) for the experimental groups

	yield	range	consistency
experimental group:			
happy mood	918 (205)	71 (34)	11.5 (7.2)
sad mood	937 (209)	52 (29)	10.9 (10.0)
control group	972 (156)	60 (30)	12.1 (6.7)

Discussion

In Experiment 2 again there was no evidence for the mood repair or resource allocation models: No drop in performance could be observed when people are induced into either a happy or sad mood. Also people in sad mood did not "repair their mood" by exploiting the resource in the first trials. After the first experiment I expected support for the motivational model. To test the model I used two indicators that had a medium correlation. However, the shared variance is too small to argue that they measure the same thing. Whereas in Experiment 1 both indicators showed evidence for the model, in the second experiment only the stock range was according to the model: it demonstrated that people in happy mood produced high and low stocks. However, the small effect of the withdrawal consistency in the first experiment disappeared in the second experiment. How can this be interpreted? From Experiment 1 to Experiment 2 I increased the amount of fish at the beginning with the assumption, that this increase makes the task easier. Indeed, in the first experiment subjects withdrew an average of 856 tons of fish and in Experiment 2 there was an average yield of 943 tons of fish. In this second version of the dilemma it was easier to reach the optimal withdrawal, therefore, both experimental groups varied their withdrawals from trial to trial. By comparing the means of withdrawal consistency across the two experiments both experimental groups varied more than in Experiment 1. In an easy task the obvious approach maybe to vary withdrawals and therefore mood effects on withdrawal consistency are obscured. However, this interpretation is problematic as the difficulty of the dilemma was varied not in the same experiment but in two separate ones.

Nevertheless, even if both experimental groups varied similarly their amounts of withdrawals, people in happy mood had a larger difference between their highest and lowest stock. Even if this difference is not significant at the 5%-level, the effect size is a medium one and is consistent across experiments. This indicates that people in either a happy or a sad mood change their strategy in this resource dilemma: People in sad mood did not risk withdrawing too many fish, whereas people in happy mood withdrew bigger amounts. They did not change the amount after every trial as first expected (withdrawal consistency), but over time they allowed themselves to reach more extreme stocks.

General discussion

Two experiments were conducted to demonstrate how the concept of mood can be related to the research on social dilemma. Hypotheses were derived from three models that explain the influence of mood on cognition. Only one model found support in the data, that is the motivational one.

Implications for the resource allocation model. My results demonstrated no drop in performance when subjects were in an induced mood. What does this mean for the resource allocation model? As was discussed at the beginning, a shortcoming of the model is its vagueness regarding what happens when the capacity limit is exceeded. Thus even changing the processing style can be integrated into the model, but doing so would start to make the model look unfalsifiable.

Another possible reason why performance was not impaired under sad mood is that moods are too weak. To reach the limits of capacity perhaps a more intense emotion is necessary. As emotions are by definition more intense than moods, more capacity should be allocated. In resource or social dilemma research, emotions can be induced by a negative feedback or defection of another player. If under such circumstances no effects could be found, serious doubt would be cast on the Ellis and Ashbrook model.

Implications for the mood repair hypothesis. In two studies (Knapp & Clark, 1991; Knapp, 1986) it was found that the worst outcomes in the problem task were due to sad subjects overexploiting the resource. My study could not replicate the effect of overexploiting, though the problem task was similar. The mood repair hypothesis argues that with negative feelings no delay of gratification is likely (Schwarz & Pollack, 1977; Seeman & Schwarz, 1974).

A similar theory to mood repair was put forward for helping behavior. In my opinion, helping behavior can be compared to cooperation, which is important for social dilemma research. Helping behavior is addressed by the negative-state relief model (Baumann, Cialdini, & Kenrick, 1981; Cialdini, Baumann, & Kenrick, 1981; Manucia, Baumann, & Cialdini, 1984). This model proposes that sad mood can be reduced by helping a person, because during socialization helping has acquired secondary reinforcement value. The parallel between the negative-state relief model and the mood repair hypothesis is that both hypotheses maintain that in sad mood people are motivated to decrease sadness either by helping or by exploiting. But many empirical studies in the field of helping behavior have shown that there are good reasons to reject the negative-state relief model (Carlson & Miller, 1987). People appear not to repair their mood by helping. In so far as the assumption of mood repair and the negative-state relief are comparable, my empirical result gains in plausibility.

Implications for the motivational model. The experiment provides evidence in favor of the motivational model: that the strategies used to handle the resource dilemma will differ with mood. In sad mood, people were more rigid as they were less likely to withdraw large amounts of fish. In happy mood, people dared to withdraw bigger amounts, thus risking the loss of some yield.

This result demonstrates an impact of mood on handling a resource dilemma through influences on the strategy.

Nevertheless, some disadvantages of the motivational model became obvious. This is a heterogenous explanation, that is, different authors describe the processing styles in different theoretical terms, therefore the choice of the relevant measure for this model is not clear. Two indicators were developed, of which one was successful and the other not. Thus an interpretation of these results remains imprecise. However, stock range and withdrawal consistency were only lowly correlated with each other. Before doing more research on this topic, it is necessary to develop specifically whether these different theoretical descriptions of the processing styles can be combined. If a unified theoretical language for the motivational hypotheses can be found, better indicators for testing the hypotheses can be developed.

Though the theoretical frame-work is still vague the results of the two experiments can be related to previous research. In the two experiments, one result was replicated: People in happy mood had a larger stock range than people in sad mood. How can this effect be interpreted? People in sad mood are said to be more rigid and error avoiding. Their behavior could be described in these terms: When they were told the starting stock they tried to conserve it. As a consequence, they never withdrew too large an amount of fish and thus they reached the optimal withdrawal by chance. In the fishing conflict game a more rigid behavior prevents overexploition of the resource. However, following this strategy they do not withdraw more fish than people in happy mood may as they are too cautious to explore whether an even higher stock would lead to more yield. In contrast the behavior of people in happy mood can be described as risk-taking and creative, as they explored a larger stock range to find the optimal withdrawal. Risk-taking may not always be successful, thus they did not have a better performance than the group in sad mood. This could explain why the findings are not consistent with earlier research, as it would be necessary to analyze each task for whether there were more creative or analysing aspects to it. Problem solving often requires both aspects.

Implications for the social dilemma research. Neither emotions nor mood have been taken into account by social dilemma researchers as a game theoretical perspective has been used to explain behavior. Characteristic of social dilemmas though are the strong emotions often arise: one gets angry about another player, disappointed about one's outcome, happy about a profit.

However, the influence of emotion on the behavior has not been taken into consideration. As a social dilemma is more complex than a resource dilemma where no other players' behavior has to be considered, research should start with resource dilemmas. In an one-player-game it can be better observed how emotions influence choices. Under less intense mood the first studies could demonstrate an impact on the strategies. In so far as a sad person can be assumed to have a rigid detail-oriented style of processing (whereas in happy mood a person varies more and takes more chances) it could be predicted that a sad person in a social dilemma would not often change her/his strategy. Once commited to a cooperating or defecting strategy, she/he will continue to use it.

Footnote

1   University of California, Department of Psychology, Los Angeles, USA

References

Abele, A. (1990a). *Kognitive und motivationale Mediatoren affektiver Einflüsse auf das Problemlösen* [Cognitive and motivational mediators of affective influence on problem solving]. Paper presented at 32. Tagung experimentell arbeitender Psychologen, Regensburg.

Abele, A. (1990b). Die Erinnerung an positive oder negative Lebensereignisse. Untersuchungen zur stimmungsinduzierenden Wirkung und zur Gestaltung der Texte [The memory of positive or negative life events]. *Zeitschrift für experimentelle und angewandte Psychologie, 37,* 181-207.

Baumann, D.J., Cialdini, R.B., & Kenrick, D.T. (1981). Altruism as hedonism: Helping and self-gratification as equivalent responses. *Journal of Personality and Social Psychology, 40,* 750-760.

Blaney, P.H. (1986). Affect and memory: A review. *Psychological Bulletin, 99,* 229-246.

Brewer, D., Doughtie, F., & Lubin, B. (1980). Induction of mood and mood shift. *Journal of*

Psychology, 26, 215-226.

Carlson, M., & Miller, N. (1987). Explanation of the relation between negative mood and helping. *Psychological Bulletin, 102,* 91-108.

Cialdini, R.B., Baumann, D.J., & Kenrick, D.T. (1981). Insights from sadness: A three-step model of development of altruism as hedonism. *Developmental Review, 1,* 207-223.

Cohen, J. (1969). *Statistical power analysis for the behavioral sciences.* New York: Academic Press.

Dawes, R.M. (1980). Social dilemmas. *Annual Review of Psychology, 31,* 169-193.

Dobson, D.J.G., & Dobson, K.S. (1981). Problem-solving strategies in depressed and nondepressed students. *Cognitive Therapy and Research, 5,* 237-249.

Ellis, H.C. (1990). Depressive deficits in memory: Processing initiative and resource allocation. *Journal of Experimental Psychology: General, 119,* 60-62.

Ellis, H.C., & Ashbrook, P.W. (1988). Resource allocation model of the effects of depressed mood states on memory. In K. Fiedler, & J. Forgas (Eds.), *Affect, cognition, and social behavior* (pp. 25-43). Toronto: Hogrefe.

Fiedler, K. (1988). Emotional mood, cognitive style, and behavior regulation. In K. Fiedler, & J.P. Forgas (Eds.), *Affect, cognition, and social behavior* (pp. 100-119). Göttingen: Hogrefe.

Hardin, G. (1968). The tragedy of the commons. *Science, 162,* 1243-1248.

Hertel, P.T., & Hardin, T.S. (1990). Remembering with and without awareness in a depressed mood: Evidence of deficits in initiative. *Journal of Experimental Psychology: General, 119,* 45-59.

Hesse, F., & Gerrards, A. (1989). Zur Wirkung emotionaler Belastung auf das Verständnis und die Lösung von Problemen [The influence of emotional strain on comprehension and problem solving]. In E. Roth (Eds.), *Denken und Fühlen* [Thinking and Feeling] (pp. 98-112). Berlin: Springer.

Holding, D.H. (1989). Adversary problem solving by humans. In K.J. Gilhooly (Ed.), *Human and machine problem solving* (pp. 83-122). New York: Plenum Press.

Isen, A.M. (1984). Toward understanding the role of affect in cognition. In R. Wyer, & T. Srull (Eds.), *Handbook of social cognition* (3, pp. 179-236). Hillsdale, N.J.: Erlbaum.

Isen, A.M. (1987). Positive affect, cognitive processes, and social behavior. *Advances in Experimental Social Psychology, 20,* 203-253.

Isen, A.M., Clark, M.S., & Schwartz, M.F. (1978). Duration of the effect of good mood on helping: Footprints on the sands of time. *Journal of Personality and Social Psychology, 36,* 1-12.

Isen, A.M., & Daubman, K.A. (1984). The influence of affect on categorization. *Journal of Personality and Social Psychology, 47,* 1206-1217.

Isen, A.M., Daubman, K.A., & Nowicki, G.P. (1987). Positive affect facilitates creative problem solving. *Journal of Personality and Social Psychology, 52,* 1122-1131.

Isen, A.M., Johnson, M.M.S., Mertz, E., & Robinson, G.F. (1985). The effects of positive affect on the unusualness of word associations. *Journal of Personality and Social Psychology, 48,* 1413-1414.

Isen, A.M., & Levin, P.F. (1972). The effect of feeling good on helping: Cookies and kindness. *Journal of Personality and Social Psychology, 21,* 384-388.

Isen, A.M., & Simmonds (1978). The effect of feeling good on a helping task that is incompatible with good mood. *Social Psychology Quarterly, 41,* 345-349.

Kahneman, D. (1973). *Attention and effort.* Englewood Cliffs, N.J.: Lawrence Erlbaum.

Kelly, G.A. (1955). *The psychology of personal constructs.* New York: W.W. Norton.

Klauer, K.C., Siemer, M., & Stöber, J. (1991). Stimmung und Leistungsniveau bei einfachen Aufgaben [Mood and level of performance in simple tasks]. *Zeitschrift für experimentelle und angewandte Psychologie, 38,* 379-393.

Knapp, A. (1986). Die Auswirkungen emotionaler Zustände auf das Lösen eines sozialen Dilemmas [The effects of emotional states on solving a social dilemma]. *Zeitschrift für Sozialpsychologie, 17,* 160-172.

Knapp, A. (1990). *Zur Beeinträchtigung der Lösegüte bei unterschiedlich schwierigen Ressourcen-Dilemma-Aufgaben durch emotionale Stimmungen* [The disturbance of performance at different difficult resource-dilemma-tasks by emotional moods]. Paper presented at 37. Kongreß der Deutschen Gesellschaft für Psychologie, Kiel.

Velten, E. (1968). A laboratory task for induction of mood states. *Behavior Research and Therapy, 6,* 473-482.

Fairness judgements in an asymmetric public goods dilemma

Jeffrey A. Joireman[1], D. Michael Kuhlman[1], and Hidetaka Okuda[2]

Abstract

Dawes (1980) and Marwell and Ames (1979) have suggested that decision making in social dilemmas is importantly influenced by considerations of fairness. The present study examined subjects' fairness judgements in an asymmetric public goods dilemma. Subjects stated the fairest possible contribution each of six persons could make to provide a public good. These six persons differed in terms of individual wealth (resource asymmetry). The subjects' attributions for resource asymmetries were manipulated so that for some, attributions were Internal (people are rich or poor due to their own efforts/abilities) and for others, External (people are rich or poor due to task difficulty/luck). This manipulation was the major independent variable. As expected, subjects making internal attributions stated that poor persons should contribute a larger proportion of their wealth than rich ones. The subjects making external attributions judged equal proportional contributions to be most fair. Fairness judgements appeared to influence subjects' own contributions and their expectations of others' contributions. The subject's Social Orientation (Cooperative, Non-cooperative) was also measured. Cooperators judged equal proportional contributions as fair, whereas Non-cooperators felt the poor should contribute a higher proportion of their wealth than the rich. Cooperators and Non-cooperators contributed equal proportions, in contrast to the hypothesis.

The present work focusses on a specific type of social dilemma known as the "Public Goods Problem" (Olson, 1965; Messick & Brewer, 1983). In public goods dilemmas, each party must decide how much (if any) of some resource (e.g., money, time, energy) they will contribute, in an effort to help provide a public good. Public goods are characterized by: (a) jointness of supply, meaning that consumption by one member of the group does not interfere with the consumption of another member, and (b) nonexcludability, meaning that all members of the group have access to the good (if provided) whether or not they personally contributed (Olson, 1968; Erev & Rapoport, 1990). These two properties generate a social dilemma, in which the tempting, individually rational, and noncooperative thing to do is contribute nothing. However, everyone would be better off if the group contributes the amount necessary to provide the good. Hence, the dilemma.

An examination of many real world public goods situations indicates that in contrast to the pessimistic prediction of economic models (Brubaker, 1975; Samuelson, 1954), groups often *do* provide public goods. Empirical studies (e.g., Marwell & Ames 1979, 1980) show that individuals will freely contribute a substantial amount of their private resources in order to provide public goods. To adapt an important point of Yamagishi and Sato (1986) to the present paper, the fact is that there *is* National Public Radio, Little League, and so on. From this perspective the question becomes: What processes, beyond economic individual rationality, guide the decision making of interdependent persons confronting public goods problems?

A number of researchers have pointed to the importance of social norms (Dawes, 1980; Marwell & Ames, 1979). In attempting to account for their subjects' success in providing public goods, Marwell and Ames state:

> Despite isolation, instructions which emphasized the monetary importance of the situation and minimized social factors, and the chance to develop full information regarding the parameters of the situation, *normative factors such as fairness* seem to have strongly influenced economic decision. (1979, p. 1359, emphasis added)

The potential importance of fairness in the public goods dilemma provides the focus for the present study. Specifically, this study will investigate subjects' judgements of the fairest contribution in a public goods dilemma with resource asymmetries (Rapoport & Suleiman, 1991) and continuous contributions.

The basic assumption of the present study is that the way people define fairness in the public goods dilemma will depend on whether the resource asymmetries are fair (equitable) or unfair (inequitable).

Fairness of resource asymmetry

In his seminal paper, Adams (1965) defines distributive justice as,

$$\frac{O_A}{I_A} = \frac{O_B}{I_B} \tag{1}$$

The numerator, O_A (O_B), denotes person A's (B's) Outcomes, while the denominator, I_A (I_B), refers to person A's (B's) *relevant* Inputs. As the formula implies, higher relevant inputs entitle an individual to higher outcomes, and distributive justice is realized when the ratio of Outcomes to Inputs is equal for all parties to the exchange.

A number of previous resource allocation studies suggest that perceptions of fair allocation are influenced by the allocator's attributional perspective (Greenberg, 1980; Harris & Joyce, 1980; Okuda & Kuhlman, 1991). In one such study, Okuda and Kuhlman had each of six persons work on an anagram task. Some subjects (Internal condition) were told that each of the six group members had been given exactly the same set of anagrams, so that differences in individual performance reflected their "ability and effort." The other subjects (External condition) were told that each person had been given different sets of anagrams, some easy and some hard, so that each individual's performance was a result of the difficulty of the task. Subjects who attributed performance differences to internal factors voted to divide the group's resources according to performance, such that tickets were directly proportional to performance, while subjects who attributed performance differences to external factors preferred to allocate the tickets equally. Okuda and Kuhlman's findings suggest that when resource asymmetries correspond to performance differences based on internal factors (effort, ability), they will be perceived as equitable; but when they correspond to performance differences based on external factors such as task difficulty and luck, they will be perceived as inequitable. The implications of equitable/inequitable resource asymmetries on fairness in the public goods dilemma are easily understood when the public goods dilemma is framed in terms of Adams' (1965) theory.

Fairness in the publics goods game

Adapting Adam's (1965) general formula (1) to the public goods game, fairness exists to the degree that the ratio in formula 2 below is equal for all persons.

$$\frac{\text{Value of the Public Good } + [\text{"Costs" or "Bonuses"}]}{\text{Contribution}} \qquad (2)$$

The "Costs"/"Bonuses" in the above expression correspond to the effect (if any) of injustice experienced in the resource allocation stage.

We assume that injustice experienced at this stage will be aversive, motivating subjects to reduce it. We further assume that subjects may construe and behave in the public goods game in ways that help to reduce this aversive state. "Costs" correspond to the negative amount by which a subject was unfairly underpaid, and "Bonus" to the positive amount by which the subject was unfairly overpaid.

If resource asymmetries are based on external factors, subjects will likely feel that the asymmetries are inequitable, and may approach the public goods dilemma as an opportunity to reduce that inequity. The poor were underpaid while the rich were overpaid. This underpayment (overpayment) could be viewed as a relevant "cost" ("bonus") to be subtracted (added) from (to) the overall reward subjects will obtain from the public good. In effect, the poor could justify giving up less and the rich might feel responsible for giving up more.

On the other hand, if resource asymmetries are based on internal factors, it seems reasonable to assume that subjects will approach the public goods dilemma with little need to reduce inequity. Put another way, equitably treated subjects will bring no previous "costs" and/or "bonuses" to bear on their decision to contribute to the public good. Assuming that the value of the public good is the same for everyone, the fairest thing for everyone to do under these circumstances would be to contribute an equal amount. In other words, the poor should give up a higher percentage of their wealth than the rich.

Compared to the "external" subjects discussed above, we can predict that the proportional contributions of this (internal) group should be less nearly equal.

A recent study by Rapoport and Suleiman (1991) provides indirect support for the hypothesis that an external attribution for resource asymmetries results in inequity which subjects attempt to redress in the public goods dilemma. In Rapoport and Suleiman's study, subjects were randomly given different amounts of money and then asked to contribute any amount they wanted to a public pool. In other words, resource asymmetries were based on an external factor, chance. If the contributions surpassed a certain provision threshold, each of the group members was awarded an equal monetary bonus. The most relevant finding for the present study was that subjects' proportional contributions were approximately the same across the different levels of endowment. Thus, it appears that when resource asymmetries are based on external factors, the fairest thing for everyone to do is to contribute a nearly equal percentage of their wealth.

Hypotheses

In the present study we will attempt to produce "Internal" attributions (people are rich and poor because of differences in their efforts and/or abilities) and "External" attributions (people are rich and poor for reasons in the environment) in others. As stated above, we expect that internal subjects will call for the poor to give up a higher proportion of their wealth than the rich, and external subjects will call for proportional contributions to be more equal.

We also hope to demonstrate that subjects' perceptions of fairness will influence two other aspects of their behavior: (a) their beliefs as to what others actually will do, as opposed to what they should do, and (b) their own individual contribution behavior. Given the task of predicting another's behavior, it seems reasonable to suggest that in the absence of any personal information about the target, relevant norms will serve as a salient reference point in making those predictions. Thus, expected contributions are predicted to take on the same pattern of result as fairness judgements.

Also, we assume that a person's actual contribution will at least partly be guided by his/her sense of fairness. To test this hypothesis, we include an additional manipulation in which we will lead some subjects to believe that they have a relatively small amount of the resource (money) and others to believe the have a large amount. To the extent to which subjects behave in a fair manner we should expect to see similar patterns for fairness judgements and contributions.

A substantial body of literature attests to the importance of Social Orientation as a variable influencing many aspects of behavior in social dilemmas (for reviews see Liebrand, 1986; Kuhlman, Camac, & Cunha, 1986). To the degree that Cooperators place higher value on group cohesion and morale than Non-cooperators[3], we might expect them to advocate resource allocation based on equality, as equality is generally considered to be the most conducive norm to the development of group cohesion and morale (Deutsch, 1975; Sampson, 1975). Non-cooperators, on the other hand, due to their interest in maximizing economic gain, would be predicted to advocate resource allocation based on performance. If the present line of reasoning is correct, we would expect Cooperators to view resource asymmetries as inequitable in general, while the Non-cooperators would see them as equitable. Thus, compared to the judgements of Non-cooperators, we would expect Cooperators' judgements of the fairest proportional contribution to be more equal in an attempt to reduce what they view as unfair resources.

In addition, the Social Orientation literature suggests that subjects with a cooperative orientation will contribute more than non-cooperative subjects (Kramer, McClintock, & Messick, 1986; Kuhlman et al., 1986; Kuhlman & Marshello, 1975; Liebrand, 1986; McClintock & Allison, 1989).

Method

Subjects. Subjects were undergraduates at the University of Delaware fulfilling a course requirement in Introductory Psychology.

Procedure. Upon arrival at the laboratory each student was greeted by an experimenter and seated in one of six separate cubicles surrounding a central room so that it was impossible to see any of the other five students. Independent of the number that actually showed up, the experimenters acted as if all 6 were present throughout the entire session.

Each student was led to believe that they had a unique ID (either A, B, C, D, E or F). In fact, half the students were (randomly) given the code of C and the other half the code of E. This was the basis for false feedback concerning the student's performance (Low or High) on the upcoming Anagrams task.

Establishing differing attributions for resource asymmetry. Following a general introduction, subjects received recorded instructions for an anagrams task. All subjects were told that they would have a chance to win some money in the experiment, and that the amount of money won would depend, in part, on their performance in the anagrams task. Half of the groups were told that each of the subjects would receive the same set of anagrams (Same Condition), and as a result, performance on the task would be a result of each individual subject's ability, effort and insight. The remaining groups were told that each subject would receive a different set of anagrams to solve (Different Condition), so that performance on the task would be a result of the easiness or difficulty of the task to which they were assigned. In fact, all subjects received the same anagrams.

Each student was given 5 minutes to solve as many anagrams as possible. Following the (ostensible) scoring of the anagrams, the experimenter announced from the central room that different students would be given different amounts of money based on their anagram performance. The experimenter announced the same amounts for every group in the study. Specifically, each group of subjects was given the following payoffs: Student A=$20; B=$6, C=$8, D=$10, E=$16, and F=$12.

After the performance feedback, subjects completed a questionnaire designed to check their knowledge of monies held by each of the six students, and to assess their attributions for the Resource Asymmetries. Subjects rated on a scale from 1 (not at all) to 5 (very much) how much effort, ability, task difficulty and luck affected the performances of the members of their group.

The public goods game. Next, subjects read along with tape recorded instructions explaining the public goods game. The instructions explained that each subject could contribute any amount of their initial (Anagrams) payoff to a public pool, and if the group's total contribution exceeded some criterion amount, each group member would receive a bonus payoff, regardless of their individual contribution. It was explained that, if provided, the bonus would be added to their initial payoff less their contribution, but if the group did not meet the goal, each subject's final payoff for the study would be their initial payoff minus any contribution they made to the public pool.

At this point, the tape recorder was turned off, and the experimenter made a series of announcements concerning specific values for the group goal and the bonus. This was an effort to make the false feedback given earlier appear valid to our subjects rather than pre-arranged. The experimenter announced that the group goal would be $36, and that the bonus, if provided would be $25.

Each subject then indicated how much of their initial payoff they wished to contribute to the public pool. Immediately following their contribution decision, and prior to any feedback, subjects wrote down what they expected the other five members of their group to contribute, and also what amount each member (including themselves) should contribute, in order to be fair.

Assessment of Social Orientation. After completion of the Public Goods task, and prior to any feedback, each student was given a set of 2-alternative decomposed games. Four of these games had a dominance structure of J.OR, and four had a dominance structure of JO.R. (Examples are given in Table 1).

Table 1

The Two Types of Decomposed Game Used to Assess Social Orientation

Type I: [J.OR]		Type II: [JO.R]	
A B		A B	
Self 119 124		Self 114 110	
Other 81 54		Other 54 31	

Note: Cooperators (J's) maximize joint gain (self plus other), Individualists (O's) maximize own gain (self), and Competitors (R's) maximize the relative difference between outcomes to self and other (self minus other). Thus, in game Type I, a J would choose A, an O would choose B, and an R would choose B. In game Type II, a J would choose A, an O would choose A, and an R would choose B.

A student was classified as a Cooperator (J) if six or more of the 8 choices maximized Joint Gain, an Individualist (O) if six or more maximized Own Gain, and as a Competitor (R) if six of more maximized Relative Gain.

Subjects were thanked for their participation, released individually to maintain anonymity, and debriefed by way of mailed feedback. Subsequently, six subjects were randomly selected and asked to report for payment.

Results

Selection of subjects for analysis

We required that subjects meet a number of criteria with respect to their knowledge of important variables for inclusion in the analysis. To be selected, subjects had to accurately report: (a) the nature of the anagram task (i.e., Same or Different) (b) the initial amounts of money of all group members, and (c) the group goal and bonus in the public goods game. Twenty-four subjects failed to meet one or more of these criteria. Of the remaining 66 subjects, 3 failed to show a consistent Social Orientation in the decomposed game task and were not included in our results. This left a total of 63 subjects. The final (between groups) design of the study was Task Type (Same vs Different) by Personal Wealth ($8 vs $16) by Social Orientation (Cooperator vs Non-Cooperator)[4].

Manipulation checks

An ANOVA conducted on subjects' responses to the "social comparison" question indicated that subjects who earned 16 points believed that they had performed better ($\underline{M}$ = 4.28) than those who had earned 8 points ($\underline{M}$ = 1.97), $F(1,54)$ = 433.47, $\underline{p}$ < .001.

Subjects' responses to the four attribution questions were analyzed in a 2 (Task Type) x 2 (Personal Wealth) x 2 (Social Orientation) Multivariate Analysis of Variance, in which the main effect for Task Type was the only one that achieved statistical significance (Rao's $\underline{F}$ = 4.52, $\underline{df}$=4,52, $\underline{p}$=0.003). A discriminant function analysis of this effect (Harris, 1975) yielded standardized coefficients of 0.324 and 0.345 for the two internal items (Ability, Effort) and -0.556 and -0.714 for the two external ones (Task Difficulty, Luck). This canonical variate is easily interpreted as a contrast between internal and external causes of resource asymmetry, such that the larger the value, the more internal the attribution. Furthermore, the means of the canonical variate for the Same (-0.641) and Different (-1.776) subjects demonstrate that our attempt to manipulate subjects' attributions for resource asymmetry was successful.

Fairness judgements

In order to allow for comparisons across Low and High subjects, we analyzed the judgements of the fairest contributions for the four other group members (targets) that Low and High subjects had in common, specifically (A=$20; B=$6; D=$10; F=$12). Judgements of fairest contributions were converted into a simple proportion. These proportions were used as the within subject dependent variables in a 2 x 2 x 2 x 4 ANOVA for repeated measures[5].

Results revealed a significant[6] Task Type (Same vs Different) by Target interaction, $F(3,165) = 2.68$, $p = .049$ (gg $p = .097$, hf $p = .09$, lb $p = .107$)[7]. The means associated with this interaction are presented in table 2.

Table 2

Mean Fairness Judgements and Expectations for Significant Effects.

| | FAIRNESS JUDGEMENTS | | | |
| | Target's Wealth | | | |
Condition	6	10	12	20
Social Orientation				
Cooperators	.53	.51	.51	.51
Non-cooperators	.63	.53	.52	.48
Task Type				
Same	.63	.54	.52	.48
Different	.54	.50	.51	.51
Overall	.58	.52	.52	.49

| | EXPECTED CONTRIBUTIONS | | | |
| | Target's wealth | | | |
Condition	6	10	12	20
Personal Wealth				
Low ($8)	.61	.50	.50	.46
High ($16)	.49	.50	.48	.51
Task Type				
Same	.63	.52	.50	.47
Different	.47	.48	.48	.50
Overall	.55	.50	.49	.49

As predicted, subjects in the Same condition (internal attributions) thought that the poor should give a higher proportion of their wealth than the rich, while subjects in the Different condition (external attributions) thought that the fairest contribution was approximately 50% for *all* targets.

The Social Orientation by Target interaction was also significant, $F(3,165) = 3.03$, $p = .031$ (gg $p = .076$, hf $p = .069$, lb $p = .087$). An examination of table 2 reveals that, as predicted, Cooperators advocated roughly equal proportional contributions while Non-cooperators thought the poor should give up a higher percentage than the rich.

A main effect for the within subject factor of Target was obtained, $F(3,165) = 5.23$, $p = .002$ (gg $p = .018$, hf $p = .014$, lb $p = .026$), indicating that subjects felt poorer targets should give up a higher percentage than rich ones.

Expected contributions

As with the analyses of fairest contributions, expected contributions were converted into proportions and the resulting data were run in a 2 x 2 x 2 x 4 ANOVA for repeated measures.

The Task Type by Target interaction was significant, $F(3,165) = 4.61$, $p = .004$ (gg $p = .011$, hf $p = .008$, lb $p = .036$). As can be seen in table 2, consistent with our earlier predictions, subjects in the Different condition expected each of the other group members to donate an equal percentage, in this case approximately 50%, while subjects in the Same condition tailored their expectations to the target's wealth, similar to the findings for fairness norms.

The Personal Wealth by Target interaction was also significant, $F(3,165) = 3.33$, $p = .021$ (gg $p = .038$, hf $p = .03$, lb $p = .073$). Table 2 shows that High subjects expected approximately equal proportional contributions, while Low subjects expected the poor to contribute a higher proportion of their money than the rich.

Actual contributions

A 2 x 2 x 2 ANOVA using the subject's proportional contribution as the dependent variable yielded only a significant main effect for Personal Wealth, $\underline{F}(1,55) = 13.17$, $\underline{p} = .001$, with the poor contributing a higher proportion (M=.76) than the rich (M=.54). Although the interaction between Task Type and Personal Wealth was not significant, the means were in the expected direction. Planned comparisons revealed that, as predicted, the difference between poor and rich subjects' proportional contributions was higher in the Same (internal attributions) condition ($M_{poor} = .84$, $M_{rich} = .55$; $\underline{F}(1,55) = 12.49$, $\underline{p} = .001$) than in the Different (external attributions) condition ($M_{poor} = .67$, $M_{rich} = .52$; $\underline{F}(1,55) = 4.58$, $\underline{p} = .037$).

Discussion

Both Dawes (1980) and Marwell and Ames (1979) have suggested that fairness plays an important role in decision making in situations of social interdependence. The primary purpose of the present study was to investigate how attributions for differences in wealth influence judgements of the fairest contribution in a step-level public goods dilemma. As predicted, individuals making internal attributions for resource asymmetries felt that the poor should give up proportionately more than the rich, while individuals making external attributions believed that more equal proportional contributions were fairest. Expected and actual contributions followed similar patterns. When resource asymmetries were attributed to internal factors, the poor were expected to contribute a higher percentage of their wealth than the rich, and they did. When resource asymmetries were attributed to external factors, subjects expected everyone to give up an equal percentage, and proportional contributions were more nearly equal in this condition.

The present study extends Rapoport and Suleiman's (1991) finding that subjects in a step-level public goods dilemma with resource asymmetries make equal proportional contributions. Subjects in the present study made more nearly equal proportional contributions when the cause of the resource asymmetries was external to the subject, generally supporting Rapoport and Suleiman's findings. However, as mentioned above, when resource asymmetries were attributed to internal factors, the poor gave up proportionately more than the rich. This is an important finding, as most of the past research on the public goods dilemma with asymmetric players has used a methodology where subjects are simply given money (e.g., Marwell & Ames, 1979; Rapoport, 1988; Rapoport & Suleiman, 1991; Wit, Wilke, & Oppenwal, in press), a procedure which has likely led subjects to hold external attributions for the resource asymmetries. The present results suggest that the creation of varying attributions for resource asymmetries in public goods research represents a potentially valuable methodology which can help increase our understanding of behavior in these situations.

The present results suggest that the public goods dilemma may be viewed as a two-stage "resource allocation" task in which fairness at the pre-dilemma resource allocation stage influences fairness at contribution stage. Over the course of these two stages, individuals may be viewed as comparing their relevant inputs (e.g., effort at a pre-dilemma task and contributions to the public good) to their outcomes (e.g., pre-dilemma endowments and the public good) to determine if the overall resources have been allocated fairly.

In addition to examining how attributions for resource asymmetries influence perceptions of fairness, the present study addressed the effect of an individual's Social Orientation on both fairness judgments and actual contributions. As predicted, Cooperators advocated more equal proportional contributions than Non-cooperators. We suggest that Cooperators' fairness judgements were advocated in the interests of maintaining group morale/cohesion, an interpretation consistent with the analyses presented by both Deutsch (1975) and Sampson (1975). Contribution decisions for the two Social Orientations did not confirm our predictions. Cooperators were expected to contribute a higher proportion of their wealth to the public good than Non-Cooperators but no significant differences were found. It is possible that the lack of an effect was due to a large number of Cooperators being assigned to the rich personal wealth condition (who contributed a lower percentage overall) and more Non-cooperators being assigned to the poor wealth condition (who contributed a higher percentage overall). An examination of the cell frequencies did not support this explanation. Another more interesting explanation centers on the type of dilemma used in the current study.

Although the public goods dilemma and the commons dilemmas are formally equivalent, it has been suggested that they may be very different psychologically (Brewer & Kramer, 1986). Our prediction that Cooperators would contribute more to a public good was based to a large extent on previous research involving the either the Prisoner's Dilemma Game (Kuhlman et al., 1986; Kuhlman & Marshello, 1975) or a form of commons dilemma (Kramer et al., 1986; Liebrand, 1986). Thus, it is possible that the framing of the dilemma as a public goods game moderated the general effect of Social Orientation prevalent in much of the past literature.

In one of the first studies to compare the two dilemmas, Brewer and Kramer (1986) found that subjects were less cooperative in the public goods dilemma than in the commons dilemma. Viewed in light of these findings, Cooperators in the present study may have been less cooperative than they normally are in the commons dilemma, while Non-cooperators may not have changed much from their generally low level of cooperation. In a more recent study, Rutte, Wilke and Messick (1987) found no differences in choice behavior between the two games. They did find, however, that in comparison to the commons dilemma, subjects enjoyed the public goods game more and anticipated more cooperation. By this argument then, it is possible that Non-cooperators in the present study were demonstrating more cooperation than normal.

Although there may be some reason to believe that the type of dilemma moderates the influence of Social Orientation on choice behavior in social dilemmas, additional research is necessary before serious pursuit of a such a framing hypothesis is justified.

One final finding deserving mention is that personal wealth did not influence fairness norms. No specific predictions were made with respect to the influence of personal wealth on advocacy of fairness norms. However, from an economically rational point of view it would seem that the rich would be more likely to call for higher proportional contributions from the poor than the rich, whereas the poor call for roughly equal proportional contributions. In contrast, the present results show that "rich" and "poor" subjects agree on fairness if their internal/external attributions are the same.

A non-critical extrapolation of this finding to the real world might lead us to expect that a random sample of poor people would on average define fairness in the same way as a group of rich ones. Such an expectation is (we think) an illusory non-correlation, based on a failure to consider the experimental conditions that produced the present results. In the present research, individual wealth depended on performance in a single well defined task with objective and clear-cut standards. Furthermore, subjects' perceptions of internality/externality were manipulated in a direct and apparently successful fashion. In a sense, we persuaded our subjects to think internally or externally, and their individual wealth did not affect the impact of our clear message about this single and clear-cut task.

In the real world however, we suspect that rich and poor tend to make internal and external interpretations of wealth differences, respectively, and no doubt, for a number of reasons. We suggest that one of them is self-interest. External attributions "call for" smaller proportional contributions from the poor than internal ones while the opposite is true for the rich.

Footnotes

1   University of Delaware, USA

2   Chukyo University, Toyota Japan

3   It is well known that Cooperators place greater emphasis on collective welfare than Non-cooperators. Thougoh not identical concepts, it seems reasonable to assume that collective welfare group cohesion/morale have common elements.

4   Students with an O or an R Social Orientation were combined in a single group of "Non-Cooperators".

5   Analyses on fairness norms, expectations and contributions using an arcsine transformed proportion (Cohen & Cohen, 1983) yielded results completely consistent with those based on the simple proportions. In the interests of clarity, only the results for the simple proportions will be presented.

6   We recognize that the alpha levels associated with the corrected degrees of freedom (i.e.,
       Greenhouse-Geisser, Huynh-Feldt, Lower bound) exceed the typically accepted level of .05.
       Cohen (1969) in his discussion of power, recommends that traditional alpha levels should
       be raised (to possibly .1) when attempting to test Null hypotheses regarding interactions,
       especially when the interaction is in the direction predicted by theory. In light of Cohen's
       suggestion, it is reasonable to reject the Null hypothesis that the Task Type manipulation
       has no effect.

7   gg = Greenhouse-Geisser; hf = Huynh-Feldt; lb = Lower bound.

References

Adams, J.S. (1965). Inequity in social exchange. In L. Berkowitz (Ed.), *Advances in experimental social psychology* (vol 2). New York: Academic Press.

Brewer, M.B., & Kramer, R.M. (1986). Choice behavior in social dilemmas: Effects of social identity, group size, and decision framing. *Journal of Personality and Social Psychology, 50*, 543-549.

Brubaker, E.R. (1975). Free ride, free revelation, or golden rule? *Journal of Law and Economics, 18*, 147-161.

Cohen, J. (1969). *Statistical power analysis for the behavioral sciences*. Academic Press: New York.

Cohen, J., & Cohen, P. (1983). *Applied multiple regression/correlation analysis for behavioral Sciences* (2nd Ed.). Hillsdale, NJ: Lawrence Erlbaum Associates.

Dawes, R.M. (1980). Social dilemmas. *Annual Review of Psychology, 31*, 169-193.

Deutsch, M. (1975). Equity, equality and need: What determines which value will be used as the basis of distributive justice? *Journal of Social Issues, 31*, 137-149.

Erev, I., & Rapoport, A. (1990). Provision of step-level public goods: The sequential contribution mechanism. *Journal of Conflict Resolution, 34*, 401-425.

Greenberg, J. (1980). Attentional focus and locus of performance causality as determinants of equity behavior. *Journal of Personality and Social Psychology, 38,* 579-585.

Harris, P.J. (1975). *A primer of multivariate statistics.* New York: Academic Press.

Harris, R.J. & Joyce, M.A. (1980). What's fair? It depends of how you phrase the question. *Journal of Personality and Social Psychology, 38,* 165-179.

Kramer, R.M., McClintock, C.G., & Messick, D.M. (1986). Social values and cooperative response to a simulated resource conservation crisis. *Journal of Personality, 54,* 576-592.

Kuhlman, D.M., Camac, C.R., & Cunha, D.A. (1986). Individual differences in social orientation. In H. Wilke, D. Messick, & C. Rutte (Eds.), *Experimental social dilemmas* (p.151-176). New York: Verlag Peter Lang.

Kuhlman, D.M., & Marshello, A. (1975). Individual differences in game motivation as moderators of preprogrammed strategic effects in prisoner's dilemma. *Journal of Personality and Social Psychology, 32,* 922-931.

Liebrand, W.B.G. (1986). The ubiquity of social values. In H. Wilke, D. Messick, & C. Rutte (Eds.), *Experimental social dilemmas* (p. 113-133). New York: Verlag Peter Lang.

Marwell, G., & Ames, R.E. (1979). Experiments on the provision of public goods I: Resources, interest, group size and the free-rider problem. *American Journal of Sociology, 84,* 1335-1360.

Marwell, G., & Ames, R.E. (1980). Experiments on the provision of public goods II: Provision points, stakes, experience and the free-rider problem. *American Journal of Sociology, 85,* 926-937.

McClintock, C.G., & Allison, S.T. (1989). Social value orientation and helping behavior. *Journal of Applied Social Psychology, 19,* 353-362.

Messick, D.M., & Brewer, M.B. (1983). Solving social dilemmas: A review. In L. Wheeler & P. Shaver (Eds.), *Review of personality and social psychology,* (vol 4, p. 11-44). Beverly Hills, CA: Sage Publications.

Okuda, H., & Kuhlman, D.M. (1991). *Evaluation of reward allocators: Relations among altruism, hedonism, and similarity effects.* Working manuscript, University of Delaware, Newark.

Olson, M. (1965). *The logic of collective action.* Cambridge, MA: Harvard University Press.

Olson, M. (1968). *The logic of collective action: Public goods and the theory of groups.* New York: Schocken.

Rapoport, A. (1988). Provision of step-level public goods: Effects of inequalities in resources. *Journal of Personality and Social Psychology, 54,* 432-440.

Rapoport, A., & Suleiman, R. (1991). *Incremental contribution in step-level public goods games with asymmetric players* (Report No. 93). Haifa, Israel: University of Haifa, The Institute for Information Processing and Decision Making.

Rutte, C.G., Wilke, H.A.M., & Messick, D.M. (1987). The effects of framing social dilemmas as give-some or take-some games. *British Journal of Social Psychology, 26,* 103-108.

Sampson, E.E. (1975). On justice as equality. *Journal of Social Issues, 31,* 45-64.

Samuelson, P.A. (1954). The pure theory of public expenditure. *Review of Economics and Statistics, 48,* 266-279.

Wit, A., Wilke, H.A.M., & Oppenwal, H. (in press). Fairness in asymmetric social dilemmas. In W.B.G. Liebrand, D.M. Messick & H.A.M. Wilke (Eds.), *Social dilemmas: Theoretical issues and research findings* (pp. 181-195). New York: Pergamon Press.

Yamagishi, T., & Sato, K. (1986). Motivational bases of the public goods problem. *Journal of Personality and Social Psychology, 50,* 67-73.

Group size effects in social dilemmas: A review of the experimental literature and some new results for one-shot N-PD games

Axel Franzen[1]

Abstract

It is often argued that group size has negative effects on cooperative behavior in social dilemmas. However, this widely accepted view does not accurately reflect the findings of the experimental research. This paper presents an updated review of the experimental findings on group size effects in various social dilemmas. Also, new results concerning group size effects in the one-shot Prisoner's Dilemma game are presented. The findings from the review and the experiment suggest that the effects of group size depend on the type of the game as well as on the experimental setting. While group size effects appear in infinitely iterated PD-type games, they do not affect the level of cooperation in the one-shot Prisoner's Dilemma game. Reasons for the observed differences and the factors that drive the group size effect are discussed.

Introduction

It seems to be common knowledge in the social sciences that large groups show less cooperative behavior than small groups. Economists who are concerned with the provision of public goods argue that large groups inhibit voluntary contributions to public goods. Thus, Olson (1965) wrote in his classical work on collective action: "The larger the group is, the farther it will fall short of obtaining an optimal supply of any collective good, and the less likely that it will act to obtain even an minimal amount of such a good"[2], and Buchanan (1965) argued: "Once the large-number dilemma is understood, the failure of the market process to produce optimal results when public goods are present is explained"[3].

Group size effects also play a major role in Psychology and Social Psychology. Many experimental studies revealed that individuals work less efficiently the larger the group. This effect was found with physical as well as with cognitive tasks. It is sometimes referred to as the Ringelmann effect, due to the early studies on group size in rope pulling experiments by Max Ringelmann (see Ingham, 1974; Kravitz & Martin, 1986). It is also referred to as social loafing (Darley & Latane, 1968), deindividuation (Festinger, Pepitone, & Newcomb, 1954), or diffusion of responsibility.

Many survey articles on social dilemma research conclude that cooperation decreases with increasing group size (Dawes, 1980; Grzelak, 1989; Messick & Brewer, 1983; Stroebe & Frey, 1982). Thus, Stroebe and Frey (1982) argue in their review article on free riding: "All in all the studies using N-person Prisoner's Dilemma or related N-person games provide strong evidence for the free rider hypothesis and for the group size effect on free riding".

This article questions the conclusion that large groups show generally less cooperation than small groups. For that purpose those experimental studies will be reviewed that were more or less designed to test the effects of group size on cooperation in a game theoretical framework. Within this body of literature more experimental evidence has accumulated during the last decade which justifies an update and a reevaluation of the effects of group size in experimental social dilemmas. Since this review is limited to experiments with decision games, its conclusions do not apply directly to the small group research in Psychology or the "real world". Such a discussion would go beyond the scope of this article.

Existing surveys on the effect of group size in experimental social dilemma research are not extensive and systematic. In particular, little attention has been given to strategic aspects of the underlying game structure of the dilemma situations. A game theoretical analysis of any decision making process has to pay careful attention to the strategic properties of the game, such as, the number of players, the strategies that are available to each player, and the rules of the game. Thus, we will pay attention to the type of game that characterizes a decision situation. Of particular importance is whether dominant strategies are available to players (as in the Prisoner's Dilemma), or whether players are faced with multiple equilibria (as in the Chicken Game). Furthermore, the strategic properties of a game will be different if players face one-shot-decisions or finitely and infinitely iterated decision situations.

It is well known that the way a dilemma is presented to subjects may affect their decision behavior. For example subjects react differently to situations that call attention to possible losses compared to decision situations that direct attention to possible gains. This evidence corroborates with Kahneman and Tversky's (1982) prospect theory. A comprehensive discussion of group size effects in social dilemmas has to take into account those consequences of presentation. It is useful to make a general distinction between two sets of criteria. On the one hand, we characterize social dilemmas by game theoretical aspects. Such an analysis is based on the objective (i.e. monetary) incentive structure of the dilemmas and might therefore be referred to as the economy of the decision situation in dilemmas. The second set of criteria is concerned with subjective aspects of the decision situations, that is, the way subjects perceive the dilemma. This second set might be referred to as the psychology of the dilemmas.

The objective incentive structure of social dilemmas has been thoroughly analyzed within game theory. We will give a short review of these findings, relate them to group size effects, and deduct a few hypotheses concerning the effects of group size on cooperation. Concerning the psychology of social dilemmas, there exists some empirical evidence on selected phenomena, such as the effects of framing or communication. However, there is no coherent theory that links subjective aspects to group size and cooperation in social dilemmas. The following review is therefore biased in such a way that a more systematic attention is given to the game theoretic structure of the dilemmas. Psychological aspects are more used as a residual category.

The remainder of this article is organized in 5 sections. Section 2 reviews the experimental evidence on group size effects in the one-shot Prisoner's Dilemma Game. It contains also a report of our own research on group size effects in one-shot games. Section 3 presents a review on one-shot provisions of public goods. Section 4 deals with group size effects in iterated dilemma games. Section 5 discusses experiments with the Commons Dilemma. Section 6 concludes the paper.

Group size and the one-shot prisoner's dilemma

Situations such as the decision whether or not to contribute to a public good, or whether or not to participate in some kind of collective action are characterized by two circumstances, viz. 1) that the actions of individuals are interdependent and 2) that individually rational actions result in inefficient and unintended collective outcomes. Due to the latter property, such situations are often referred to as social dilemmas'. A special case of a social dilemma is the Prisoner's Dilemma. Buchanan (1965) and Hardin (1971) have argued that the logic of collective action may be demonstrated by the Prisoner's Dilemma Game. Subsequently, many authors (e.g., Hampton, 1987; Taylor 1987; Taylor & Ward 1982;) argued that in reality many public goods could be better perceived as step level goods, which are more adequately modelled by the so-called Chicken Game or the Battle of the Sexes Game. The Prisoner's Dilemma Game, however, received most attention among social scientists as a model of decision making concerning collective goods or, more generally, concerning decision-making in social dilemmas. This is not surprising, since the Prisoner's Dilemma is the most prominent example of a paradoxical situation in which individual rationality results in collectively inefficient consequences. The Prisoner's Dilemma is therefore a good starting point to analyse the question of why group size could or should affect the cooperation rate.

Let us assume that N individuals face a one-shot decision situation in which every player has to chose between cooperation (C) or defection (D). Denote the payoff to a cooperating player, given that m players cooperate (including actor i), by $C(m)$. The payoff to a defecting player is represented by $D(m-1)$. The PD Game is characterized by two properties: 1) The payoff that is associated with a defecting choice is always larger than the payoff that results from cooperation, that is $D(m-1) > C(m)$; 2) If all players cooperate, the payoff every player receives is larger than the payoff every player receives if all defect, that is $C(N) > D(0)$. A representation of the N-person PD Game is shown in figure 1:[5]

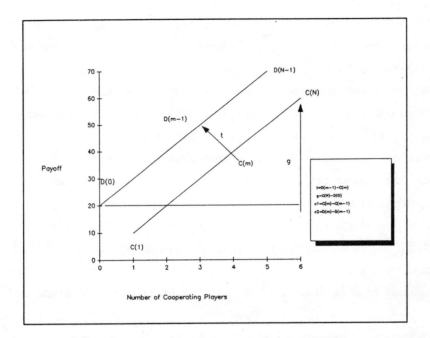

Figure 1: Graphical Presentation of an N-Person Prisoner's Dilemma Game

The pattern in figure 1 may be characterized by four payoff parameters. The parameter t ($t=D(m-1)-C(m)$) indicates player i's payoff difference between his cooperative and defecting choice. Since the payoff for defection is (by definition) always larger than the payoff for cooperation, t may be interpreted as player i's incentive to defect. The parameter c_1 ($c_1=C(m) - C(m-1)$) denotes the amount of the positive external effect each cooperating player transfers to all other players. On the other hand c_2 ($c_2=D(m)-D(m-1)$) may be interpreted as the negative external effect that every defecting player imposes on all other players. Thus, if a player switches from cooperation to defection, she increases her own payoff by t and lowers the payoff of other cooperating actors by c_1 and the payoff of defecting others by c_2. Finally, the parameter g indicates the cooperative gain all players receive by mutual cooperation versus the payoff they receive by mutual defection.

Game theory prescribes that rational actors should not cooperate in a one-shot Prisoner's Dilemma because the defecting choice dominates the cooperative choice. Thus, no matter which choices the other players make, a player always will receive a higher payoff if she defects. Mutual defection is therefore the only Nash-equilibrium in the PD. This outcome is, however, Pareto-inefficient. A descriptive interpretation of the game theoretic structure would therefore predict that subjects will not cooperate when they are confronted with a Prisoner's Dilemma. This hypothesis is often referred to as the (strong) free rider hypothesis (Marwell & Ames, 1979). A variation of group size should not affect the prediction of zero cooperation. However, many experiments with 2-person PD Games found that some subjects usually cooperate even in one-shot games and that the cooperation rate depends partly on the payoff structure of the PD Game[6]. Since the normative model does not hold in 2-person games, the question raises whether group size has an effect on the cooperation rate in PD Games, and if so, how this effect can be explained.

A difficulty of testing group size effects in the one-shot PD Game lies in the fact that a variation of group size implies a covariation of some payoff parameters as well. This fact was often misconceived in the literature but can actually easily be seen in the representation of the N-person PD Game shown in figure 1. If we assume for simplicity that $c1 = c2$[7], than a variation of group size may be independent from t, but it implies a variation of either $c1$ or g as well. Generally, a variation of group size implies necessarily a covariation of one of the payoff parameters $c1$, g or t. If we are now concerned with the determinants of group size effects in the one-shot PD Game, one crucial question refers to the parameters being chosen to be held constant, or, equivalently, the question must be answered which parameters are chosen to covary with group size. We have three alternative hypotheses of why larger groups produce lower cooperation rates in experimental games. In the first two explanations we hypothesize that the effect of a variation of group size depends on the covariation of one of the payoff parameters. The third hypothesis argues that group size effects do not result from utility considerations of subjects, but that a separate psychological process is at work. The hypotheses may be derived and stated as follows.

1) According to the assumption that individuals maximize their private utility, no cooperation should occur in the one-shot Prisoner's Dilemma. However, the assumption of zero cooperation may be relaxed if we assume that some subjects cooperate because they perceive secondary utility (utility that is not contained in the explicit payoff matrix) from cooperation. A psychological justification for this assumption is that subjects want to be fair or friendly to their co-players (see Selten, 1978; de Vries, 1991). If subjects perceive secondary utilities, then the

cooperation rate should depend on the payoff differentials between cooperation and defection (t). In other words, cooperation causes opportunity costs to individuals, the monetary gain foregone by not defecting. The larger these costs of primary utilities, the lower the cooperation rate should be. Thus, the larger the incentive to defect, the lower the cooperation rate. According to this "weak" free rider hypothesis, a variation of group size should not affect the cooperation rate, if t remains constant. Put differently, if t decreases with increasing group size, then cooperation should rise and if t increases with increasing group size, then cooperation should decrease.

2) However, if subjects consider and value the incremental external effect that results from their cooperative choice (c1), a variation of group size that decreases c1 (and keeps t and g constant) should produce lower cooperation rates. This second hypothesis suggests that the cooperation rate is affected by the influence each individual has on the result of the group. It might be taken as an abstract version of Olson's and Buchanan's arguments[8].

3) In past experimental research, group size effects were often explained by deindividuation[9] (Hamburger, Guyer, & Fox, 1975) or social loafing[10] (Latane, Kipling, & Harkins, 1979). In contrast to the explanations that group size effects are a consequence of the payoff variation, both terms denote a separate psychological process that occurs within individuals and produces lower cooperation. Hence, if group size effects cannot be attributed to a payoff change, deindividuation, social loafing or a pure members-in-the-group effect might be present. However, since a variation in group size is necessarily related to at least one changing payoff parameter, this third hypothesis can not be falsified in a single experiment. This third hypothesis would be supported however, if larger groups would always produce lower cooperation rates in different experiments, no matter which payoff parameter is held constant.

There are at least two studies (Dawes, McTavish, & Shaklee, 1977; Komorita & Lapworth, 1982) in which group size effects were investigated in one-shot PD Games. In the experiment by Dawes et al., which was originally designed to test communication effects, group size varied due to absenteeism from 5 to 8 participants. The decision situation was explained and shown to subjects with a payoff table. Strategies and payoffs were symmetric and common knowledge among players. Subjects had the option to choose between X (defecting choice) and O (cooperative choice). Both payoff functions were linear with equal slopes and dependent on the number of cooperators, like the example shown in figure 1. The incentive to defect (t) was $8, irrespective of group size. Further, the impact of each individual's defecting choice on payoffs (which was $1.50) remained constant in different groups. Thus, the two payoff parameters t and c1 remained constant while g increased with increasing group size. In the condition that is of interest here, subjects were in one room, but were not allowed to communicate. Choices were made in private and subjects were dismissed separately. Summed over all group size conditions, Dawes et al. report a cooperation rate of 27%. No effect of group size was found.

In the Komorita et al. study a very similar design was used. Again subjects had two choices, which they made anonymously. Payoff matrices were symmetrical and known to all players. The payoff parameter t increased, c1 decreased, and g remained constant when group size varied between 2, 3, and 6 participants. However, it is not clear from the authors' description of the experiment by which absolute monetary amount the defecting choice dominated the cooperative choice, since subjects could accumulate points over a series of one-shot decisions. Subjects (undergraduate students) could then transform their accumulated points into school supplies that were worth up to $2. Thus, the monetary incentive to defect in a single decision was rather low. A significant decrease of cooperation was found from 59% in the 2-person group, to 50% in the 3-person and to 44% in the 6 person group. Komorita et al. conclude that this group size effect is due to deindividuation or a diffusion of responsibility effect.

The evidence from the two reported studies is not conclusive. In the experiment by Dawes et al. the two payoff parameters t and c1 were held constant and the changing of g produced no group size effect. In the experiment by Komorita et al., c1 and t covaried with the variation of N, so that the group size effect cannot be attributed unambiguously to either of the two parameters' variation.

In order to differentiate between the effects of externalities (c1) and the costs of cooperation (t) (and therefore between the above mentioned hypothesis 1 and 2), Franzen (1990), and Diekmann and Franzen (1991) conducted experiments with one-shot Prisoner's Dilemma Games. As in the other studies, Franzen (1990) recruited college students (N=203) and presented them the decision situation via payoff matrices. In this experiment only c1 decreased with increasing group size, while the payoff parameters t and g remained constant over all group size conditions. Subjects in this study faced an incentive to defect of about $2. Since the range of the group size variation might have an important effect on the result of the study, group size was varied from 2 to 101-person groups[11]. Overall, the author found an average cooperation rate of 13% with no group size effect being observable[12]. The study by Diekmann and Franzen (1991) consisted of a series of three one-shot Prisoner's Dilemma Games. All three decision situations were again presented to subjects via payoff matrices. In the first PD Game, the payoff parameters varied as in Franzen (1990), that is, t and g remained constant, while c1 decreased with increasing group size. However, the incentive to defect (t) was lowered by $1 in order to increase the average level of cooperation. This time the average cooperation rate was at about 45%. Again, overall group size had no significant effect on the cooperation rate (Chi-square=13.62, df=9, p>.20, N=329). The results of this experiment are presented in figure 2:

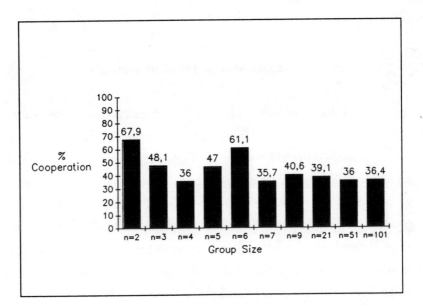

Figure 2:   Cooperation and group size in the one shot PD.

In the second and third decision situation of Diekmann and Franzen's study, the payoff matrices were constructed in such a way, that the parameter c1 remained constant, while t and g increased with increasing group size. The two games differed only in the presentation of the decisions. Again, in both of these decision situations no group size effect was observed. Thus, these data support the conclusion, that group size does not affect the cooperation rate in the one-shot

Prisoner's Dilemma, in which no communication is possible and in which decisions are anonymous. However, in regard to the question of the relative effects of the payoff parameters c1 and t the results from Franzen (1990), and Diekmann and Franzen (1991) are not conclusive either.

It might be possible that in the second and third decision of study 2, the effects of the parameters t and g cancelled each other out. While an increase of the parameter t motivates subjects to defect more, an increasing g might have created the competing motive to cooperate more. The interplay of both parameters might thus have produced the absence of the group size effect. Whether this reasoning is correct and whether the result of Komorita et al can be reproduced, is left to further research.

Group size and one-shot provisions of public goods

In reality, not all social dilemmas correspond to the logic of the Prisoner's Dilemma. Moreover, situations in which the payoffs are linear functions of the number of cooperators are particularly unrealistic. Some authors (Taylor 1987, Taylor & Ward 1982, Hampton 1987) argue, therefore, that most public goods for instance are characterized by provision points. If the total amount of contributions is below the provision point, the goods are of almost no value to the users and contributors receive no gain from their provisions. Contributions beyond the provision point are superfluous and add no further value to the good. Examples are roads, tunnels or bridges, which are either valuable if complete, or useless if incomplete. If goods are characterized by provision points, then defection is not the best individual choice, as in the Prisoner's Dilemma. It may be individually advantageous to contribute if others do not and to abstain from contributing if others do the job. Potential contributors to step level goods are therefore confronted with multiple equilibria. In Harsanyi's (1977) terminology, players face the "coordination problem" of who should make the contribution.

Marwell and Ames (1979) designed an experiment for such a situation. Each participant was told that she was either a member of a four person or of an 80 person group. Every group member received 225 tokens with the option to allocate any amount of the endowment to either a private account or a public account. Every token invested in the private account was worth one cent, such that subjects who kept all their tokens received $2.25 for certain. The amount of money that returned from the tokens invested into the public account was dependent on the amount of the total contribution by all group members. It was equally divided among all members including those who did not contribute. If the public account reached more than 400 tokens (8000 in the large group) of contributions, the money return exceeded the return from the private accounts. Thus, the average contribution rate had to be 100 tokens per person to be profitable for the group. To contribute is the best strategy of a subject if her contribution made the public account exceed its critical value of 400 tokens. Otherwise, it is always better to save one's own tokens and have others contribute to the public account. In the experiment, subjects contributed an average of 127.6 tokens (or every group invested 57% of its total resources) into the public account. Group size just failed (p > .10) to have a significant effect.

Similar results are reported from experiments by Kerr (1989), and Rapoport and Bornstein (1989). In Kerr's experiment group size varied between 9, 54, and 324 subjects (within subject variation). Participants' endowment were $10 which could be either kept or invested in the public good. Once the provision point was reached, every subject received $20 from the public good[13]. Provision points were varied between 1/3 and 2/3 of the group's resources. Although participants perceived themselves to be more efficacious in smaller groups than in larger ones, this perception of self-efficacy had no influence on their contribution behavior. No significant group size effects were found. A second experiment basically replicated the finding that group size had no effect on the observable cooperation behavior of subjects, even though individuals' perception of self-efficacy decreased with increasing group size.

Rapoport and Bornstein (1989) had two groups of different size (3 and 5 participants) compete for a public good. Both groups started with identical endowments. Individuals in the small groups received 5 units each and subjects in the large group received 3 each. The group that contributed most received the public good. Similar to Kerr's results, subjects who were in large groups perceived themselves to be less effective. However, this perception did not significantly influence the cooperation behavior. About 56% of individuals contributed irrespective of group size.

A special case of a social dilemma with a step level payoff function is Diekmann's Volunteer's Dilemma. The Volunteers Dilemma is a model of a situation in which the contribution of a single group member is sufficient for its provision. A real life example of such a situations is helping behavior as described in the research by Darley & Latane (1968). The assumptions of the game are that there are N group members each of which is able to provide help to a victim. If the victim receives help, every group member realizes utility (U). Helping incurs, however, costs (K) to the individual who helps. Since $U > K$ and therefore $U\text{-}K > 0$, it is individually advantageous to help if none of the others helps, but since $U > U\text{-}K$, every individual has an incentive not to help but to wait and see if another group member helps. If the players of the Volunteer's Dilemma could communicate, the volunteer could be chosen by some rule like a probability mechanism. Under the restriction of no communication, the players face a coordination problem. The dilemma has a Nash-equilibrium in mixed strategies, namely to defect with a probability of $q = (K/U)1/N\text{-}1$ (Diekmann, 1985). Accordingly, cooperation should decline in a curvilinear fashion with increasing group size.

This is exactly the result that Diekmann (1986) obtained in an experiment in which group size was manipulated by a within subject design. Subjects were asked whether they would cooperate if they had 1, 2, 3, and so on group members. The results were replicated in a study of Franzen (1990) in which the payoff structure was represented by a payoff matrix. The percentage of participants that chose to cooperate dropped from 65% in the two person group to below 30% when subjects were told that they have 50 or 100 co-players.

Group size effects in iterated social dilemmas

Regarding experimental research on the effects of group size on cooperation, the infinitely iterated Prisoner's Dilemma (PD supergames) received a great deal of attention. The result of the analytical work with iterated games (e.g. Friedman, 1970) is that conditional cooperative strategies might be in every player's best self-interest if the players are not too myopic, that is, if the long term advantage of mutual cooperation outweighs the short term advantage of the defecting choice. In terms of the notation used in figure 1, mutual cooperation is for instance advantageous if

$$\sum_{t=1}^{\infty} C_t(N) > \sum_{t=1}^{T-1} C_t(N) + D_T(N-1) + \sum_{t=T-1}^{\infty} D_t(0) \qquad (1)^{14},$$

were trials run from 1 to infinite. If players are assumed to discount future payoffs, the payoff for mutual cooperation converges to

$$U = \sum_{t=1}^{\infty} a^{t-1} C(N) = C(N) / (1-a), \quad (0 < a < 1) \qquad (2)$$

$(0 < a < 1)$, were a denotes the discount parameter. If discounting is taken into account, mutual cooperation will be in the players' best interest if each player's discount parameter

$$a^* \geq [D(N-1) - C(N)] / [D(N-1) - D(0)] \qquad (3)^{15}$$

If the discount parameter gets smaller than a*, then the defecting choice becomes a player's best reply.

Group size could now affect the probability of cooperation in a number of different ways[16]. First of all, group size might be confounded with the cost of cooperation or the cost of conflict in such a way that the defecting choice becomes a best reply for some players. Second, players' time horizon could be more heterogeneous in larger groups. This might lead to an inflation of defecting choices. Third, the risk that an actor deviates by accident from cooperation increases with larger groups. Due to the assumption of no communication actors cannot detect other players' motives. Hence, an escalation of defection might result.

There are six studies that tested group size effects in the iterated Prisoner's Dilemma Game (Bonacich & Light, 1978, Fox & Guyer, 1977; Hamburger, Guyer, & Fox, 1975; Komorita et al., 1980, 1982; Marwell & Schmitt, 1972;). Of particular interest is the study by Bonacich et al. because these authors tried to separate group size effects that are driven by a change of the payoff constellation from other mechanisms. Bonacich et al. varied group size between 3, 6, and 9 participants, and they varied the payoff structure in such a way that 1) t and g were both held constant, 2) both payoffs increased with increasing group size and 3) the parameter g increased while t remained constant. Similar to the hypothesis concerning one-shot games, the authors hypothesized that the two payoff parameters would counteract each other. Cooperation will be promoted with larger g, but will be inhibited with larger t. Thus, under the first and second payoff condition the authors expected no group size effects. However, if t remains constant and g increases with group size, there should be higher rates of cooperation in the larger groups. The number of trials was unknown to subjects[17]. The payoff matrices were presented via computer terminals, and it was only through these terminals that subjects received feedback concerning the number of cooperators and defectors in each trial. Thus, there was complete anonymity. The average cooperation rate dropped from 45% in the 3-person group to 25% in the 9-person group in the first and second payoff condition. Only when gain (g) increased and t was constant the cooperation rate did increase from 15% in the 3-person group to 35% in the 9-person group. Therefore, the first two results contradict the authors' hypothesis while the last result fits the prediction.

Bonacich et al. give two explanations for the decrease of cooperation in the first two conditions. The first explanation is that larger groups contain more likely non-cooperators than smaller groups and the authors found evidence in the data that a non-cooperative choice reduced the probability of continuous cooperation by others. Thus, a few non-cooperators might have caused the erosion of universal cooperation. The second possible explanation is that strategies lost their informational content in larger groups. Thus, the authors found that the influence of the proportion of others that chose cooperatively on a subject's own choice decreased with group size. Subjects seemed to influence each other less in larger groups.

Bonacich et al. did not take discounting of future payoffs into account. However, constancy of the parameters t and g implies a constant a* as well, if the payoff functions for cooperation and defection are parallel to each other (which was the case in this experiment). Also, the other two payoff constellations led to the same prediction as would have been suggested by a*.

The experiments by Hamburger et al., Fox and Guyer, and Marwell and Schmitt used a payoff constellation in which the parameters t and g did not vary with different group size. All of these studies report declining rates of cooperation. An exception are the findings of Komorita et al. (1980, 1982). Komorita et al. proposed an index K' (K' = C(N)-D(0)/D(N-1)-C(1)) as an index of cooperation. K' is an extension of a cooperation index that was proposed by Rapoport (1967) for the two person PD Game. The numerator of K' is identical with the parameter g. The denominator takes two motivational forces into account, viz. the greed to exploit other players D(N-1), and the fear to be the lone cooperator C(1). In the first experiment Komorita et al. varied the payoff structure such that K' remained more or less stable between different group sizes. In terms of the payoff parameters c1, g and t, this payoff variation implied that g remained constant while t increased with increasing group size. Although the cooperation rate for the small group (N=4) was somewhat larger (31%) than for the larger group (27%, N=8), the difference was not statistically significant. However, a replication of their payoff variation (Komorita et al., 1982) with g again remaining constant while t increased, produced declining cooperation rates, as would have been expected from the studies by Bonacich et al.

In some of the experiments on iterated games that we reviewed so far, none of the authors mentioned whether or not players knew the definite end of the game. However, this piece of information is highly important from a game theoretical point of view. If the end of a game is known, then players have an incentive to defect in the last trial, since no retaliation is possible. Accordingly, every player will expect her co-players to defect in the last trial. However, if mutual defection is expected in the last trial anyway, then a defecting choice becomes attractive in trial number t-1. By backward induction, mutual defection is expected from the very first trial in finitely iterated games (Luce & Raiffa, 1957). However, as with one-shot situations, experimental evidence contradicts game theoretical reasoning: subjects are often found to cooperate even in finitely iterated games. Different authors have tried to reconcile empirical evidence with game theoretic reasoning (Kreps, D.M., Milgrom, P., Roberts, J., & Wilson, R., 1982; Selten 1978; ; for a review see Holler & Illig, 1991). The basic result is that cooperative equilibria are feasible if players expect their co-players for some reason (e.g. a taste for simple strategies, incomplete information) to be committed to conditional cooperative strategies.

There are two experiments that tested group size effects in finitely iterated games (Isaac & Walker, 1988; Liebrand, 1984[18]). Isaac and Walker (1988) tested group size effects on the provision of public goods in a finitely iterated game. Group size was varied between 4 and 10 participants. Every subject received an endowment of 25 tokens for every decision trial. Subjects knew that the game would terminate after 10 trials. In each trial subjects had to decide how many of the 25 tokens they wanted to invest in the public good. Every token that subjects kept was worth one cent. Tokens that were invested in the public good paid either 0.3 or 0.75 cents back to subjects (thus, the marginal per capita return (MPCR) was either low or high)[18]. This payoff schedule was therefore structured according to a Prisoner's Dilemma, since it is individually best to keep all tokens privately. However, a Pareto-efficient result will only be reached if all group members invest all their tokens into the public good.

There are two relevant findings from the experiment: 1) The cooperation rate varied according to whether groups had a low or a high MPCR rate and 2) no other effect of group size appeared. The four person groups contributed on average 14.5%, whereas the ten person groups gave up 15.5% of their initial endowment of 25 tokens per trial. Hence, large groups were more cooperative than small groups. However, the difference was statistically not significant. The authors take this finding as conclusive evidence that group size effects are driven by changes of the MPCR and not by a mere presence of larger numbers of individuals in a group.

If provision to public goods does not involve all or nothing decisions, then there is no direct way to apply the payoff parameters t and g. However, if choices get truncated into all or nothing decisions (if subjects had to contribute all or no tokens) the parameters can be calculated. Such a re-analysis of the results of Isaac and Walker reveals that t varied between experimental conditions. The lowest average cooperation rate is found in the group with the largest t and the highest cooperation rate in the two groups with the lowest t. Thus, the experiment supports hypothesis 1, according to which the cooperation rate depends on the opportunity costs of cooperation.

In contrast to the previously reviewed studies, the evidence from studies with infinitely repeated Prisoner's Dilemma Games supports the notion that large groups cooperate less than small groups. The question whether games are finitely or infinitely iterated seems to be crucial for the appearance of the group size effect. The study by Isaac and Walker, which used a finitely iterated game, did not find group size effects.

Group size effects and the commons dilemma

The logic of decision making in social dilemmas inhibits not only the efficient production of public goods, but also the efficient use and maintenance of common goods and resources. It was Hardin

(1968) who reintroduced the term "Commons Dilemma" by describing the behavior of herdsmen who had access to the so-called Commons - commonly owned pasture land - in the states of New England[20]. Other examples of common resources are the atmosphere, oceanic fishing grounds or clean water supplies. The analog to free riding behavior is the extensive use by every individual, which will collectively result in overharvesting and destruction of the "Commons".

From a game-theoretical point of view, the incentive structure of a commons dilemma is similar to the incentive structure of other social dilemmas. As in other dilemmas, it is individually advantageous not to cooperate, but to withdraw as much as possible from the common resource. Psychologically, however, it may make a difference for people's behavior whether they have to contribute own endowments or have to restrict own taking in order to cooperate (Kahneman et al., 1982). Experimental studies on cooperation and group size effects in the commons dilemma deserve therefore a separate review. As with social dilemmas in general, not all commons dilemmas need to be characterized by a dominant strategy. Similar to the provision of step level goods, a common resource may reach its critical value by a single further withdrawal. Thus, it seems to be more similar to a Chicken-type Game[21] than a PD-type game. There are four experimental studies in which the effects of group size on the management of a commons were investigated (Allison & Messick, 1985; Brewer & Kramer, 1986; Liebrand, 1984; and Messick & McClelland, 1983). All four studies model the commons as a PD situation, in which it is individually always better to use the resource rather than to save it.

The Commons is usually represented to subjects by a pool of points or tokens. Subjects can withdraw points in each trial and can transform the accumulated number of points into money. In the study of Messick and McClelland (1983), the pool contained 10 points per subject. Each subject could withdraw between 0 and 4 points on every trial. After each trial the pool was renewed by 30% of the points that were left in the pool. The pool never exceeded the maximum of 10 points per subject. The game ended as soon as no points were left in the pool. Therefore, the end of the game was dependent on the groups' harvest behavior. The cooperative choice that maximizes the points for all participants is for every individual to withdraw an equal share of that proportion, which allows the pool to reach its maximum size again after each trial. In the study of Messick and McClelland the average withdrawal of 2.5 points per trial and individual was found. The authors varied group size from 1, 3 to 6-person groups. Though subjects could harvest the pool for an indefinite time, one-person groups depleted the pool on average after 30 rounds, the 3-person groups kept the pool for about 10 trials, and the 6-person groups finally depleted the pool after 9 trials.

Very similar group size effects were found by Allison and Messick (1985) where the pool contained 100 points per subject and would renew itself by 20% after each trial. Again 1-person groups maintained the pool longest (on average by 19 trials), followed by 3-person groups (about 18 trials), and 6-person groups (8 trials). The small difference between 1 and 3-person groups disappeared however, when subjects had, prior to the group condition, individual experiences with harvesting the pool. The authors took this as evidence for the conclusion that individuals in the commons dilemma face the difficulty of obtaining information on the relation between their personal harvest behavior and the maintenance of the pool.

No group size effect was found in the other two studies. In Liebrand's (1984) study, the common resource pool did not replenish. Subjects were either in 7 or 20-person groups and could withdraw any amount from $1.50 to $9.00 in five consecutive trials from the pool. Players knew that the game would end after five trials. However, players did not know the exact pool size. The pool size was determined after the game by a chance mechanism familiar to the players. If the sum of the players' withdrawal over the five trials exceeded the determined pool size, none of the players would receive anything. If the sum of claimed withdrawals was lower than the determined pool size, each player received the amount she claimed. Obviously, the cooperative strategy is to claim a moderate amount (here $13). Individuals in 20-person groups withdrew slightly more money from the pool than subjects in the small group, but the difference was not significant. However, the variance in the large group was bigger, suggesting that some subjects exploited others in this larger group.

Brewer and Kramer (1986) used a replenishable resource game from which either 8 or 32 subjects could withdraw between 0 and 25 points each trial. The replenishment rate of the pool varied by chance between 1% and 10%. The maximum and initial pool contained 150 points per subject and the game terminated as soon as the pool was depleted (actually the experimenter simulated a breakdown of the pool after twenty trials). Subjects in both group size conditions harvested at the same rate and took on average 11 points per trial out of the pool. In a second variation of the experiment, 8 and 32-person groups could not withdraw points from a pool but received an endowment of 25 points per trial instead. Then, subjects had to decide whether they kept the points or contributed them to a common pool which was reduced by every trial. Again the game terminated (the end was simulated again after 20 trials) if the pool was depleted. The cooperative strategy in this second condition was to contribute enough points to maintain the pool. Under this new condition a group size effect appeared. Subjects in the larger groups kept more points to themselves (M=13.90) than subjects in the small groups (M=11.47). The authors conclude that social dilemmas that are framed in such a way that subjects have to provide some of their endowments to maintain or provide a good are more sensitive to group size effects than decision tasks which are framed as a commons dilemma.

Thus, the evidence concerning effects of group size in the commons dilemma is not conclusive. Two out of four experiments do report declining cooperation rates. All of the experiments were conducted in a very similar manner so that there is no known factor that differentiates the experiments. Thus, to clarify the question why and when group size effects appear in the commons and what might override them must be left to future research.

Conclusion

Over the last decade new empirical evidence on group size effects within experimental game theory has accumulated, so that a revision of the conclusions of former surveys is timely. From a game-theoretical point of view, cooperation depends on 1) the type of the game and 2) whether players are faced with one-shot or iterated decision situations. If the players are faced with iterated decision situations, then the further distinction between finitely iterated and infinitely iterated games is vital. In this review of the experimental evidence we paid attention to the structure and the rules of games. In table 1 the reviewed studies are summarized according to the sections of this review.

A. Franzen

Table 1

Summary of experimental studies on group size effects in social dilemmas

Author	Presentation of dilemma	game type	group size	number trials	finitely vs. infinitely	parameter constellation	result
Dawes, McTavish Shaklee (1977)	Take some Game	N-PD	5,6,7,8	1	one shot game	t constant g increases	no effect on cooperation
Diekmann, Franzen (1991)	Presentation by payoff matrix	N-PD	2,3,4,5,6 7,9,21,51 101	1	one-shot game	1) t & g constant 2) t & g increases	no effect on cooperation
Franzen (1990)	Presentation by payoff matrix	N-PD	2,3,5,7,9, 21,51,101	1	one-shot game	t constant g constant	no effect on cooperation
Komorita & Lapworth (1982)	Presentation by payoff matrix	N-PD	2,3,6	1	one shot game	t increases g constant	cooperation declines
Kerr (1989)	Public Good	MCS	1) 9,54, 324, 2) 9,30	1 1	one shot game one shot game	t constant g increases	no effect on cooperation
Marwell & Ames (1979)	Public Good	MCS	4, 80	1	one shot game	t constant g increases	no effect on cooperation
Rapoport Bornstein (1989)	Public Good	MCS	3, 5	1	one shot game	t decreases g decreases	no effect on cooperation
Diekmann (1986)	Nominal groups Presentation by payoff - matrix	VOD		1	one shot game		coopertion declines
Bonacich, Shure, Kahan, Meeker (1976)	Presentation of payoff matrices by computer terminal	N-PD	3,6,9	15	not clear	1) t and g constant 2) t constant g inceases 3) t increases g increases	cooperation declines cooperation increases cooperation declines
Fox and Guyer (1977)	Take Some Game Presentation by matrix	N-PD	3, 12	200	infinitely	t constant g constant	cooperation declines
Hamburger, Guyer, Fox (1975)	Take Some Game Presentation by matrix	N-PD	3, 7	150	not clear	t constant g constant	cooperation declines
Komorita & Lapworth (1982)	2) Presentation by payoff matrix	N-PD	2, 6	45	45	t increases g constant	cooperation declines
Komorita & Lapworth (1980)	Presentation by payoff matrix	N-PD	4, 8	60	not clear	t increases g constant	no effect on cooperation
Marwell & Schmitt (1972)	Presemtation by payoff matrix	N-PD	2, 3	150	not clear	t constant g constant	cooperation declines
Isaac and Walker (1988)	Public Good	N-PD	4, 10	10	finitely	t constant g increases	no effect on cooperation
Allison, Messick (1985)	Commons Dilemma Presentation by computer terminal	N-PD	1,2,3,	max.20	infinitely	pool size increases with N	cooperation declines
Brewer, Kramer (1986)	1) Commons Dilemma. presentat. by terminal 2) Public Good presentat. by terminal	N-PD N-PD	8, 32 8, 32	pool end after 20 trials	infinitely infinitely	pool size increases with N	no effect on cooperation cooperation declines
Liebrand (1984)	Commons Dilemma	N-PD	7, 20	5	finitely	pool size varies with N	no effect on cooperation
Messick & McClelland (1983)	Commons Dilemma	N-PD	1, 3, 6	50	infinitely	pool size varies with N	Cooperation declines

Section 1 contains the studies that tested group size effects in one-shot Prisoner's Dilemma Games. We formulated basically two conjectures why group size effects might be expected in one-shot PD Games. In the first line of reasoning (hypothesis 1 and 2) we argued that group size effects depend on the incentive structure of the games. This structure is described by the payoff parameters c1, g and t. The second conjecture reasoned that not utility considerations, but other psychological processes as deindividuation, diffusion of responsibility etc. produce lower cooperation rates. With the exception of the study by Komorita (1982), none of the studies that tested group size effects in one-shot PD Games report declining cooperation rates. Also, group size effects were not observed in one-shot provisions of public goods games (see section 2 of table 1). The empirical evidence lends support to the conclusion that the size of a group does not affect the level of cooperation in one-shot social dilemmas. There is no support for the hypothesis that individuals cooperate less in larger groups because of deindividuation or any other psychological process. However, there is also no conclusive evidence on the effects of various payoff parameters. The comparison between different experiments (e.g. Diekmann & Franzen, 1991; Franzen, 1990) suggests that the level of cooperation is strongly affected by the payoff parameter t. Though, there is no convincing proof on the effect of t within a single experiment.

An exception to the general notion that group size effects are absent in one-shot social dilemmas, is the observed behavior in the one-shot Volunteer's Dilemma. In the Volunteer's Dilemma the cooperation rate declined almost as it is predicted by the Nash-equilibrium.

The studies that are grouped into section 3 of table 1 reveal that group size effects did appear in infinitely iterated Prisoner's Dilemma games. As in one-shot games, there is no straightforward way to experimentally isolate the mechanisms that produces the decline in cooperation. In addition to the difficulty of separating the effects of different payoff parameters, individuals form expectations about the length of the game. The shorter the expected number of trials is, the larger is the incentive to defect in infinitely iterated games. Larger groups might contain more likely individuals with shorter time expectations. The defecting choice of these individuals might then produce an escalation of defecting choices in the whole group.

No group size effects were observed in the study by Isaac and Walker (1988) as well as in the study by Liebrand (1984). Both studies used finitely iterated games. Thus, finitely iterated games seem to be less sensitive to group size effects. This conclusion is, however, severely limited by lack of data.

The experimental studies that tested group size effects within the Commons Dilemma frame are grouped into section 4 of table 1. Two out of four studies found group size effects. Thus, the evidence on group size effects in the Commons Dilemma is not as conclusive as it is in other social dilemmas.

The main goal of this article was to provide an updated review on the findings of group size effects in experimental social dilemmas. We set out to question the general conclusion of previous reviews (e.g. Stroebe & Frey, 1982), that large groups show usually a lower cooperation rate. The main finding from the studies discussed here support the conclusion that group size does not affect the level of cooperation in one-shot Prisoner' s Dilemma games. Also, larger groups are not more susceptible to the free rider problems than small groups in one-shot public goods games.

Footnotes

1   University of Berne, Department of Sociology, Berne, Switzerland

2   Mancur Olson (1965): The Logic of Collective Action. Cambridge, Mass. Harvard University Press. (p. 36)

3   James M. Buchanan (1965): Ethical Rules, Expected Values, and Large Numbers. Ethics, Vol. LXXVI. (p.9)

4   The term "social dilemma" was first introduced by Dawes (1980). Dawes, however, discusses the Prisoner's Dilemma which is defined by the two properties 1) that every player has a strictly dominant response and 2) that the actors' use of this dominant response results in an inefficient collective outcome. This definition excludes other interesting situations in which rational actors fail to reach the collective optimum such as in the Chicken Game (Rapoport et al. 1966) or in the Volunteer's Dilemma (Diekmann 1985), but lack dominant strategies. Thus, we use the term "social dilemma" more generally to refer

to any situations that is subject to efficiency problems. See Harsanyi (1977) and Liebrand (1983) on the issue of classifying social dilemma games.

5   Similar presentations of the N-PD are used by Kelley & Grzelak (1972), Schelling (1971), Hamburger (1973) and Dawes (1975).

6   See Murningham & Roth (1983) for a discussion of different payoff parameters in the PD.

7   This implies that the two payoff graphs C(m) and D(m) are parallel to each other. This means that all players in a given group face the same incentive to defect (t). There are no positional effects.

8   Note, however, that the experiments beeing discussed in the text are not a test of Olson's or Buchanan's theory. On the one hand, Olson and Buchanan do not explicitly distinguish between iterated and one-shot decision situations. On the other hand, both authors argue that larger groups imply less communication and more anonymity, which increases the incentive to defect to the point that it dominates cooperation. Thus, in Olson's and Buchanan's view, large numbers create a PD-situation that is not present if the group is small.

9   The term "deindividuation" was introduced by Festinger et al. (1952) and refers to the observation that individuals behave in a less morally restricted manner and engage more readily in self beneficial behavior if they find themselves in anonymous situations (e.g., as a member in large crowds).

10   "Since people are likely to work hard in proportion to the pressure they feel to do so, we should expect increased group size to result in reduced efforts on the part of individual group members. These reduced efforts can be called "social loafing"- a decrease in individual effort due to the social presence of others". Bibb Latane, Kipling Williams, Stephen Harkins (1979).

11   Group size was varied by telling subjects that they had a certain number of co-players who were like them randomly chosen from the college population. Hence, there were no real groups, but only nominal groups.

12   The results of this experiment are reported in Diekmann (1991).

13   However, not every subject received monetary payoffs. Some groups and some subjects were determined randomly to actually receive the monetary payoffs after the experiment. Thus, the expected monetary reward for subjects was rather low.

14   Discounting of future payoffs is not taken into account here. Furthermore, it is assumed that a defecting choice by one player results in mutual defection of all other players in all remaining trials.

15   See Axelrod (1984) and Raub (1988) for the derivation of this equation.

16   See Raub (1988) for a discussion of this issue.

17   Actually the authors do not explicitly mention whether subjects knew the number of trials or not. However, since knowing the number of trials would change the logic of decision making drastically, it may be assumed they used infinitely iterated games.

18   Liebrand's study will be discussed in the next section.

19   The marginal per capita return of an individual's contribution corresponds to an individual's external effect of cooperation that was denoted as c1 in figure 1.

20   The problem of the Commons was already analyzed by Lloyd in 1833 (see Hardin 1968).

21   Think of Schelling's example of an electricity shortage during hot summer seasons. It is collectively rational to use as many air conditioners as possible. However, the additional use of a single air conditioner may bring the undesirable blackout. If an individual would know that her withdrawal is critical, she probably would abstain from using her air conditioner.

References

Allison, S.T., & Messick, D.M. (1985). Effects of experience on performance in a replenishable resource trap. *Journal of Personality and Social Psychology, 49/4,* 943-948.

Axelrod, R.(1984). *The evolution of cooperation.* New York, Academic Press.

Bonacich, P., Shure, G., Kahan, J., & Meeker, R. (1976). Cooperation and group size in the n-person prisoner's dilemma. *Journal of Conflict Resolution, 20/4.*

Bonacich, P., & Light, J. (1978). Laboratory experimentation in sociology. *Annual Review of Sociology, 4,* 145-70.

Bray, R.M., Kerr, N.L., & Atkin, R. (1978). Effects of group size, and sex on group performance and member reaction. *Journal of Personality and Social Psychology, 36/11,* 1224-1240.

Brewer, M.B., & Kramer, R.M. (1986). Choice behavior in social dilemmas: Effects of social identity, group size, and decision framing. *Journal of Personality and Social Psychology, 60,* 543-549.

Buchanan, J.M. (1965). Ethical rules, expected values, and large numbers. *Ethics, 1,* 1-13.

Chamberlin, J. (1974). Provision of collective goods as a function of group size. *The American Political Science Review, 68,* 706-717.

Colman, A. (1982). *Game theory and experimental games. The study of strategic interaction.* Pergamon Press.

Darley, J.M., & Latane, B. (1968). Bystander intervention in emergencies: Diffusion of responsibility. *Journal of Personality and Social Psychology, 8,* 377-383.

Dawes, R. (1975). Formal models of decision making. In N. Kaplan & S. Schwartz (Eds.), *Human judgement and decision processes: Formal and mathematical approaches* (pp 88-107). New York: Academic Press.

Dawes, R. (1980). Social dilemmas. *Annual Review of Psychology, 31*, 169-193.

Dawes, R. (1988). *Rational choice in an uncertain world.* Harcourt Brace Jovanovich, Inc.

Dawes, R., McTavish, J., & Shaklee, H. (1977). Behavior, communication and assumptions about other peoples behavior in a commons dilemma situation. *Journal of Personality and Social Psychology, 35/1*, 1-11.

Diekmann, A. (1985). Volunteer's dilemma. *Journal of Conflict Resolution, 29/4*, 605-610.

Diekmann, A. (1986). Volunteer's dilemma. A social trap without a dominant strategy and some empirical results. In A. Diekmann & P. Mitter (Eds.), *Paradoxical effects of social behaviour* (187-197).

Diekmann, A. (1991). Soziale Dilemmata, Modelle, Typisierungen und empirische Resultate. In H. Esser & G. Troitzsch (Eds.), *Modellierung sozialer Prozesse* (417-456).

Diekmann, A., & Franzen, A. (1991). Group size effects in the one-shot Prisoner's Dilemma. Unpublished manuscript.

Festinger, L., Pepitone, A., & Newcomb, T. (1954). Some consequences of de-individuation in a group. *Journal of Abnormal and Social Psychology, 68*, 359-366.

Fox, J., & Guyer, M. (1977). Group size and others' strategy in an N-person game. *Journal of Conflict Resolution, 21/2*, 323-338.

Franzen, A. (1990). *Die Gruppengröße und das Problem der Kooperation in sozialen Dilemmata.* Diplomarbeit, University of Mannheim, unpublished manuscript.

Friedman, James W. (1970). A non-cooperative equilibrium for supergames. *Review of Economic Studies, 30*, 1-12.

Frohlich, N., & Oppenheimer, J.A. (1970). I get by with a little help from my friends. *World Politics, 23*, 104-20.

Grzelak, J. (1989). Conflict and cooperation. In M. Hewstone, W. Stroebe, P. Codol, & G.M. Stephenson (Eds.), *Introduction to social psychology* (pp. 288-312). Basil Blackwell.

Hamburger, H. (1973). N-person prisoner's dilemma. *Journal of Mathematical Sociology, 3*, 27-48.

Hamburger, H., Guyer, M., & Fox, J. (1975). Group size and cooperation. *Journal of Conflict Resolution, 19/3*, 503-531.

Hampton, J. (1987). Free rider problems in the production of public goods. *Economics and Philosophy, 3*, 245-273.

Hardin, G. (1968). The tragedy of the commons. *Science, 162*, 1243-1248.

Hardin, R. (1971). Collective action as an agreeable n-person prisoner's dilemma. *Behavioral Science, 16*, 472-481.

Harkins, S.G., Latane, B., & Williams, K. (1980). Social loafing: Allocating or taking it easy? *Journal of Experimental Social Psychology, 16*, 457-465.

Harsanyi, J.C. (1977). *Rational behavior and bargaining equilibrium in games and social situations*. Cambridge: Cambridge University Press.

Holler, M., & Illig, G. (1991). *Einführung in die Spieltheorie*. Berlin, Heidelberg: Springer Verlag.

Ingham, A.G. (1974). The Ringelmann Effect: Studies of group size and group performance. *Journal of Experimental Social Psychology, 10*, 371-384.

Isaac, R.M., & Walker, J.M. (1988). Group size effects in public goods provision: The voluntary contributions mechanism. *Quarterly Journal of Economics, 103*, 179-199.

Kahneman, D., Slovic, P., & Tversky, A. (1982). *Judgement under uncertainity: Heuristics and biases*. Cambridge: Cambridge University Press.

Kelly, H.H., & Grzelak, J. (1972). Conflict between individual and common interest in an n-person relationship. *Journal of Personality and Social Psychology, 21/2*, 190-197.

Kerr, N.L. (1989). Illusions of efficiency: The effect of group size on perceived efficiency in social dilemmas. *Journal of Experimental Social Psychology, 25*, 287-313.

Kerr, N.L., & Bruun, S.E. (1983). Dispensability of member effort and group motivation losses: Free rider effects. *Journal of Personality and Social Psychology, 44/1*, 78-94.

Komorita, S.S., & Lapworth, W.C. (1982). Cooperative choice among individuals versus groups in an n-person dilemma situation. *Journal of Personality and Social Psychology, 42/3*, 487-496.

Komorita, S.S., Sweeney, J., & Kravitz, D.A. (1980). Cooperative choice in the n-person dilemma situation. *Journal of Personality and Social Psychology, 38/3*, 504-516.

Kravitz, D.A., & Martin, B. (1986). Ringelman rediscovered: The original article. *Journal of Personality and Social Psychology, 50/5*, 936-941.

Kreps, D.M., Milgrom, P., Roberts, J., & Wilson, R. (1982). Rational cooperation in the finitely repeated prisoner's dilemma. *Journal of Economic Theory, 27*, 245-252.

Latane, B., Kipling, W., & Harkins, S. (1979). Many hands make light the work: The causes and consequences of social loafing. *Journal of Personality and Social Psychology, 37/6*, 822-832.

Latane, B., & Nida, S. (1981). Ten years of research on group size and helping. *Psychological Bulletin, 89/2*, 308-324.

Liebrand, W.B.G. (1983). A classification of social dilemma games. *Simulation and Games, 14/2*, 123-138.

Liebrand, W.B.G. (1984). The effect of social motives, communication and group size on behavior in an n-person multi-stage mixed-motive game. *European Journal of Social Psychology, 14*, 239-64.

Luce, R.D., & Raiffa, H. (1957). *Games and decisions*. New York: Wiley.

Marriot, R. (1949). Size of working group and output. *Occupational Psychology, 26*, 47-57.

Marwell, G., & Ames, R.E. (1979). Experiments on the provision of public goods. I. Resources, interests, group size, and the free rider problem. *American Journal of Sociology, 84/6*, 926-937.

Marwell, G., & Schmitt, D.R. (1972). Cooperation in a three-person prisoner's dilemma. *Journal of Personality and Social Psychology, 21/3*, 376-383.

Messick, D.M. (1973). To join or not to join: An approach to the unionization decision. *Organizational Behavior and Human Performance, 10*, 145-156.

Messick, D.M., & Brewer, M.B. (1983). Solving social dilemmas: A review. In L. Wheeler & P. Shaver (Eds.), *Annual review of personality and social psychology* (pp. 11-44) 4. Beverly Hills: Sage.

Messick, D.M., & McClelland, C.L. (1983). Social traps and temporal traps. *Personality and Social Psychology Bulletin, 9/1*, 105-110.

Murnigham, K.J., & Roth, A (1983). Expecting continued play in prisoners dilemma games. *Journal of Conflict Resolution, 27/2*, 279-300.

Olson, M. (1968). *The logic of collective action*. Cambridge, Mass.: Harvard University Press.

Olson, M. (1982). *The rise and decline of nations*. Cambridge, Mass.: Harvard University Press.

Rapoport, A., & Bornstein, G. (1989). Intergroup competition for public goods: Effects of unequal resources and relative group size. *Journal of Personality and Social Psychology, 56/5,* 748-756.

Rapoport, A. (1966). *Two person game theory. The essential ideas*. Ann Arbor: The University of Michigan Press.

Rapoport, A. (1967). A note on the index of cooperation. *Journal of Conflict Resolution, 11,* 101-103.

Raub, W. (1988). Problematic social situations and the "large-number dilemma". A game-theoretical analysis. *Journal of Mathematical Sociology, 13,* 311-357.

Schelling, T. (1971). On the ecology of micromotives. *The Public Interest, 25,* 61-98.

Selten, R. (1978). The chain store paradox. *Theory and Decision, 9,* 127-159.

Steiner, I.D. (1966). Models for inferring relationships between group size and potential group productivity. *Behavioral Science, 11,* 273-283.

Steiner, I.,D. (1972). *Group process and productivity*. New York, London: Academic Press.

Stroebe, W. & Frey, B.S. (1982). Self-interest and collective action: The economics and psychology of public goods. *British Journal of Social Psychology, 21,* 121-37.

Taylor, M. (1987). *The possibility of cooperation*. Cambridge University Press.

Taylor, M., & Hugh, W. (1982). Chickens, whales, and lumpy goods: Alternative models of public-goods provision. *Political Studies, 3,* 350-370.

Thomas, E.J., & Fink, C.F. (1963). Effects of group size. *Psychological Bulletin, 60/4,* 371-384.

Umino, M. (1987). Formulation of commons dilemma: Dawes' model reconsidered. *Journal of Mathematical Sociology, 14,* 237-246.

Vries de, S. (1991). *Egoism, altruism, and social justice. Theory and experiments on cooperation in social dilemmas*. Rijksuniversiteit Groningen.

Acknowledgment

This research was supported by the "Deutsche Forschungsgemeinschaft" grant DI 292/3-1 to Andreas Diekmann and Anatol Rapoport. I would like to thank Norman Braun, Andreas Diekmann, Michael Conway and an anonymous reviewer for helpful comments on an earlier version of this article.

Provision of step-level public goods:
Effects of different information structures

Amnon Rapoport[1] and Ido Erev[2]

Abstract

We report the results of two experiments on social dilemmas in which each of n players receives an endowment and then decides privately whether to contribute it for the provision of a monetary public good. The good is provided if and only if at least m group members contribute. Decisions are made sequentially. We present and then test an equilibrium model under two different information conditions in which players are informed of 1) the previous decisions in the sequence; 2) either the number of previous contributions or the number of previous non-contributions. When the equilibrium solution yields unique predictions, most of the subjects behaved in accordance with it.

Introduction

Problems of public goods provision constitute a class of social dilemmas characterized by two basic properties (Barry & Hardin, 1982; Olson, 1965; Taylor, 1987). The first property, called jointness of supply means that once the public good is provided, any given amount of the good can be made available to or "consumed" by any member of the group. The second property, called nonexcludability, means that regardless of the magnitude of their contribution to the provision of the good, members of the group cannot be prevented from consuming it. Bridges, roads, public parks, libraries, charity drives, unpolluted air, rain forests, as well as nonphysical goods such as ideas published in scientific journals and social status of a given profession are examples of public goods possessing these two properties.

The problem posed by the voluntary provision of public goods is as old as the history of social groups organizing their members in order to achieve some common goal. Because group members seeking to enhance their own benefit will recognize opportunities to "free ride" on the contributions of others, a basic prediction derived from the standard economic model of rational, single-period individual choice is that public goods will be underprovided relative to demand or, in more extreme cases, will not be provided at all. Libraries, churches, charity drives, public parks, and other goods of this nature produced by voluntary contributions seem to refute this pessimistic prediction. There is ample evidence in many natural and experimental settings that mechanisms exist for the voluntary provision of some public goods and the rate of free riding is not as high as predicted. If this evidence is cavalierly dismissed as a manifestation of atypical altruism, then there is a serious question whether the economic theory of public goods consists of any refutable hypotheses. For explanations proposed to reconcile this evidence with the basic prediction of economic theory concerning the provision of public goods see, for example, Hampton (1987), Harrison and Hirshleifer (1989), Margolis (1982), Miller and Andreoni (1991), and Taylor (1987).

Field observations cannot refute the free rider hypothesis because in most cases we do not know the optimal quantity of the public good that was actually provided. They only point out an incongruity which, in turn, has stimulated experimental studies of public goods provision. These experiments have taken various forms depending on the nature of the good (e.g., binary vs. incremental), type of contribution (e.g., binary or continuous), population of players, group size, and payoff structure (see, e.g., Andreoni, 1988; Dawes, Orbell, Simmons, & Van de Kragt, 1986; Isaac, McCue, & Plott, 1985; Isaac & Walker, 1988; Isaac, Walker, & Thomas, 1984; Marwell & Ames, 1981; Palfrey & Rosenthal, 1988, 1991; Rapoport & Bornstein, 1989; Rapoport & Eshed-Levy, 1989; Rapoport & Suleiman, in press; Van de Kragt, Orbell, & Dawes, 1983).

The present study employs a simple research paradigm introduced by Van de Kragt et al. (1983) in which contributions are binary and the public good is all-or-none. This research paradigm, referred to as the minimal contributing set (MCS) game (Rapoport, 1985), is an n-person noncooperative game with the following structure: The game is played once by a group of n players. Communication before, during, and immediately after the game is prohibited. Each of the n players in the group is provided with a fixed sum (a promissory note) worth \$e (e > 0). She must then decide privately and anonymously whether to contribute her entire endowment to the benefit of her group. The public good -- a prize worth \$r (r > e) -- is provided to each member of the group if at least m group members contribute (1 < m < n); it is not provided, otherwise. The value of m is common knowledge. Player i (i = 1,...,n) never learns how many players contributed, only whether the public good was provided. Depending on her individual decision (to either contribute or not) and the number of contributors (smaller than m, equal to or greater than m), each player ends up the game with a payoff of either \$0, \$e, \$r, or \$(r+e), as shown in Table 1. Note that, unlike the n-person Prisoner's Dilemma game, the decision not to contribute (denoted by D) is not dominant. If exactly m-1 of the remaining n-1 members contribute (choose C) then, as shown by Table 1, the focal player is better off choosing C rather than D.

Table 1

Payoff Matrix for the MCS Game

Player i's Decision	Number of Other Players Choosing C		
	m-2 or fewer	m-1	at least m
C	o	r	r
D	e	e	e + r

All the MCS experiments referred to above as well as most studies of social dilemmas have implemented the simultaneous protocol of play (Harrison & Hirshleifer, 1989) in which, on each trial, players make their decisions privately and anonymously. With very few exceptions (Rutte, Wilke, & Messick, 1987; Erev & Rapoport, 1990), there have been no attempts to implement the sequential protocol of play in which decisions are made one after the other in a prespecified order. Erev and Rapoport (1990) pointed out that the experimental investigation of the sequential protocol in social dilemma situations is important for at least two reasons. First, in many social dilemmas occurring in real life the decision whether to contribute or how much to contribute is made sequentially rather than simultaneously. This is often the case when people are asked to contribute voluntarily to United Way campaigns, public radios, libraries, hospitals, etc. Very often, when they consider what decision to make, group members know the total amount of money already contributed by their predecessors. A second, related reason is that in many social dilemmas some of the players may be tempted to bind themselves irrevocably to noncooperation. This incentive derives from the expectation of a player that an irrevocable commitment on her part will induce some of the other group members to cooperate. (Other players may not share this incentive if they believe that irrevocable commitment to noncooperation may induce other group members, who are yet to make their decisions, retaliate by noncooperation). Irrevocable binding to noncooperation when preplay communication is prohibited can be studied experimentally when the protocol of play is sequential, not simultaneous.

Models for different information structures

When the MCS game is played under the sequential protocol of play several information structures can be distinguished. We consider below two different structures depending on the information acquired by or provided to the player when it is her turn to play. To describe these information structures, assume without loss of generality that the players are ordered from 1 to n with player i occupying the i-th position in the sequence. Under the full information (FI) structure, each player i is fully informed about the decisions of players $1,2,...,i-1$, when it is her turn to make a decision. She is also informed of her serial position in the sequence. Under the partial information (PI) structure, player i is only informed of the previous number of contributions or noncontributions. In particular, in Condition C player i is informed that k members have already contributed $(k=0,1,...,i-1)$, but not how many players have not contributed. In Condition D player i is informed that k members have not contributed, but not how many players have actually contributed. In neither condition player i is informed of her exact position in the sequence, nor can she deduce it from the information she has acquired. She can only deduce that $i > k$. (If she knew her position in the sequence, player i could calculate how many of her predecessors had contributed and how many had not. In this case, the PI structure would reduce to the FI structure.)

Full information. Our investigation of the different information structures is motivated by a model developed and tested in a previous study by Erev and Rapoport (1990). To explain this model, consider the game tree in Fig. 1 for the MCS game played under the sequential protocol with full information. Figure 1 assumes n=4 and m=2. Each player can make one of two decisions labeled C and D. Player 1 is shown at the top of the figure, player 2 is shown below, and so on. The signs + and - at the bottom of the figure indicate provision or nonprovision of the good, respectively. The subgame perfect equilibrium (SPE) solution is derived by backward induction. To illustrate the derivation, assume that player 4 has been informed that players 1, 2 and 3 chose C, D, and C, respectively. If player 4 chooses D she will gain \$(r+e), whereas if she chooses C her payoff will be \$r. Hence, the optimal decision in this case is D. This decision is marked by a heavy line in the figure. If player 4 is informed that players 1, 2 and 3 chose C, D, and D, respectively, she will do better by choosing C and getting \$r than choosing D and receiving \$e. Consider next player 3, and assume that she is informed that player 1 chose C and 2 chose D. Assuming that player 4 will behave rationally, given any of her two decisions, player 3's optimal decision is D. The optimal decision at each decision point of the game tree is indicated by a heavy line. The equilibrium path is (D,D,C,C).[3]

At the individual player level the equilibrium strategy is to choose C if and only if the number of previous D decisions is exactly 2. This strategy is a subgame perfect (Nash) equilibrium since it specifies the equilibrium decision for player i even if one or more of players preceding him in the sequence are known to depart from the equilibrium path. The equilibrium model is not restricted to the specific values of n and m. The subgame perfect equilibrium for the general game is to choose C if and only if the number of previous D decisions is exactly n-m. Three predictions can be derived from the model. Ordered in terms of their specificity, these predictions are:

1. The public good will be provided.
2. The public good will be provided efficiently.
3. The first n-m players in the sequence will choose D and the remaining players will choose C.

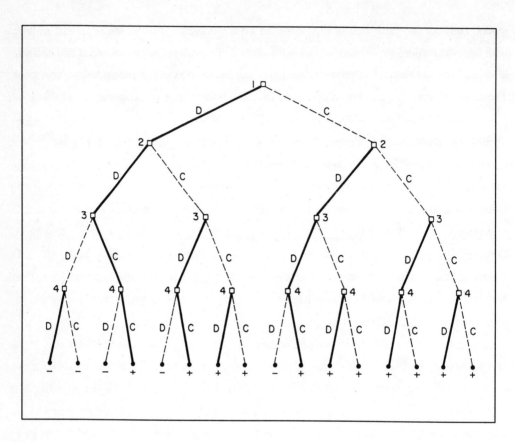

Figure 1:   Equilibrium solution to the MCS game with n=4 and m=2.

Note that in deriving the solution by backward induction, the model invokes the assumption that when making her decision player i assumes that players i+1, i+2,...,n will behave rationally. This assumption may seem to be too strong. Supposing that player i is informed that some or all of the players preceding her in the sequence departed from their equilibrium decisions. Will this information lead her to suspect the rationality of players i+1,i+2,...,n and consequently change her behavior? Or will she ignore this information and adhere to her equilibrium decision? Experiment 1 below was designed in part to answer this question.

   Partial Information. Consider Conditions C and D, which we defined above, where only partial information about previous decisions is provided. A natural question, which has practical implications for the construction of mechanisms for enhancing contributions to public goods, in which of the two conditions will generate more contributions. A social psychological theory incorporating the notion of conformity, which assumes that a player will be influenced by and tend to imitate the decisions that members of the group have already made, predicts more contributions under Condition C than D. Reciprocal altruism arguments result in the same prediction. Extending the equilibrium solution described above to the PI structure, Erev and Rapoport (1990) derived the opposite prediction.

Rather than going through the derivation, we illustrate their model by Fig. 1. Consider first Condition D. If a player is informed that $k=0$, she can deduce that her position in the sequence, i, is either the first, second, third, or fourth. Figure 1 shows that she should choose D, given any of these four positions. If the player is informed that $k=1$, then she can deduce that $i=2,3$, or 4. Figure 1 shows that the optimal decision for any of these three positions is again D. Consider next the case where the player is informed that two of her predecessors did not contribute ($k=2$). She can deduce that either $i=3$ or $i=4$. In either case, Fig. 1 shows that her optimal decision is C. Finally, if $k=4$, then $i=4$ and the optimal decision is again D. It follows from this analysis that in condition D (with $n=4$ and $m=2$), player i should choose C if and only if $k=2$ (and, in the general case, if and only if $k=n-m$). If all the n players behave rationally in Condition D, then players $1,2,...,n-m$ will choose D and players $n-m+1, n-m+2,...,n$ will choose C. Thus, the model yields the same predictions for Condition D as for the FI structure.[4]

The situation is quite different for Condition C. For example, supposing that a player is informed that $k=0$. As before, she should conclude that $i=1,2,3$ or 4. Figure 1 shows that after observing zero C's, the player should choose D in positions 1,2, and 4, and C in position 3. The predicted decision in this case is indeterminate. Unless distributional assumptions are made by player i about her position in the sequence (e.g., that positions 1,2,3 and 4 are equally likely, if $k=0$), her decision remains indeterminate. The same is true when $k=1$, but not when k m. Because information about previous contributions in Condition C does not result in unambiguous predictions, Erev and Rapoport (1990) argued that the public good will be provided less often in Condition C than D. Their results support this prediction. A major purpose of Experiment 2 below is to replicate the results of Erev and Rapoport with larger values of n and m, which render the backward induction calculations to be beyond the computational ability of most subjects.

Experiment 1

Experiment 1 was designed 1) to test the SPE solution described above for the FI structure with no restrictions on play; 2) to test the same model when the decisions of the first two players in the sequence are fixed in advance by the experimenter.

Method

Subjects. Subjects were 70 male and female students at the Technion - Israel Institute of technology. They were recruited by advertisements promising monetary reward contingent on performance in a group decision making experiment. Depending on the game, to be described below, the subjects were divided randomly into either 10 groups of 7 members each or 14 groups of 5 members each.

Procedure. With a few changes, the procedure was identical to the one of Erev and Rapoport (1990). Subjects arrived at the laboratory individually and were each given a set of written instructions (in Hebrew) and seven cards (one for each game) with the subject identification number written on their back. The subjects were told that the study concerned decision making in small groups with monetary reward contingent on performance. They were further instructed that they would participate in seven different games, and that they would be grouped with different players on different games. Their task in each game would be to place the card for the game (with the game number written on its back) in one of two boxes colored blue (B) or red (R).

The instructions made no reference to contribution or noncontribution in order not to bias the subjects. Rather, the subjects were instructed that their payoff for each game would be determined as follows:

You receive 20 NIS for participation in the game.

You lose 12 NIS, if the Blue box contains more than 3 cards.

You win 6 NIS, if the Blue box contains your card.

The resulting individual payoff for each game was either 14 (Blue box contains at least four cards and own card is in the Blue box), 8 (Blue box contains at least four cards and own card is in the

Red box), 26 (Blue box contains no more than three cards and own card is in the Blue box), or 20 (Blue box contains no more than three cards and own card is in the Red box). In terms of the parameters of the MCS game, placing a card in either the Red or blue box corresponds to contribution (C) or noncontribution (D), respectively. The payoff structure defines an MCS game with $n=7$, $m=4$, $e=6$, $r=12$, and an additional 8 NIS for participation ($1 = 2.4$ NIS). The ratio $r/e = 2$ is the same as the one used previously by Van de Kragt et al. (1983) and Erev and Rapoport (1990).

The subjects were instructed that in some of the games both boxes would be opaque and in some both would be transparent, so that they could count the number of cards already placed in each box. (The seven cards of each group were of different length, so that cards could be counted easily without taking them from the box.) The subjects were further instructed that their position in the sequence (1-7) would vary from one game to another.

The experiment consisted of the following seven games[6]:

Game 1.   Both boxes are transparent.

Game 2.   Both boxes are transparent. Two cards are placed initially in the Red box.

Game 3.   Both boxes are transparent. One card is placed initially in each of the two boxes.

Game 4.   Both boxes are transparent. Two cards are placed initially in the Blue box.

Game 5.   Both boxes are opaque. Each player is only told his/her position (1-7) in the sequence.

Game 6.   Same as Game 5.

Game 7.   Same as Game 1.

Half of the subjects played Games 1 through 7 in this order. For the other half the order of Games 2 and 4 was reversed. The entire experiment lasted approximately 30 minutes.

Each of the seven group members in Game 1 had full (and correct) information about the decisions of his/her predecessors. No attempt to manipulate this information was made. We replicated this condition in Game 7 in order to assess the effects of experience in playing the MCS game under different information conditions. Games 2, 3, and 4 presented false information about the decisions of players 1 and 2 in the sequence. Whereas each player in these games believed that he/she was a member of a seven-player group, in fact only positions 3 through 7 were assigned to the players. Consequently, the 70 subjects in Games 2, 3, and 4 were divided into 14 groups of 5 members each rather than 10 groups of 7 members each.

To allow the subjects to check their understanding of the payoff structure, a brief questionnaire was included as part of the instructions. In each question, the subject was asked to compute his/her payoff for a different contingency (number of cards in the Blue or Red box) depending on his/her decision. Subsequently, the correct answers were given and explained in the instructions.

Each subject was instructed to maximize his/her payoff in each of the seven games separately. The subjects were told that at the end of the experiment one of the seven games would be chosen randomly to determine their payoff for the experiment.

Results

Table 2 presents the results of Games 1 and 7. The first column identifies the group for the game, and the second shows the decisions of all seven group members in order. For example, players assigned positions 1, 3, and 5 in Group 10 of Game 1 chose D, C, and C, respectively. Column 3 shows whether the public good was provided.

The seven right-hand columns of Table 2 compare each of the observed decisions to the equilibrium prediction. A plus indicates confirmation of the model (C if the number of previous D decisions is 3, D otherwise), and a minus a violation of the model. To interpret these results, consider for example Group 2 in Game 1. In equilibrium, player 1 should choose D. In violation of the model, this player actually chose C. Anticipating that players 5, 6, and 7 will play rationally and choose C, players 2, 3, and 4 in the sequence should each choose D. All three of them chose D as predicted. However, in violation of the model, player 5 chose D rather than C. Because only a single C choice was made by their predecessors, players 6 and 7 chose D, as they should.

The prediction that when fully informed about the decisions of their predecessors, the first $n-m$ players in the sequence will choose D and the remaining m players will choose C was violated by all ten groups in Game 1 and six of the ten groups in Game 7. The weaker prediction that the public good will be provided efficiently was supported by two of the ten groups in Game 1 and six of the ten groups in Game 7. Eleven of the 70 subjects (15.7%) violated the model in Game 1 compared to only six violations (8.6%) in Game 7. The difference between these two proportions of model violation is not significant ($z = 1.29$, $p > .05$).

Table 2

Individual Choices under the Sequential Protocol of Play with full Information (Exp. 1)

Game 1 Group	Choice	Outcome	1st	2nd	3rd	4th	5th	6th	7th
1	DDDDDDD	–	+	+	+	–	+	+	+
2	CDDDDDD	–	–	+	+	+	–	+	+
3	DDDDDDD	–	+	+	+	–	+	+	+
4	DDDCCDD	–	+	+	+	+	+	–	+
5	DDCDCCC	+	+	+	–	+	+	+	+
6	DDDCCDD	–	+	+	+	+	+	–	+
7	DDDCCDD	–	+	+	+	+	+	–	+
8	DDDCDDD	–	+	+	+	+	–	+	+
9	DDDCCDD	–	+	+	+	+	+	–	+
10	DDCDCCC	+	+	+	–	+	+	+	+

Game 7 Group	Choice	Outcome	1st	2nd	3rd	4th	5th	6th	7th
1	DDDDDDD	–	+	+	+	–	+	+	+
2	DCDDCCC	+	+	–	+	+	+	+	+
3	DDDCCCC	+	+	+	+	+	+	+	+
4	DDDCCDD	–	+	+	+	+	+	–	+
5	DDCDCCC	+	+	+	–	+	+	+	+
6	DDDDDDD	–	+	+	+	–	+	+	+
7	DDDDDDD	–	+	+	+	–	+	+	+
8	DDDCCCC	+	+	+	+	+	+	+	+
9	DDDCCCC	+	+	+	+	+	+	+	+
10	DDCCCCC	+	+	+	+	+	+	+	+

The subgame perfect equilibrium solution for Condition FI can be violated in two different ways: the player may choose C when the solution prescribes D, or choose D when the solution prescribes C. Of these two kinds of violations the latter is more serious as it threatens the provision of the good; The former kind of violation results in overprovision. Of a total of 17 violations of the solution, 5 are of the first type and 12 of the second type.

Figures 2, 3, and 4 display the equilibrium decisions for players 3 through 7 in Games 2,

A. Rapoport and I. Erev

3, and 4, respectively. Each of these figures is drawn in the same format and should be interpreted, therefore, in the same manner as in Fig. 1. Inspection of these figures shows that the equilibrium path differs from one game to another. Predicted decisions off the equilibrium path also differ from one game to another. In each game the model predicts that the public good will be provided efficiently.

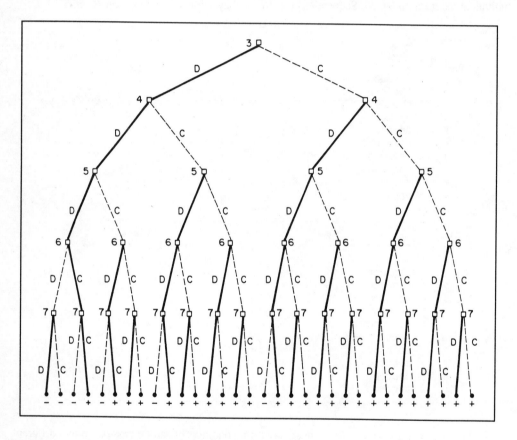

Figure 2:   Equilibrium solution to the CMS game, given that the first two sequences chose C(n=7, M=4).

Tables 3, 4, and 5 present the individual decisions of all the subjects in Games 2, 3, and 4, respectively. Each of these tables has the same format as Table 2. The only difference is that each group in Games 2, 3, and 4 has five rather than seven members. Tables 3, 4, and 5 show that the public good was provided by 13, 12, and 10 (out of 14) groups in Games 2, 3, and 4, respectively. This is a very high rate of provision. Provision of the good was efficient in all 35 cases. The number of subjects violating the models was 5 (7.1%), 5 (7.1%) and 8 (11.4%) in Games 2, 3, and 4, respectively. Pairwise comparisons of the proportions of model violation in the three games yielded no significant differences (t < 1 in both cases).

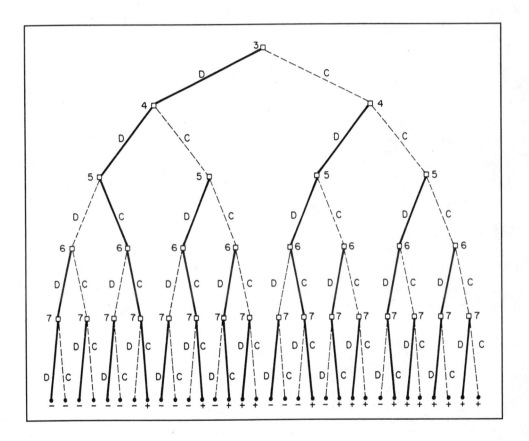

Figure 3:   Equilibrium solution to the MCS game, given that one of the first two players chose C and the other chose D (n=7, m=4).

Table 3

Individual Choices under the Sequential Protocol Following Two C Decisions (Exp. 1)

Game 2 Group	Choice	Outcome	Position in the Sequence 3rd	4th	5th	6th	7th
1	DCDDC	+	+	−	+	+	+
2	DDDCC	+	+	+	+	+	+
3	DDCDC	+	+	+	−	+	+
4	DDDCC	+	+	+	+	+	+
5	CDDDC	+	−	+	+	+	+
6	DDDDD	−	+	+	+	−	+
7	DDDCC	+	+	+	+	+	+
8	DDDCC	+	+	+	+	+	+
9	DDDCC	+	+	+	+	+	+
10	DDDCC	+	+	+	+	+	+
11	DDDCC	+	+	+	+	+	+
12	DDDCC	+	+	+	+	+	+
13	DDCDC	+	+	+	−	+	+
14	DDDCC	+	+	+	+	+	+

Table 4

Individual Choices under the Sequential Protocol Following One D and One C Decision (Exp. 1)

Game 3 Group	Choice	Outcome	Position in the Sequence 3rd	4th	5th	6th	7th
1	DCDCC	+	+	−	+	+	+
2	DDCCC	+	+	+	+	+	+
3	DDCCC	+	+	+	+	+	+
4	DDCCC	+	+	+	+	+	+
5	DDCCC	+	+	+	+	+	+
6	DDCDD	−	+	+	+	−	+
7	DDDDD	−	+	+	−	+	+
8	CDDCC	+	−	+	+	+	+
9	DDCCC	+	+	+	+	+	+
10	DDCCC	+	+	+	+	+	+
11	DDCCC	+	+	+	+	+	+
12	DDCCC	+	+	+	+	+	+
13	DCDCC	+	+	−	+	+	+
14	DDCCC	+	+	+	+	+	+

Table 5

Individual Choices under the Sequential Protocol Following Two D Decisions (Exp. 1)

Game 4 Group	Choice	Outcome	Position in the Sequence				
			3rd	4th	5th	6th	7th
1	CCDCC	+	−	−	+	+	+
2	DCCCC	+	+	+	+	+	+
3	DCDDC	−	+	+	−	+	−
4	DCCCC	+	+	+	+	+	+
5	DCCDD	−	+	+	+	−	+
6	DCCCC	+	+	+	+	+	+
7	DCCCC	+	+	+	+	+	+
8	DCCCC	+	+	+	+	+	+
9	CDCCC	+	−	+	+	+	+
10	DCCCC	+	+	+	+	+	+
11	DCCCC	+	+	+	+	+	+
12	DCCCC	+	+	+	+	+	+
13	DDDDD	−	+	−	+	+	+
14	DDDDD	−	+	−	+	+	+

Discussion

Comparison of Tables 2, 3, 4, and 5 indicates that the information provided to the subjects about the decisions of the first two players had no effect on the percentage of equilibrium decisions. The overall percentages of model violations in Games 2, 3, 4, and 7 were 7.1, 7.1, 11.4, and 8.6, respectively. Even when finding themselves off the equilibrium path, most subjects behaved according to the model's predictions. The decisions of the first two players in Games 2, 3, and 4 were manipulated in an attempt to create different propensities toward contribution by social conformity. The results show that this manipulation had no effect on the provision rate or percentage of players behaving rationally. It could be argued that the effects of this manipulation should be best tested with the decisions of the players occupying the third position in the sequence, because later subjects observed the results of both fictitious and real players. Examination of the decisions of the players assigned the third position in the sequence supports the previous conclusion of no differences between Games 2, 3, and 4. Of the 15 players in each game assigned the third position, only 1, 1, and 2 players violated the model in Games 2, 3, and 4, respectively (see Tables 2, 3, and 4).

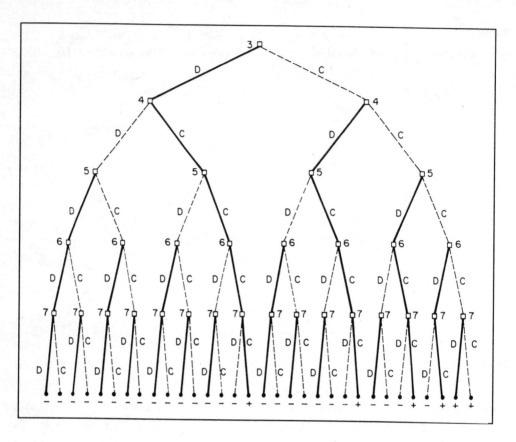

Figure 4:   Equilibrium solution to the MCS game, given that the first two players in the sequence chose D (n=7, m=4).

Experiment 2

Experiment 2 was designed in part to test the equilibrium solution for Conditions C and D where only partial information about previous decisions of one type or another is available.

Method

Subjects. Subjects were 70 male and female students at the Technion - Israel Institute of Technology. As in Experiment 1, the subjects were recruited by advertisements promising monetary reward contingent on performance. None of the subjects had taken part in Experiment 1. The 70 subjects were divided into groups of six or seven members each, depending on the game they played, as explained below.

Procedure. The parameters of the MCS game, instructions, and payoff scheme were the same as in Experiment 1. The only differences between the two experiments were in the characteristics of the games and the assignment of subjects to positions. The subjects in Experiment 2 participated in the following seven games[7]:

Game 1.   Both boxes are opaque. Each player is only told his/her position in the sequence.

Game 2.   Same as Game 1.

Game 3.   Both boxes are transparent.

Game 4.   The Red box is transparent and the Blue box is opaque.

Game 5.   The Red box is opaque and the Blue box is transparent.

Game 6.   Same as Game 1.

Game 7.   Same as Game 1.

Half of the subjects played the seven games in this order. For the other half the order of Games 3 and 5 was reversed. The experiment lasted about 35 minutes.

Game 3 in Experiment 2 (FI structure) is identical to Games 1 and 7 in Experiment 1. Game 4 implements Condition C (PI structure) in which without knowing his/her serial position in the sequence, a subject is only informed about the number of group members preceding him/her in the sequence who have already contributed. Game 5 implements Condition D.

Results

The individual choices in Game 3 are presented in Table 6. The organization of Table 6 is the same as Table 2. Comparison of Tables 2 and 6 shows that support for the equilibrium model was stronger in Experiment 2 than 1. The prediction that when they are fully informed about the decisions of their predecessors, the first n-m players in the sequence would choose D and the remaining m group members would choose C was supported by eight of the ten groups. Only two players violated the equilibrium model: the sixth player in Group 4 and the fourth player in Group 6. Both players chose D rather than C.

Table 6

Individual Choices under the Sequential Protocol of Play with Full Information (Exp. 2)

Game 3 Group	Choice	Outcome	Position in the Sequence						
			1st	2nd	3rd	4th	5th	6th	7th
1	DDDCCCC	+	+	+	+	+	+	+	+
2	DDDCCCC	+	+	+	+	+	+	+	+
3	DDDCCCC	+	+	+	+	+	+	+	+
4	DDDCCDD	−	+	+	+	+	+	−	+
5	DDDCCCC	+	+	+	+	+	+	+	+
6	DDDDDDD	−	+	+	+	−	+	+	+
7	DDDCCCC	+	+	+	+	+	+	+	+
8	DDDCCCC	+	+	+	+	+	+	+	+
9	DDDCCCC	+	+	+	+	+	+	+	+
10	DDDCCCC	+	+	+	+	+	+	+	+

The individual decisions in Game 5 (Condition D) are shown in the upper part of Table 7. Recall that the equilibrium model yields the same predictions for Condition D and the FI structure. Support for the model is impressive: only 4 of the 70 subjects violated the model in Game 5. Two of these violations involve a choice of D instead of C and two involve a choice of C instead of D.

The individual decisions in Game 4 (Condition C) are presented in the lower part of Table 7. Because the predictions of the model are ambiguous in this condition, the optimality of the decisions cannot be determined. Table 7 shows that the public good was provided by five of ten groups, and that the provision was always efficient. Efficiency is expected because a subject who understands the payoff scheme would not contribute after counting four cards in the Red box. In this respect, efficiency of the provision serves as a manipulation check.

Table 7

Individual Choices under the Sequential Protocol of Play with One Opaque and One Transparent Box (Exp. 2)

Game 5 Group	Choice	Outcome	1st	2nd	3rd	4th	5th	6th	7th
1	DDDCCCC	+	+	+	+	+	+	+	+
2	DDDCCCC	+	+	+	+	+	+	+	+
3	DDDCCCC	+	+	+	+	+	+	+	+
4	DDCDCDD	–	+	+	–	+	+	–	+
5	DDDCCCC	+	+	+	+	+	+	+	+
6	DDDCDDD	–	+	+	+	+	–	+	+
7	DDDCCCC	+	+	+	+	+	+	+	+
8	DDDCCCC	+	+	+	+	+	+	+	+
9	CDDDCCC	+	–	+	+	+	+	+	+
10	DDDCCCC	+	+	+	+	+	+	+	+

Game 4 (Condition C) Group	Choice	Outcome
1	DCCDDDC	–
2	DDCCCCD	+
3	DCDDDDD	–
4	CDCDCDC	+
5	CDCCCDD	+
6	DDCDDDD	–
7	CDCDDCC	+
8	DCDDDCC	–
9	DCCCCDD	+
10	CDDDDDC	–

Of the 70 subjects who participated in Game 4, 30 contributed their endowment. The number of contributors is seen to be distributed more or less evenly over the seven positions -- 4, 4, 7, 3, 4, 3, and 5 in positions 1, 2, 3, 4, 5, 6, and 7, respectively. Inspection of the lower part of Table 7 shows that of the 18 players who observed no cards in the Red box, 10 (55.6%) contributed. Of the 28 players who observed a single card in the Red box, only 8 (28.6%) contributed. Of the 13 players who observed two cards in the Red box, 7 (53.8%) contributed. And of the 6 subjects who observed three cards in the Red box, 5 (83.3%) contributed. Efficiency implies no contribution after observing four cards in the Red box. Indeed, none of the five players who observed four cards in the Red box contributed.

In an attempt to explain the subjects' behavior in Condition C, Erev and Rapoport (1990) formulated the hypothesis that the relative frequency of contributors in Condition C increases as the probability of being critical for the group success in achieving the Pareto optimal outcome increases. This hypothesis implies that the probability of contribution after observing k C's (k < m) is larger than the probability of contribution after observing k-1 C's. The nonmonotonic change in the percentages of contribution reported immediately above is inconsistent with this hypothesis.

General discussion

The games in Experiments 1 and 2 were designed to test the predictive power of the equilibrium solution under two different conditions. Deliberate attempts were made not to bias the subjects by framing the task in terms of contribution and non-contribution. To motivate the subjects, we followed the now common procedure of rendering individual payoff contingent on (both individual and group) performance. It was, therefore, quite natural to instruct the subjects to maximize payoff rather than increasing between-subject variability by leaving the issue of the payoff scheme ambiguous. The FI structure in which the decisions of the first two players are experimentally manipulated is novel to the present study. Both the games implementing the PI and FI structures were designed to extend the previous results of Erev and Rapoport to a different population of subjects and a larger group size.

Comparison of the two studies with respect to the FI structure yields strikingly similar results. When the subjects were first exposed to the sequential protocol of play with full information without having any previous experience in playing the MCS game the percentage of model violation was relatively high. Of the 75 subjects in Experiment 1 of Erev and Rapoport (conducted in the USA), 20 (26.7%) violated the model. And out of 70 subjects who played Game 1 in Experiment 1 of the present study, 11 (15.7%) violated the model. In contrast, when the FI game was played later in the sequence, after the subjects had an opportunity to realize the strategic implications of the game, the percentage of model violation dropped considerably. When the FI game was played as the sixth game in Experiment 2 of Erev and Rapoport, only 10% of the subjects violated the equilibrium model. Similarly, the percentage of model violation in Game 7 of Experiment 1 and Game 3 of Experiment 2 of the present study are 8.6 and 5.7, respectively. Taken together, the results of both studies suggest that with more experience in playing the MCS game subjects learn the strategic implications of the game and play the equilibrium strategy. Because of the relatively low percentage of model violation, a larger number of iterations of the FI game is required to test for convergence.

Support for the equilibrium model actually improved when the subjects were only given partial information about previous decisions. Of the 60 subjects who participated in Condition D in the previous study, only 4 (6.7%) violated the model. The comparable percentage of violation of the model in Experiment 2 is 5.7. Similarly, out of 12 groups who participated in Condition C in the previous study, only 3 provided the public good to their members. In Experiment 2 of the present study the public good was provided in 5 out of 10 cases. Twenty-four (40%) of the 60 subjects who participated in Condition C in the previous study contributed compared to 30 (42.9%) out of 70 (see Table 7) in the present study. The latter comparison is meaningful because both studies maintained the same r/e ratio.

Because the equilibrium solution to the sequential protocol is derived by backward induction, the model implies that when playing the FI game player i should not be influenced by the information she has already acquired about the rationality or irrationality of the players preceding her in the sequence. In contrast, traditional social psychological theories invoking notions of conformity and group pressure imply that this kind of information will affect behavior. The results of Games 2, 3, and 4 in Experiment 1 tend to support the SPE solution. Additional experiments are needed to determine whether this finding is generalizable to other interactive situations with a strong strategic component.

The present study together with the previous study of Erev and Rapoport constitute a small part of a considerably larger research program whose major aim is to construct a behavioral theory of interactive decisions. Game theory is the cornerstone of this program. Opposition to this line of experimental investigation stems in part from the perception, shared by many behavioral scientists, that game theory is a normative theory attempting to prescribe decisions for ideal "agents" who have no restrictions in their cognitive systems and little resemblance to reality. Recent studies of bounded rationality in two-person repeated games and attempts to integrate irrationality into game theory strongly suggest that this perception is inaccurate. In modeling the strategic considerations of the players in interactive situations, we agree with Rubinstein that a game should be "a comprehensive description of the relevant factors involved in a specific situation as perceived by the players, rather than as a presentation of the physical rules of the game" (1991 p. 917). A major task that behavioral scientists should undertake is the discovery of these factors.

Footnotes

1   University of Arizona, Department of Management and Policy, Tucson, USA

2   Technion - Israel Institute of Technology, Faculty of Industrial Engineering and Management, Haifa, Israel

3   The derivation assumes that subjects attempt to maximize individual payoff and that the utilities are ordinal.

4   Technically, the game under Condition D does not have a proper subgame, and, hence, the solution is sequential equilibrium rather than subgame perfect equilibrium.

5   The ability of players to perform backward induction calculations plays a major role in problem solving experiments and studies of two-person sequential bargaining with time discounting and finite horizon (see, e.g., Ochs & Roth, 1989).

6   Experiment 1 was designed in part to study the effects of another information structure -- called the Positional Order Structure (POS) -- in which each player i is only informed of her serial position in the sequence and information about the decisions of players i through i-1 is withheld. Games 5 and 6 implement the POS. Because of space limitations, the results of this information structure will be reported elsewhere.

7   Similarly to Games 5 and 6 in Experiment 1, Games 1, 2, 6, and 7 in Experiment 2 were
      introduced to study the effects of the POS. The results of these four games, too, will be
      reported and discussed elsewhere.

References

Andreoni, J. (1988). Why free ride? Strategies and learning in public good experiments. *Journal of Public Economics, 37,* 291-304.

Barry, B., & Hardin, R. (Eds.). (1982). *Rational man and irrational society?* Beverly Hills, CA: Sage.

Dawes, R.M., Orbell, J.M., Simmons, R.T., & Van de Kragt, A.J.C. (1986). Organizing groups for collective action. *American Political Science Review, 80,* 1171-1185.

Erev, I., & Rapoport, A. (1990). Provision of step-level public goods: The sequential contribution mechanism. *Journal of Conflict Resolution, 34,* 401-425.

Hampton, J. (1987). Free-rider problems in the production of collective goods. *Economics and Philosophy, 3,* 245-273.

Harrison, G.W., & Hirshleifer, J. (1989). An experimental evaluation of the weakest-link/best-shot models of public goods. *Journal of Political Economics, 97,* 201-225.

Isaac, R.M., McCue, K.F., & Plott, C.R. (1985). Public goods provision in an experimental environment. *Journal of Public Economics, 26,* 51-74.

Isaac, R.M., & Walker, J.M. (1988). Group size effects in public goods provision: The voluntary contribution mechanism. *Quarterly Journal of Economics, 53,* 179-200.

Isaac, R.M., Walker, J.M., & Thomas, S.H. (1984). Divergent evidence on free riding: An experimental examination of possible explanations. *Public Choice, 43,* 113-149.

Margolis, H. (1982). *Selfishness, altruism and rationality.* Cambridge, England: Cambridge University Press.

Marwell, G., & Ames, R.E. (1981). Economists free ride, does anyone else? *Journal of Public Economics, 15,* 295-310.

Miller, J.H., & Andoni, J. (1991). Can evolutionary dynamics explain free riding in experiments?

Economics Letters, 36, 9-15.

Ochs, J., & Roth, A.E. (1989). An experimental study of sequential bargaining. *American Economic Review, 79,* 355-384.

Olson, M. Jr. (1965). *The logic of collective action.* Cambridge, MA: Harvard University Press.

Palfrey, T.R., & Rosenthal, H. (1988). Private incentives and social dilemmas: The effects of incomplete information and altruism. *Journal of Public Economics, 28,* 309-322.

Palfrey, T.R., & Rosenthal, H. (1991). Testing game-theoretic models of free riding: New evidence on probability bias and learning. In T.R. Palfrey (Ed.), *Laboratory research in political economy* (pp. 239-268). Ann Arbor: University of Michigan Press.

Rapoport, A. (1985). Provision of public goods and the MCS experimental paradigm. *American Political Science Review, 94,* 74-83.

Rapoport, A., & Bornstein, G. (1989). Solving public goods problems in competition between equal and unequal size groups. *Journal of Conflict Resolution, 33,* 460-479.

Rapoport, A., & Eshed-Levy, D. (1989). Provision of step-level public goods: Effects of greed and fear of being gypped. *Organizational Behavior and Human Decision Processes, 44,* 325-344.

Rapoport, A., & Suleiman, R. (in press). Incremental contribution to step-level public goods games with asymmetric players. *Organizational Behavior and Human decision Processes.*

Rubinstein, A. (1991). Comments on the interpretation of game theory. *Econometrica, 59,* 909-924.

Rutte, C.G., Wilke, H.A.M., & Messick, D.M. (1987). Scarcity or abundance caused by people or the environment as determinants of behavior in the resource dilemma. *Journal of Experimental Social Psychology, 23,* 208-216.

Taylor, M. (1987). *The possibility of cooperation.* Cambridge, England: Cambridge University Press.

Van de Kragt, A.J.C., Orbell, J.M., & Dawes, R.M. (1983). The minimal contributing set as a solution to public goods problems. *American Political Science Review, 77,* 112-122.

Acknowledgement

The research reported in this paper was supported in part by the Technion and Haifa University Joint Research Fund. The authors wish to thank Iris Lapman and Jacob Seagull for their help in running the experiments.

Please address all correspondence to: Dr. Amnon Rapoport, Department of Management and Policy, McClelland Hall, Room 405, University of Arizona, Tucson, AZ 85721.

Conditional contributions and public good provision

Eric van Dijk[1] and Henk Wilke[1]

Abstract

The present article focuses on the effect that conditional contributions can have on the provision of public goods. First, a theoretical analysis is presented. It is argued that since promises will often be conditional, making promises can be regarded as a strategic move that alters the payoff structure of public good dilemmas. Second, an experiment is reported in which one member supposedly committed him/herself to contribute if at least one other member contributed too. The main focus in the experiment was on the reactions of the members confronted with this conditional contribution.

Conditional contributions and public good provision

An important property of public goods is the "impossibility of exclusion" (Samuelson, 1954, 1955), i.e., no member of the public can be excluded from consumption. This property of non-exclusion raises the question how people can be induced to contribute to the provision of public goods, when they realize they benefit from the public good even without contributing to its provision. In the present study we present a theoretical analysis and an experimental demonstration of how conditional contributions may affect choice behavior of members facing the dilemma whether or not to contribute to a public good.

During the thirty years of experimental research on social dilemmas numerous factors affecting choice behavior in such dilemmas have been identified. Part of this research has focused on the role of communication among members. In general it was shown that free communication among members increases cooperation (see e.g., Caldwell, 1976; Dawes, McTavish, and Shaklee, 1977; van de Kragt, Orbell and Dawes, 1983; Orbell, van de Kragt & Dawes, 1988). Little or no attention has been given, however, to the process by which communication may influence choice behavior. In the present article we try to fill this gap by focusing on the role of conditional contributions.

As Orbell, van de Kragt, and Dawes (1988) suggested, discussions may be effective by offering members the possibility to make promises to cooperate. According to Orbell et al., 'discussion provides an opportunity for subjects to offer and extract from each other promises that they will cooperate and, despite the fact that promises do nothing to change the dominance of defection' ... 'such promises could explain discussion's effect' (Orbell et al., 1988, p. 812). In other words, according to Orbell et al. discussion can work since members make promises which they intend to keep. Orbell et al. (1988) also observed that during periods of discussion, there were 'frequent assertions, e.g., that people would not make a promise themselves unless *everyone* did. And subjects frequently observed that the whole understanding they established would collapse if *anyone* broke a promise.' (Orbell et al., 1988, p.818). Although Orbell et al., did not interpret it as such, these findings suggest that subjects perceived their promises to be conditional on others' behavior.

One of the first to deal with promises was Schelling (1980). For two-person games, Schelling described promise-making as a strategic move with the objective "to set up for one's self and communicate persuasively to the other player a mode of behavior (including conditional responses to the other's behavior) that leaves the other a simple maximization problem..." (Schelling, 1980, p.160). As Schelling noted most promises are conditional, and coupled with some sort of threat. A promise to cooperate, for example, is usually coupled with a threat to defect should the other member decide to defect.

As we already noted, in the case of public good provision, experimental research has shown promises to be conditional in the sense that members promise to contribute on the condition that a certain number of their fellow group members will contribute too (see e.g., van de Kragt et al., 1983; Orbell et al., 1988). Put differently, promises appear to be conditional in the sense that they carry the threat that one will not contribute when the condition posed is not met. This would mean, however, that promise-making lowers the number of possible outcomes.

I.e., communication might alter the payoff structure by lowering the number of possible outcomes.

In the present study we wanted to demonstrate the structural consequences that the posing of conditional promises may have. In contrast to other studies on promise-making our main focus was not on the promise makers themselves. We studied a situation in which one member promised to contribute when a certain condition was fulfilled. The promise could not be broken, however. If the condition would be fulfilled, the 'conditional contributor' had to contribute, i.e., the present study was not as much focused on the effect of conditional promises (which may or may not be kept), but on the effect that conditional contributions have on choice behavior of the other members. Of course, such commitments are not restricted to experimental settings. For example, conditional contributions can be observed regularly in real life situations, such as international conferences on environmental control.

In order to demonstrate the consequences conditional contributions may have on public good provision, the present study employed a continuous public good setting, i.e., a setting in which the value of the public good is positively related to the contributions of the individual members (cf. Hardin, 1982). An example is a collective advertisement campaign that becomes more effective, the more money individual firms contribute to this campaign.

In experimental research on continuous public goods individual members possess a certain number of endowments (x_i), which can be contributed to the public good. The endowments not contributed accrue to the individual, but individual contributions are multiplied by a certain factor (m). The resulting outcomes are distributed among all group members: Regardless of their individual choice behavior each member receives a certain share (I_i) (see e.g. Van Dijk & Wilke, 1993) of this public good. The structure of a continuous public good game is usually that of an n-Person Prisoners' Dilemma Game (n-PDG). Thus, (a) the group obtains higher outcomes when all contribute than when no member contributes, but (b) each individual member obtains higher outcomes by not-contributing than by contributing. This implies (a) that the multiplication factor is greater than one (m > 1) and (b) that for the individual members the outcomes obtained by not-contributing (O_{NCi}) exceed the outcomes obtained by contributing (O_{Ci}).

By not-contributing, the individual member i will receive x_i (plus outcomes resulting from eventual contributions of other members). By contributing, member i will receive his/her share I_i of his multiplied individual contribution ($x_i * m$) (plus outcomes resulting from eventual contributions of other members). In such situations the difference between the outcomes obtained by contributing (O_{Ci}) and the outcomes obtained by not-contributing (O_{NCi}) then will be denoted by:

$$O_{Ci} - O_{NCi} = (I_i * x_i * m) - x_i < 0 \qquad (1)$$

What will be the outcomes structure if a specific member makes a conditional contribution, committing him/herself to contribute his/her endowments only when a certain number of the other group members will contribute their endowments too? How will this affect the structure of the dilemma for the other members? For these members, the dominance ordering will not be changed (a) if the condition is already fulfilled or (b) if the condition can not be fulfilled even by contributing. Thus, for members who are *not decisive* for fulfilling the condition, the difference between the outcomes obtained by contributing and the outcomes obtained by not-contributing will still be described by eq. (1), and they will still obtain higher outcomes by not-contributing than by contributing.

For members whose contribution is *decisive* for fulfilling the condition, the situation may be different. For decisive members the condition will be fulfilled when they contribute, but not when they do not contribute. Thus, for decisive members contributing will result in extra outcomes: The outcomes resulting from the contribution of the conditional contributor. Can these extra outcomes make contributing more attractive than not-contributing for the decisive members? By not-contributing, a decisive member i will receive x_i (plus outcomes resulting from eventual contributions of other members). By contributing, however, a decisive member i will induce the conditional contributor j to contribute his/her endowments too. As a result, member i will receive his/her share (I_i) of the outcomes resulting from his/own contribution ($m * x_i$), and the conditional contributor's contribution ($m * x_j$) (plus outcomes resulting from eventual contributions of other members). Consequently, for a decisive member the difference between the outcomes obtained by contributing and the outcomes obtained by not-contributing may be expressed as:

$$O_{Ci} - O_{NCi} = (I_i * (x_i + x_j) * m) - x_i \qquad (2)$$

In our present experiment, we demonstrate that conditional contributions may transform the social dilemma outcomes structure for other members depending on (a) their interest position and (b) the factor by which the individual contributions are multiplied (establishing the value of the public good). In order to demonstrate the structure of the dilemma at hand, we also manipulated whether members confronted with the conditional contribution were decisive or not. This was done by manipulating the feedback they received about others' choice behavior.

The experimental study

In the experiment we employed 5-person groups, with subjects either in the Low Interest position (receiving 15%) or in the High Interest position (receiving 25%). The Multiplication Factor was either Low (2.5) or High (3.5). As a member of the group, the subjects were confronted with a promise by one of the members, stating that s/he would only contribute if one other member would contribute too. Half of the subjects received Feedback that no other member contributed (i.e., implying that the subject was Decisive). The other half of the subjects received Feedback that already one other member contributed (i.e., implying that the subject was Not Decisive).

In Figure 1 the difference between the outcomes obtained by contributing and the outcomes obtained by not-contributing (O_{Ci}-O_{NCi}), is plotted against the Feedback[2]. The Figure shows that (a) for High-Interest subjects it is more attractive to contribute than for low-interest subjects, (b) it is more attractive to contribute when one is decisive than when one is not decisive, and (c) contributing is more attractive when the multiplication factor is 3.5 than when it is 2.5. Consequently, we expected:

1. High-Interest subjects to contribute more often than Low-Interest subjects (Hypothesis 1)
2. Decisive subjects to contribute more often than subjects who are Not Decisive (Hypothesis 2)
3. subjects to contribute more often when the Multiplication factor is High than when it is Low (Hypothesis 3)

Figure 1 also shows that in the Low Interest/Low Multiplication Factor conditions, members are always better off by not contributing (O_{Ci}-O_{NCi} < 0). Thus, with not-contributing being the dominating strategy, the Low Interest/Low Multiplication Factor condition can be described as an n-persons' prisoners dilemma, with subjects obtaining the highest outcomes when they do not contribute, irrespective of the choice behavior of the fellow group members. Consequently, we expected that most subjects in this conditions would opt not to contribute, irrespective of the Feedback one received.

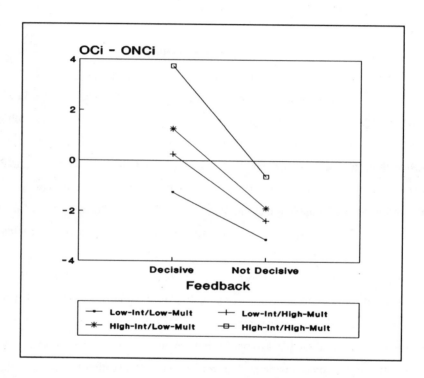

Figure 1:   The difference between the outcomes obtained by contributing (OCi) and the outcome obtained by not-contributing (ONCi) as a function of Multiplication Factor, Interest position, and Feedback.

In the other three combinations of Interest and Multiplication Factor, others' choice behavior is very important, since in these conditions the highest outcomes can be obtained by contributing if one is decisive, but by not-contributing when one is not decisive. Consequently, we expected the Feedback to have more effect in these three conditions. We expected:

4.   The effect of Feedback to be weaker in the Low Interest/Low Multiplication Factor than in the other conditions (Hypothesis 4)

Method

Subjects. The subjects, 146 Social science students at the University of Leiden, participated voluntarily and were promised 10 Dutch Guilders per hour (1 Dfl = $ 0.60).

Procedure. The subjects were invited to take part in a study on group decision making. Upon arrival in the laboratory they were placed in separate cubicles, each containing an Apple Macintosh computer, connected to a server.

First, the subjects received some written instructions. They were informed that they were a member of a 5-person group. They would never learn the true identity of their fellow group members, but each member would be identified by a letter: A, B, C, D, and E. In reality, all subjects learned that they were assigned the letter E.

After this, the rules of the game were explained. All members were said to have 5 Dutch Guilders at their disposal. Each member could make the binary decision whether or no to invest these 5 guilders. Subjects in the Low Multiplier conditions learned that each individual contribution would be multiplied by 2.5 whereas subjects in the High Multiplier condition learned that it would be multiplied by 3.5. The group payoff that would result from the individual contributions would be divided among all group members. Subjects in the Low Interest conditions were informed that as group member E they would receive 15%. Member D would also receive 15%, whereas A and B would receive 25%, and C would receive 20%. Subjects in the High Interest conditions were led to believe that they received 25%. Member D would receive the same percentage, whereas A and B would receive 15%, and C would receive 20%.

The subjects were further informed that member C, the member receiving 20%, could opt for making a conditional contribution. This would mean that s/he would only contribute when one or more fellow group members would contribute. Member C could indicate whether or not s/he wanted to make such a conditional contribution at the end of the written instructions, so the experimenter could determine which version of the experiment would be played on the computer. Before starting the experiment on the computer, all subjects were informed that member C had opted for making the conditional contribution, a feature that was to be taken into account in the version that they would be confronted with. Before making their contribution decision, the subjects received Feedback about their fellow group members' choices. Being assigned the letter E, the subjects were led to believe that they were the last to decide. In the Decisive conditions, the subjects learned that no fellow group member had contributed. In the Not-Decisive conditions, the subjects learned that one fellow group member had invested.

At the end of the experiment, the subjects were thoroughly debriefed and paid the standard amount of Dfl 10. All subjects agreed to this procedure.

Results

Contributions

In Figure 1, the proportion of the subjects contributing is presented. a log-linear analysis on these data indicated that all our hypotheses were confirmed. In line with hypotheses 1, 2, and 3, the analysis revealed main effects for Interest, Multiplication factor and Feedback: The subjects contributed (a) more often in the High-Interest conditions (56/73 = 78%) than in the Low-Interest conditions (29/73 = 40%; χ^2 = 22.2, df = 1, p < .0001) (b) more often in the High-Multiplication conditions (48/72 = 67%) than in the Low-Multiplication conditions (37/74 = 50%; χ^2 = 4.6, df = 1, p < .04) and (c) more often in the Decisive conditions (52/75 = 69%) than in the Not Decisive conditions (33/71 = 47%; χ^2 = 9.2, df = 1, p < .003).

Moreover, the loglinear analysis indicated a significant Interest X Multiplication Factor interaction (χ^2 = 9.6, df = 1, p < .002). Further testing showed that subjects in the Low-Interest/Low Multiplication Factor conditions (7/38 = 18%) contributed less often than subjects in the other three combinations of Interest and Multiplication Factor (percentage$_{\text{Low-Int/High-Mult}}$ = 63% (22/35); percentage$_{\text{High-Int/High-Mult}}$ = 70% (26/37); percentage$_{\text{High-Int/Low-Mult}}$ = 83% (30/36)).

More interestingly, the results corroborated hypothesis 4. We predicted that the effect of Feedback would be weaker in the Low Interest/Low Multiplication Factor than in the other conditions. Although this interaction did not reach significance (p < .4), further testing corroborated hypothesis 4. As Figure 2 shows, Feedback did not influence the contributions in the Low-Interest/Low Multiplication factor conditions, (percentage$_{Decisive}$ = 16% (3/19), percentage$_{Not\ Decisive}$ = 21% (4/19), χ^2 = .18, df = 1, p < .7). In contrast, in the other conditions, however, subjects contributed less often when they were Not Decisive than when they were Decisive (Low-Int/High-Mult: percentage$_{Decisive}$ = 78% (14/18), percentage$_{Not\ Decisive}$ = 44% (8/17), χ^2 = 3.5, df = 1, p < .07; High-Int/Low-Mult: percentage$_{Decisive}$ = 94% (18/19), percentage$_{Not\ Decisive}$ = 70% (12/17); χ^2 = 3.8, df = 1, p < .06; High-Int/High-Mult: percentage$_{Decisive}$ = 89% (17/19), percentage$_{Not\ Decisive}$ = 50% (9/18); χ^2 = 6.9, df = 1, p < .009).

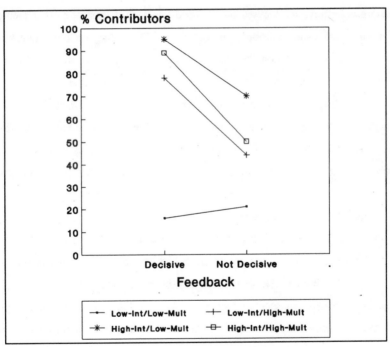

Figure 2: Percentage contributors as a function of Multiplication Factor, Interest position, and Feedback.

Discussion

The present experiment demonstrated the transformational consequences of making conditional contributions. In particular, it was shown that the assertion of Orbell et al., that promise making leaves the dominance ordering unchanged, may be false. The data suggest that conditional contributions have the strongest effect on others' choice behavior when they alter the dominance ordering. In this case others' choice behavior becomes very important, since then the highest outcomes can be obtained by contributing when one is decisive, but by not-contributing when one is not decisive. When this dominance ordering is not changed (i.e., when one can still obtain higher outcomes by not-contributing than by contributing) one can expect that group members will not contribute and that others' choice behavior will have less of an effect.

In the present study, we focused on the condition that at least one other member should contribute for the conditional contributor to contribute. Depending on the interest position of group members, the multiplication factor, the n-persons prisoners' dilemma turned into a dilemma without a dominated strategy. I.e., for certain members the highest payoffs were obtained by contributing when no other member contributed, but when at least one other member contributed, the highest payoff would be obtained by not-contributing. In other words, for certain members the dilemma could be described as a chicken game in which the alternative of not-contributing yielded the highest payoffs only when no other player contributed (cf. Liebrand, 1983). Other conditions may result in different structures. When for example, the requirement would be that all members should contribute, the members may face a trust dilemma in which contributing only becomes attractive when all other members contribute (cf. Liebrand, 1983). Of course, other conditions can be posed too. In situations in which universal cooperation is virtually impossible, one could expect members to pose conditions that will induce part of the members (subsets) to contribute. Also, in the case of public step goods, i.e., public goods that are provided when a certain level of contribution is reached, overprovision provides the members with lower outcomes than optimal provision. In that case one may expect (conditional) promises (see Van de Kragt et al., 1983) that specify the number of contributors that is required.

Previous studies focusing on the process by which communication (e.g. Van de Kragt et al., 1983; Dawes et al, 1987; Orbell et al, 1988) may affect choice behavior, also studied the effect of promise-making. They did not pay attention, however, to the point that promises are likely to be conditional. Orbell et al. (1988) noted that promises 'do nothing to change the dominance of defection'. Their results suggested that communication influences choice behavior by creating some sort of 'group identity' (see Dawes et al., 1987), and is especially effective when all members promise to cooperate (see also Orbell et al., 1988). The present study, however, focused explicitly on the consequences of *conditional* contributions. Conditional contributions can fundamentally change the problem that group members face by changing the dominance structure. In this respect, we feel that this change of dominance may also be responsible for the success of communication. Consequently, we pose that the possibility to make conditional promises can be regarded as a structural solution (cf. Messick and Brewer, 1983).

In the present experiment we investigated the effect of one member making a specific condition: The condition that at least one other member should cooperate. A logical course for future research would be to investigate which members are most likely to make conditional contributions. At this point, it is worthwhile to speculate about possible answers to this research question. As for the identity of the conditional contributor, a relevant aspect would be his/her interest position: are members having more interest more likely to make conditional contributions than members having less interest? One could expect such a result when one views the making of conditional contributions as a benevolent move, i.e., when one stresses that it is a conditional *contribution*. However, when one views conditional contributions as a non-cooperative move, i.e., when one stresses the fact that the contribution is only *conditional*, one can also reason that the members having less interest will be more likely to make a conditional contribution. In other words, conditional contributions are somewhat ambivalent: they can be interpreted as a cooperative move, or as a non-cooperative move.

The general conclusion of the present study is that when communication allows for conditional contributions or promises, it can provide a structural solution to the public goods dilemma. Of course we realize that the present study only describes a small part of the process by which conditional contributions may promote public good provision. For example, we only studied the effect of one member making a conditional contribution while the other members could only decide whether or not to contribute. We did not study a situation in which members could make proposals *to each other*. However, we do feel that the present study has made clear that the circumstance that promises are often conditional needs further attention in research on communication and public good provision.

Also, in the present experiment, all hypotheses were based on the premise that group members strive to maximize their own outcomes. The hypotheses were corroborated. The results also show, however, a considerable part of the subjects contributing even when they were not-decisive. Clearly this indicates that group members were not solely concerned with maximizing their own outcomes. Future research may be needed to relate such choice behavior to, for example, considerations of fairness. Group members may very well feel induced to contribute even when they are not-decisive out of concerns of fairness. In the present experiment, for example, (part of) the subjects may have felt they were obliged to contribute since already two other members (including the conditional contributor) contributed.

Footnotes

1   Rijksuniversiteit Leiden, Faculty of Social and Behavioral Sciences, The Netherlands

2   This Figure can easily be derived from eq. 1 and eq. 2. E.g., in the Low Multiplication Factor conditions, the outcomes for a High-Interest member are derived as follows:

   a)   When the member is Decisive (i.e., when no other member contributes), see eq. 2:

   $OC_i - ONC_i = (25\% * DFl10 * 2.5) - Dfl5 = DFl\ 1.25$

   b)   When the member is Not Decisive (i.e., when already one other member contributes), see eq. 1:

   $OC_i - ONC_i = (25\% + 2.5) - DFl5 = -Dfl\ 1.90$

References

Caldwell, M.D. (1976). Communication and sex effects in a five-person Prisoner's Dilemma Game. *Journal of Personality and Social Psychology, 33*, 273-280.

Dawes, R.M. (1980). Social Dilemmas. In M.R. Rozenzweig & L.W. Porter (Eds.), *Annual review of psychology, 31*, 169-193.

Dawes, R.M., McTavish, J. & Shaklee, H. (1977). Behavior, communication, and assumptions about other people's behavior in a commons dilemma situation. *Journal of Personality and Social Psychology, 35*, 1-11.

Dawes, R.M., van de Kragt, A.J.C., & Orbell, J.M. (1988). Not me or thee but we: the importance of group identity in eliciting cooperation in dilemma situations: experimental manipulations. *Acta Psychologica, 68*, 83-97.

Hardin, R. (1982). *Collective action*. Baltimore, MD: Johns Hopkins University Press.

Liebrand, W.B.G. (1983). A classification of social dilemma games. *Simulation and Games, 14*, 123-138.

Messick, D.M., & Brewer, M.B. (1983). Solving social dilemmas: a review. In L. Wheeler & P. Shaver (Eds.), *Review of personality and social psychology, 4*, 11-44.

Orbell, J.M., van de Kragt, A.J.C., & Dawes, R.M. (1988). Explaining discussion-induced cooperation. *Journal of Personality and Social Psychology, 54*, 811-819.

Schelling, T.C. (1980). *The strategy of conflict*. Cambridge, Mass., Harvard University Press.

Van Dijk, E., & Wilke, H.A.M. (1993). Differential interests, equity, and public good provision. *Journal of Experimental Social Psychology, 29*, 1-16.

Van de Kragt, A.J.C., Orbell, J.M., & Dawes, R.M. (1983). The minimal contributing set as a solution to public goods problems. *American Political Science Review, 77*, 112-122.

Acknowledgement

The Netherlands organization for scientific research (NWO) is gratefully acknowledged for funding this project. This research was conducted while E. van Dijk was supported by a PSYCHON-grant of this organization (560-270-034), awarded to Dr. H. Wilke.

Convergence in the orange grove:
Learning processes in a social dilemma setting

Ido Erev[1]

Abstract

In a controlled social dilemma experiment conducted in an orange grove, Erev, Bornstein and Galili (in press) found that behavior converges to the game theoretical equilibria points. The present paper summarizes these results and explores learning models by which they can be described. Simulation results favor an imitation based learning rule over a fictitious play rule. In addition, it was found that the imitation heuristics can be learned by a simple reinforcement based learning rule.

Introduction

In a recent paper Erev, Bornstein and Galili (in press) have demonstrated that a simple game theoretical model provides accurate predictions of workers' behavior in an orange grove. In accordance with the game theoretical predictions a collective reward rule was found to reduce personal investments (to increase free riding), and intergroup competition was found to eliminate the tendency to free ride to the extent that the subjects' were crucial[2] for their group success. In addition to these predicted tendencies, Erev Bornstein and Galili (EBG) observed consistent changes in the workers' behavior over time. Whereas production dropped with time when the workers were collectively rewarded, the opposite trend was observed in the intergroup competition condition. EBG suggested that these trends may reflect a learning process -- with experience the workers seemed to converge to the game theoretical equilibria.

The main goal of the present paper is to present and evaluate learning processes that could give rise to the observed time effects. The paper starts with a summary of EBG's game theoretical model and experimental results. Three learning models that might account for the observed time effects are then presented and evaluated using computer simulations. Immediate implications and future research problems are discussed.

General presentation of EBG's game theoretical model

EBG considered a team of n orange pickers (workers) who fill the same container. The team receives a reward $r for each orange picked (unit produced). Whereas the payment per orange is a public good and is equally divided among the n workers such that each gets $r/n per orange, the cost of picking an orange (i.e. in terms of energy loss and risk of injuries) is privately paid by the worker who picks the orange. Assuming that the oranges pickers have decided to pick oranges anyway, the analysis can be restricted to the additional costs resulting from the intensity of work. These costs (per orange) are assumed to be an increasing function of work speed.

It is easy to see that this incentive structure can lead to a social dilemma (Dawes, 1980). Whereas the group maximizes payoff if all workers pick as many oranges as they can (in a certain speed range), rational workers will not invest more than $r/n per orange. Thus, a free riding problem arises. Each Worker is motivated to slow down while hoping that his/her fellows will provide the public good. As a result, the group will fail to maximize payoff.

Based on previous work (Bornstein, Erev and Rosen, 1990; Parlfry and Rosenthal, 1983), EBG suggested that in a one-shot version of this game (if workers are assumed to decide how many oranges they pick in advance) the incentive to free ride can be eliminated by the introduction of constructive intergroup competition. If subgroups of workers are competing to win "the most productive subgroup" bonus, rational workers may be willing to invest more than $r/n per orange, The equilibrium strategy in this case depends on the bonus ($b) promised to the most productive subgroup, and on the players ability to affect the competition outcome. When all players are critical to their subgroup success, optimal bonus can lead to a Pareto efficient equilibrium.

For a numerical example, consider a group of four orange pickers (n = 4) that receives a cent for each orange they pick (r = $.01). The cost per orange in cents is c = $S/25$, where S is speed as measured by the number of oranges picked per minute of work.

Table 1 presents Player (Worker) i's payoffs for a 100 minutes of work in this hypothetical situation under three simplifying assumptions: (1) each worker sets his work speed once, prior to the beginning of the work, (2) the workers are symmetrical, and (3) only two work speeds are possible: Low -- 5 oranges per minute, and High -- 10 oranges per minute. Worker i's expected payoffs are presented as a function of his/her effort investment and the number of other high-effort investors in his/her team. The table is an example of the prisoner dilemma game. It shows that the team as a whole is better off if all its members invest maximal effort (choose High speed). The total team payoff in this case is $24, $6 for each team member. But the table also shows that each individual group member is better off investing minimum effort (Low speed). Regardless of what the others do, each worker can increase his/her earnings by $1.75 if he/she decides to take a "free ride". However, if all group members invest minimum effort, the group's payoff is $16 and each earns only $4.

Table 1

An hypothetical orange grove dilemma: Player i's payoffs as a function of his/her effort investment and the number of other high-effort investors in his/her team.

		Number of high effort investors among the other 3 workers			
		0	1	2	3
Player i's investment	Low	4.00	5.25	6.50	7.75
	High	2.25	3.50	4.75	6.00

Consider now the case in which an intergroup competition is introduced; the workers are divided into two dyads and each member of the more productive dyad wins a bonus of $4 (each worker gets $2 in case of a tie). Table 2 presents Player i's payoffs in the modified game as a function of his/her partner's effort and the number of high effort investors in the competing dyad. The table shows that the game has only one equilibrium point in which all workers invest maximal effort.

Table 2

Constructive intergroup competition: Player i's payoffs as a function of his/her effort investment, his partner's effort, and the number of high-effort investors in the competing dyad.

		Player i's partner's investment					
		Low			High		
# of investors in the competing dyad		0	1	2	0	1	2
Player i's investment	Low	6.00	5.25	6.50	9.25	8.50	7.75
	High	6.25	5.50	4.75	7.50	8.75	8.00

EBG also noticed that in a repeated decisions version of the game (when each worker can change his behavior based on observation of his/her co-workers' behavior), the relative size of the minimal bonus needed to eliminate the incentive to free ride decreases. Thus, the effectiveness of intergroup competition increases. For example, assume that the orange grove dilemma presented in Table 1 is divided into 40 rounds, where each round consists of 2.5 minutes work, and is equivalent to the original game with the payoffs divided by 40. In this "supergame" a relatively minor bonus of $.20 paid to the members of the more productive subgroup is sufficient to support an efficient subgame perfect equilibrium strategy in which all workers invest maximum effort as long as the game is tied.

Finally, EBG showed that in accordance with Rapoport and Bornstein's (1987) analysis, the intergroup competitions can be successful only when the workers believe that they can affect the competition outcome. Thus, the effectiveness of the competition was predicted to decrease with an increase in differences in abilities between the competing dyads. In order to examine the game theoretical predictions, EBG ran a controlled experiment in an orange grove.

EBG's experiment

Subjects (forty-eight male high-school students from an Israeli suburban town) were run in groups of four. Each group participated in three experimental conditions.

Each condition lasted 40 minutes and a ten minute break was scheduled between conditions. In all three conditions the subjects' task was to pick oranges (fill containers), and the group's total payoff was based on a fixed fee of IS 8 ($1 = IS 2.4) and a piece-work pay of IS 24 per container. Thus, for each condition the 4 group members were paid a total of IS 8 + 24P, where P is the portion of the container filled by the group.

The three conditions differed in the way the two components of the group's payoff were allocated to the four subjects: In the *Personal condition*, the container was divided into four equal sections and each subject was asked to fill up his personal section. The individual payoff in this condition consisted of (a) a flat payment of IS 2, and (b) a fee of 6P, where P is the portion of the personal section filled by the subject.

The container used in the *Team condition* was not divided. Each worker received a payment of IS 2 bonus plus 1/4 of the group's piece-work pay.

In the *Competition condition* the container was divided into two equal parts. Each group of four subjects was randomly divided into two dyads, and each dyad was assigned one section of the divided container. At the end of the competition, the quantities of oranges in the two sections were compared and each member of the more productive dyad earned a bonus of IS 4. Members of the less productive dyad received no bonus. In the case of equally productive dyads, a bonus of IS 2 was paid to each subject. After the outcome of the competition was determined, the divider was removed and subjects received a piece-work payoff identical to that in condition Team (that is, 24P/4).

Figure 1 presents the average performance in the three conditions as measured after 20 minutes and 40 minutes of work. As can be seen in this figure, there is a sharp decrease in productivity over time in condition Team, a sharp increase in productivity over time in condition Competition, and no time effect on productivity in condition Personal. On the average, a group in condition Team picked 160 kg in the first 20-minute period, as compared with 120 kg in the last 20 minute period (t[11] = 4.65, p < .01). In the Competition condition, on the other hand, the average group picked 172 kg in the first half of the competition, and 208 kg in the second half (t[11] = 4.26, p < .01). The difference between the two conditions was not significant in the first 20 minutes (160 vs. 172), but highly significant (t[11] = 8.3, p < .01) in the last 20 minutes (120 vs. 208). These results suggest that, with experience, the workers converged to the game theoretical predictions: minimal investment in condition Team, and maximal investment in condition Competition.

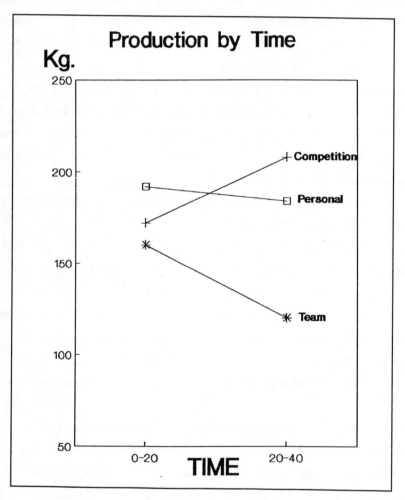

Figure 1:   The average performance in the three conditions as measured after 20 minutes and 40 minutes of work in EBG study.

To examine the effect of differential abilities, the correlation between an objective measure of the difference in abilities (as measured in condition Personal) and the effect of the competition (the difference between condition Competition and Team) was calculated. In accordance with the game theoretical prediction, the correlation was negative ($r = -.74$) and significant ($p < .01$).

The learning processes

As noted above, EBG's results seem to suggest that, with experience, workers learned to behave in accordance with the game theoretical equilibria. In order to evaluate this suggestion and discuss itsimplications, the present paper examines three learning models that could give rise to these results. The three models are representative of a larger family of plausible adaptive learning models. All these models share the assumption that individuals modify their behavior in an adaptive fashion.

At first glance, the study of learning processes in games may seem counterproductive. Traditional game theorists could argue that since learning leads to equilibrium, social scientists who are interested in predicting behavior should focus on the equilibrium and can ignore the exact learning process. Recent developments in evolutionary game theory (e.g., Maynard Smith, 1984; Harley, 1981; Nelson & Winter, 1982; Boyd & Richerson, 1985; Selten, 1991; Roth & Erev, 1993) suggest, however, that the study of learning rules can be fruitful. This is particularly true when games with more than one equilibrium point are considered. In addition, better understanding of situations in which learning rules lead behavior to converge to equilibrium may help us predict when they are likely to fail. As Roth and Erev (1993) have demonstrated the fact that behavior converges to equilibrium is not always informative because the converges can take 10 rounds in certain games and 1,000,000 rounds in other games. Better understanding of the learning process is needed to determine if the convergence is likely to occur in our lifetime... It is this latter usage of learning rules that motivated the present investigation. Indeed, I believe that the study of learning rules is necessary in order to advance psychology of decision making from the focus on demonstrations that people are not always rational, to useful predictions of behavior. The models presented below can be thought of as sets of sufficient conditions to the observed rational behavior in the orange grove.

Method

In order to present and evaluate the models, a repeated play variants of the game presented in Table 1 (the orange grove dilemma) was considered. A "Team" supergame simulated the Team condition in EBG experiment. In each of the 40 rounds in this supergame, each of four players chooses a work speed. As in the original dilemma, Player i earns .25 cent for each orange picked by the team, and pays a cost of S/25 cents (S = speed) per each orange he or she picks.   A "Competition" supergame simulated EBG's Competition condition. This game is equivalent to the Team game with the addition of an intergroup competition; the players are divided into dyads and at the end of the last round a bonus of $4 is awarded to each member of the more productive dyad. Each worker receives $2 if the difference in the outputs of the two dyads is not noticeable. For calculation purposes, a noticeable difference is defined as a difference of 5 or more oranges.

To examine the effect of the players abilities, the models' predictions were derived for five groups of hypothetical workers with different abilities distributions. To avoid unnecessary notations the groups are referred to by their members' maximum work speed. For example, the group "14,14,6,6" includes two members that can pick up to 14 oranges per minute, and two slower members that cannot pick more than 6 oranges per minute. In the competition condition, the first two numbers represent the abilities of the members of one dyad, and the last two represent the members of the second dyad. Thus, a competition in group "14,14,6,6" is between two fast (14) players and two slow (6) players. Five hypothetical groups were considered: "10,10,10,10," "7,13,9,11," "14,6,14,6," "13,11,9,7," and "14,14,6,6." The ability distributions were arbitrarily chosen to reflect a wide variety of differences, all are normalized to a sum of 40.

A simplified fictitious play model

The simplest model (at least according to the number of assumptions made) involves the notion of fictitious play (Brown, 1951; Robinson, 1951; Monderer & Shapley, 1988). According to this model, every Player i assumes that the other players use mixed strategies and do not update their behavior during the game. Under this (wrong) belief, Player i tries to learn his/her co-workers strategies and to answer with the best response. To the traditional fictitious play assumption, the present simulation adds the assumption that work speed in the first round is randomly selected and is in the "higher" side of the worker ability range. This assumption was added to facilitate comparison between simulations (although it is not natural to the fictitious play logic), it was operationalized as follows:

(1.1)   Player i's work speed in the first round is randomly selected from uniform distribution over the interval $[S^m_i/2, S^m_i]$, where S^m_i is Player i's maximum work speed.

The prediction for the Team game is trivial. In this game the player's best response is always 3.125 oranges per minute, the work speed that maximizes the worker payoff from his/her own effort:

(1.2)   Following the first round in the Team game, Player i sets his/her work speed to 3.125 oranges per minute.

To simplify the prediction for the Competition game, it is also assumed that the workers believe that their assessment of their co-workers' speeds are error-free. Under this assumption the following rule, used by the simulation, makes sense:

(1.3)   To determine his/her work speed in the Competition game Player i calculates the minimal winning speed (MWS) -- the minimal speed that promises the bonus under his/her beliefs in round t:

$$MWS = (E[Diff] + 5)/(40 - t + 1)$$

where E[Diff] is the expected difference in the number of oranges picked by the end of the supergame by the competing dyad and Player i's partner, 5 is the minimal noticeable difference, and $40 - t + 1$ is the number of rounds left to play (including round t). The actual work speed is MWS if $3.125 < MWS < S^m_i$, and 3.125 otherwise.

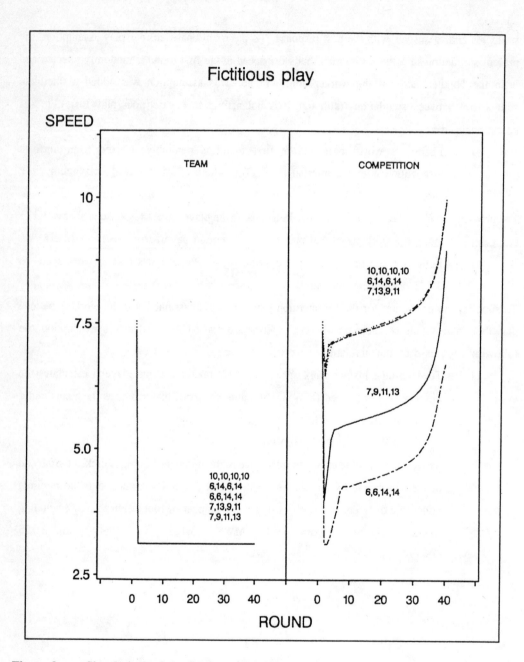

Figure 2: Simulations of the fictitous play model

Figure 2 presents the results of the simulation for each of the five hypothetical groups in the two games. Each curve represents an average work speed of the four workers in twenty simulations. (Each simulation was started with a different randomly selected work speed). The model predicts immediate learning to free ride in the Team game. The simulation provides a more interesting pattern, and a better fit to EBG's data in the Competition game. The simulated work speeds increase with time, and are sensitive to differences in abilities. When the dyads are of equal abilities (10,10,10,10; 14,6,14,6, and 7,13,9,11) workers learn to invest maximum effort. When one of the dyads is stronger (6,6,14,14 and 7,9,11,13) the members of the weaker dyad invest maximum effort, and the members of the stronger dyads invest the minimal effort necessary to win the game.

The fictitious play model has two main limits as a descriptive model in the present context. First, on the light of previous results (see review by Dawes & Thaler, 1988) the prediction of immediate learning to free ride in the Team game is probably too strong. Experimental and field studies show that even if the tendency to cooperate decreases with experience it does not disappear (e.g., Isaac, McCue, & Plott, 1985; Issac, Walker, & Thomas, 1984; Andreoni, 1988; Cooper, DeJong, & Ross, 1992). A second and related problem arises as the model ignores the possibility of reciprocal cooperation (Axelrod, 1984). In contradiction to the model's predictions, players in both the Team and the Competition games may be motivated to invest effort in order to affect other players.

The imitation model

The basic idea behind the second model is that imitation can have a dual role in the present setting. It can facilitate reciprocal cooperation and lead to a symmetrical equilibrium. To encourage his/her co-worker to cooperate in the Team game while learning the best response, Player i is assumed to follow a "defensive imitation" strategy. Specifically, Player i sets his/work speed to exceed the work speed of his/her slower co-worker by half an orange per minute:

(2.1)   In the Team game Player i sets his/her work speed in round t to be: $\text{Min}(t-1) + .5$, where Min(t-1) is the work speed of i's slowest co-Worker in round t-1. (two constraints are kept -- the minimum work speed is 3.125, and the maximum is $S^m{}_i$). Note that the defensive imitation heuristic has the main characteristics of the TIT FOR TAT (TFT) strategy (Axelrod, 1984). Indeed, it is a "TIT minus half an orange FOR TAT" strategy. The small, unconditional cooperation (half orange) was added to increase the robustness of the strategy to random events. The defensive imitation strategy can lead to full cooperation even if one of the players errs and does not cooperate in one of the rounds.

The defensive imitation strategy protects Player i from being a "Sucker," and is consistent with the well known "Sucker effect" (Kerr, 1983). Indeed, Kerr's distinction between the Sucker effect and imitation does not hold in the present context if subjects are not aware of their co-workers abilities. Additional support to the defensive imitation strategy comes from the incidental observation that the subjects in the EBG study tried but failed to coordinate their behavior. In the Team condition, EBG's subjects made promises to help each other and decided to maximize production. However, after a few minutes of good work, one or more of the workers slowed down and the others followed.

In the Competition game, imitation of the slower co-worker might be a costly way to learn -- a player who follows this strategy is likely to lose the competition. Thus, Player i is assumed to encourage his/her co-workers to cooperate by adopting a "competitive imitation" strategy. According to this strategy Player i imitates his/her faster competitor while using the work speed prescribed by the fictitious play rule (1.3) as a lower bound:

(2.2)   In round t of the Competition game Player i's desired work speed is the maximum of (A) the work speed prescribed by rule 1.3, and (B) the work speed of Player i's faster competitor in round t-1. If Player i cannot achieve the desired work speed he or she works as fast as possible.

Finally, to facilitate comparison with the first model the assumption concerning the work speed in the first round (1.1) is kept.

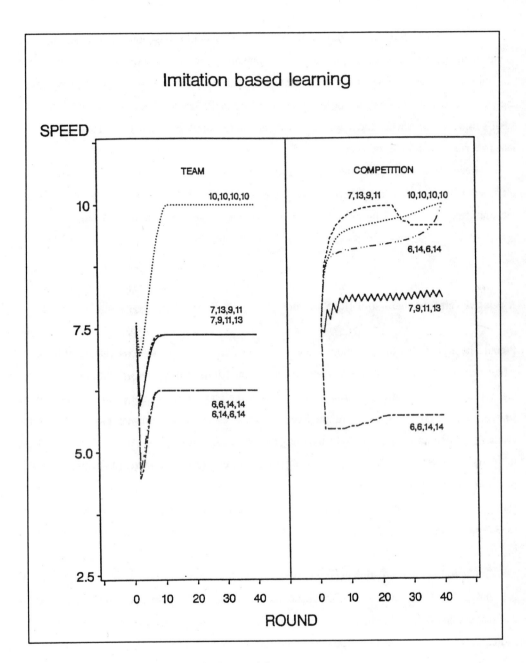

Figure 3: Simulations of the imitation model

Figure 3 presents the simulation of the imitation model. The organization of this figure is identical to the organization of Figure 2. The simulation shows that work speeds in the Team condition convergence to the slower player's maximal ability. Thus, variability in abilities impairs the effectiveness of reciprocal cooperation, and increase inefficiency. This results is consistent with EBG's findings. Only when the players are symmetrical (group 10,10,10,10) does the model predict that free riding will be eliminated.

Reconstruction of EBG main results is also achieved in the Competition game. Work speed increases with time until the maximum work speed of one of the two dyads is reached. Overall, the simulated groups work faster under the imitation model than under the fictitious play rule. This is a result of the reciprocal cooperation achieved by the imitation.

A relative reinforcement sum (RRS) model

It could be argued that the two models presented above describe a superficial change in behavior rather than a real learning process. These models demonstrate that it is possible to find strategies that replicates EBG's results, but say nothing about the way subjects may learn to choose these strategies. As a first stage toward modeling strategy selection, the present model utilizes the principle of operant conditioning: It assumes that the probability that a certain strategy will be followed increases when the choice is positively reinforced (e.g., Skinner, 1953). To apply this principle to our games, a version of Harley's relative payoff sum (RPS) model is used. Whereas Harley's model was originally proposed to describe the behavior of simple animals, Roth and Erev (1993) have recently showed that it can be modified to provide a useful description of experimental results.

The following simulation examines which of the four heuristics considered above (1.2, 1.3, 2.1, and 2.2) are favored by such a simplistic learning rule in each of the two games. It is assumed that players choose a random work speed in the first round (in accordance with assumption 1.1), and can choose one of the four strategies in each of the remaining rounds:

(3.1)   In each round $t > 1$ each player can choose one of the following strategies: 1.2, 1.3, 2.1 or 2.2.

The probability that a certain strategy will be chosen is assumed to be equivalent to its relative reinforcement sum (RS). To simplify the simulation, the exact starting value of the reinforcement sums were arbitrarily set to 1000 (changing this value will not effect the main results but will increase variance -- if the value is decreased, or slow the learning -- if the value is increased). Thus,

(3.2) The probability that strategy k will be chosen ($P(s_k)$) in a certain round $t > 1$ is:

$$P(s_k) = RS_k/[\sum_{j=1}^{4}(RS_j)].$$

(3.3) In the beginning of the game $RS_k = 1000$ for all k.

Learning is achieved through updating of the reinforcement sums. At the end of each round the chosen strategy's assessed success is added to its reinforcement sum. Success is quantitatively defined in the simulation as the payoff the player expects to receive if no change in strategies will take place until the end of the supergame. That is,

(3.4) If strategy k is chosen in round t, the player's expected outcome is added to RS_k. The expected outcome is calculated as the player's final profit in the supergame under the assumption that all four group members will not change their strategy until the end of the supergame (will play their strategies in round t from then on).

Table 3 presents the probability that each strategy will be selected at the beginning of the simulation (round 1), middle (round 20) in 100, and end (round 40) in 100 simulations. Since no group effect was observed the data are averages over the five hypothetical groups. As can be seen in this table, the RRS rule favors the heuristics prescribed by the imitation model. In the Competition game, the probability of a competitive imitation (2.2) increases to .28, while the probability of free riding decreases to .21. In the Team game the probability of defensive imitation (2.1) increases to .28 on the expense of competitive imitation. Whereas the learning is slow, the directions are clear. The RRS model appears to converge to the imitation model heuristics.

Table 3

The simulation of the RRS model: The probability for each of the four strategies in the beginning (round 1), middle (round 20), and end (round 40) of the two simulated games.

	Game					
	Team			Competition		
Round	1	20	40	1	20	40
Strategy:						
(1.2) Free riding	.25	.27	.27	.25	.22	.21
(2.1) Defensive imitation	.25	.27	.28	.25	.26	.26
(1.3) Competitive fictitious play.	.25	.25	.26	.25	.25	.24
(2.2) Competitive imitation	.25	.21	.19	.25	.27	.28

Discussion

The present paper demonstrates that simple learning heuristics can give rise to the finding that workers in an orange grove seem to converge to the game theoretical equilibria (EBG's results). This demonstration is consistent with the view that game theory can provide useful predictions of behavior even if people are not entirely rational (e.g., Maynard Smith, 1984; Harley, 1981; Nelson & Winter, 1982; Boyd & Richerson, 1985; Selten, 1991).

The paper also suggests that when social dilemmas are involved, imitation based learning heuristics have three advantages over fictitious play rules. First, whereas the fictitious play rule predicts an immediate learning to free ride, the imitation heuristics are consistent with the observation that the strong free riding hypothesis is rarely supported (Dawes & Thaler, 1988; Erev & Rapoport, 1990). Secondly, whereas a fictitious rule ignores the possibility of reciprocal cooperation, the imitation heuristics facilitate it. Finally, the latter advantage of the imitation heuristics makes them "learnable" by a simple reinforcement based learning rule of the type studied by Harley (1981) and Roth and Erev (1993).

The suggestion that people may use imitation heuristics to converge to adaptive behavior in natural social settings has nontrivial implications; it can be used to relate three important concepts: the TFT strategy (Axelrod, 1984), the Sucker effect (Kerr, 1983), and the effect of communication (Braver & Wilson, 1986; Orbell, van de Kragt, & Dawes, 1988).

Note first that in natural settings in which discrete alternatives and games are not always defined, imitation heuristics are often the only possible operationalization of the TFT strategy. As noted above, in the Team game the defensive imitation can be thought of as an "Almost TFT" strategy. At the same time, the defensive imitation strategy is also consistent with, or, if you wish, leads to the Sucker effect. While protecting the players from being exploited by free riders, it can lead to a suboptimal outcome in which one incapable worker slows a capable group. Figure 3 presents such an unfortunate results. It can also be shown that in an extreme case the use of a defensive imitation strategy can lead to a paradoxical outcome which is worse than a complete free riding.

A natural tendency for defensive imitation can also explain why the free communication had little effect in EBG study. Whereas their subjects were able to communicate and made promises to cooperate, promises were not kept. Under the defensive imitation hypothesis this finding is a demonstration that the Sucker effect can be stronger than the effect of the communication. Whereas subjects may be motivated to keep their promises, they do not do so if they wrongly believe that other players (the less capable ones) do not keep their promises. This suggestion is consistent with Orbell et. al.'s (1988) analysis, and with the observation that the Sucker effect arises when subjects believe that their co-worker do not work as hard as they can (Kerr, 1983).

According to stronger interpretation of the present results, imitation is selected by its consequences; thus, it is more likely to be observed when it has strategic value (when it leads to efficient equilibrium). This interpretation is in line with the finding that imitation is not observed when it is strategically counter productive (Rapoport & Erev, 1992).

In summary, then, the present work demonstrates that the study of learning in social settings can lead to interesting testable predictions. Whereas this demonstration is not sufficient to determine the value of this new approach, it does show its potential.

Footnotes

1   Faculty of Industrial Engineering and Management, Technion -- Israel Institute of Technology, Haifa, Israel.

2   When one of the competing group had a decisive lead and the players could not effect the outcomes of the competition, the competition was less effective.

References

Andreoni, J. (1988). Why free ride? Strategies and learning in public good experiments. *Journal of Public Economics, 97,* 291-304.

Axelrod, R. (1984). *The Evolution of Cooperation.* New York: Basic Books.

Brown, G.W. (1951). Iterative solution of games by fictitious play. In *Activity analysis of production and allocation.* New York: Wiley.

Bornstein, G., Erev, I., & Rosen, O. (1990). Intergroup competition as a structural solution for social dilemma. *Social Behavior, 5,* 247-260.

Boyd, R., & Richerson, P.I. (1985). *Culture and the Evolutionary Process.* Chicago\London: University of chicago Press.

Braver, L.B., & Wilson, L.A. (1986). Choices in social dilemmas: Effect of communication within subgroups. *Journal of Conflict Resolutions, 30,* 51-62.

Dawes, R.M. (1980). Social dilemmas. *Annual Review of Psychology, 31,* 169-193.

Erev, I., Bornstein, G., & Galili R. (in press). Constructive intergroup competition as a solution to the free rider problem in the workplace. *Journal of Experimental Social Psychology.*

Harley, C.B. (1981). Learning the evolutionarily stable strategy. *Journal of Theoretical Biology, 89,* 611-633.

Isaac, R.M., Mccue, K.F., & Plott, C.R. (1985). Public goods provision in an experimental environment, *Journal of Public Economics, 26,* 51-74.

Isaac, R.M., Walker, J.M., & Thomas, S.H. (1984). Divergent evidence on free riding: An experimental examination of possible explanations. *Public Choice, 43,* 113-1149.

Kerr, N.L. (1983). Motivation loss in small groups: A social dilemma analysis. *Journal of Personality and Social Psychology, 45,* 819-828.

Maynard Smith, J. (1984). Game theory and evolution of behavior. *Behavioral and Brain Sciences, 7,* 95-125.

Monderer D., & Shapley L. S. (1988). Potential games. Mimeo.

Nelson, R., & Winter, S. G. (1982). *An Evolutionary Theory of Economic Change.* Cambridge, MA\London: Belknap Press of Harvard University Press.

Orbell, J. M., van de Kragt, A J. C., & Dawes, R. M. (1988). explaining discussion induced cooperation. *Journal of Personality and Social Psychology, 54,* 811-819.

Palfrey, T. R., & Rosenthal, H. (1983). A strategic calculus of voting. *Public Choice, 41,* 7-53.

Rapoport, A., & Bornstein, G. (1987). Intergroup competition for the provision of binary public goods. *Psychological Review, 94,* 291-299.

Rapoport, A., & Erev, I. (1992). Provision of step-level public goods: Effects of different information structures. Paper presented at the Fifth International Conference on Social Dilemmas, July, 11-15, 1992, Bielefeld, Germany.

Robinson, J. (1951). An interative method of solving a game. *Annals of mathematics, 54,* 296-301.

Roth A. E., & Erev, I. (1993). Learning in extensive form games: Experimental data and simple dynamics models in the intermediate term. Paper to be presented at the Nobel symposium on Game Theory, June 18-20, 1993, Bjorkborn, Sweden.

Selten, R. (1991). Evolution, learning, and Economic behavior. *Games and Economic Behavior, 3,* 3-24.

Skinner, B. F. (1953). *Science and Human Behavior.* Macmillan Press.

Acknowledgement

The research reported in this paper was supported in part by the B. & L. Blumfild Research Fund. The author wishes to thank Carolyn Tal, Gary Bornstein and Rachely Galili for their useful comments.

Leadership and group identity as determinants
of resource consumption in a social dilemma

Margaret Foddy[1] and Andrew Crettenden[1]

Abstract

Leaders who act on behalf of a group to access a common resource have been shown to "manage" the resource better, in that the average amount of the resource taken per persion is smaller, and distribution of resources in the group more equitable. However, research on leadership has usually involved only one group, thus eliminating any competition for the resource when the leader alone can access it. If several groups with leaders have access to a resource, will good management continue, or will leaders attempt to take more for their own group members? In this paper, we examine factors which might make the leader more or less resource conserving, with an emphasis on accountability to a subgroup, and on level of social identity. We predict that better management by leaders will be undermined if subgroup membership is made salient, but that conditions promoting dual accountability will also promote a more cooperative and resource conserving strategy.

An experiment was conducted to examine the relative impact of subgroup identification and leadership on resource use. Psychology undergraduates were led to believe they were connected by a computer network to a data-base in the Library, along with five other Psychology students (ingroup), and six Education students (outgroup); in a fourth, control condition, Psychology students believed they were in a network with 11 other unidentified students. Total time available on the data base was insufficient to meet the needs of all students, who required the data base to complete an assignment. In the first, baseline, phase, subjects made a booking for themselves individually; in the second phase, subjects were assigned to one of four conditions: ingroup leader, outgroup leader, individual ingroup member, or individual, non-ingroup member (n=20 subject per cell). Leaders made bookings on behalf of their group members in the second phase; individual booked only for themselves.

Results showed that both ingroup and outgroup leaders booked significantly fewer hours/person than did non-leaders; there was no difference between the two leader conditions. On the whole, leaders distributed hours equally, although need was also an important criterion. While our results suggest that the leadership effect overrides the effect of ingroup identification, our manipulation of group membership (common college major) may have made competition among individual ingroup members more salient than intergroup competition. Further research using a variety of means to create group identification is needed to establish the impact of leaders on resource consumption.

Introduction

In the last decade, considerable attention has been given to so-called "structural" solutions to social dilemmas (Messick & Brewer, 1983; Yamagishi (1986); Samuelson, 1993). These solutions may 1) *alter* the incentive structure to make cooperation more attractive, or 2) completely *eliminate* interdependence among individuals with access to the common resource (Samuelson & Messick, 1993). Changes of the first sort, which alter the payoff structure include the imposition of fines and sanctions for overuse (Sato 1987; Yamagishi 1986), changes in group size, or number of people with access to the resource (Franzen, this volume; Komorita & Lapworth, 1982; Stroebe & Frey, 1982); and imposition of quotas or ceilings on the amount than can be taken from a resource pool (Samuelson, 1993). These solutions retain the structure of interdependence which defines it as a social dilemma[2], but alter the extremity of the differences in payoffs for the cooperative and non-cooperative choices[3]. So long as the level of cooperation increases to a level which will sustain the common resource, the dilemma has been "solved" or "managed".

Privatization of common resources and appointment of a leader or manager with sole access to the resource are two examples of structural changes which radically alter the interdependence structure, effectively "dissolving" the dilemma, rather than "solving" it by inducing higher levels of primary or secondary cooperation. Both privatization and the appointment of a leader to manage a resource are seen as structural solutions since they remove the social aspects of the dilemma, leaving only the question of management of the resource over time, and the distribution of resources across the group (Rutte & Wilke, 1984, 1985; Wilke, Rutte, Wit, Messick, & Samuelson, 1986; Wit & Wilke, 1988). While it is not certain that the leader will be able to manage a temporal trap better than a collective of decision makers (Ostrom, 1990) there is some experimental evidence that leaders do better than individuals (Rutte & Wilke, 1984). Messick and McClelland (1983) demonstrated that individuals performed a resource maintenance task better than groups. Researchers tend to assume that the leader should be able to manage the resource more effectively, since its management becomes transparently simple once the social aspect of the dilemma is removed. Despite the possibility of greater efficiency, people do not always prefer a leader-manager as a solution to the commons dilemma, since this alternative restricts individual freedom and may be judged to be inequitable and undemocratic (Wilke, de Boer, Karst, & Liebrand, 1986; Samuelson & Messick, 1993).

Interest in leaders in social dilemmas has been largely restricted to assessing the conditions under which the leadership option will be preferred (Samuelson, 1993; Samuelson, Messick, Wilke, & Rutte, 1986), and to questions of leader performance and fairness (Wit & Wilke, 1988). Both of these dealt with "solved" dilemmas, in the sense that the leader was given sole access to a common resource. An important but neglected possibility is that there will be two or more "leaders" who represent subgroups with access to a resource. For example, heads of corporations may act on behalf of the members of their organization in a social field with a small number of other such representatives who may decide, for example, whether to increase or decrease production. There are also many natural groups, such as fishing communities, and users of water supplies (Ostrom, 1990), who may appoint a small number of representatives to access a common resource, and to negotiate with other groups about shared access. The appointment of leaders in this case does not dissolve the dilemma, but retains the defining features (dominance of the non-cooperative choice, deficiency of the dominant strategy, etc.).

In this paper, we will outline some of the processes which may be activated when the common resource can be accessed by a small number of individuals who are leaders or representatives of subgroups of individuals. We will first discuss variables which might make the leader *more resource conserving and cooperative* than individuals; we will then consider why subgroup leaders might be *less conserving and less cooperative*. In particular, we will examine the possibility that acting as a leader of a group will induce strong ingroup identification, and that this will subsequently lead to intergroup competition, with negative effects on the common resource. Analysis of the effects of level of identity also leads to suggestions about the conditions under which the leadership role may *individuate* the leader from the rest of the group members, and actually produce more cooperative behaviour which benefits all subgroups (the superordinate group). Finally, we report the results of a study which is the first to examine the effects of appointing subgroup leaders, on resource use in a social dilemma. The study introduces a research paradigm in which shared access to scarce information bases creates a social dilemma.

Leaders with access to a common resource

What would happen if a leader were still confronted with a dilemma structure? Let us take the simplest case, two leaders of two groups in a "take-some" dilemma; the leaders have to decide how much of a resource to take from a common pool, to meet the needs of their group members. The arguments we make should apply to "give-some" dilemmas as well, and for simplicity we will not pursue the possible distinctions between them here.[4]

A) The leader will be more resource conserving

1. Better understanding of the relationship between individual demand and threat to the commons. In studies of single leaders (Rutte & Wilke, 1984; Wit & Wilke, 1988), one reason given for the better performance of leaders is that they have an overview of the demands made on the resource by all of the individuals in their groups, and can assess the aggregate level of demand in relation to what the commons can sustain. To the extent that collapse of a resource results largely from the difficulty of coordinating demand, then the leaders of two subgroups should also be in a better position to conserve the resource. In particular, dilemmas which are largely problems of coordination (Caporael, Dawes, Orbell, & van de Kragt, 1989) should show better management when only two actors have access to the commons. Messick and McClelland (1983) have suggested that individuals are better able to see their effects on the resource pool, and can learn more quickly how and when to moderate demand. Even in one-shot dilemmas, where learning is not possible, leaders of subgroups may show higher levels of cooperation, because they are simply in a better position to see the relationship between preservation of the common good and satisfaction of individual demand.

2. Greater impact on the common resource. In analyses of social dilemmas, one of the most agreed upon assumptions is that individuals are less likely to contribute to common goods, or refrain from accessing common resources, as group size increases (Hamburger, Guyer, & Fox, 1975; Kerr, 1989; Komorita, & Lapworth, 1982; Stroebe & Frey, 1982;). This is because the impact of any one individual is usually smaller, the larger the number of individuals in the group. Conversely, smaller groups are more cooperative (Komorita & Lapworth, 1982). Two-person groups in particular are considered more likely to be cooperative, because in addition to greater efficacy, the actors cannot "free-ride" in anonymity; if they compete or "defect", the other person knows who has made this choice. In repeated dilemmas, two people can engage in tacit communication through adoption of an clear strategy, which in many cases leads eventually to mutual cooperation (Axelrod, 1984). To the extent that leaders of two groups resemble the two-person dilemma, a greater sense of responsibility for maintaining the resource, and a greater sense of identifiability may produce higher levels of cooperation compared with larger aggregates of individuals.

Not only is the leader in a better position to evaluate the relationship between group and individual outcomes, there is a normative expectation that the leader *should* consider the collective good. Impartiality, and the capacity to see beyond the demands of the moment, are characteristics considered desirable in leaders.

The effects of these first two factors, greater understanding, and greater responsibility for the fate of the common resource, will of course depend on the state of the commons. In cases of extreme scarcity, greater understanding may simply increase the realization that the commons cannot be saved. When conditions are not so severe, the leader may be uniquely situated to balance the desire for gain for group members, and the desire to use the resource intelligently.

3. Accountability to a constituency. Samuelson and Messick (1993) have suggested that the reason subjects in social dilemma experiments dislike giving a leader exclusive access to a resource, is that they fear the leader may exploit the resource for his or her individual gain, or may fail to manage the resource intelligently (see also Wit & Wilke, 1988). Little is known about the actual behaviour of group leaders in social dilemmas (whether accountable or not), but research on leader accountability in negotiation settings provides some suggestions. In this section we will consider factors which might make a leader or representative more resource conserving; in section B 1) we will take up the conditions in which accountability may have the opposite effect.

Tetlock (1992) examined the effect of "accountability" to known and unknown audiences, on judgments and impression formation. In this research, the focus is on the *expectation* of having to account for one's actions and choices, which is assumed to motivate people to perform in such a way as to ensure positive evaluations from the group or constituency. Across a variety of tasks, Tetlock and his colleagues have shown that predecisional accountability can motivate complex, vigilant and self-critical decision making, particularly when the views of the audience are unknown. In settings of interdependence, such as negotiation in mixed motive games, this decision-making style may not just "motivate thought", but also encourage decision-makers to take the role of the other, and consider the impact of their behavior on the outcomes of others. Extending this process to leaders in dilemmas, if more complex information processing and perspective taking produces more thorough consideration of resource conserving alternatives, leaders should be more likely than individuals to endorse cooperative solutions. This is a big "if", for two reasons. First, dilemmas are so-named because the "best" solution is contentious-- the cooperative solution may be heavily dominated by the non-cooperative one (as in finite resources under high demand).

Second, accountability to a known constituency with definite views can produce the opposite effect: accountable decision makers take the path of least cognitive effort and adopt a view acceptable to their audience or constituency. We will discuss the potentially negative impact of this "acceptability heuristic" (Tetlock, 1992, p. 341) below.

In his review of the effects of accountability of group representatives on intergroup negotiations, Carnevale (1985) states that representatives of groups may develop *dual accountability*. Because they interact over time with the outgroup representative, they may develop positive ties, and a concern for the welfare of the outgroup, as well as for their own constituents. This dual concern leads, according to Carnevale, to more complex thinking about issues, and makes it more likely that the representatives will "seek and adopt integrative solutions that reconcile their own group's interests with those of the other group" (Carnevale, 1985, p. 227). Applying this to the case of subgroups with access to a common resource, we suggest that if the leader role produces a sense of dual accountability, then collectively rational solutions will be more salient, desirable, and chosen.

4. Salience of superordinate group identity. Brewer and Kramer (1984, 1986) have explored the effects of enhancing identification with superordinate groups on behavior in resource dilemmas. They employ Turner's (1987) distinction among three levels of self-categorization: the superordinate or collective level, the intermediate level of ingroup-outgroup categorizations, and the subordinate level of personal self-categorizations based on differentiation between oneself as a unique individual and other members of one's group (Turner, 1987, p. 45). Kramer and Brewer (1986) argue that when collective level identity is salient, "subgroup comparisons become less relevant and impactful, thus reducing or eliminating intergroup competition. Under these conditions, more cooperative decisions are likely" (p. 229). The personalized or individual level of identity is predicted to produce levels of cooperation intermediate between the other two, in the same way that individualistic motivational orientation leads to behavior mid-way between that of competitors and cooperators (Kuhlman, Camac, & Cunha, 1986; McClintock & Liebrand, 1988).

In a series of experiments, Kramer and Brewer demonstrated that, when a resource was rapidly deteriorating, superordinate or collective orientation did indeed produce greater restraint compared with a salient subgroup identification. This was so whether the salient level of identity was induced by drawing attention to natural category memberships (e.g. "university students" compared with "psychology students versus economics students"), or using a "common fate" manipulation which emphasised subgroup or superordinate group boundaries. Brewer and Kramer (1984) also contrasted superordinate and individual levels of identity, using the common fate manipulation, and found higher levels of cooperation in the superordinate condition, in a take-some dilemma.

Although Kramer and Brewer originally proposed that the higher levels of cooperation under conditions of collective orientation would be mediated by positive perceptions and higher levels of trust in other group members, measures of these variables did not support this explanation. More recently, Kramer (1993) found that subjects who identified strongly with their group did show higher levels of group based trust. Kramer also argued that a salient collective identity has the effect of transforming motivational orientation in the direction of greater cooperativeness. Regardless of individual motivational orientation, group identification manipulations shifted all subjects in the direction of greater cooperative behavior.

What are the implications of these findings for the behavior of subgroup leaders? While the more common effect of the leader role may be to emphasize subgroup identification, when leaders see themselves as having dual responsibility (Carnevale, 1985), the effects may be similar to those found for superordinate identity. Further, when the leader is singled out as an individual who is different from the group, in the sense of having a unique role, then the personalised or individual level of identity may be most salient; this should produce greater levels of cooperation than when ingroup-outgroup identity dominates. This prediction is consistent with the finding that individuals are less competitive than groups in a range of social dilemmas (Insko & Schopler, 1987).

B) The leader will be less resource conserving

The four factors discussed in the previous section are also relevant to understanding the conditions under which a leader will be less restrained than individual group members. Greater knowledge, and greater access to a resource may provide a leader with the means to exploit a common resource on behalf of his or her group; accountability and ingroup identification may provide the motivation to do so. We will focus our discussion on the latter two factors.

1. Accountability to constituencies. In a survey of research concerned with the effects of accountability to "audiences" who were dependent on a negotiator to obtain good outcomes in bargaining, Rubin and Brown (1975) concluded that audiences "generate pressures toward loyalty, commitment, and advocacy of their preferred positions" (pp. 50-51). In most cases, the preferred positions were for tough bargaining (extreme initial bids, and slow concessions), on the assumption that better outcomes would result. Rubin and Brown added that increasing commitment to a constituency reduces the negotiator's capacity to perceive alternatives posed by an opposing party, so that strong subgroup identification actually increases the competitiveness of the intergroup relations. Highly accountable representatives may thus adopt strategies which are not in the group's best interests, insofar as tough stances frequently lead to stalemate and sub-optimal agreements.

Carnevale's (1985) analysis of group representatives also suggested that high accountability and surveillance by the constituents would produce tougher bargaining, as the representatives strive to please the group members for whose outcomes they are responsible. Failure to produce good outcomes can lead to loss of face and status. Although Carnevale notes that the default assumption is that constituents prefer a competitive stance, and representatives act to please the constituents, should the group desire a cooperative or conciliatory stance, the accountable representative will oblige. Tetlock (1992) similarly concluded that, in a desire to please constituents and to maintain a successful social identity, representatives would take a stance which was consistent with the views of the group members. In common resource settings, these views are likely to reflect a desire for gain, as well as a desire to maintain the resource. If there are two identifiable groups accessing the resource, then competitive tendencies are emphasised, and the leader may reasonably assume (if s/he does not actually know) that there is an expectation that s/he will act to keep the group equal to or better than the outgroup. Under conditions of high ingroup identification, and competitiveness between groups, it may in fact be better if leaders are *less* accountable, since they will be more likely to consider more complex and integrative solutions to the commons problem.

In order to predict whether leaders will be more or less conserving than individuals, it is necessary to pay attention to the nature of their relationship to the group; this includes the *structural* relationship (e.g. what can the group do to sanction the leader?), and the *psychological* relationship (do the leaders see themselves as separate from, or identified with, their constituents?). We turn now to the latter process.

 2. Ingroup identification and outgroup bias. Studies of accountability place a strong emphasis on the role of identification with one's group in creating competitive relations *between* groups. This is consistent with the predictions from social identity theory (Tajfel & Turner, 1979; Turner, 1987). Strong identification with an a group has been shown to lead to a positive bias in evaluation of ingroup members, and behavior which advantages the ingroup. These effects occur when the basis for group membership is arbitrary and minimal, but are stronger when there is an existing common membership in a social category whose members interact with one another, and share a common fate. When a leader is chosen because s/he is seen to represent the views and characteristics of the subgroup (i.e., is prototypical), conditions are right for maximal identification with the ingroup. Subsequent actions in the role of representative of the group may reinforce this sense of identification. What is not known, is whether the definition of the leader *as against the rest of the group* also invokes a strong personalised identity, which may cancel to some extent the identification with the group.

 The work of Brewer and Kramer, reviewed above, showed that subjects in subgroups, created by common category membership, or by common fate, were less resource conserving than subjects for whom a superordinate group identity was salient, especially under rapid depletion of resource. Komorita and Lapworth (1982) also found that when a larger collective was subdivided into smaller subgroups, the positive effects created by having fewer people in the group, were attenuated by the intergroup competition which this subdivision engendered.

 Kramer and Brewer (1986; see also Brewer & Schneider, 1990) have argued that salient subgroup identity activates positive bias toward the ingroup, and negative bias toward the outgroup. Higher levels of competitive choices (lack of restraint) then presumably reflect a desire to prevent the outgroup from doing well, even though such competitive choices also reduce the outcomes for the ingroup. To date, Kramer and Brewer have not simultaneously compared subgroup identification (when there are several subgroups in competition), with the level of personalized or individual identity. This contrast is important, because the more competitive choices of the subgroup members *could* reflect higher levels of competitiveness toward individual *ingroup members*. That is, the more self-centered choices of ingroup members may in fact not represent actions to provide relative advantage to the ingroup, but rather, be equivalent to individualistic choices of undifferentiated individuals in the commons. Given the many studies done in the social identity tradition which show negative evaluation and competitiveness toward outgroup members when subgroup identity is salient, this interpretation does not seem highly plausible. Nevertheless, empirical studies are needed to establish which behaviors are associated with all three levels of social identity.

Leadership and levels of identity

In our review of factors affecting the behavior of leaders or group representatives, it is clear that there is no simple answer to the question: "Will group leaders be more or less resource conserving than individuals?". A crucial variable is the nature of the relationship of the leader to the group, and *how leaders think of themselves in relation to the group.* Depending on the nature of the relationship of the leader to the group, s/he may see him or herself as set off and above the group, or as a prototypical member. We have suggested that the level of social identity may be the mediating variable in how leaders behave, but it is still necessary to delineate the antecedent conditions which produce a given level of identity--personalised, group, or superordinate. If the leader role serves to separate the leader from the group, and to de-emphasise group identification, then the leader may show greater concern for the superordinate groups' welfare. If, on the other hand, leadership arises from and highlights identification with an ingroup, and sharpens the apparent differences between ingroup and outgroup, higher levels of competition should be evident.

The specification of the factors which produce different orientations in leaders of subgroups is a task which is beyond the scope of this paper, but we would suggest that theory building should begin by exploring a) the relationship of the leaders to other members of their groups (intragroup structure), and b) the nature of the relations between groups (intergroup relations). At the intragroup level, it will be useful to consider the way in which the leader is chosen (random, election, self-selection, etc.), how similar the leader is to others in the group, the nature of the leader's accountability to the other group members (can they apply sanctions?), the frequency and necessity of communication between the leader and the group, and the extent to which group members share a common fate. Aside from distinctions between the leader and the people he represents, group members may vary in the extent to which they perceive their interests as shared or in conflict, and it may therefore be more or less difficult for a leader to coordinate to actions of group members toward a common cause, even if the most efficient strategy is apparent. The literature on bargaining and negotiation provides a range of research paradigms in which these variables can be manipulated; their impact on the use and management of common resources needs to be explored in future research.

A second set of factors which is likely to affect the way in which a leaders identify with their groups is the nature of *intergroup* relations. Important factors are likely to be the degree of conflict or shared interest between the groups (defined in terms of past equality/inequality of outcomes, as well as structural inequality of access and opportunity), the possibility of communication and interaction between the groups and their leaders, and the availability of superordinate identities which can transform intergroup difference to common cause. Hinkle and Brown (1990) have made the interesting suggestion that there are many cases in which comparison between subgroups is not salient, and where one would not expect the negative effects of intergroup competition to interfere with the desire to maintain a valued common resource. A better understanding of these non-comparative contexts may be relevant to predicting the impact of subgroup leaders on social dilemmas.

Moderating the effects of intragroup and intergroup relations on leadership will be the nature of the commons itself. Recent reviews of social dilemmas (Messick & Brewer, 1983; Van Lange, Liebrand, Messick, & Wilke, 1992; Yamagishi, 1986) draw attention to the importance of framing effects (is the dilemma a "give some or take some"), the relative strength of fear and greed in the payoff structure (Caporael, et al., 1989), external threats to the resource, and so on. These need to be explored to reveal whether they improve the chances of subgroup leaders to manage a resource, or hinder them.

In an initial attempt to examine the variables influencing the behavior of leaders compared with individuals, we conducted an experiment in which we compared choices of leaders of their own natural ingroup, with leaders of an outgroup, to separate the effects of being a leader per se, with the effects of common category membership. We contrasted the behavior of leaders with that of individuals for whom subgroup identity was made salient, and individuals who acted neither as leaders, nor as subgroup members. This is a preliminary study, which serves to introduce the array of research questions which arise from a consideration of subgroup leaders in social dilemmas.

Method

Subjects. Subjects were 75 undergraduate Psychology students (60 females and 15 males) at La Trobe University in Melbourne, Australia (mean age=22 years).

Resource dilemma task. For the *dilemma*, we made use of an existing scarce resource, namely, a CD-ROM information base (PsychLit), available for use in the university library. Students were already aware that another common resource, the remote access general library catalogue, was available but difficult to log on to, and so had some familiarity with the problems of accessing a scarce common resource. At the time of the study, the CD-ROM was not available from remote terminals, and could only be accessed by using a booking sheet in the library to reserve half-hour time slots on one of two computers. The library administration was planning to network the data base to relieve pressure on space and computers in the library building.

Subects were told that the library was assessing the viability of networking the CD-ROM to remote terminals in various departments on campus. The experiment was introduced as a study of how students would use such a resource, and whether problems of overuse might arise. After being briefed about their need to book time on a restricted-access data base, subjects indicated the number of hours they wanted to book for an assignment (*Phase 1*). They then attempted to log on to the data base, but were uniformly unsuccessful. Then, according to the condition to which they had been assigned, subjects either accessed the data base to book hours on behalf of themselves and five other members of their subgroup, or they booked time for themselves individually (*Phase 2*).

Procedure. On arrival at the laboratory, subjects were seated in one of several small rooms, and given a written description of the study, which outlined the nature of the library access task, and stressed that they were one of twelve subjects in the session. After showing the subject how to use the computer terminal, the experimenter moved from room to room, to reinforce the impression that there were several subjects in the session. In fact, only two subjects were tested at one time, and each of these was presented with the task at a stand-alone personal computer in separate rooms. These were made to look as if they were in a network, with cables leading to a false computer bus. In all but the individual-no-ingroup condition, subjects were informed that they were one of 6 Psychology students participating in the session, and that another 6 Education students were similarly connected from another building on the campus.

Subjects in all conditions completed 2 independent "one shot" dilemmas. Motivation to book hours on the CD-ROM was created by providing subjects with a scenario in which they were asked to imagine that they had to write an essay worth 30% of their course requirements, and that they would need to spend approximately 1.5 to 2.5 hours on the data base to access the references needed to write the essay. The topic concerned changes in community attitudes to AIDS over the last 10 years, and was a plausible topic for both Education and Psychology students, which would require a substantial amount of time on the data base.

For all conditions, the number of hours available to be booked was 16--eight hours on each of two days, with the remaining three days blocked out. Since the number of people trying to use the data base was 12, there were insufficient blocks of time for everyone to book even the minimum recommended time of 1.5 hours. Subjects were informed that if more hours were requested than were available, the system would crash, and no one would be able to log on to the system at all. This cover story was designed to create the impression that hours were scarce, and that there was a conflict between the individual's and the total group's interests. Since only one-hour blocks could be booked, subjects had to make a decision to cooperate (book one hour only), or to defect (book two or more hours). The structure of the dilemma was such that if eight people booked one hour each, four could book two hours, and still maintain the resource.

Given that there was no communication allowed, this is a difficult coordination problem; the most straightforward "cooperative" response was to book one hour.

Leader manipulation. Subjects assigned to the "leader" roles in Phase 2 were told, after Phase 1, that they had been randomly assigned to be the leader of a group of six students, and that they would make bookings on the data base on behalf of their group. Half of the leaders were assigned to act for a group of Psychology students (ingroup leader); the other half were made leaders of a group of Education students (outgroup leader). These two leader groups were created to separate the effects of ingroup membership and leadership: the Psychology students who were leaders of the Education group should exhibit only the "leader" effect, while the leaders of the Psychology students should show the combined influence of leadership and ingroup membership.[5] The operationalization of "leader" in this study was a deliberately nominal one; the subjects were selected randomly, as opposed to being elected or chosen on merit. Further, they were not directly accountable to the other members of their subgroups, and could not communicate with any other participants. We chose this simplified procedure to reduce the number of variables which might affect the leaders' decisions. Future research will need to vary systematically the relationship of the leader to his or her subgroup.

The remaining half of the subjects were assigned to one of two individual access conditions, in which the Phase 2 task was a repeat of that for Phase 1 (see below).

Group identity manipulation. Subjects were assigned to one of four conditions: Ingroup leader; Outgroup leader; Individual ingroup member; and Individual with no salient (sub)group identity. Group identity was operationalized by using Psychology students, who at this University form a relatively small subgroup (400 students on a campus of 12,000), with strong ingroup identification[6]. Subjects were led to believe that they were one of 12 students taking part in a trial run of the CD-ROM network. In the first three conditions, subjects' ingroup category membership was emphasized. S's computer terminals had a prominent label (e.g. "PSYCHOLOGY: STATION 3), and instructions made frequent reference to the fact that there were 6 students from Psychology, and 6 from Education in the study. Education students were chosen as they were the second highest users of the CD-ROM facility, after Psychology students. Subjects in the fourth condition were also Psychology students, but this subgroup identity was not made salient. No labels were present on the equipment, and no reference was made to Psychology and Education subgroups. The scenario presented to them was that 12 students were participating in a feasibility study for the library concerning remote access by students to the data base.

We chose to use common category membership, and not common fate, as the sole means of activating ingroup identity in this study. Tajfel and Turner (1979), as well as Brewer and Kramer (1984), have shown that simple categorization is sufficient to produce positively biased ingroup evaluations and reward distributions. To the extent that acting as a leader induces ingroup identification, it is probably through a sense of common fate, and we did not wish to confound this with the manipulation of ingroup or category membership.[7]

After *Phase 2*, when subjects had accessed the data base for themselves or for their groups, the "leader" subjects replied to questions presented on the computer screen. These were concerned with how they would distribute the hours among group members, expectations about the other leader's behaviour, reasons for booking as they did, and their preference to lead each of the two groups. Subjects in the individual conditions simply booked time on the timesheet presented on the computer screen, and indicated the factors they considered in making their bookings.

The experiment was a 4 (condition) X 2 (phase) design; the former was a between groups factor, the latter a repeated measure. While it would have been desirable to have a fully crossed factorial design (with leader-no leader as one factor, and ingroup-outgroup as the other), the choice of appropriate contrasts is not so simple. It was not plausible to have an "individual-outgroup" condition, since this is theoretically equivalent to the "individual-ingroup" condition. Further, if non-Psychology students were used to be outgroup members, a number of extraneous variables related to vocational orientation might be introduced. There are a number of other candidates for control conditions--leaders of one superordinate group, or leaders of groups with no existing category identification are two examples. Since the present study was the first investigation of leaders of subgroups, we decided to concentrate on the contrast between ingroup and outgroup leaders, using the individual conditions as control or baseline groups.

Hypotheses: We hypothesized that leaders would be more cooperative (book fewer hours) than individuals, but that leaders of the ingroup would be less cooperative than outgroup leaders, because of heightened subgroup identity. We further predicted that ingroup individuals would be less cooperative than individuals for whom no subgroup was salient.

Results

A two-way ANOVA was performed on the number of hours booked per person by subjects in the four conditions in Phases 1 and 2. For leaders, the total number of hours they booked was divided by 6 to give the number of hours per person. (See Table 1 for means and standard deviations of hours booked.)

Table 1

Means and standard deviations of hours booked per person

	Individual baseline	Booking task	Difference
Leader Condition			
Ingroup leader[a]	3.16 (1.7)	1.16 (0.3)	-1.94
Outgroup leader[a]	2.60 (1.1)	1.23 (0.3)	-1.37
Individual condition			
Ingroup member[a]	3.00 (1.2)	2.90 (1.5)	-0.10
Non-ingroup individual[b]	2.73 (1.4)	2.53 (1.1)	-0.20
Total	2.87 (1.36)	1.92 (1.99)	

a: n = 20

b: n = 15

The results revealed a significant effect for experimental condition ($F_{3,71} = 4.43$, $p < .01$), and for phase ($F_{1,71}$) $= 39.57$, $p < .001$). These effects need to be considered in light of a significant interaction between experimental condition and phase ($F_{3,71} = 10.09$, $p < .001$). Simple main effects analyses indicated that there were no differences among subjects in Phase 1 (prior to the leadership manipulation). After the leadership manipulation, subjects in the two leader conditions booked significantly fewer hours compared with Phase 1; there were no differences between the two leaders in Phase 2. In the individual conditions, subjects booked a similar amount in both phases, and there were no differences between subjects in the individual condition in either phase.   The results support the hypothesis that leaders would be more cooperative than individuals, but do not support the prediction of lowered cooperation as a result of ingroup identification. Subjects who acted as leaders booked, on average, a small enough number of hours to avoid collapse of the resource; individuals booked almost twice as much as the system could support.[8]

Questionnaire responses from subjects in leader conditions revealed no differences between ingroup and outgroup leaders. In both conditions, half indicated that they would distribute hours equally, while half indicated they would use need and ability to use the resource as the basis for distribution. Both groups predicted that the other group leader would book a similar number of hours to what the subject had taken, and neither thought his/her group was more deserving. In both leader groups, a majority of leaders said that they considered the welfare of *both* subgroups in making their bookings, although more Psychology leaders indicated that they thought their own subgroup's interest was paramount (7 vs 3). The only tangible indication of ingroup bias was seen in the response to the question of who subjects would prefer to lead; no one chose the Education group; 20 chose the psychology group, and 20 indicated no preference.

Discussion

The results of our experiment suggest that individuals given the role of group leader, are more influenced by factors which encourage them to act to conserve the common resource, than those which would make them attempt to exploit the commons for the benefit of their constituency. Leaders of both ingroups and outgroups made significantly lower demands on the information base than did individuals, and accessed it at a rate which would ensure its continuation. In doing so, they provided a slightly less than optimal level of the resource to their group members, but ensured that they would get something rather than nothing.

These results should be interpreted in light of the theoretical analysis presented in the earlier parts of this paper. The leaders in this experiment were only minimally accountable to their groups--indeed, they may have met Tetlock's conditions for flexible, complex thinking, in that they did not know the views of their constituents, but would be motivated to be able to justify their actions. Not anticipating interaction with others in the group, the leaders would not have been strongly influenced to gain their approval, or have been fearful of sanctions should they not maximize outcomes. Thus, our experiment represents one endpoint of a continuum, with leaders who are minimally accountable, able to coordinate access to a common resource (greater knowledge), with a role which separates them from other members of their group.

While it might be tempting to conclude that the leadership role cancels the effects of ingroup identity, such a conclusion would be premature. First, as noted above, our study created the conditions under which leaders are most likely to take a superordinate view, and adopt a prominent, collectively rational solution. Second, the manipulation of common category membership may not have been sufficiently strong to induce a desire to protect the interests of ingroup members over the interests of the outgroup. Although our experimental procedures were similar to those employed by Kramer and Brewer in their experiments which used common category membership as a means of inducing ingroup identity, it is possible that the scenario which presented the library as testing ways of dealing with excessive student demand for the data base, may have created a superordinate identity of "student", so that leaders of both groups were anxious to show that they could manage the information resource responsibly. The subjective measures of ingroup bias did not support the predictions, but Kramer and Brewer (1986) also did not obtain evidence for subjective perceptions as mediating the ingroup effects they obtained.

In the individual conditions, we predicted that subjects for whom subgroup identity was made salient, would attempt to access the data base more, than would subjects who were not made aware of ingroup identity. However, subjects in the two individual conditions behaved very similarly, booking more hours than they needed, and more than the common resource could bear. A possible explanation of the high level of consumption by individuals in the individual-ingroup condition, is that they felt competitive towards other Psychology students. Such ingroup competition might be as strong, or stronger than, competition with an outgroup (Education students). Subjects in the individual-ingroup condition may have been motivated to prevent their nearest rivals (other Psychology students) from booking hours on a data base which would help them do better in a common university course. Turner (1987) has noted the factors which are likely to lead to a personalized level of identity are those which lead ingroup members to feel private, isolated, separate, distant, and anonymous, conditions which prevailed in both of our individual conditions. However, if this was true of the individual ingroup condition, it was also true of the undifferentiated individual condition, in that the subjects behaved very similarly. It is puzzling that deliberate attempts to make category membership salient did not appear to lead to the effects which have been shown in many other studies (more positive evaluation of the ingroup, more negative evaluation of the outgroup, desire to reward the ingroup). Future research will need to create clear distinctions between these conditions, or use a common fate manipulation to induce ingroup identity. Our experiment has served to highlight an interesting disjunction between common category membership and common fate--it is quite possible that ingroup members will feel more strongly competitive to one another than to members of an outgroup, in which case the dynamics of their behavior toward these two categories of others will be very different from conditions in which common fate and common category coincide.

Because our experiment was an explicit simulation, in which subjects were asked to imagine some of the independent variables, we would not wish to draw overly strong conclusions from it. It was not an extreme dilemma, and there was a reasonably prominent solution to be coordinated by the leaders. The leadership manipulation could be more realistic and thorough going, so that the leader not only was responsible for the group, but felt some accountability to the group members. As we have indicated earlier in this paper, there is a large array of variables which will condition the leader's behaviour, and these require systematic study. Although the leaders in this experiment were resource conserving, one should not regard leaders as a solution to all social dilemmas; we have suggested a number of conditions which would make them poor managers. In addition, the leader may have acquired that position with the intention of exploiting the resource for his or her own individual benefit; while such possibilities are difficult to study in the laboratory, experience suggests that this may constitute a significant subset of leaders-of-dilemmas.

Our experiment introduced the idea of shared information as a scarce resource, and we believe it has potential as a paradigm for studies of dilemmas. The use of data bases offers two different dilemmas--one could manipulate the remote access to a data base as the dilemma (here, logging on to the computer is the behavioral option), and one can also consider the proportion of time people try to take for themselves. This paradigm is suitable for the study of sanctions for overuse, as well as for various structural arrangements for management of the resource.

Conclusion

Although not much is known about the impact of subgroup leaders on the management of common resources, it is a topic worthy of future research, given the potential of leaders to orient to superordinate outcomes, and to coordinate difficult commons problems. Our analysis suggested a number of variables which will determine whether the leader will be able to provide more efficient resource management, focusing on the level of social identity of the leader engendered by intragroup and intergroup variables.

Footnotes

1   La Trobe University, Department of Psychology, Melbourne, Australia

2   We define the common properties of social dilemmas in accordance with Liebrand's
       (1983) analysis; 2) the non-cooperative over the cooperative choice; 2) the non-
       cooperative choice by an individual reduces the outcomes of others sharing the resource;
       and 3) the total outcome to the group is less if all fail to cooperate than if all cooperate.

3   Changes to features of the dilemma might also alter the *subjectively perceived utility* of
       the cooperative and defecting choices. For example, open communication prior to choice
       may increase expectations of cooperation from other players, thereby increasing the
       subjectively expected utility of the cooperative alternative. Changes such as cooperation,
       and open commitment to a given choice are not usually treated as structural changes,
       because they do not alter the "given matrix" of outcomes (Kelley**) which define the
       dilemma.

4   Komorita and Carnevale (1992) note that the differences in levels of cooperation between
       "give-some" and "take-some" games are not the same across all dilemmas, and further,
       that there is no consensus about the mechanisms involved in the framing effects (p. 222).

5   Education students were chosen because of the plausibility of their interest in a similar
       essay topic.

6   This is based on anecdotal knowledge of the subject population; ingroup identity was not
       directly measured.

7   It may be argued that *all* of the subjects would feel a "common fate", in that the library
       resource would collapse if they overused it, but this is not the usual meaning of the
       term, and further, this common fate was constant for all conditions.

8   The maximum number of hours per person which could be booked by leaders as 2.67 hours/person. While this might have created an artifactually low ceiling on group leaders, they in fact booked less than half of what was possible.

References

Axelrod, R. (1984). *The evolution of cooperation.* New York: Basic Books.

Brewer, M.B., & Kramer, R.M. (1986). Choice behavior in social dilemmas: Effects of social identity, group size and decision framing. *Journal of Personality and Social Psychology, 50,* 543-549.

Brewer, M.B. & Schneider, S.K. (1990). Social identity and social dilemmas: A double-edged sword. In D. Abrams & M. Hogg, (Eds.), *Social identity: Constructive and critical advances.* Hemel Hempstead, U.K.: Harvester Wheatsheaf.

Brown, R. (1988). *Group processes: Dynamics within and between groups.* Oxford: Basil Blackwell.

Carnevale, P.J.D. (1985). Accountability of group representatives and intergroup relations. *Advances in Group Processes, 2,* 227-248.

Caporael, L.R., Dawes, R., Orbell, J.M., & van de Kragt, A.J.C. (1989). Selfishness examined: Cooperation in the absence of egoistic incentives. *Behavioral and Brain Sciences, 12,* 683-99.

Dawes, R. (1980). Social dilemma. *Annual Review of Psychology, 31,* 169-193.

Hamburger, H., Guyer, M., & Fox, J. (1975). Group size and cooperation. *Journal of Conflict Resolution, 19,* 503-531.

Hinkle, S. & Brown, R. (1990). Intergroup comparisons and social identity: Some links and lacunae. In D. Abrams, & M. Hogg, (Eds.), *Social identity: Constructive and critical advances.* Hemel Hempstead, U.K.: Harvester Wheatsheaf.

Insko, C.A., & Schopler, J. (1987). Categorization, competition, and collectivity. In C. Hendrick, (Ed.), *Review of personality and social psychology: Group processes, 8,* 213-251. New York: Sage.

Kerr, N.L. (1989). Illusions of efficacy: The effects of group size on perceived social dilemmas. *Journal of Experimental Social Psychology, 25*, 287-313.

Komorita, S.S., & Carnevale, P.J.D. (1992). Motivational arousal vs. decision framing in social dilemmas. In W.B.G. Liebrand, D. Messick, & H. Wilke (Eds.), *Social dilemmas: Theoretical issues and research findings (pp. 209-224).* Oxford: Pergamon Press.

Komorita, S.S., & Lapworth, W.C. (1982). Cooperative choice among individuals versus groups in an N-person dilemma situation. *Journal of Personality and Social Psychology, 42*, 487-496.

Kramer, R.M. (1993). Helping the group or helping one's self? Cognitive-motivational determinants of cooperation in resource conservation dilemmas. In D. Schroeder, (Ed.), *Social dilemmas: Social psychological perspectives*. Praeger.

Kramer, R.M., & Brewer, M.B. (1984). Effects of group identity on resource use in a simulated commons dilemma. *Journal of Personality and Social Psychology, 46*, 1044-1057.

Kramer, R.M., & Brewer, M.B. (1986). Social group identity and the emergence of cooperation in resource conservation dilemmas. In H.A. Wilke, D.M. Messick, & C.G. Rutte (Eds.), *Psychology of decisions and conflict: Experimental social dilemmas*. Frankfurt, Verlag Peter Lang.

Kuhlman, D.M., Camac, C.R., & Cunha,D.A. (1986). Individual differences in social orientation. In H.A.M. Wilke, D.M. Messick, & C. Rutte (Eds.), *Experimental social dilemmas*. Frankfurt: Verlag Peter Lang.

Lancaster, S., & Foddy, M. (1988). Self-extensions: A conceptualisation. *Journal for the Theory of Social Behaviour, 18*, 77-94.

McClintock, C.G., & Liebrand, W.B.G. (1988). The role of interdependence structure, individual value orientation and other's strategy in social decision making: A transformational analysis. *Journal of Personality and Social Psychology, 55*, 396-409.

Messick, D.M., & Brewer, M.B. (1983). Solving social dilemmas: A review. *Review of Personality and Social Psychology, 4*, 11-44.

Messick, D.M., & McClelland, C.L. (1983). Social traps and temporal traps. *Personality and Social Psychology Bulletin, 9*, 105-110.

Ostrom, E. (1990). *Governing the commons: The evolution of institutions for collective action.* Cambridge: Cambridge University Press.

Pruitt, D.G., & Kimmel, M.J. (1977). Twenty years of experimental gaming: Critique, synthesis, and suggestions for the future. *Annual Review of Psychology, 28*, 363-392.

Rabbie, J.M. (1982). The effects of intergroup competition and cooperation on intragroup and intergroup relationships. In V.J. Derlega, & J. Grzelak (Eds.), *Cooperation and helping behavior: Theories and research (pp. 123-149).* New York: Academic Press.

Rubin, J.Z., & Brown, B.R. (1975). *The social psychology of bargaining and negotiation.* New York: Academic Press.

Rutte, C.G., & Wilke, H.A.M. (1984). Social dilemmas and leadership. *European Journal of Social Psychology*, 105-21.

Rutte, C.G., & Wilke, H.A.M. (1985). Preference for decision structures in a social dilemma situation. *European Journal of Social Psychology, 15*, 367-370.

Samuelson, C.D. (1993). When do people want to change the rules for allocating shared resources? In D. Schroeder (Ed.), *Social dilemmas: Social psychological perspectives.* New York: Praeger.

Samuelson, C.D., & Messick, D.M. (in press). A multi-attribute evaluation approach to structural change in resource dilemmas. *Organizational Behavior and Human Decision Processes*, forthcoming.

Samuelson, C.D., Messick, D.M., Wilke, H.A.M., & Rutte, C.G. (1986). Individual restraint and structural change as solutions to social dilemmas. In H.A. Wilke, D.M. Messick, & C.G. Rutte (Eds.), *Psychology of decisions and conflict: Experimental social dilemmas.* Frankfurt: Verlag Peter Lang.

Sato, K. (1987). Distribution of the cost of maintaining common resources. *Journal of Experimental Social Psychology, 23*, 94-104.2

Stroebe, W., & Frey, D. (1982). Self-interest and collective action: The economics and psychology of public goods. *British Journal of Social Psychology, 21*, 121-137.

Tajfel, H., & Turner, J.C. (1979). An integrative theory of intergroup conflict. In W.G. Austin, & S. Worchel (Eds.), *The social psychology of intergroup relations.* Monterey, California: Brooks-Cole.

Tetlock, P.E. (1992). The impact of accountability on judgment and choice: Toward a social contingency model. In M.P. Zanna (Ed.), *Advances in Experimental Social Psychology, 25*, 331-376.

Turner, J.C. (1987). *Rediscovering the social group: A self-categorization theory.* Oxford: Basil Blackwell.

Wilke, H.A.M., de Boer, K.L., Karst, L., & Liebrand, W.B.G. (1986). Standards of justice and quality of power in a social dilemma situation. *British Journal of Social Psychology, 25*, 57-65.

Wilke, H.A.M., Rutte, C.G., Wit, A., Messick, D.M., & Samuelson, C.D. (1986). Leadership in social dilemmas: Efficiency and equity. In H.A. Wilke, D.M. Messick, & C.G. Rutte (Eds.), *Psychology of decisions and conflict: Experimental social dilemmas.* Frankfurt: Verlag Peter Lang.

Wit, A., & Wilke, H.A.M. (1988). Subordinates' endorsement of an allocating leader in a commons dilemma: An equity theoretical approach. *Journal of Economic Psychology, 9*, 151-168.

Yamagishi, T. (1986). The structural goal/expectation theory of cooperation in social dilemmas. *Advances in Group Processes, 3*, 51-87.

Acknowledgement

We would like to thank Marilynn Brewer for helpful suggestions for this paper, and Paul Polidori for writing the computer program for the library dilemma.

Prisoner's dilemma networks:
Selection strategy versus action strategy

Toshio Yamagishi[1], Nahoko Hayashi, and Nobuhito Jin

Abstract

To date, most research on Prisoner's Dilemmas has dealt with isolated dyads. However, most PD-like relations in the real world take place in a network of relations where each player has a choice of partners. In this research project, we have created a situation where (1) every member of a group selects a partner (that is, two parties form a relationship by mutual choice, and each is free to leave the relationship), and (2) a PD game is played by members who have selected each other. We call this situation a *prisoner's dilemma network*. We invited social dilemmas researchers to a computer contest of strategies. Nine strategies participated, and the winner of the contest was PURGE submitted by T. Kameda, which was a simple *out-for-tat strategy*. The major findings of this study are: (1) Action strategy (how to decide between C and D) is not as important as selection strategy (how to select a partner). (2) Out-for-tat seems to be the best strategy in PD networks. (3) In the situation where actions of the partner can be "mistaken," forgivingness to defection in out-for-tat is important.

Prisoner's dilemma networks

Prisoner's dilemmas and other interdependence games are often considered to be models of social phenomena (e.g., Hamburger, 1979). However, most experimental gaming studies are limited to dyadic relations. To generalize the findings of experimental gaming research, it is obvious that we need to overcome this limitation. One way of extending the experimental gaming research beyond dyadic relations is to study n-person mixed motive situations such as the n-person prisoner's dilemma or social dilemma situations. This avenue has been fairly well pursued by now (see Dawes, 1980; Edney & Harper, 1978; Messick & Brewer, 1983; Orbell & Dawes, 1981; Stroebe & Frey, 1982; Yamagishi, 1989, in press, for reviews of social dilemmas research). However, n-person mixed motive games are not the only possible research paradigm for extending the experimental gaming tradition beyond dyadic relations. Another possible research paradigm is what we call the "prisoner's dilemma network," in which dyadic relations are embedded in a larger network structure.

What makes interdependent relations embedded in a larger network structure distinct from isolated relations between two actors is the possibility of choosing partners. In isolated dyadic relations, actors can choose actions (usually a choice between cooperation and defection), but they cannot choose interaction partners. Past theoretical developments and empirical findings concerning iterated interdependent relations require that the two partners be locked into a particular relation. Many interdependent relations in the real world, such as the U.S.-U.S.S.R. relation before the disorganization of the Soviet Union, are actually of this kind; the two partners are "forced" to interact with each other and cannot leave the relation. However, many other interdependent relations in the real world are not of this sort. We often choose to interact with our partners by mutual choice, and each has the freedom (more or less) to leave the relationship. In fact, most dyadic interdependent relations in the real world, even the most long-lasting ones such as marriage and friendship, involve possible alternatives. How generalizable are the findings of experimental gaming research on isolated dyadic interdependent relations to the type of situation in which actors have a choice of partners? If the findings of the research on isolated dyadic relations are not easily generalizable to situations where actors have a choice of partners, then what should we study, and how should we study it? These are the questions that motivated us to launch a research project on prisoner's dilemma networks.

Our research project on prisoner's dilemma networks started with two preliminary studies, one simulation study (Hayashi, Jin, & Yamagishi, 1993) and one experiment (Jin, Hayashi, & Shinotsuka, 1993). Let us first summarize the major findings of these two studies.

Hayashi, Jin, and Yamagishi, 1993.[2] The question addressed by Hayashi, Jin, and Yamagishi (1993) is whether or not the tit-for-tat (TFT) strategy, which has proven to be effective in generating cooperative relations in an iterated PD, is also as effective in prisoner's dilemma networks. In a computer simulation of 28-person groups, she assigned each of the 28 simulated actors a unique combination of 4 types of "selection strategy" and 7 types of "action strategy." Selection strategies were used to select partners whom the actor wished to interact with in each trial. A PD game for that particular trial was played between two partners who wished to interact with each other. Actors selected targets of their interaction based on their selection strategies at the beginning of each trial, so that different sets of pairs could interact in each trial. Each actor selected two partners each trial. When more than one pair were formed involving the same actor, a pair was randomly chosen. Those who were not chosen by anyone else could not play a PD game on that trial. Once a PD-pair was formed based on mutual selection, their choice in that PD game was determined by their action strategies. Each simulated actor could use information about its own experience (who was the partner and the action of that partner) in making either partner selection or action decisions. They had no information about other PD pairs (i.e., no "reputation" existed at all). The simulation was replicated 300 times, each lasting 300 trials. Two types of payoff matrix (high and low in payoff) were used in the simulation. The high payoff matrix represented a situation where the "sucker's payoff" was better than the outcome of being left out (i.e., a zero point). The low payoff matrix represented a situation where the "sucker's payoff" was worse than the payoff of being left out. Two of the 7 action strategies were unconditional strategies (unconditional defection and unconditional cooperation), and the other five were variants of the TFT strategy. The four selection strategies and the 7 action strategies used in Hayashi et al.'s (1993) simulation are listed in Table 1.

Table 1

Average scores of the 28 actors in Hayashi et al.'s simulation

SELECTION STRATEGY	ACTION STRATEGY							
	0	1	2	3	4	5	6	Total
RANDOM	0.31	0.33	0.33	0.33	0.32	0.31	0.32	0.32
	0.12	0.11	0.10	0.08	0.05	0.04	0.03	0.08
CUMULATIVE	1.08	1.54	1.62	1.77	1.87	1.86	1.92	1.67
	0.45	0.49	0.54	0.50	0.53	0.53	0.52	0.51
COMMITMENT	0.86	1.36	1.39	1.50	1.69	1.73	1.67	1.46
	0.23	0.36	0.36	0.37	0.31	0.30	0.25	0.31
SHORT MEMORY	0.54	0.73	0.91	1.20	1.32	1.31	1.36	1.05
	0.23	0.24	0.23	0.36	0.38	0.40	0.38	0.32
Total	0.70	0.99	1.06	1.20	1.30	1.30	1.32	1.12
	0.26	0.30	0.31	0.33	0.32	0.32	0.30	0.31

The upper entry of each cell is the average score in the simulation with the high payoff matrix, and the lower entry is with the low payoff matrix.

Selection Strategies:

RANDOM: Randomly selects two other members.

CUMULATIVE: Selects two members who have cooperated the most in the previous PD games played with this strategy.

COMMITMENT: Selects two members who have most frequently played PD games with this strategy.

SHORT MEMORY: Selects the partner in the last trial if he cooperated there, and another member randomly. If he defected in the last trial, randomly select two members.

Action Strategies:

0: Unconditional defection.

1: Cooperates when and only when the partner has cooperated in all of the last three encounters with him. Otherwise, defects.

2: Cooperates when and only when the partner has cooperated in both of the last two encounters with him. Otherwise, defects.

3: Tit-for-tat.

4: Tit-for-two-tats.

5: Tit-for-three-tats.

6: Unconditional cooperation.

Summary results of this simulation are also shown in Table 1. The major findings of that simulation are: (1) The effect of the partner selection strategy on the actor's total points was several times stronger than the effect of the action strategy. That is, whom to play with was much more important than how to play in this simulation. (2) The action strategy and the selection strategy had an interaction effect on the actor's total earnings, ostensibly because the consequence of actions affected the chances of that actor's being selected by others. (3) There was no single action strategy that "performed" best in all situations. That is, which action strategy was the best depended on the partner selection strategy taken by the actor and the nature of the payoff matrix. The overall conclusion of this study is that more attention needs to be given to partner selection strategies when we analyze dyadic interdependent situations embedded in larger network structures.

Jin, Hayashi, and Shinotsuka, 1993.[3] In an experiment on a PD network, Jin, Hayashi, and Shinotsuka (1993) allowed subjects to choose their partners for a PD game from the other three members of a four person group. As in Hayashi et al.'s (1993) simulation study, the choice of partners was made at the beginning of each trial. Each subject could choose up to three potential partners (without ordering them). A PD pair was formed first by mutual selection. When more than one mutually selecting pair existed in the group, one pair was randomly chosen and the existence of a mutual choice was examined in the remaining two. However, when one pair was formed by mutual selection, the second pair was forced to play a PD game even when they did not choose each other as desired partners.[4] That is, the second pair could be either a mutually selecting pair or a "forced" pair. When no pair was formed by mutual choice, two pairs were randomly formed. A PD game played in each trial did not include dichotomous choices, but rather multi-level choices. Each subject decided how much they would give to their partner, ranging from 0 yen to 10 yen (about 9 cents). The amount contributed by the subject was doubled and then provided to the partner. This decision was repeated 65 times, but the subject was not informed of the total number of trials. Results of this experiment showed that commitment (repeated interactions with the same partner by mutual choice) increased over time. One interesting finding of this study is that subjects who have succeeded in forming a mutually committed relationship with another subject maintained an extremely high level of cooperation; they almost always contributed all of the 10 yen available on each trial. But, only a slight deviation from this high level of mutual cooperation was enough to terminate the committed relationship. In other words, a substantial proportion of the subjects in Jin et al.'s (1993) experiment adopted a special form of tit-for-tat, involving both action *and* selection strategies; "if you keep cooperating, I will keep choosing you as my partner and fully cooperate; if you fail to cooperate fully, I will desert you and turn to someone else." This peculiar form of tit-for-tat, which may be called "out-for-tat," seems to be much more effective than the simple TFT in producing a high level of mutual cooperation, because it would not start a conflict spiral of mutual defection.

PD network contest

Results of the above two initial studies of PD networks point to the need for further research on the partner selection strategy. However, since there are practically no systematic studies of selection strategies so far, we did not know what selection strategies would be possible and what ones were often used. As a means to find out what selection strategies could be used in PD network situations, we held a contest of computer programs of strategies to be used in a PD network. Participants at the Fourth International Conference on Social Dilemmas and members of the Japanese Mathematical Sociological Association (and a few additional people) were invited to participate in this contest. Nine strategies were proposed. Brief descriptions of the nine strategies are included in Table 2.

Table 2

Summary of the 14 strategies participated in the contest. (Note that the actual strategies may be more complicated than the ones summarized here.)

The following terms will be used in the description.

Strangers:	whom the strategy has not interacted in the past.
Enemies:	who defected at least once in the past interaction.
Friends:	who always cooperated in the past interactions.

Priorities in the first trial were randomly assigned to all partners, except in Nepotism.

ANSF (All You Need is Some Friends)
(1) Selection strategy. Assign first priorities to friends (according to the frequency of the past interactions), and then to strangers (randomly). Never select enemies.
(2) Action strategy. Unconditional cooperation when the number of friends is less than three. When there are three friends, cooperate with friends and defect against strangers. (The stranger against whom ANSF defected is then classified as an enemy.)

D-KEN
(1) Selection strategy. Assign priorities randomly to all except enemies.
(2) Unconditional cooperation.

ENDER
(1) Selection strategy. Divide members into three categories: "high-cooperators" who cooperated 49% or more, "low-cooperators" who cooperated less than 49%, and "strangers" with no past interactions. Assign first priorities to high-cooperators (according to their cooperation rates), and to strangers (randomly), and finally to low-cooperators (according to their cooperation rates).
(2) Action strategy. TFT with a modification; tolerate the first defection.

HIFI (High Fidelity)
(1) Selection strategy. Assign first priorities to friends (according to the frequency of past interactions), and then to strangers (randomly). If the partner in the previous trial cooperated, then assign the first priority to that partner. Never select enemies.
(2) Action strategy. Unconditional cooperation.

NAKAYOSHI (Friendship)

(1) Selection strategy. Assign first priorities to friends (based on the frequency of past interactions), then to strangers (randomly), and finally to enemies (according to the *average* score obtained from interactions with the partner).

(2) Action strategy. TFT.

NEPOTISM

(1) Before starting interactions, divide partners *a priori* randomly into two categories of equal size: "insiders" and "outsiders." Assign first priorities to insiders; first, to the ones who always cooperated with a history of more than two interactions, then to the ones who defected just once in the past but cooperated in the most recent interaction, and then to the ones with less than three interactions, and finally to others (random assignment within each category). Then, assign the remaining priorities to outsiders.

(2) Action strategy. TFT with insiders. Unconditional defection against outsiders.

ODA

(1) Selection strategy. Assign first priorities to friends (according to the frequency of past interactions), and (when the number of friends is less than five) to strangers (randomly, only up to the 5th priority). If the partner in the previous trial cooperated, then assign the first priority to that partner. Never select enemies.

(2) Action strategy. Unconditional cooperation.

SUITOR

(1) Selection strategy. Assign priorities to N-3 actors. Divide members to "priority partners" (who cooperated in the most recent interaction) and "random partners" (others). Assign choice priorities among priority partners according to the duration of the most recent consecutive cooperations. When the number of priority partners is less than N-3, randomly assign the remaining priorities to random partners.

(2) Action strategy. TFT.

PURGE

(1) Selection strategy. Assign priorities randomly to all except the ones who defected in the previous PURGE trials. (The PURGE trial number was set to one in the current simulation.) If the partner in the previous trial cooperated, then assign the first priority to that partner.

(2) Action strategy. Unconditional cooperation.

Summary of the contest rules

Participants in the contest were told that there would be several hundred periods, not exceeding one thousand. In each period, each actor assigned a preference order to the other members for forming a PD-pair. An actor who did not want to play with a particular member could avoid that member. Pairs for the period were formed based on the preference orders assigned by the members.[5] Once a pair was formed, each actor decided whether to cooperate or to defect. Each received a score for that period based on the choices of the two partners using a prisoner's dilemma matrix, in which CC=1, CD=-1, DC=2, and DD=0. With this matrix (corresponding to the low-payoff matrix in Hayashi et al., 1993), those who failed to play a game (i.e., failed to form a PD-pair with someone else) received no score for the period, which was identical to the payoff of mutual defection. The actors could find out and "remember" with whom they formed pairs and what decisions the partners made. They did not know, however, on what strategy the partner's choice was based, or what decisions other actors made in other relations (i.e., no reputations existed).

Submitted strategies

One conspicuous feature of the submitted strategies is the niceness of action strategies. The action strategies adopted by the participants were mostly either the unconditional cooperation strategy (D-KEN, HIFI, ODA, and PURGE) or the TFT strategy (ENDER, SUITOR, and NAKAYOSHI). These two action strategies were "nice" in the sense that they never initiated defection (cf, Axelrod, 1984). The other two strategies, ANSF and NEPOTISM, involved an element of "nastiness" (Axelrod, 1984) and applied the unconditional defection strategy against "strangers" (ANSF) or "outsiders" (NEPOTISM). Even they were nice, however, and unconditionally cooperated with "friends" (who have never defected in past interactions) in the case of ANSF, or applied the TFT strategy to "insiders" in the case of NEPOTISM (see Table 2 for the distinction between insiders and outsiders in NEPOTISM). Furthermore, the actual use of the unconditional defection strategy was relatively rare even with these strategies (since other strategies avoided interacting with these strategies once they had been betrayed by them). This niceness of the strategies may partly reflect the findings of Axelrod's (1984) simulation, in which niceness was an important ingredient of a successful strategy. It may also reflect the nature of the PD network situation compared to an isolated dyadic PD situation; there is a strong incentive to be selected by others as an interaction partner when actors can choose partners.

The submitted selection strategies can be classified by the following three factors. (1) Whether or not the selection strategy is based on the principle of "out-for-tat" (OFT). According to the out-for-tat principle, the strategy assigns the first priority to the partner of the last trial unless the partner defected on that trial. HIFI, NAKAYOSHI, ODA, and PURGE are characterized by OFT. (2) Whether or not the selection strategy never interacts with "enemies" (who have defected at least once in past interactions). ANSF, D-KEN, HIFI, and ODA are characterized by this "unforgivingness of enemies." The other strategies are more forgiving and give some chance of future interactions even to "enemies." (3) Priority assignment method. PURGE and D-KEN disregard the distinction between "friends" and "strangers," and randomly assign priorities to "friends" and "strangers" (and even to previous "enemies" in the case of PURGE) alike. ANSF, HIFI, NAKAYOSHI, and ODA assign higher priorities to "friends" than to "enemies." These four strategies assign priorities among friends according to the frequency of interactions (in which partners always cooperated). The other three strategies, ENDER, NEPOTISM, and SUITOR, are unique in their priority assignment methods (see Table 2 for details).

Contest results

Table 3 lists the average score for each strategy. The winner of this contest was PURGE submitted by T. Kameda of Toyo University. HIFI submitted by A. Diekmann of Bern University was the second, closely followed by ODA submitted by T. Oda of the Institute for Social Research.

Table 3

Contest Results

Strategy Name	Characteristics of the Strategies				Av. Score	SD	Frequency distribution of the excluded trials				
	1	2	3	4			0-100	100-199	200-299	200-399	400-500
1 PURGE	C	OFT	F	R	496.7	11.0	100	0	0	0	0
2 HIFI	C	OFT	U	F	490.6	28.2	97	3	0	0	0
3 ODA	C	OFT	U	F	482.9	53.3	94	2	4	0	0
4 NAKAYOSHI	T	OFT	F	F	478.9	74.9	93	2	3	2	0
5 ENDER	T	no	F	other	477.8	44.1	90	9	1	0	0
6 SUITOR	T	no	F	other	468.8	55.2	87	11	2	0	0
7 ANSF	CD	no	U	F	450.4	82.3	74	16	10	0	0
8 NEPOTISM	TD	no	F	other	447.0	113.4	80	4	13	3	0
9 D-KEN	C	no	U	R	204.1	188.2	23	11	10	10	46

Characteristics of the strategies

1) Action strategy.

TFT: tit-for-tat

UC: Unconditional cooperation

CD: Unconditional cooperation with "insiders"; unconditional defection against "outsiders."

2 TD: TFT with friends; unconditional defection against some strangers

2) Out-for-tat

3) Forgiveness

F: Forgiveness to enemies

UF: unforgivingness to enemies

4) Priority Assignment Method

F: Higher priorities to "friends"; priorities among friends based on the frequency of past interactions

R: Random assignment of priorities

Table 3 also shows how each strategy is classified according to the four distinguishing features of the submitted strategies discussed above, (1) type of action strategy, (2) OFT, (3) forgiveness to "enemies," and (4) priority assignment method. Some systematic relations are found in the table between these features of the strategies and the strategies' performance levels. First, all four strategies with the OFT feature performed better than the other strategies. In addition, the action strategy of the top three strategies, PURGE, HIFI, and ODA, was the unconditional cooperation strategy. Whether the action strategy is TFT or unconditional cooperation does not make a difference insofar as the selection strategy is the OFT strategy, because, with either action strategy, the strategy always cooperates with a consistently cooperative partner. In other words, insofar as selection of the partner is done with the OFT principle, the TFT action strategy is redundant. NAKAYOSHI, the fourth performer with the TFT action strategy, can thus be considered an out-for-tat strategy. All of the top four strategies were out-for-tat strategies which dealt with the same partner and always cooperated insofar as the partner was cooperative.

The effectiveness of the OFT feature is further demonstrated by a comparison of the scores of D-KEN and PURGE. These two strategies are similar in their priority assignment method and in their action strategy; they both randomly assign priorities to "friends" and "strangers" disregarding the distinction, and always cooperated. Despite the similarity between the two, PURGE was the best performer and D-KEN was by far the poorest performer. Besides the difference in OFT, however, these two strategies were different in forgiveness; therefore, the huge difference in the score between the two may not be due solely to the OFT feature of PURGE and the lack of it in

D-KEN. In order to examine the pure effect of OFT, we conducted an additional simulation in which PURGE was replaced with UNFORGIVING-PURGE. UNFORGIVING- PURGE was the same as PURGE except for one difference; it never interacted with actors who ever defected in past interactions. In this additional simulation (30 replications with 500 trials), the difference between the score of UNFORGIVING-PURGE (482.70) and D-KEN (310.07) was still quite large. This result clearly shows that the OFT feature is an extremely important ingredient in a successful strategy in PD networks.

Another interesting finding is the negative relationship between the average score and the standard deviation; the lower the score, the greater the standard deviation. This suggests that the existence (or non-existence) of a few replications in which the strategy failed to find partners and thus performed extremely poorly was the major determinant of the overall performance level. Table 3, which also shows the frequency distribution of trials in which each strategy failed to find a partner, confirms this interpretation.

Effect of the action strategy. In order to examine how important a role the action strategy played, we conducted an additional simulation (100 replications with 500 trials) in which all actors made the cooperation-defection decisions based on the unconditional cooperation strategy. That is, the action strategies of ANSF, ENDER, NAKAYOSHI, NEPOTISM, and SUITOR were converted into the unconditional cooperation strategy in this simulation. The only significant change in the score from the original contest occurred for D-KEN (from 204.11 to 151.75, t = 2.00, p < .05). Only minor changes occurred by changing the TFT strategy to the unconditional cooperation strategy, confirming the conclusion in Hayashi et al.'s (1993) study that the action strategy is not as important as the partner selection strategy.

Robustness of the strategies. In order to examine the robustness of the above findings, we conducted several more simulations each with some variations (see Table 4 for the results of these additional simulations). First, we conducted a simulation in which each strategy had a clone. We suspected that the results of the original contest might be unique to odd-number groups in which at least one strategy was excluded on any trial. The result of the second simulation in which group size was even (9 x 2 = 18 strategies) confirmed this suspicion. The difference in the average score between the best performer (HIFI) and the poorest performer (D-KEN) was much smaller in this simulation (498.8 vs. 472.6; a difference of 22.6) than in the original simulation in which the difference between the best performer, PURGE, and the poorest performer, D-KEN, was 292.7. The difference between the second best performer and the second poorest performer was also much smaller in the second simulation (12.5) than in the original simulation (43.6).

Table 4

Results of the Five Simulations

Strategies	Original Contest	With Clones	With Randoms	Mistaken Identities	Mistaken Actions	Overall Average
PURGE	(1) 496.7	(4) 497.1	(4) 474.5	(1) 496.1	(1) 457.1	(1) 484.3
HIFI	(2) 490.6	(1) 498.8	(2) 490.2	(2) 491.9	(6) 294.3	(5) 453.2
ODA	(3) 482.9	(5) 496.6	(1) 494.7	(3) 488.8	(7) 286.6	(6) 449.9
NAKAYOSHI	(4) 478.9	(6) 489.5	(7) 453.3	(4) 484.2	(3) 433.9	(4) 468.0
ENDER	(5) 477.8	(3) 497.9	(3) 489.1	(5) 482.9	(5) 431.6	(2) 475.9
SUITOR	(6) 468.8	(2) 498.0	(5) 474.3	(6) 468.6	(2) 442.2	(3) 470.4
ANSF	(7) 450.0	(7) 488.0	(6) 469.9	(7) 421.7	(9) 192.5	(8) 404.4
NEPOTISM	(8) 447.0	(8) 485.5	(8) 445.7	(9) 265.7	(4) 433.0	(7) 415.4
D-KEN	(9) 204.1	(9) 476.2	(9) 362.1	(8) 340.6	(8) 222.2	(9) 321.0
Average	444.1	492.0	463.1	437.8	354.8	438.1

Next, we added four strategies to the original nine strategies, all of which were based on random selection: Random_D, Random_C, Random_T, and Random_R. All of these strategies randomly assigned selection priorities to all partners; the difference among these four strategies was in the action strategy. Random_D's action strategy was the unconditional defection, Random_C the unconditional cooperation, Random_T the TFT strategy, and Random_R randomly chose between C and D. With these four random selection strategies included, the range of scores among the nine submitted strategies became smaller (132.6) than in the original contest (292.6). This change in the range of scores is considered to be the result of the "randomness" in the process of finding steady partners.

In the next two simulations, we introduced two types of errors. In one simulation, actors mistook the identity of their interaction partners with the probability of 3%. This error of mistaken identities of the partners significantly depressed the scores of ANSF (from 450.0 to 421.7, t=1.98, p<.05), and NEPOTISM (from 447.0 to 265.7, t=8.68, p<.01), and significantly improved the score of D-KEN (from 204.1 to 340.6, t=5.07, p<.01).[6] It did not affect the scores of other strategies very much. In another simulation, actors mistook the actions of their partners, again, with the probability of 3%.[7] The effect of these mistaken actions was much more pronounced than the effect of mistaken identities. Scores of most strategies declined as a result of the mistaken actions, and the decline was especially great for HIFI (from 490.6 to 294.3, t=19.41, p<.01), ODA (from 482.9 to 286.6, t=19.30, p<.01), and ANSF (from 450.0 to 192.5, t=24.12, p<.01). These were unforgiving strategies that never interacted with "enemies" (who defected at least once). It is thus suggested that the total unforgivingness to "enemies" depressed the scores of these strategies and, indirectly, the scores of other strategies interacted (or failed to interact) with these strategies. In order to test the hypothesized negative effect of the total unforgivingness in the above simulation, we conducted an additional simulation in which the four unforgiving strategies ANSF, D-KEN, HIFI, and ODA were made more forgiving. Specifically, these four strategies in this simulation forgave enemies after one trial as in PURGE. All strategies performed in this simulation (with 30 replications) almost as well as in the original contest; the overall average score in this simulation was 440.3, which was as good as the overall average in the original contest.

The last column of Table 4 reports the overall ranking based on the average scores across the five simulations. PURGE, which was the winner of the contest, was again the best overall performer. HIFI and ODA, which were the second and the third best performers in the original contest, were not very strong overall. In contrast, SUITOR and ENDER, which were mediocre performers in the original contest, consistently performed relatively well in the other four simulations and became the third and the second best overall performers. NAKAYOSHI, the fourth in the original contest, kept the same position in the overall result.

Discussion

The major findings of the simulations we have conducted so far may be summarized as follows. (1) Action strategy is not as important as partner selection strategy. (2) The OFT strategy seems to be the best strategy in PD network situations. (3) In an uncertain situation where identity and, especially, action of the partner can be mistaken, "forgivingness" is a necessary feature for being a successful strategy. "Forgivingness," which was considered by Axelrod (1984) to be an important ingredient of a successful (action) strategy, was again suggested, by the results of the current simulations, to be an important factor in making a selection strategy successful, especially in socially uncertain situations.

The winner of the contest, PURGE, which was also the most robust performer throughout the series of simulations, had both of these two features, OFT and forgivingness. It was actually a simple out-for-tat strategy: "I will keep choosing you as my partner and cooperate if you keep cooperating; otherwise, I will desert you and turn (randomly) to someone else." These features of PURGE also characterized the winning strategy, CONCO, in Schuessler's (1989) simulation. Schuessler concluded that the forgiving out-for-tat strategy (which he termed CONCO) was the best strategy in an anonymous group situation with an "exit" option. In addition to confirming this, the results of our study further demonstrate that the effectiveness of the out-for-tat strategy is not limited to groups consisting of totally anonymous members who have no memory at all. The results also indicate that remembering partners' past actions is not of much help; very short-term memory (i.e., the memory of success or failure on the previous trial) is enough to form an effective selection strategy. Out-for-tat is quite similar to tit-for-tat in this respect.

In conclusion, simple was the best in this PD network simulation as in Axelrod's (1984) dyadic PD simulation. Actually, the excellent performance of PURGE points to the same set of conclusions proposed by Axelrod (1984). Axelrod (1984) lists three features of the TFT strategy, the winner of his computer contest of strategies in isolated PD relations: simpleness, responsiveness, and forgivingness. The overall winner of the contest, PURGE, was also characterized by these three features. The forgiveness of PURGE put it above the other OFT strategies (e.g., HIFI and ODA) in a situation where partners' actions can be mistaken, and made it the overall winner of the contest.

Footnotes

1 Hokkaido University, Dept. of Behavioral Sciences, Sapporo, Japan.

2 The study was conducted as a part of Hayashi's Bachelor's Thesis project in 1989.

3 The study was conducted as a part of Jin's Bachelor's Thesis project in 1989.

4 This aspect was different from the procedure used in Hayashi et al.'s (1993) simulation.

5 Pairs are matched according to the following procedure. The procedure is based on the general idea that pairing occurs conjunctively. That is, how likely a pair is to form is based on the priority given by the less eager partner. This principle will be easy to understand in the case of dating. A man is eager to take a woman for a date. The woman is not eager at all. Then, there will be no dating. In this example, eagerness of the man is less important than the degree of reluctance shown by the woman. Whether or not dating occurs depends mainly on the less eager partner's (in this example, the woman's) willingness to agree. The actual procedure is as follows: (1) First, list all the potential pairs, in which the two partners have chosen each other as potential partners, disregarding their preference order. (2) Give those pairs priorities according to the preference order of the "less eager" player. The "less eager" player is the one whose preference order is the lower. (3) When there are more than one pair that have received the same priority level according to the above criterion, those pairs are given secondary priorities according to the preference order by the "more eager" player. (4) When there are more than one pair that have received the same primary and secondary priorities, those pairs are randomly given priorities.

6 D-KEN enjoyed a better outcome in this simulation because the error did not affect its random selection and, at the same time, the relative failure of other strategies in finding partners gave it a better chance.

7 Each actor recorded the cooperative choice of a partner as non-cooperative, and a non-cooperative choice as cooperative, with the probability of 3%. However, the cumulative score was calculated based on the true choices.

References

Axelrod, R. (1984). *The evolution of cooperation*. New York: Basic Books.

Dawes, R.M. (1980). Social dilemmas. *Annual Review of Psychology*, *31*, 169-193.

Edney, J.J., & Harper, C.S. (1978). The commons dilemma: A review of contributions from psychology. *Environmental Management*, *2*, 491-507.

Hamburger, H. (1979). *Games as models of social phenomena*. San Francisco: Freeman.

Hayashi, N., Jin, N., & Yamagishi, T. (1993). Prisoner's Dilemma network: A computer simulation of strategies. *Research in Social Psychology*, *8*, 33-43. (In Japanese)

Jin, N., Hayashi, N., & Shinotsuka, H. (1993). An experimental study of Prisoner's Dilemma network. *Japanese Journal of Experimental Social Psychology*, *32*, in press. (In Japanese)

Messick, D.M., & Brewer, M.B. (1983). Solving social dilemmas: A review. In Wheeler (Ed.), *Review of personality and social Psychology, Vol. 4* (pp.11-44). Beverly Hills, CA: Sage.

Orbell, J.M., & Dawes, R.M. (1981). Social dilemmas. In G. Stephenson & J. H. David (Eds.), *Progress in applied social psychology, Vol. 1* (pp. 37-65). Chichester: Wiley.

Stroebe, W., & Frey, B.S. (1982). Self-interest and collective action: The economics and psychology of public goods. *British Journal of Social Psychology*, *21*, 121-137.

Yamagishi, T. (1989). Major theoretical approaches in social dilemmas research. *Japanese Psychological Review*, *33*, 64-96. (In Japanese)

Yamagishi, T. (In press). Social dilemmas. In K. Cook., G. Fine, & J. House (Eds.), *Sociological perspectives on social psychology*. Allyn and Bacon.

Acknowledgement

The research reported in this chapter was supported by a Ministry of Education Scientific Grant to Toshio Yamagishi and Hiromi Shinotsuka.

Choice of strategies in social dilemma supergames

Motoki Watabe[1] and Toshio Yamagishi[1]

Abstract

The purpose of the studies reported in this chapter is to examine if people prefer trigger-type payoff structure over NPD structure, and if trigger-type payoff structure is created at the supergame level as a result of strategy choices. Results of two experiments reported below are generally negative to these questions, and thus are inconsistent with the result of an earlier study (Watabe, 1992). Result of a computer simulation, however, suggests that trigger-like-payoff structures are more likely to result in larger groups than in smaller groups. This may explain the difference of the current result involving 4-person groups from the result of Watabe's (1992) study involving a 10-person group.

Introduction

There is a large body of literature on the effectiveness of various strategies for achieving mutual cooperation in two-person, iterated Prisoner's Dilemmas. Strategies are decision rules prescribing when to cooperate and when to defect. One of the simplest strategies is the unconditional cooperation strategy; "Always cooperate no matter what the others do." Another simple strategy is the strategy of unconditional defection. Other strategies are strategies of conditional cooperation; "Cooperate when such and such conditions exist; otherwise, do not cooperate." One of the simplest conditional cooperation strategies is the tit-for-tat strategy, which prescribes: "Cooperate when and only when the partner cooperated in the previous round; otherwise, do not cooperate." This strategy, despite its simplicity, has proven very effective in inducing the partner to taking cooperative actions (cf., Axelrod, 1984; Oskamp, 1971; Wilson, 1971). However, as Dawes (1980) points out, the effectiveness of the tit-for-tat strategy is primarily limited to dyadic relations. When there are more partners it is difficult to detect who is cooperating and who is defecting. Furthermore, the effectiveness of one's action is distributed across many partners so that one's action does not have a strong impact on specific others. Finally, strategic actions may have negative "externalities" (Yamagishi, 1989). If one decides to defect as a means to punish a defector, other cooperators might interpret his or her strategic action as exploitative, and might try to punish him or her by defecting themselves. On the other hand, some game theorists believe that an effective strategy of conditional cooperation can be developed for N-person social dilemma situations (Taylor, 1976, 1982; Friedman, 1986). One possible strategy might be the "trigger strategy" (Friedman, 1986): "Cooperate if and only if all others cooperate; otherwise, do not cooperate." This strategy is similar to the tit-for-tat strategy in the sense that if everybody else has adopted this strategy, it is rational to cooperate. Any attempt to free ride, then, "triggers" an avalanche of defection, and immediately produces unanimous defection. In addition, once unanimous cooperation is achieved, no one has an incentive to defect. This is, unanimous cooperation is the Nash-equilibrium. Furthermore, the risk of being a sucker does not exist with this strategy. When there is at least one other member who is not willing to cooperate, one will not cooperate either; then, one will not be exploited by free riders.

A problem remains, however. The trigger strategy (to be called TS below) is an individually better strategy than D if the choice is provided between TS and D. This is not usually the case in iterated social dilemmas. Some people may think of the advantage of the trigger strategy, but others may not. Some of the group members may adopt the unconditional cooperation strategy, some others the strategy of unconditional defection, and yet others may adopt other versions of strategy of conditional cooperation. For example, let us assume a 5-person PD situation in which one player has adopted the unconditional defection strategy and three have adopted a conditional cooperation strategy in which the necessary and sufficient condition for cooperation is a maximum of one defector in the group. If the last player adopted the unconditional cooperation strategy, there will be four cooperators in the group. On the other hand, if the last player adopted the trigger strategy, he or she would defect. And his or her defection will prompt the other three conditional cooperators to defect as well. The result is the unanimous defection. Adoption of the trigger strategy thus involves a risk of turning a near unanimous cooperation into a unanimous defection. Given this risk, people may hesitate to adopt the trigger strategy. Once the choice is provided between TS and D, people would choose TS over D. However, in actual social dilemma situations, people may or may not prefer to adopt the trigger strategy because of the fear that it may turn a near unanimous cooperation into a unanimous defection.

As a first attempt to provide an empirical basis for answering the question of whether people would prefer the trigger strategy over other strategies, Watabe (1992) conducted an iterated social dilemma experiment in which subjects decided on the choice of strategies rather than actions. A 10-person iterated social dilemma was used in the experiment, in which each subject's contribution of ten yen (about eight cents) per trial was tripled and evenly distributed among all group members. The task of the subject, however, was not to decide whether to contribute or not in each trial; rather the subject was asked to submit his or her own strategy to be applied throughout the iterated social dilemma (which will be called the "supergame" in this chapter). The experiment lasted over eleven days. Instructions were given on the first day. In the morning of each of the following ten days, subjects submitted their own strategies to be used in the day's supergame. Their actions in the day's supergame (iterated over 45 to 70 trials) were determined based on their submitted strategies. The strategies subjects submitted were not devised by the experimenter; subjects themselves invented the strategies. This process was repeated ten times over the next ten days.

Subjects' strategies during the last two days finally produced a trigger-type payoff structure at the supergame level, not at the constituent game. The payoff structure of each constituent game was the 10-person social dilemma described above. The payoff structure of the supergame, on the other hand, consisted of the final outcome resulting from the combination of submitted strategies. The trigger-type payoff structure of the constituent game would mean the step-level social dilemma in which the provision point is located at the unanimous cooperation. Minimal contributing set as discussed by van de Kragt, Dawes, and Orbell (1983) is an example of the trigger-type payoff structure (TTPS). The trigger-type payoff structure of the supergame, on the other hand, is created by a combination of strategies. The combination is such that it is impossible to convert one of the strategies to the unconditional cooperation strategy without triggering an avalanche of defections in others. That is, it is a situation in which the unconditional cooperation of one player results in a unanimous or near unanimous defection. When the combination of strategies constitutes the trigger-type payoff structure of the supergame, no one can free ride. In the above experiment, most subjects came to adopt some form of strategy of conditional cooperation, and the condition for cooperation became stringent in the last two supergames (during the last two days); but the strategies they adopted were by no means the exact trigger strategy. However, the combination of strategies in the last two supergames was such that unilateral change of one member's strategy to the unconditional defection strategy triggered an avalanche of defection on the part of other members. These results suggested that people facing iterated supergames in fact come to adopt, under certain conditions, strategies that transforms an N-person PD structure of the constituent game to the trigger-type payoff structure at the supergame level.

Although the above result of Watabe's (1992) experiment is stimulating and indicative of the possibility that group members facing an iterated social dilemma come to voluntarily adopt a set of strategies that produces the trigger-type incentive structure at the supergame level, the result is far from conclusive because only one group was involved. In addition, subjects in Watabe's (1992) experiment could not change their strategies during each supergame. Subjects submitted new strategies each time when a new supergame was started. In the real world, on the other hand, iterated social dilemmas are not likely to be divided into a set of iterated games; each member may change his or her strategy anytime during an iterated game, and changes of strategies of the group members are not likely to occur simultaneously as in Watabe's (1992) experiment. The following studies were designed to provide more systematic evidence concerning the possibility of voluntary adoption of the trigger strategy, or of the set of strategies that produces the trigger-type incentive structure at the supergame level. In Experiment 1, which was a more systematic replication of Watabe (1992), we examined whether subjects come to choose a set of strategies that produces the trigger-type payoff structure at the supergame level. In Experiment 2, we examined whether people prefer the trigger-type payoff structure over an N-person PD structure at the constituent game level by letting subjects choose between the two payoff structures instead of letting them choose among strategies.

Experiment 1

Subjects. One hundred and ninety-two students (in 48 4-person groups) of Hokkaido University were used as subjects. These subjects were recruited from a pool of about 650 students who had filled out application forms. The students in the subject pool all filled out an eight-item trust scale developed by Yamagishi (1986, 1988a, 1988b) with their application forms. Most subjects participated in the experiment at least a couple of weeks after they filled out the application form and the trust scale.

Design. The design involved two factorially crossed between-subjects factors; Type of Choices (the behavior choice condition, the strategy choice condition, and the iterated supergames condition) and Trust (high and low). Subjects were classified into low- and high-trusters based on their scores of the trust scale. Approximately the middle 20% of the distribution of the trust scores in the subject pool was not used for the experiment. In the behavior choice condition, subjects' choice was between C (cooperation) and D (defection) at each trial; this was a simple iterated social dilemma situation commonly used in many social dilemma experiments. In the strategy choice condition, subjects were asked to choose a strategy (i.e., a set of conditions to be used for the C-D choices in the supergame), not an action (between C and D) per se. They could change their strategies anytime they wanted during the 600 trials in the experiment. In the iterated supergame condition, subjects chose their strategies as in the strategy choice condition. The 600 trials were, however, divided into 40 "supergames" each consisting of 15 trials, and subjects could change their strategies only between supergames. This last condition was similar to the condition used in Watabe's (1992) experiment, in that the choices of strategies by group members occurred simultaneously.

Procedure. The experiment was run in 4-person groups. Prompts and feedbacks were displayed on a microcomputer (IBM/PS2-Model 30) located on a desk in front of the subject, and the subject's decisions were entered through the computer's keyboard. Subjects' computers were connected to a host computer (IBM/PS2-Model 80), and the subjects' responses were sent to and stored there. As subjects arrived at the laboratory, they were individually escorted to small isolation rooms. They could not meet other subjects or talk to each other before, during, or after the experiment. An instruction booklet was given to the subject as he or she was escorted to an isolation room. The experimenter visited subjects' rooms several times while they were reading the instructions, and questions about the instructions were individually answered in the subject's room. However, doors of the subjects' rooms were not completely closed while the experimenter visited subjects' rooms so that other subjects could overhear the voice (not the content) of the conversation between the experimenter and other subjects. This was to convince subjects that there were in fact other subjects and that they were not interacting with the computer. After all four subjects finished reading instructions and all questions were answered, the experiment was started. When all trials were over, they were asked to fill out a post-experimental questionnaire. Then, they were paid the amount they had earned in the experiment (mostly between 500 yen and 1,500 yen), and individually released. Cares were taken to prevent subjects to meet outside the laboratory after they were released.

Incentive structure of the constituent game. Each constituent game in this experiment was a 4-person prisoner's dilemma. That is, in each trial subjects decided whether or not to contribute one yen (about 0.8 cents) for the group. Their contributions were tripled in value and evenly allocated to the other three members of the group. When all four contributed, each thus received three yen; when no one contributed, each kept their original one yen.

The strategies. Subjects in the strategy choice and the iterated supergames conditions selected one of the following five strategies. C0: the strategy of unconditional cooperation. D0: the strategy of unconditional defection. C1, C2, and C3: conditional cooperation strategies; the subject cooperates if at least one (C1), two (C2), or three (C3) other member(s) cooperated in the previous trial. In addition, two one-time-only strategies, OTO-C (one-time-only cooperation strategy) and OTO-D (one-time-only defection strategy), were used in the strategy choice condition. The adoption of these strategies affected the choice (between C and D) of the current trial only; in the next trial, the subject resumed the strategy he or she used in the previous trial. One unique feature of this experiment was that unless the subject decided to change his or her choice (of actions in the behavior choice condition or of strategies in the other two conditions), his or her choice in the immediately preceding trial was automatically continued in the new trial. Each trial lasted only three seconds.

Screen display. During the experiment, all relevant information was graphically shown on the display screen of a microcomputer. In all conditions, the feedback information included the subject's own choice (C or D), how many cooperated among the four members including the subject him or herself, the amount of benefit given by the other three subjects, the amount of total benefit the subject received in the previous trials. These pieces of information were graphically displayed on a line, which scrolled as trials went on up to 15 lines. That is, subjects could see at a glance the above information for the past 15 trials. The display was designed in such a way that subjects could easily grasp changes over repeated trials. In addition, subjects in the iterated supergame condition were provided, between supergames, summary information of the previous supergame (the total amount of benefit, the strategy each of the other three subjects adopted, the average number of cooperators, the average benefit the subject was given by the other three).

Each trial lasted three seconds. With the start of a new trial, the display scrolled, adding information of the immediately preceding trial. Subjects in the behavior choice condition could change their choices of C or D by pressing a key corresponding to their new choice. Unless the subject pressed a key during the three second, it was assumed that he or she did not want to change his or her choice. Similarly, subjects in the strategy choice condition could change their strategy (from the aforementioned seven strategies) in each trial. And, as in the behavior choice condition, unless a subject indicated his or her new strategy by pressing a corresponding key, it was assumed that he or she did not want to change his or her strategy. When OTO-C or OTO-D was selected, the subject cooperated or defected in that trial, but resumed to the previous choice in the next trial. Subjects in the iterated supergames condition, on the other hand, could not change their strategies in each trial. They could select their strategies from the five strategies (C0, C1, C2, C3, and D0) only before a new supergame was started. Once a supergame was started, they could only watch the screen scrolled every three seconds until the supergame finished after 15 trials.

Results

In the following analysis, 600 trials and 40 supergames (in the iterated supergame condition) were aggregated into five trial blocks (120 trials and eight supergames per trial block). Unless otherwise mentioned, groups rather than individuals were used as the unit of analysis due to the interdependent nature of the subjects' responses within the group.

Cooperation rate. The average overall cooperation rate was 41.3% in the behavior choice condition, 33.1% in the strategy choice condition, and 48.9% in the iterated supergame condition. In the Type of Choice x Trust x Trial Block ANOVA, the main effect of Type of Choices was significant, $F(2, 42) = 3.37$, $p < .05$. The main effect of Trial Block was also significant, $F(4, 168) = 32.24$, $p < .01$. The average of cooperation rate declined over time from 54.9% in the first trial block, to 43.4% in the second trial block, 38.9% in the third trial block, 35.7% in the fourth trial block, and finally to 32.7% in the fifth trial block. The main effect of Trust was significant, too, $F(1, 42) = 6.07$, $p < .05$. The average cooperation rate was 35.0% among low-trusters and 47.2% among high-trusts, replicating the difference between the two observed in other studies using the same trust scale (Yamagishi, 1986, 1988a, 1988b). Finally, the Trust X Trial Block interaction was significant, $F(4, 168) = 2.78$, $p < .05$; the difference between high-trusters and low-trusters diminished over time, replicating the finding of Sato (1988). None of the other interaction effects was significant.

Frequency of the selected strategies. We analyzed the average frequency of each strategy (excluding OTO-C and OTO-D) in each trial block using Type of Choice x Trust x Trial Block ANOVAs. Since strategies were selected only in the strategy choice and the iterated supergame conditions, the analysis included only the two conditions. The values reported below are the average numbers of subjects in the group of four who adopted the strategy per trial. The overall frequencies of lenient strategies, C0 (0.55), C1 (0.68), were generally lower than more conservative strategies, C2 (0.86), C3 (0.82), and D0 (0.90).

C0: The significant effects were the main effect of Trust, $F(1, 28) = 3.56$, $p < .05$, the main effect of Trial Block, $F(4, 112) = 9.17$, $p < .01$, and Trust x Trial Block interaction, $F(4, 112) = 3.18$, $p < .05$. High-trusters (0.70) adopted the unconditional cooperation more often than low trusters (0.40). The frequency of this strategy declined over time, and the decline was greater among high-trusters than among low-trusters. The unconditional defection strategy was adopted by 0.55 subjects per group. In addition, the average of 0.18 subjects in the strategy choice condition adopted OTO-C strategy.[2]

D0: No effect was significant.[3]

CC1: No effect was significant.

CC2: The only significant effect was the main effect of Trial Block, $F(4, 112) = 3.16$, $p <$ .05; the frequency of this strategy increased from 0.84 in the first block to 1.03 in the last block.

CC3: The only significant effect was the main effect of Trial Block, $F(4, 112) = 2.13$, $p <$ .05; the frequency of this strategy increased from 0.69 in the first block to 0.85 in the last block.

Decomposition of cooperative choices. The overall cooperation was higher in the iterated supergame condition (48.9%) than in the strategy choice condition (33.1%). The result of the above analysis shows that this difference cannot be attributed to the difference in the frequencies of strategies selected in the two conditions. Furthermore, the difference in the cooperation rate between the two conditions was not due to the difference in the frequency of the strategy of unconditional cooperation. The relative frequency of the strategy of unconditional cooperation was about 16% in both conditions. There was a slight and insignificant difference in the relative frequency of the strategy of unconditional defection; about 28% in the strategy choice condition and 23% in the iterated supergame condition. This difference in the relative frequency of the strategy of unconditional defection alone, however, cannot explain the difference in the cooperation rate. Most of the difference in the cooperation rate came from the proportion of cooperation accompanied by the strategies of conditional cooperation in the two conditions. Only 30% of subjects who adopted a strategy of conditional cooperation (C1, C2, or C3) cooperated in the strategy choice condition, whereas 54% of the conditional cooperators did cooperate in the iterated supergame condition. That is, the set of strategies of conditional cooperation adopted by subjects in the iterated supergame condition was more conductive to cooperative choices than the set adopted in the strategy choice condition.

Was the trigger-type payoff structure created at the supergame level? It was shown above that the higher overall cooperation rate in the iterated supergame condition than in the strategy choice condition came mainly from the higher cooperation ratio among conditional cooperators in the first condition than in the second condition. Does it mean that the trigger-type payoff structure was created more often in the iterated supergame condition than in the strategy choice condition? In order to answer this question, we analyzed the size of the "multiplier effect" in the two conditions. The trigger-type incentive structure implies that one member's change in the strategy affects other member's choices to a large degree. Thus, how much change in the overall cooperation rate one member's unilateral change in his or her strategy is induced (the "multiplier effect") can be used as an indicator of the "triggerness" of the payoff structure at the strategy choice level. In this analysis, the multiplier effect (how many others would alter their choices as a result of one member's unilateral change in his or her strategy) was used as the dependent variable. First, each subject's strategy at each trial was changed to the strategy of unconditional defection when his or her choice there was C, or to the strategy of unconditional cooperation when his or her choice was D. Then, we ran a simulation with the set of strategies (the subject's unconditional C or D, and the strategies of the other three subjects in that trial) unchanged for the next four trials. How many others changed their choices after the four trials would indicate the multiplier effect of that subject's action in the set of strategies existed in that particular trial. The overall average of the multiplier effect was 0.69; one subject's change would not have made much difference in the sets of strategies adopted by the subjects in this experiment. In addition, no effect was significant in the Choice Type x Trust x Trial Block ANOVA. The difference between the two conditions cannot be attributed to the degree to which the trigger-type payoff structure was created.

Effect of consistency. The above results suggested that the difference in the overall cooperation rate in the strategy choice and the iterated supergame conditions cannot be attributed to differences in the nature of the adopted strategies (and their combinations). The only remaining explanation for the difference between the two conditions is the fact that subjects' strategies did not change within a supergame in the iterated supergame condition. In order to examine if the observed difference in the overall cooperation rate in the strategy choice and iterated supergame conditions would not have existed if subjects in the strategy choice conditions had had a chance to change their strategies only at every 15 trials, we conducted the following simulation. In this simulation, we treated the strategy choice condition as if it had been the iterated supergame condition. That is, subjects' strategies in the every 15th trial replaced their strategies during the following 14 trials. In addition, all strategies except D0 started each "supergame" with C in both conditions. The overall cooperation rate in this simulation was 0.53 in the strategy choice condition, and 0.60 in the iterated supergame condition. The difference was not significant. It was thus suggested that more frequent and uncoordinated changes in strategies in the strategy choice condition were mostly responsible for the lower cooperation rate in that condition.

Experiment 2

In the first experiment, we examined whether or not subjects voluntarily provide a set of strategies that produced a trigger-type payoff structure at the supergame level. The answer provided by the result of the experiment was generally negative; the set of strategies adopted by the subjects failed to produce a trigger-type payoff structure. A question remains; did subjects prefer a trigger-type payoff structure over a PD structure, but failed to produce it? Or, did subjects not prefer such a payoff structure? The second experiment was conducted to answer this question. In the second experiment, subjects chose between two types of payoff structures instead of choosing between strategies.

Subjects. One-hundred and thirty Hokkaido University students selected from a subject pool of about 800 students, recruited from various classes on campus, were used as subjects. Monetary rewards were emphasized when they were recruited.

Design. A 4 (hypothetical group membership) x 2 (hypothetical group size) x 2 (payoff structure) x 2 (stimulus presentation order) design was used. All factors except the last one were within-subjects factors; the only between-subjects factor was the stimulus presentation order.

Procedure. The experiment was conducted in groups of three to six. When less than three subjects showed up, confederates were called in to create the appearance of a three-person group. The experiment was divided into three sessions. The first and the second sessions were identical in procedure except the difference in the payoff structure involved (trigger-type payoff structure or N-person PD or NPD structure). Which payoff structure was used in the first session constituted the only between-subjects factor, the stimulus presentation order. The choice between the two payoff structures was made in the third session.

Each of the first and the second sessions started with explanations of the payoff structure involved in the session. Then, they were given a chance actually to play with the incentive structure involved. Subjects were each given 100 yen (about 80 cents), and asked to contribute the money for the group. When the NPD structure was involved, the contributed money was tripled and evenly distributed to all group members. When the trigger-type payoff structure (TTPS) was involved, each member received 300 yen if all members contributed 100 yen each. Feedback of the result, however, was not provided until the end of the experiment (after the third session). The main purpose of this process was to have subjects experience the payoff structure involved in the following vignette.

After experiencing the payoff structure involved by actually making a decision themselves, subjects were given a vignette. The vignette contained eight scenarios representing the eight combinations of two within-subjects factors; subjects were asked to imagine that they were in a 5-person or a 100-person group consisting of (1) ordinary people, (2) college students, (3) *yakuza* or gangsters, or (4) housewives. For each combination of the two factors, they were asked whether they would contribute 10,000 yen (about $80) when the group involved the same payoff structure as they had experienced. For example, subjects were asked if they would contribute 10,000 yen if they were in a group of 100 gangsters. In addition to the hypothetical decision makings as mentioned above, subjects were asked, for each combination, to estimate the number of cooperators, and how many of the members did not understand the situation, were more interested in competition than in earning as much money as possible, and were not rational (not interested in earning money). Subjects responded to these questions for the eight combinations. One half of the subjects played in the first session a TTPS game and then responded to these questions involving TTPS. Then, in the second session, they were given a chance to play an NPD game and then responded to the above questions involving NPD. The other half of the subjects played and responded to NPD in the first session, and again played and responded to TTPS in the second session.

Finally, in the third session, they were asked which payoff structure, TTPS or NPD, they preferred if they were to make a decision of whether or not to contribute 10,000 yen in a 5-person or 100-person group of ordinary people.[4] In addition, subjects were asked if they would contribute 10,000 yen in the two types of payoff structures.

Results

Actual decision. Subjects actually played each of the TTPS and NPD games involving real money. The cooperation rates in the TTPS and NPD conditions were 77.42% and 67.74%. The difference was not significant.

Choice of payoff structures. The central dependent variable in this experiment was the preference for the payoff structure. Majority (83.8%, 109 subjects) of the subjects preferred the ordinary n-person PD structure (NPD) rather than the trigger-type structure (TTPS).[5] The proportions were significantly greater than 50%, binomial test, $p < .01$.

Decisions in hypothetical groups and choice of structures. Next, we examined how subjects' decisions in the hypothetical groups were related to their choice of structures. During the first and the second sessions, subjects provided a total of 16 decisions; 4 (hypothetical membership) x 2 (size) x 2 (payoff structure) = 16. In addition, they answered four estimation questions (see above) for each hypothetical group. In total, each subject answered a total of 80 questions (16 decisions and 16 x 4 = 64 estimation questions) during the first and the second sessions. These questions were factor analyzed, yielding six factors. Then, the choice of the strategy was dummy coded and regressed on these six factors. In this regression analysis the following three factors were found to be strongly related to the choice of strategies. (Because of the violation of the assumptions for the ordinary regression analysis, no statistical testing was conducted in this analysis. (1) The "trigger factor" consisting of decisions and estimations of cooperators involving the TTPS situation. (2) The "gangsters factor" consisting of decisions and estimations of cooperators in the gangsters' group, including both payoff structures. Finally, (3) the "non-rational factor" consisting of estimations of the "dummies" and "non-rational" members. Three binary variables were then created based on the sign of the factor scores of these factors, and the effect of these three variables on the choice of the strategy were tested with a multi-variate chi-square analysis (CATMOD in SAS). The only factor significant in this analysis was the "trigger factor," $X^2(1) = 4.13$, $p < .05$. Subjects who contributed in the hypothetical trigger-type payoff groups and estimated a large proportion of cooperators in such groups preferred the trigger-type payoff structure (TTPS) over the ordinary NPD structure.

Actual decisions and the choice of payoff structures. There was no significant relationship between either of their actual decisions and their choice of payoff structures.

Discussion

The results of the two experiments were clear and consistent. Majority of the subjects in these experiment did not prefer the trigger-type payoff structure over NPD payoff structure at the constituent game level (Experiment 2), nor did they adopt the set of strategies that would transform an N-person PD of the constituent game to the trigger-type payoff structure at the supergame level (Experiment 1). On the other hand, these findings are inconsistent with the findings of the aforementioned study by Watabe (1992). This inconsistency may have been produced by differences in the experimental settings. Watabe's (1992) experiment lasted over eleven days. Subjects had enough time to examine strategies of other members and think about implications of their own strategies. In contrast, decision periods went on very fast in Experiment 1, and subjects did not have enough time to think through the implications of their strategies. To think about implications of strategies carefully may be important for the emergence of the trigger-type payoff structure at the supergame level.

There is another possible explanation for the inconsistency, however, which seems to be more viable. That is, the trigger-type payoff structure may be easier to produce without communication in 10-person groups than in 4-person groups. The multiplier effect mentioned earlier can be represented by the horizontal distance between a critical mass and the lower equilibrium (cf., Granovetter, 1978; Schelling, 1978). When there are at least m people who are willing to cooperate insofar as there are m-1 or more other cooperators, these people can maintain cooperation among themselves. If one additional defector in the group triggers an avalanche of defections among these members, m is called the critical mass. The difference between m and the number of cooperators after the avalanche of defections indicates how much change in the overall cooperation in the group can be produced by a single member's triggering defection. We conducted a simulation to see if group size would affect the size of this multiplier effect. In this simulation, we let each simulated player in the group adopt a strategy of conditional cooperation. The condition for cooperation (the minimum number of other cooperators for a cooperative choice) for each player was randomly distributed from zero (unconditional cooperation) to the group size N (unconditional defection). The number of replications for each condition was 1,000. When the group size was four, the average multiplier effect (m-1 minus the lower equilibrium) was 0.18.

That is, the ratio of this multiplier effect to the group size (let us call this the multiplier ratio) was $0.18/4 = .05$. When the group size was ten, the multiplier ratio was 0.12. When the group size was 100, it was 0.25. Thus, it was shown that even when the distribution of the condition for cooperation was uniform, the multiplier ratio increases as does group size. The effect of group size on the multiplier ratio was even stronger when the distribution of the condition for cooperation was a normal distribution with the mean of $n/2$ and the standard deviation of $n/5$. The multiplier ratio was 0.07 in the 4-player group, 0.22 in the 10-player group, and 0.47 in the 100-player group. When the conditions for cooperation are congregated rather than evenly distribution as in Experiment 1 or in Watabe's (1992), even random distribution of the condition among group members may often produce the trigger-strategy or trigger-like-strategies at the supergame level. Although group members may not be likely to prefer the trigger-type incentive structure over NPD structure at the constituent game, a trigger-like-strategy may yet be produced in large groups as a consequence of uncoordinated selections of conditional cooperation strategies. The condition for facilitating the production of a trigger-like-strategy is that members select similar conditions for cooperation. This was actually what happened in Watabe's (1992) experiment in which subjects became to adopt similar conditions for cooperation over repeated supergames.

Footnotes

1   Hokkaido University, Dept. of Behavioral Sciences, Sapporo, Japan

2   We performed the same ANOVA using the sum of C0 and OTO-C as the dependent variable. The only change from the reported significant effects was that the effect of Trust became marginal ($p < .07$) in this analysis.

3   An average of 0.22 subjects in the strategy choice condition adopted OTO-D. We performed the same ANOVA using the sum of D0 and OTO-D as the dependent variable. No effect was significant, as reported, except the main effect of Trial Block ($p < .05$).

4   All subjects answered the question concerning the preference for the payoff structures involving a 100-person group. However, only 60 of the 130 subjects answered the question when a 5-person group was involved. This was because the question concerning a 5-person group was added in hindsight in the middle of the experiment. Data involving a 5-person group, thus, will be footnoted when referenced.

5   When the hypothetical group size was five, the proportion of NPD choices was slightly lower, 26.7% (44 of the 60 subjects who responded to this question).

References

Axelrod, R. (1984). *The evolution of cooperation*. New York: Basic Books.

Dawes, R.M. (1980). Social dilemmas. *Annual Review of Psychology, 31,* 169-93.

Friedman, J.W. (1986). *Game theory with applications to economics*. New York: Oxford University Press.

Granovetter, M. (1978). Threshold models of collective behavior. *American Journal of Sociology, 83,* 1420-1443.

Oskamp, S. (1971). Effects of programmed strategies on cooperation in the prisoner's dilemma and other mixed motive games. *Journal of Conflict Resolution, 15,* 225-229.

Sato, K. -(1989). Trust and group size in a social dilemma. *Japanese Psychological Research, 30,* 88-93.

Schelling, T.C. (1978). *Micromotives and macrobehavior*. New York: W.W. Norton.

Taylor, M. (1976). *Anarchy and cooperation*. New York: Wiley.

Taylor, M. (1982). *Community, anarchy and liberty*. New York: Cambridge University Press.

van de Kragt, A.J.C., Orbell, J.M., & Dawes, R.M. (1983). The minimal contributing set as a solution to public goods problems. *American Political Science Review, 77,* 112-122.

Watabe, M. (1992). Choice of strategies in social dilemma supergames. *Japanese Journal of Experimental Social Psychology, 32,* 171-182. (In Japanese)

Yamagishi, T. (1986). The provision of a sanctioning system as a public good. *Journal of Personality and Social Psychology, 51*, 110-16.

Yamagishi, T. (1988a). The provision of a sanctioning system in the United States and Japan. *Social Psychology Quarterly, 51*, 264-270.

Yamagishi, T. (1988b). Seriousness of social dilemmas and the provision of a sanctioning system. *Social Psychology Quarterly, 51*, 32-42.

Yamagishi, T. (1989). Unintentional effects in solution of social dilemmas. *Sociological Theory and Methods, 5*, 21-37. (In Japanese)

Acknowledgement

The research reported in this chapter was supported by a Ministry of Education Scientific Research Grant to T. Yamagishi and H. Shinotsuka. The experiments reported in this chapter were conducted jointly with Kyoko Ito (Experiment 1) and Kyoko Yoshikawa (Experiment 2) as a part of their Bachelor's Thesis projects. We would like to thank their contributions to our research project.

Social dilemmas exist in space

Andrzej Nowak[1], Bibb Latane[2], and Maciej Lewenstein[3]

Abstract

Proper representation of many kinds of social dilemmas requires the consideration of social space. Social interdependence is mainly limited to other people located in a local neighborhood. The concept of social space may be more fruitfull in some instances than the network description. Several geometries that may be usefull describing the social space are discussed: Euclidean, City Block, Fractal, One-dimensional, Railroad, Random, Probabilistic, and Multiple spaces metric. The outcomes of the conformity game for several types of the geometries of the social space are discussed.

Social dilemmas exist in social space, very much as do the societies that the dilemmas concern. The nature of this space should be taken into consideration when analyzing a social dilemma, since both the nature of the dilemma and social processes in the groups affected by the dilemma are dependent on the properties of the social space. In this chapter, we will use computer simulations to show some effects of space on social processes and propose some geometries relevant to representing social space. In the next chapter, the effects of the geometry of social space in an experimental setting with human subjects will be presented.

Importance of space for social dilemmas

To appreciate the basic importance of space for social dilemmas, let us consider in some detail a variation of a classic dilemma of smog. Let us imagine a spread out town consisting of small houses. Each house may be heated by coal or by electricity. The nature of the dilemma is simple; coal is cheaper but produces repulsive smoke, electricity is much more expensive, but clean. The smoke from a single house is not very upsetting, but as more people decide to use coal, the air becomes more and more unbearable. The nature of the dilemma appears very simple indeed: for each individual separately it is preferable to use coal, but for the group it is better to use electricity.

If we look at this situation in somewhat greater detail, the nature of the interdependencies is not so simple. Clearly the smoke of each house does not affect everyone in the same way. Neighbors are affected most (unless the chimneys are very high). This effect of the choice of a single individual decreases with distance. This situation is illustrated in Figure 1.

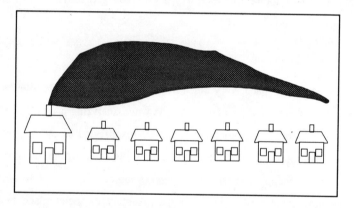

Figure 1:   Amount of smoke decreases with distance

The simple observation that the effect of people's choices depends on the distance presents a problem for classical approaches to social dilemmas. In both theoretical and empirical studies concerning social dilemmas, one of the crucial factors affecting the nature of the dilemma and influencing human choices in it is the size of the group. In the above example with smog, it is not clear what size group we should assume. Usually we assume that the group is composed of people who are mutually interdependent in their choices. If the interdependencies are the same for all group members and symmetrical, the situation is clear: starting from every person and listing all the group members that are interdependent with this person we get the same list: the whole group. In our smoke example, this is not the case.

The first difficulty comes from the graded nature of the interdependence relations between group members. The further apart in space are two individuals, the less the choices of one affect the other. So for each individual, as we draw circles of growing radius, we include within the circles others who are less and less dependent on his or her choice. The number of people affected by this choice depends on what degree of interdependence we consider meaningful. We can deal with this difficulty alone without using the concept of space. Either we can assume an arbitrary cut-off point and dichotomize the varied strength of the relationships, or we can represent the graded nature of group membership with the concepts of fuzzy sets theory (see Zadeh, 1965).

The second difficulty has to do with defining who belongs to the group of interdependent individuals. It is much harder to solve without the concept of space. Even if we establish who should be included as dependent on a given person, for each group member we get a different set of persons (see Figure 2).

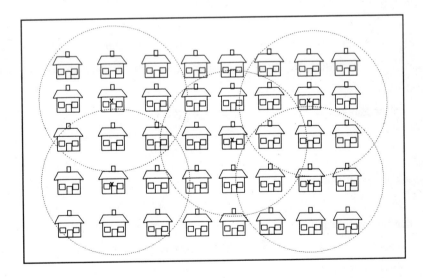

Figure 2:   Nearest neighbors are encircled as dependent on persons located centrally

If we start from a person and enlist in the first step everybody affected by this person's decisions in the second step we include everybody who is affected by the person from the first list and so on, in a finite (and usually small) number of steps we will include everybody in town. This estimate of group size clearly does not have to correspond to the number of persons affected by a single individual and the number of persons that are considered by this individual when making choices. It is clear in the extreme example where an individual affects only four closest neighbors. By including people that are dependent on the neighbors and by repeating this procedure, we can enlist the whole group.

Not only interdependency but also the spread of information is usually affected by space. In the smog example described below, it may be difficult or virtually impossible to remember all the individual choices of everybody in town. Everybody can easily see whether their neighbor's chimney smokes or not. It is almost as easy to see their second row neighbors but more and more difficult as the distance grows. Unless some town statistics are available, each individual knows mostly of her or

his neighborhood. In social dilemma theory we usually assume that everybody has the same knowledge of the facts and other people's behavior. In real situations, it is usually not the case. People know best what is going on in their immediate vicinity. It is much more likely that I know my neighbors choices than those of people on the other side of town.

People can influence each other's behavior. Whether the influence comes about by sharing information or by more direct forms of persuasion, those close in space are usually more easily influenced. When people coordinate their behavior in a social dilemma, it is easier to coordinate within a local neighborhood then in the whole large group.

The concept of social space

The idea that human interactions are affected by physical space has been put forward in a number of empirical studies. Bossard (1932) has shown on the basis of the analysis of marriage records that the probability that two persons will marry depends on the distance between their home locations. Most of the studies conducted in this area concern a gravity model of social interaction. In analogy to Newton's gravity theory, it is assumed that the amount of interaction between two places (in empirical research, often cities) is directly proportional to the product of the populations of the two cities, and inversely related to the square of the distance between the two cities. Most of the studies have been able to show the inverse relationship with distance (Steward, 1941), but the exponent has not always been two (see Bradford & Kent, 1990). The function linking distance with the amount of interaction is called *the distance decay function* and varies with such factors as transport technology. Most of the studies conducted in the tradition of the gravity model have concerned migration, but this model has also been applied to such data as attendance at universities (Tinto, 1973), telephone communication, or visiting shopping centers (Zipf, 1949; see also Olsson, 1965).

The two dimensional representation of social space used so far in our examples was obviously oversimplified. Although the physical distances are very important components of social space they in no way exhaust the list of factors deciding about the distances in social space. In reality, the distribution of smoke depends not only on distance but also on the prevailing direction of the wind, differences in elevation, which side of the building the windows are facing and so on.

If we consider dilemmas other than our example of smoke, many other factors in addition to physical distance shape the geometry of social space. In cities, towns, and villages, there are walls and fences. Cities may be divided by a river, where the other bank, although physically close, may be difficult to access. There are streets where we can go, and buildings that we have to go around. These are some physical factors determining why the space affecting people is not simply a two dimensional Euclidean space.

There are some social factors as well. Economic racial or cultural segregation may divide the city by social factors rather than physical ones. Some areas are easily accessed by public transportation, some are difficult to access. Places located in the vicinity of major communication routes seem closer than places away from such routes. In fact, human subjective estimates of the distance between two places in a city are strongly influenced by the number of turnings that one has to traverse to move from one place to the other (Hillier & Hanson, 1984). Some areas of the city are more socially central (integrated) than others because they are more densely connected with the rest of the city. Different locations may also vary with respect to their integration with the local neighborhood.

Such an understanding of the distances allows to accurately predict on the basis of a map of the city, the flow of both pedestrians and vehicles on various streets, as well as locations of business and residential neighborhoods (Penn & Dalton, 1993).

Summarizing, the concept of social space lies somewhere between the physical space and the psychological space as understood by Lewin (1951).

Geometries for social space

Traditionally, the social distances between people are characterized as social networks and analyzed by graph theory. This approach leads to interesting predictions concerning behavior in social dilemmas. Social networks are very useful for representing relations between people, especially in small groups.

For many situations, representation in the form of a social space may be more useful. We characterize the relation of a given person to other group members by specifying coordinates of the person's locations in space. Knowing the positions of others in this space, we can calculate the distances between all group members. It makes sense to talk about social space instead of social networks when we can adequately approximate the relation between group members by assigning to them positions in some space. In such a space, knowing the relationship to some other objects and the metric of the space, we can infer relations to all the other objects in the space. This presents at least a negative criterion for using spatial representation: when the relations with all objects are independent it makes no sense to build a spatial representation of these relations.

One advantage of the spatial approach over the network approach is clear: to characterize as a network all the relations between people in an N-person group we need to specify N^2 relations, which for larger groups may become cumbersome or technically impossible. Using a spatial representation, we need only N spatial locations to specify all the relations between group members. This is useful not only in the coding of the data, but may become especially attractive during the data collection. There is a strong relationship between properties of social space and the dynamics of social processes (Lewenstein, Nowak Latane, 1992). Thus if we can use a spatial representation, then we can predict the dynamics of social processes from the properties of this social space .

The considerations in the previous section have shown first, that the geometry of the space lived by humans is much more complex than the simple two dimensional matrix used in our simulations and, and second that social space is not simply equivalent to physical space. On the other hand, unlike Lewin's concept of a psychological space, physical distance is a strong component constituting the social space. Spaces can be characterized by a topology (which describes its very general properties) and a metric (which defines distances in the space). Although, in reality, the geometry of social space is probably very complex, we can use several simplified models to represent the global properties of different kinds of social space.

Euclidean space. The most obvious geometry for human interaction is a two dimensional Euclidean space which approximates local areas of the surface of the Earth. One could doubt, if in modern times with telephone communications, easy airline connections, high social mobility physical distance still is an important predictor of patterns of social interactions. Recently (Latane at al., 1993) have shown that the probability that two persons will discuss matters important to them decreases with the square of the distance between their home locations. This result was obtained in both US and China and replicated in Poland (Kapusciarek, Nowak 1993).

Humans do not really live on the two flat dimensional surface, the Earth is round so the space could be more adequately represented as a sphere. The social space in apartment buildings is three-dimensional where people have neighbors not only to the north, east, south and west but also above and below.

City block metric. In a city, the distance to travel from one place to another is not equal to the aerial, pigeon's flight, distance between the two places. The distance a human has to travel is the sum of the distances traversed by streets and avenues. The City Block metric mimics this property by computing the distance between two points as the sum of the differences on all the axis spanning the space. In a well laid out city like New York, with North- South avenues and East-West streets, the East-West distance between any two city locations needs to be added the North-South distance.

Fractal dimension. In some cases (like a residential neighborhood), we can reasonably assume equal density of population. In reality, especially at larger scales, the population density is clearly uneven. There are houses where several people live close to each other. Those are organized into small residential neighborhood, those in turn into cities, which, in turn, are organized into urban agglomerations. Such a distribution has property of being self-similar. On different scales of magnification, the structure looks equivalent: with higher units resembling the lower units they are composed of.

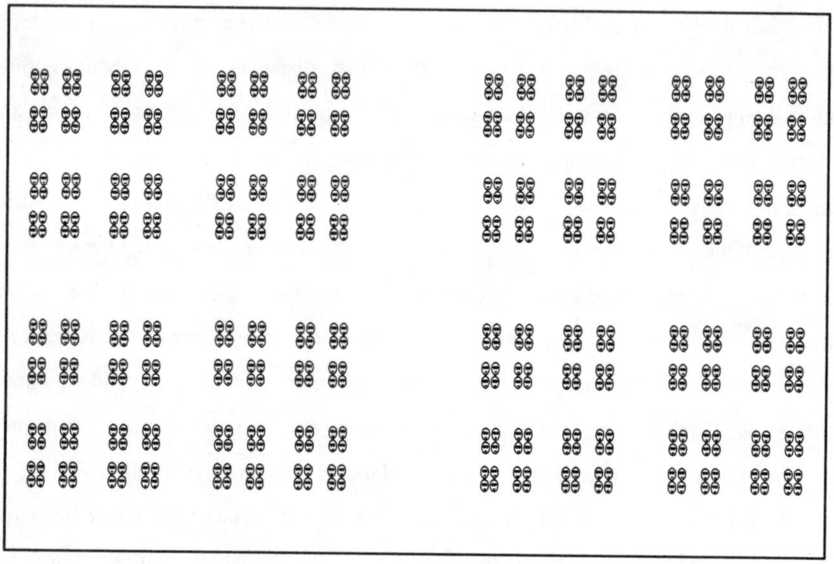

Figure 3:   Fractal structure of human settlements.

Such a structure may be characterized as having fractal dimension. (Mandelbrot, 1982, Peitgen Jurgens, & Souppe, 1992).

The dimension of such a social configuration in the two dimensional space would be between one and two, where the exact value of the dimension would depend on the way such a distribution of habitats is structured, especially what is a proportion of inhabited to uninhabited space on each level of organization.

Fully connected models. In some, especially smaller groups everybody may interact with everybody else with approximately equal frequency. We can represent such a group as a network where everybody is connected to everybody by connections of equal strength. In a way, such structure may be described as non-spacial, since all the distances are equal.

One-dimensional space. In rural settlements, especially in less developed countries or historical times, the human settlements often developed along a river or a road. Such settlements may be adequately described by one dimensional space. In a one dimensional space the passage of messages is much more difficult than in a higher dimensional space, since their is only one path between any two places. It is sufficient that one place in such a line stops transmitting messages for the flow of information to stop.

Hierarchical geometry. Often the social space may depend on other than physical distance dimensions, especially when we analyze groups composed of people located close together in physical space. One of the social structures of most interest to social psychologists are organization, which can be represented as hierarchies of overlapping groups (see Figure 4).

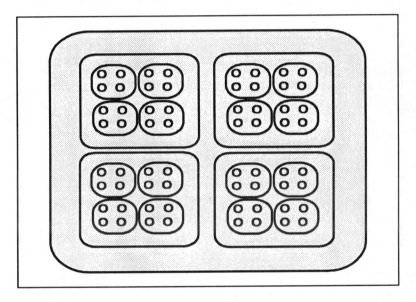

Figure 4: Hierarchical geometry.

The distance between two individuals is a decreasing function of the lowest hierarchy level in which they both belong to the same group. If they both belong to the same lowest subgroup the distance between them is minimal, for example, 1. If a group common to both of them is one level higher, the distance is larger, for example, 2, and so on. Such a geometry corresponds to an organizational structure where people working in the same subgroup are nearest to each other, the people working in the same division are relatively close, the people in the same organization are further apart, and the people working in the same group of organizations (like state employees) are still further apart.

Railroad metric. People travelling larger distances rarely go directly. Instead they usually go to a communication center (like a railroad station or airport) and then connect to another communication center before going to their final destination. In fact, the distance they have to travel is the sum for the distances to the first and from the second communication center plus the distance between those centers (see Figure 5).

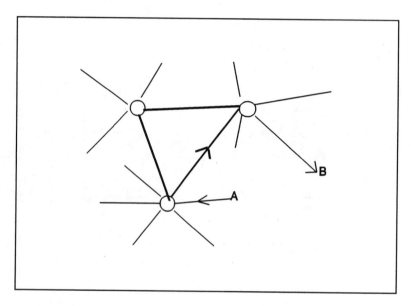

Figure 5:   Railroad metric

The distance between the centers or "hubs" may be additionally weighted to represent the fact that it is usually much more quickly travelled. In such a metric, it may be quicker to go from New York to Los Angeles on opposite coasts, than from Kill Devil Hills to Chapel Hill , North Carolina.

Probabilistic space. In real world it often may not be possible to find a single metric that can adequately describe the distances between people. For example, a different distance separates two persons if they have to drive to see each other than if they can call each other on the telephone.

Such a social space may be represented as a probabilistic space, where, with a given probability, the distance is computed using one metric, with another using a different metric and so on. Figure 6 shows schematically an Euclidean space of human habitats with some links of telephone connections.

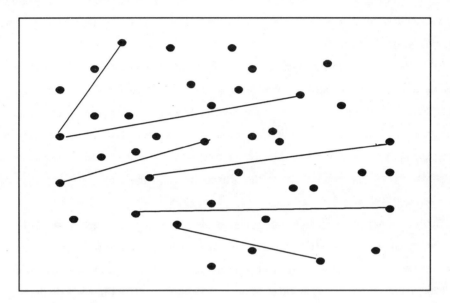

Figure 6: *Probabilistic space*

Random geometry. There may be no order in social relations between people. The structure of communications between people may change in a disordered way, as for example in a milling crowd. Such structure of relations may be described as random.

Multiple spaces metric. Humans are mobile. They change locations even in the course of the day. Different geometries may represent the work environment (for example, hierarchical), the home environment (for example, fractal), and a different one the social entertainment environment (for example, city block).

Then distances between two persons should equal to be some weighted function of the distance in all the relevant spaces.

The conformity game

It is often beneficial and in some cases vital (in the direct meaning) for a person to be in the majority. In many historic wars, one of the critical skills for survival was the ability to tell which would be the winning side. Today, the same skill seems crucial for the careers of many politicians. Often the truth is socially decided upon by voting. Avoiding being in the minority is a good strategy for safety in most social situations.

The idea that the spread of a social group in space is crucial to the evolution of social processes has been demonstrated in computer simulations of the theory of dynamic social impact (Nowak, Szamrej & Latane, 1990). The computer simulations were based on well tested theory of social impact (Latane, 1981). It has been shown that for a variety of situations the magnitude of impact a group exerts on a person is directly proportional to the strength and number of people in the group and inversely proportional to the distance between the group and the target person (Latane & Wolf, 1981).

In most of our computer simulations, the euclidean geometry was used, where social groups were represented as a square grids, with each person occupying one cell of the grid. Each person has one of two possible opinions (such as pro and con or for a democrat vs. republican). Each individual opinion is represented as either an open or a closed face (see Figure 7). In the beginning of simulations, opinion is assigned at random to people.

In the following picture, we can see the randomly intermixed 60 percent majority (open faces) and 40 percent minority (closed faces). What is not visible is that the individuals modelled in the simulations differ in strength. Some are more visible, articulate, have higher status, are more credible than are others. In the simulations, strength is represented as a value between 0 and 100, randomly assigned at the beginning of the simulations.

The rules of the simulation, originally were interpreted as a model of attitude change (Nowak, Szamrej, & Latane, 1990). For our purposes, the simulation may be described as a conformity game, where everybody wants to be in the majority with respect to the opinion held.

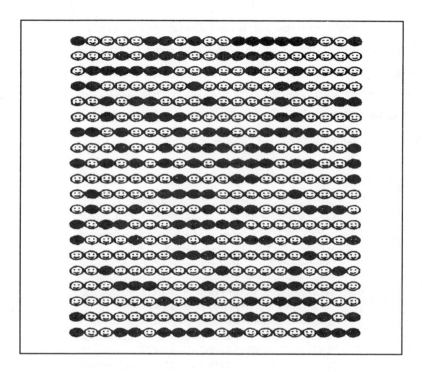

Figure 7: Random distribution of opinions at the start of a simulation

Everybody, however, exposed only to locally biased information, is not aware of opinion of everybody else in the group, but mostly of their closest neighbors, then their next row of neighbors and so on. The awareness of somebody else's opinion may be described as an inverse square function of distance $1/d^2$, where "d" denotes the distance from that person. The person is also aware of her or his own opinion.

After the initial opinions have been randomly assigned, one randomly selected person assesses on the basis of locally available information which opinion is more popular. This is achieved by summing up the availability of information for each opinion. If there is more evidence available for the popularity of ones own opinion, the person stays with that opinion. If, however, it looks like the other opinion may be more popular, the person switches opinion. In more technical terms, the sum of the individual impacts of the members of each opinion group is calculated as the square root of the sum of squares of strength of each person divided by their square distance. The opinion of the self is also added to the appropriate group. If such a sum of impacts is greater for the opposite opinion, the person adapts the opposite opinion. Otherwise the person stays with his or her current opinion. After the first person has had an opportunity to change her or his opinion, the second quasi-randomly selected person has a chance to change his or her opinion and so on until the simulation achieves equilibrium (i.e. nobody changes opinion anymore). The final equilibrium configuration is displayed in Figure 8.

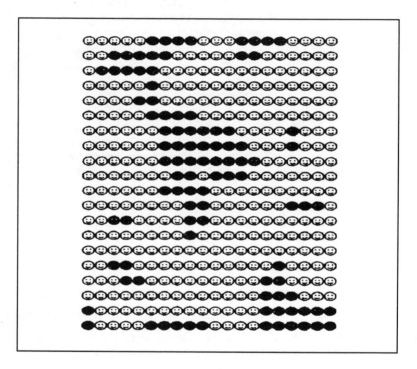

Figure 8:   Equilibrium state, after 6 simulations steps

Two important changes have taken place since the initial random distribution. First, the initial 40 percent minority has shrunk to 24 percent in the equilibrium solution. Second, the minority has clustered, i.e. grouped in coherent islands or pockets. This has happened only though opinion changes, without any person moving in space.

Clustering is possible only because the group exists in space. It is a direct consequence of the fact that the accessibility of information decreases with distance. In the beginning of a simulation, due to chance mechanism, there are more people holding the global minority opinion (closed faces) in some local areas of the simulation matrix than those holding majority opinion (open faces). In those local areas, judging by the information available to them, everybody thinks that the closed faces are in the majority. Everybody tries to be in the majority, but due to biased information in different areas, there are different judgments about which opinion is in the global majority. This phenomenon may be interpreted as the result of a sampling error, where the sampling of information depends on one's location in space. Because of clustering, the minority may survive, even if everybody wants to be in the majority.

To understand better the mechanism by which a minority may survive in stable clusters, let us examine in somewhat more detail the dynamics of the development and decay of a single cluster. Initially, several minority members are located close together. Early in the simulation, most of the people in this neighborhood switch to the global minority (but local majority) opinion. Within this neighborhood, a cluster develops. Outside of this cluster almost everybody switches to the majority opinion (unless there is another cluster). After the cluster has formed, those inside the cluster are sheltered from the influence of the majority, and only those on the border of the cluster are subjected to majority pressure.

To begin with, the cluster is not very regular due, among other factors, to the irregular shape of the random aggregation that underlaid its creation. Most of its borderline is convex, some may be concave. Those located on the convex edge are surrounded by more people of the opposite opinion than those who share the same opinion. The convex parts tend to erode, minority members are converted to majority position, while the concave parts tend to fill up, so, in general, the cluster gets more regular in shape. What happens then depends on individual differences. If there are no individual differences, the cluster will tend to shrink and finally vanish, unless one's own opinion is given a great deal of weight (see Figure 9).

Individual differences can stop the decay of the cluster. The border will involute till a minority member is reached that is strong enough to withstand minority pressure. The strong person will give support to weaker members. At some distance, the weaker minority members will again be converted to the majority viewpoint. A majority may "eat into" the cluster until again a stronger minority member is encountered. The border will then resemble an irregular wall, where stronger

A. Nowack, B. Latane, and M. Lewenstein

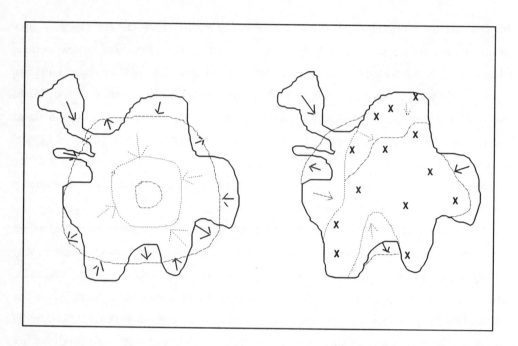

Figure 9: Decay of clusters in the presence of noise. On the left, cluster with no individual differences. vanishes. On he right, individuals high in strength (displayed by x) stop decay of the cluster.

group members located on the borders may stop the decay of the cluster. If there is no forces other than the influence of other group members, the achieved clustered configuration will be stable, i.e. there will be no more changes. If, however, we assume, that forces external to social pressures of other group members contribute to opinion changes, the resulting dynamics will be more complex. The external forces, which may be interpreted as such factors as: media influences, mood swings, new experiences etc. may be represented as random factors, so called *noise*. Such factors may cause one of the stronger persons yield to the pressure of the majority. This will cause a number of weaker persons to follow until a new wall is established. This mechanism, in the presence of some random factors disturbing weak equilibria, will cause a so called staircase dynamics, where periods of relative stability are interleaved with periods of rapid decay (for the analytic derivation of the staircase dynamics, see Lewenstein, Nowak & Latane 1992).

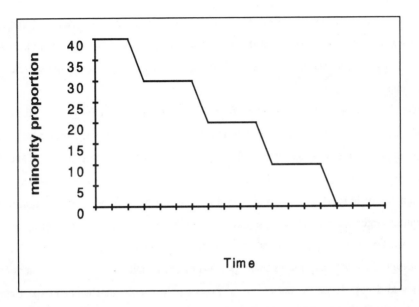

Figure 10. Staircase dynamics of the decay of the minority opinion in the presence of noise

With the geometric analysis conducted above, it is clear that the dynamics of clusters, and thus of the simulated conformity game, depend strongly on the properties of the spatial configuration that we can call geometry of social space. For example, the tendency for the minority to decay depends on the minority clusters having convex borders. If the geometry is such that smaller groups do not have convex borders, then there should be no tendency for minority clusters to decay. If, on the other hand, due to the properties of the space, in which they interact, minority can not cluster, then in most conditions it will decay.

In fact, in fully connected models the decay of minority can stop only due to self supportiveness. If we assume that the value of self-supportiveness is not to large and constant such a system will quickly unify. Even for high values of self supportiveness its relative contribution gets smaller with the growth of the size of the group, since the magnitude of the impact received from other group members is proportional to the size of the group. Even for a very high self-supportiveness its contribution is negligible for large groups.

Minority opinion may resist the majority pressure for all group sizes only if we assume that self-supportivness scales with the size of the group. This class of models, in the presence of noise will display a staircase dynamic; first the weakest members of the minority will switch to the majority viewpoint, this will constitute the first step, then somewhat stronger individuals, and so on till everybody is converted to the majority side. Between each steps the system will display very slow dynamics.

One-dimensional space has also specific properties in the conformity game described earlier. Everybody has two closest neighbors: one to the left and one to the right. Further neighbors may have some impact, but due to the drop in the impact proportional to some power of the distance, only next few neighbors have significant influence. Those located between two persons of the opposite opinion or in small clusters, have good reason to believe they are in the minority. Those located within larger clusters are well shielded from the contact with the opposite opinion. Those located on the border of larger clusters have no clue as to which opinion is in the majority since looking in each direction they see as many persons of each opinion. Minority clusters thus have no tendency to decay. From the above considerations it is obvious that we can expect clustering, but not polarization in a one-dimensional geometry.

It has been proven analytically (Lewenstein, Nowak & Latane 1992) that in a hierarchical geometry, minority clusters tend to fill up the geometrical clusters, and are very stable once formed. In some of the low level groups, due to the chance, there is more individuals holding minority Opinion. The probability that, in a given group, minority clusters will be formed, according the Central Limit theorem, is much lower than the probability of a majority cluster and depends on the initial proportion of the minority and the size of the group. Each low level group will quickly unify. The majority of the groups will unify on the majority opinion. Those groups, however, where there was more minority members to begin with, have higher chance of unifying on the minority opinion. Once a group has unified, it is stable even in the presence of low Noise. If everybody in the same group shares the same opinion, then each individual has strong evidence for the popularity of her or his point of view, even when weak signals arrive that people in other groups have different opinions.

In a random geometry, in each round of interaction a few random individuals are selected as interaction partners for the subject. If in the selected sample individuals presenting an opposite opinion have enough influence, the subject will change opinion. Even if the majority and the minority fractions are not very different in numbers, in the process of sampling sometimes samples containing an overwhelming majority or an overwhelming minority proportion will be drawn. There is much higher probability (due to the Central Limit Theorem) that in such samples the majority opinion will be prevalent. The result of such a sampling process is that in a finite time, even for very strong individuals, such a sample will be drawn, that will cause them to change their opinion. This will happen more often in the direction of the majority opinion. The clusters can not form in the random geometry because there is no locality or local neighborhood and the majority will prevail (for analytical derivation of this prediction see Lewenstein, Nowak & Latane 1992).

Conclusion

In most social dilemmas, people do not affect each other in a uniform way. For a single individual, some people are more visible than others. Consequences of our actions for some people are much more direct then for others, for whom the interdependence relations are less strong. Such differences can be captured by the assumption that social dilemmas exist in a space, in which each individual has a location. The location of an individual determines his or her relations to other people.

The properties of this space are crucial to both the nature of the dilemmas and human responses to them. In the present chapter, we have described how space affects the conformity game. The conformity game can be understood as an abstract model for many real life situations, such as an attitude change.

Due to the fact that dilemmas exist in space, local neighborhood effects, such as clustering, are possible. In reality, social space is much more complex than the two- dimensional matrix we have been using in our simulations. We have presented several geometries that can be used to approximate different types of social space. If we can describe both the nature of the social process (such, as for example, maximizing outcome) and the geometry of the social space, then we may be able to describe the outcome of the process much better than we could do it without the use of the concept of social space. Furthermore, there is reason to believe, that in more complicated spaces those processes are accentuated rather than reduced.

Footnotes

1   University of Warsaw, Institute for Social Studies, Warsaw, Poland

2   Florida Atlantic University, Department of Psychology, USA

3   Polish Academy of Sciences, Center for Theoretical Physics, Poland

References

Bossard, ., (1932). Residential propinquity as a factor in marriage selection. *American Journal of Sociology, 38*, 219-244.

Bradford, M.G., & Kent, W.A. (1990). *Human Geography: theories and applications.* Oxford: Oxford University Press.

Hillier, B., & Hanson J. (1984). *The social logic of space.* London: CUP.

Kapusciarek, I., & Nowak, A. (1992). The social space of Polish students, unpublished technical raport.

Latane, B. (1981). The psychology of social impact. *American Psychologist, 36*, 343-365.

Latane, B., Liu, J.H., Nowak, A., Bonevento, M., & Long Zheng (1993). Distance matters: physical space and social influence. Submitted.

Latane B., & Wolf, S. (1981). The social impact of majorities and minorities. *Psychological Review, 88*, 438-453.

Lewenstein, M., Nowak, A., & Latane, B. (1992). Statistical mechanics of social impact. *Physical Review A., 45*, 763-776.

Lewin, K. (1951). *Field theory in social science.* New York: Harper & Row.

Mandelbrot, B.B. (1982). *The fractal geometry of nature.* New York: Freeman.

Nowak, A., Szamrej J., & Latane, B. (1990). From private attitude to public opinion: Dynamic theory of social impact. *Psychological Review, 97*, 362-376.

Olsson, G. (1965). Distance and human interaction: A review and bibliography (Regional Science Research Institute Philadelphia).

Peitgen, H.-O., Jurgens, H., & Souppe (1992). *Fractals for the classroom: Part one, introduction to fractals and chaos*. Berlin: Springer.

Penn, A., & Dalton, N. (1993). The architecture of society: stochastic simulation of urban movement. In N. Gilbert (Ed.), *Simulating societies*. Guilford: University of Surrey.

Steward, J.Q. (1941). An inverse distance variation for certain social influences. *Science, 93*, 89-90.

Tinto, V. (1973). Colledge proximity and rates of attendance. *American Educational Research Journal, 10*, 277-293.

Zadeh, L.A. (1965). Fuzzy sets. *Information and Control, Vol 8*, 338- 353.

Zipf, G.K. (1949). *Human behavior and the principle of the least effort*. New York: Hafner.

Acknowledgement

This research was suppported by the Polish Goverment Grant 1 113 91 02 and National Science Foundation Grant NS9009198.

Commuting by car or by public transportation?
An interdependence theoretical approach

Mark Van Vugt[1], Ree M. Meertens[2], & Paul A. M. van Lange[3]

Abstract

Subjects from two different populations -- daily commuters and students -- were asked to make a single choice between going by car or by public transportation in a hypothetical commuting situation. On the basis of interdependence theory (Kelley & Thibaut, 1978), we assumed that the choice for car versus public transportation would be affected by the perceived structure of interdependence underlying the decision situation. Consistent with our predictions, it was found that commuters primarily perceived the decision situation as an accessibility problem -- with the basic structure of an N-person Chicken Dilemma -- whereas students primarily perceived the decision situation as an environmental problem -- with the basic structure of an N-person Prisoner's Dilemma. Relative to commuters, students exhibited a greater preference for commuting by public transportation, and exhibited a weaker tendency to take expectations regarding others' choices into consideration. These and other findings are discussed in terms of interdependence theory.

Commuting by car or by public transportation?

The choice between commuting by car versus commuting by public transportation may be affected by several variables, such as efficiency, convenience, or financial costs. A comparative survey conducted in major cities revealed that in Amsterdam 58% commuted by car, 14% by public transportation and 28% cycled or walked. In Washington DC, on the other hand, 80% commuted by car, 14 % by public transportation, and only 6% cycled or walked, whereas in Tokyo only 16% commuted by car, 59% by public transportation, and 25% cycled or walked (Newman & Kenworthy, 1989). It is clear that such choices are affected by structural variables, such as the scarcity of parking space, the quality of public transportation, or the likelihood of traffic jams. These variables influence the relative efficiency of cars versus public transportation. In addition to such criteria of accessibility, the choices to commute by car or by public transportation may also be evaluated in terms of how much they pollute the environment. Over the past five years more and more attempts have been made by the Dutch government to promote commuting by public transportation in order to decrease environmental pollution and accessibility problems. But these efforts -- primarily through the use of campaigns -- have not been very fruitful yet. So far, the conclusion seems to be that it is hard for people to change the habit of using the car and to start commuting by public transportation.   The current chapter reports a study on individuals' preferences for car versus public transportation as two different means to commute. In part, this study was conducted in light of the belief that excessive car use may ultimately lead to a disastrous situation much the same as the "Tragedy of the Commons" described by Hardin (1968). By employing an hypothetical -- single-trial -- commuting situation, we focus on the different ways in which such decision situations may be construed, and on factors that may promote commuting by public transportation. More specific goals of this study are, first, to examine how individuals may assign different meanings to the identical hypothetical situation, and exhibit different preferences for car versus public transportation on the basis of their dependence on the car versus public transportation. Second, we examine how people respond to information regarding the choices of other individuals.

The choice between car and public transportation is made in situation of *interdependence*. An individual's own choice not only affects his or her own well-being, but also that of other individuals. For example, it is clear that excessive car use has a negative impact on others' well-being, because excessive car use causes higher levels of pollution, traffic congestion, and noise. The current chapter is based on the assumption that the type of interdependence individuals perceive to underlie this decision situation -- commuting by car versus public transportation -- may vary as a function of the salience of self-interest versus collective interest, and how much individuals think they are dependent on the car versus public transportation. As stated most explicitly in Kelley and Thibaut's (1978) interdependence theory, it is unlikely that all or most individuals merely make their choices on the basis of the "objective" decision situation, or the given matrix that represents an individual's immediate outcomes. Indeed, one may assume that any given structure of interdependence undergoes a series of transformations so as to result in an effective matrix that is more directly predictive of behavior in interdependent situations. Such transformations may be dictated by an individual's personal motives, such as a concern for comfort, or individual freedom. On the other hand, such transformations may also be dictated by a concern for the collective welfare, the willingness to contribute to a good future, or a motivation to be a good "example" to other individuals. We propose that such "pro-social" or "pro-society" transformations are greater to the extent that self-interest is less salient, and to the extent that individuals think they are -- or actually are -- less dependent on the car.

The role of the perceived interdependence structure

In what ways may the decision between car and public transportation be construed, and what are the characteristics of different interdependence structures individuals may perceive? We propose that individuals may interpret this decision situation in at least two distinct ways. First, an individual may interpret the decision situation as a choice between *personal convenience* and *our environment*. According to this interpretation (hereafter referred to as an environmental interpretation), the option of going by car is attractive from an individual short-term perspective. Relative to public transportation, traveling by car is considered to have greater benefits in terms of convenience, such as flexibility, independence, and comfort. The option of going by public transportation, however, may be relatively more attractive from a collective long-term perspective. Relative to cars, public transportation is cleaner, and therefore less damaging to our environment. The structure of interdependence underlying an environmental interpretation shows similarities to the *N-person Prisoner's Dilemma* (Hamburger, 1979; Rapoport & Chammah; Van Lange, Liebrand, Messick & Wilke, 1992) or to the *social trap*

(Platt, 1973): The option of going by car (i.e.. noncooperative choice) is always more attractive to an individual regardless of other individuals' choices. However, if all individuals opt for the car, then each individual is eventually worse off than if all individuals had opted to go by public transportation (i.e., cooperative choice). The simple fact that this environmental interpretation comes into being when individuals realize the long-term detrimental effects associated with car use, suggests that such individuals essentially make a *pro-social* or *pro-society* transformation of the given situation: They will view the decision situation not only in terms of their own immediate payoffs, but also consider the situation in light of long-term effects for all individuals involved. Hence, those who spontaneously consider the decision situation as an environmental problem will be more concerned with the collective interest than those who do not.

A second possible interpretation of the decision between car versus public transportation is more strongly affected by the criterion of *accessibility*. According to this accessibility interpretation, an individual does not so much view the decision situation in terms of long-term or societal implications, but focuses on the immediate costs or benefits for self: "What is the most efficient or quickest way to travel?". An accessibility interpretation reflects a structure of interdependence that is fundamentally different from the structure of interdependence underlying an environmental interpretation. According to the accessibility interpretation the option of going by car is more attractive to the extent that *fewer* other individuals go by car, because of a lower probability of traffic jams and/or parking problems. The option of going by public transportation is more attractive to the extent that *more* other individuals go by car, and traffic jams and parking problems could be avoided. From this point of view, an individual's choice should be strongly influenced by his or her expectations regarding the probable behavior of other individuals. The structure of interdependence underlying an accessibility interpretation resembles the so-called *N-person Chicken Dilemma* (Liebrand, 1983). As opposed to the N-person Prisoner's Dilemma there is *no* dominant option in the N-person Chicken Dilemma. Individuals are better off by a car choice (i.e., noncooperative choice) than by a public transportation choice (i.e., cooperative choice) when a sufficient number of other individuals do not opt for the car. If a great number of other individuals opt for the car, then the option of public transportation is more attractive. Thus, when individuals construe the decision situation as an accessibility problem, then the expectations regarding other individuals' choices should be an important determinant of their choices.

To summarize; we propose that the choice to commute by car or by public transportation could be interpreted spontaneously in two different ways; (1) as an environmental problem with the features of a N-person Prisoner's Dilemma, and (2) as an accessibility problem with the features of an N-person Chicken Dilemma. Whereas the environmental interpretation is assumed to be instigated by a salience of collective interest, the accessibility interpretation is instigated by a greater salience of self-interest.

Dependence on the car versus dependence on public transportation

The line of reasoning above provides a conceptual framework that allowes us to understand how individuals may construct different interdependence situations. We propose that the interpretation of the decision situation, at least in part, depends on the salience of the individual interest versus collective interest, which in turn is influenced by how much individuals think they are *dependent* on the car versus public transportation. Put differently, the salience of self-interest [versus collective interest] should be affected by the level of dependence on the car (or public transportation), i.e., "how much one needs the car [versus public transportation]. The level of dependence on the car or public transportation is likely to be influenced by a variety of more specific factors. Examples are the extent to which one is used to the car or public transportation, fully aware of the pros and cons regarding the car or public transportation, and poorly informed about the pros and cons regarding alternative means of transportation. Therefore, we assume that people who tend to use the car on a daily basis -- the majority of *commuters* in the Netherlands (Central Bureau of Statistics, 1991) -- not only feel more dependent on or attached to the car, but also have more experience with the advantages and disadvantages of the car than people who never or very infrequently use the car -- most of the *students* in the Netherlands. The ease with which luggage can be taken, the comfort and individual freedom could be mentioned as favorable aspects of the car. On the other hand, daily commuters also have experience with some aversive aspects of the car, particularly the *frustration* due to *ending up in a traffic jam* or due to *not finding parking space.* To individuals who frequently go by car, these advantageous and disadvantageous aspects may be highly salient, and therefore we assume that commuters are likely to perceive the decision situation as an accessibility problem.

Individuals who less frequently use the car and presumably feel they are less dependent on the car -- students -- are less likely to construe the decision situation as a problem of accessibility. In the Netherlands, most students are very much dependent on public transportation because they usually do not have enough money to buy a car, and they have free access to public transportation. Most students evaluate the pros and cons of public transportation in the absence of viable alternatives, and are therefore likely to take most of the disadvantages associated with public transportation for granted. They also experience a clear advantage of public transportation over the car: Public transportation is *less damaging* to the *environment*. The negative implications regarding excessive car use (e.g., pollution, smell) are even more salient, because students frequently use the bike. Therefore, we assume that students are likely to emphasize the environmental aspects regarding the decision situation. Because commuters are more dependent on their cars than students -- who are more dependent on public transportation -- we predict that commuters exhibit a greater tendency to prefer the option of going by car than students who should exhibit a greater tendency to prefer the option of going by public transportation (Hypothesis 1).

The role of expectations regarding other individuals' choices

We have asserted that commuters are likely to perceive the decision situation primarily as an accessibility problem, and that -- through their personal experience -- they are fully aware of the advantages and disadvantages of the car as a means to commute. It is important to note that some (if not most) of the disadvantages (e.g., traffic jams, problems findings parking space), at least in part, are caused by *interdependent others*. Hence, commuters are likely to construe the decision as an N-person Chicken Dilemma, in which going by car (i.e., the noncooperative option) is only more attractive than going by public transportation (i.e., the cooperative option) to the extent that fewer other individuals choose to go by car. Therefore, if commuters perceive the decision problem primarily as an N-person Chicken Dilemma, then their preferences should be influenced to a great extent by what they think other individuals will choose.

In contrast, we have asserted that students are likely to perceive the decision situation as an environmental problem which resembles the properties of an N-person Prisoner's Dilemma. From a game theoretical point of view, the expectations regarding the behavior of other individuals should *not* influence own preferences in the situation. Whether the majority of other individuals decides to commute by car or by public transportation, in either case the option for commuting by car is the relatively more attractive one. However, there may be a variety of psychological factors that lead individuals to prefer the same option as what they think other are going to choose (e.g., normative or conformative pressures; cf. Liebrand, Wilke, Vogel & Wolters, 1986; Kerr, 1989). But, unlike the perception of an N-person Chicken Dilemma, the perception of an N-person Prisoner's Dilemma should not lead to a stronger motivation to prefer the cooperative option as the actor thinks that fewer other individuals will choose for this cooperative option. Therefore, among students preferences for public transportation should be greater when they think that the majority will choose for commuting by public transportation than when they think that the majority will choose for commuting by car. In contrast, among daily commuters preferences for public transportation should be greater when they think that the majority will choose for commuting by car than when they think that the majority will choose for commuting by public transportation (Hypothesis 2).

Finally, the perception of the structure of interdependence could also be influenced by the presentation of the "objective" structure of interdependence (cf. McClintock & Liebrand, 1988). By presenting the decision problem as an accessibility problem an individual's self-interest may become more salient. Conversely, by presenting the decision situation as an environmental problem the collective interest may become more salient. This allowes us to test the hypothesis that students have a stronger preference for commuting by public transportation when many other individuals are expected to commute by public transportation and the situation will be presented as an environmental problem. As opposed to students, commuters will have a stronger preference to go by public transportation when many people are expected to go by car and the situation is presented as an accessibility problem (Hypothesis 3).

Method

Subjects. The experiment was conducted using two different samples. The first sample consisted of undergraduate students of the Faculty of Health Sciences at the University of Limburg in Maastricht. A questionnaire was administered as part of social science class. In total, eighty-six subjects participated: 72 women and 14 men. The second sample consisted of employees of a large insurance company in Utrecht. All of these employees usually commuted by car. Of the 120 questionnaires that were distributed, 88 were returned (73%), 60 by men and 28 by women.

Overview of the design. The questionnaire contained a hypothetical commuting situation. There were six different versions of the commuting situation. First, the expectations regarding others' choices were manipulated: One group was led to believe that the majority commutes by car, and the other group was led to believe that the majority commutes by public transportation. Second, the situation was presented in one of three ways: as an environmental problem, an accessibility problem, or as both an environmental and accessibility problem. The experimental design was thus a 2 (Group: Commuters vs. Students) by 2 (Expectation: Majority Car vs. Majority Public Transportation) by 3 (Presentation: Environmental problem, Accessibility problem, vs. Combined problem). The main dependent variable was the preference for car versus public transportation.

The commuting situation

A description of a hypothetical commuting situation -- with a distance of 30 kilometers between home and work -- was given on paper. The subjects were asked to imagine that they were commuters for a *single* day in this situation. They could state their preference either to commute by car or to commute by public transportation.

Manipulation of expectation. Subjects were given information about the travel-mode choices that were supposedly made in earlier research with the same commuting situation. It was suggested that in each of the earlier studies either a majority (60%) chose to go by car or a majority (60%) chose to go by public transportation.

Manipulation of presentation. In the presentation of the situation as an Environmental problem it was stated that there would be serious environmental damage when a majority were to go by car in the commuting situation. Specifically, it was stated that "the vegetation at the side of the road will decrease slowly as a consequence of acid rain produced by cars. Moreover, a contribution is made to the greenhouse effect which may threaten mankind in the future". In contrast, it was stated that "regardless of the number of commuters, public transportation will hardly cause any damage to the environment". In the presentation as an Accessibility-problem it was argued that there would be a serious time delay due to congestion when a majority were to go by car. Normally it would take 40 minutes by car. However, when a majority would choose to go by car the travel time would be 70 minutes. The travel time by public transportation was always 50 minutes -- including the time of pre- and post-transportation. In the presentation as a Combined problem both information about potential environmental damage and about a potential delay was given.

Dependent measures

Subjects stated their preferences for the car or public transportation on a seven point bipolar scale, ranging from 1 (strong preference to commute by car) to 7 (strong preference to commute by public transportation). In order to examine more closely how the decision situation was construed, we asked each subject to write down the main reasons for his or her preference. By focusing on spontaneous use of arguments related to environment (e.g., environmental pollution, environmental damage) or accessibility (e.g., travel time, traffic congestion), we counted the number of subjects that either mentioned environment or accessibility as a major reason for their preference.

Results

Car versus Public Transportation preferences were analyzed in a 2 (Group: Students vs. Commuters) by 2 (Expectation: Majority Car vs. Majority Public Transportation) by 3 (Presentation: Environmental problem, Accessibility problem, vs. Combined problem) ANOVA. This analysis revealed a strong main effect for Group, $F(1,162) = 53.15$, $p<.001$. As predicted by Hypothesis 1, Commuters had a stronger preference for car ($M = 3.30$) than did Students ($M = 5.26$). Further testing revealed that each of these means differed significantly from 4, the midpoint of the preference scale. Commuters preferred commuting by car above the neutral point, $t(87) = 3.74$, $p<.001$, whereas Students did the opposite, $t(85) = 6.30$, $p<.001$.

In addition to the main effect for Group, the analysis revealed an interaction of Group and Expectation, $F(1,162) = 10.72$, $p<.001$. The means associated with this interaction are shown in Table 1.

Table 1

Interaction Effect of Group and Expectation.

	Expectation	
	Majority Car	Majority Public Transp.
Group		
Students	5.07[a]	5.44[a]
Commuters	3.98[b]	2.61[c]

Note. The preference scale ranges from 1 (strong preference for car) to 7 (strong preference for public transportation).
Means with a different superscript differ significantly, $p<.05$

As can be seen in Table 1, commuters exhibit a weaker car preference when they are led to believe that the Majority commutes by Car than when they are led to believe that the Majority commutes by Public Transportation. This finding is consistent with the idea that commuters construe this decision situation as an N-person Chicken Dilemma.

Preferences of students were not significantly influenced by our manipulation of Expectation, although there is a tendency towards greater Public Transportation preferences when they think that the majority chooses to commute by public transportation. Thus, Hypothesis 2 is supported for the commuter-sample, but not or marginally at best for the student-sample.

This lack of support for a part of Hypothesis 2 could be due to the fact that many students did not have a driver's license (which is not uncommon in the Netherlands). Therefore, using the *student sample*, we performed an analysis of variance and added the factor Driver's License (License versus No license) to the design. The analysis revealed a significant interaction of Driver's license and Expectation, $F(1,74) = 16.83$, $p < .03$. The means associated with this interaction are presented in Table 2.

Table 2

Interaction Effect of Driver's License and Expectation for Student-sample

		Expectation	
Driver's License	n	Majority Car	Majority Public Transp.
License	55	4.39[a]	5.30[b]
No License	31	6.33[c]	5.69[c]

Note. The preference scale ranges from 1 (strong preference for car) to 7 (strong preference for public transportation).
Means with a different superscript differ significantly, $p < .05$

The means in Table 2 reveal that there is a difference in stated preference between the Expectation-conditions only for students who possess a Driver's License. When students with a License expect a Majority to commute by Public Transportation they also have a stronger preference to go by public transportation than when they expect a Majority to go by Car. Thus, Hypothesis 2 is supported for students with a driver's license. This finding illustrates that students (with a driver's license) perceive the decision situation as an -- prosocially transformed -- N-person Prisoner's Dilemma.

Finally, we were interested in examining the idea that students would exhibit a stronger public transportation preference when the majority was expected to commute by public transportation and the decision problem was presented as an environmental problem, and the idea that commuters would exhibit a weaker car preference when the majority was expected to commute by car and the situation was presented as an accessibility problem (Hypothesis 3). Ideally, support for this hypothesis would be revealed by a significant interaction of Group, Expectation, and Presentation. However, this three-way interaction was not found to be significant, F $(2,162) < 1$. To provide a more precise test for each of these predicted interactions separately, we conducted two 2 (Expectation) by 3 (Presentation) ANOVAS, one using the student sample, the other using the commuter sample.

Using the *student sample*, this analysis did not reveal evidence for an interaction of Expectation and Presentation, $F(2,74) < 1$.

Using the *commuter sample*, a 2 (Expectation) by 3 (Presentation) ANOVA revealed a marginally significant interaction of Expectation and Presentation, $F(2,80) = 3.90$, $p<.06$. The means associated with this interaction effect are presented in Table 3.

Consistent with Hypothesis 3, commuters' car preference was lowest when the decision situation was presented as an Accessibility problem or a Combined problem and when commuters were led to believe that the majority would commute by car. Interestingly, when commuters were led to believe that the majority would commute by public transportation, then their car preferences were not in the least influenced by the three different presentations.

Table 3

Interaction Effect of Presentation and Expectation for Commuter-sample

Presentation	Expectation	
	Majority Car	Majority Public Transp.
Environmental problem	3.50[a]	2.64[a]
Accessibility problem	4.31[b]	2.60[a]
Combined problem	4.20[b]	2.60[a]

Note. The preference scale ranges from 1 (strong preference for car) to 7 (strong preference for public transportation).
Means with a different superscript differ significantly, $p < .05$.

After the subjects in both samples had stated their car versus public transportation preferences, they were asked to write down the reasons for their preferences. A chi-square analysis on the frequencies of these reasons revealed some clear-cut differences between the samples in mentioning environmental and accessibility arguments, Chi-square(2) = 37.37, $p < .001$. Environmental arguments are given by 46% of the students and by only 9% of the commuters, whereas travel time and traffic congestion is mentioned as an argument by only 14% of the students and by 47% of the commuters. Apart from environmental arguments, 40% of the students gave practical reasons for their preference, like having free access to public transportation. A considerable amount of commuters mentioned convenience and freedom, besides travel time as arguments for their preference (33%).

Discussion

This study was conducted in light of the belief that excessive car use may ultimately lead to a disastrous situation, or at least a situation most of us rather do not like to think about. We have used Kelley and Thibaut's (1978) interdependence theory to analyze how individuals may construct different interdependence situations on the basis of the same decision situation (i.e., a commuting situation). Because of their felt dependence on cars as a means to commute, we claimed that commuters would primarily perceive this decision situation as an accessibility problem, with a structure very similar to an N-person Chicken Dilemma. Conversely, students who were expected to feel a greater dependence on public transportation were assumed to perceive the decision situation primarily as an environmental problem, with a structure very similar to an N-person Prisoner's Dilemma. The results were quite consistent with these claims.

One major finding of this study is that the subjects in the two samples -- students and daily commuters -- responded differently to expectations regarding the choices of other individuals. Students -- at least those students with a driver's license -- tended to have a weaker preference for commuting by public transportation when a majority of the others was expected to commute by car than when a majority was expected to commute by public transportation. This finding, in support of Hypothesis 2, is reminiscent of a very robust relationship between expectations and choice observed in experimental research on prisoner's dilemmas, in particular in those studies in which the expectations of others' cooperation were manipulated (e.g., Liebrand et al., 1986; Schroeder, Jensen, Reed, Sullivan, & Schwab, 1983). The present findings may very well be explained in terms of conformity and normative pressures associated with beliefs regarding others' concern with environmental pollution. It is morally more acceptable to commute by car when one believes that a majority commutes by car than when one believes that a minority commutes by car.

Also consistent with Hypothesis 2, commuters exhibited a weaker preference for commuting by car when they believed that the majority commuted by car than when they believed that the majority commuted by public transportation. This provides some evidence for our claim that commuters are likely to transform the given decision situation into an accessibility problem, with an N-person Chicken Dilemma structure. From this "effective matrix," it indeed is more rational to cooperate when one believes that a greater number of others do not cooperate. Moreover, it appeared that in the condition in which the majority prefers to commute by car, commuters exhibited virtually identical preferences for commuting by public transportation when the situation was presented as an accessibility problem only and when the situation was presented as an accessibility plus environmental problem, and both of these conditions yielded stronger public transportation preferences than when the situation was merely presented as an environmental problem. This suggests that commuters were more persuaded by the accessibility interpretation than by the environmental interpretation. Finally, the reasons commuters described for their preferences were consistent with an accessibility interpretation: About half of them (47%) spontaneously reported travel time as a reason, whereas only 14% of the students reported this reason. These findings provide convergent evidence in support of the claim that commuters tend to perceive the decision situation as an accessibility problem, rather than an environmental problem.

The current findings did not reveal unequivocal support for Hypothesis 3, that students' preference for commuting by public transportation would be especially greater when both they expected a majority to commute by public transportation and the situation was presented as an environmental problem. One post-hoc interpretation of this finding is that the type of presentation had little influence on students' perceptions of the decision situation. It seems plausible that students are quite convinced in advance that the choice between car and public transportation is an environmental issue, and the environmental presentation (by the experimenter) does not further strengthen this conviction.

The study revealed some support for the idea that commuters' preferences for commuting by car would be especially low when they believe that the majority commutes by car, and when the presentation includes the accessibility interpretation. The interesting result here is that for commuting purposes public transportation can be better promoted by stressing the limits of the accessibility of cars than by stressing the environmental advantages of public transportation.

Throughout the chapter we have analyzed the decision "car versus public transportation" in terms of interdependence theory (Kelley & Thibaut, 1978), in particular accentuating the role of transformation processes. Although interdependence theory is in essence focused on dyadic relations, and may not be so easily applicable to multiperson situations, the current findings underline the usefulness of an interdependence analysis. Indeed, individuals tend to construct different interdependence situations on the basis of broader goals, whereby students are more likely than commuters to make a pro-social or pro-society transformation of the decision situation, because students are relatively less dependent on cars, and more dependent on public transportation. It should be noted that this analysis does not preclude any other (better) theoretical analysis. However, the experiment was designed not so much to test interdependence theory, but to use interdependence theory as a conceptual framework.

In the current study we also found strong support for Hypothesis 1: Commuters exhibited a stronger preference for commuting by car than did students who exhibited a stronger preference for commuting by public transportation. This finding was anticipated on the basis of differential levels of experienced dependence on cars versus public transportation. However, as an alternative explanation, one might argue that this finding reflects sex differences -- the vast majority of students were women, whereas the majority of commuters were men. Indeed, the current study cannot rule out the interpretation that women are more in favor of public transportation than men who might be more in favor of cars, and that women and men may respond differently to expectations regarding others' choices. However, in prior social dilemma research sex-differences in choice behavior are rather inconsistent (Van Lange, 1992). Thus, it seems not plausible that the current results are due to the stereotypical idea that women are more cooperative than men. Another stereotype -- that men like car driving better than women -- may provide a more plausible explanation.

Before closing, we wish to outline a few strengths and limitations of the current research. One limitation is that the study employed a hypothetical decision situation. It may therefore be that tendencies toward social desirability or favorable self-presentation, at least in part, colored the findings obtained. Second, the current study cannot rule out several alternative explanations for the obtained differences between commuters and students. In addition to the interpretation based on sex-differences, it is also possible that differences in age, income, or other more or less unforeseen differences related to the distinction commuters versus students help to explain the results.

A major strength of the current study is that we concentrated on a real-life dilemma situation, using a sample of subjects (commuters) whose commuting behavior at the moment is of utmost importance to the future quality of the environment. The finding that these individuals are inclined to perceive the decision situation as an accessibility problem with the structure of an N-person Chicken Dilemma helps to understand why campaigns stressing the concern for the environment are in fact less effective than we had hoped. This suggests that, in designing campaigns aimed at reduction of car use, one has to take into account the interpretations people assign to such situations of interdependence. A moral appeal to the collective interest of a clean environment is more likely to change the behavior of an individual who does not feel dependent on the car than the behavior of an individual who feels very much dependent on the car. These latter individuals may be more sensitive to arguments that emphasize the personal benefits associated with public transportation, or the disadvantages associated with commuting by car, such as travel time and perhaps the greater financial costs of the car.

Footnotes

1   University of Limburg, Department of Health Education, Maastricht, The Netherlands

2   University of Limburg, The Netherlands

3   Free University of Amsterdam, Amsterdam, The Netherlands

References

CBS (Central Bureau of Statistics, 1991). *De mobiliteit van de Nederlandse bevolking.* (The mobility of the Netherlands population). Voorburg/Heerlen (Neth.): Centraal Bureau voor de Statistiek.

Dawes, R.M., McTavish, J., & Shaklee, H. (1977). Behavior, communication and assumptions about other people's behavior in a common's dilemma situation. *Journal of Personality and Social Psychology, 35,* 1-11.

Hamburger, H. (1979). *Games as models of social phenomena.* San Fransisco: W. H. Freeman and company.

Hardin, G. (1968). The tragedy of the commons. *Science, 162,* 1243-1248.

Kelley, H.H., & Thibaut, J.W. (1978). *Interpersonal Relations: A Theory of Interdependence.* New York: Wiley.

Kerr, N.L. (1989). Illusions of efficacy: The effects of group size on perceived efficacy in social dilemmas. *Journal of Experimental Social Psychology, 25,* 287-313.

Liebrand, W.B.G. (1983). A classification of social dilemma games. *Simulation & Games, 14,* 123-138.

Liebrand, W.B.G., Wilke, H.A.M., Vogel, R. & Wolters, F.J.M. (1986). Value orientation and conformity: a study using three types of social dilemma games. *Journal of Conflict Resolution, 30,* 77-97.

McClintock, C.G., & Liebrand, W.B.G. (1988). Role of interdependence structure, individual value orientation, and another's strategy in social decision making: a transformational analysis. *Journal of Personality and Social Psychology, 55,* 396-409.

Newman, P., & Kenworthy, J. (1989). *Cities and automobile dependence: an international sourcebook.* Aldershot: Gower, England.

Platt, J. (1973). Social traps. *American Psychologist, 28,* 641-651.

Rapoport, A., & Chammah, A.M. (1965). *Prisoner's Dilemma: A study in conflict and cooperation.* Ann Arbor: University of Michigan Press.

Schroeder, D.A., Jensen, T.D., Reed, A.J., Sullivan, D.D., & Schwab, M. (1983). The actions of others as determinants of behavior in social trap situations. *Journal of Personality and Social Psychology, 19,* 522-539.

Van Lange, P.A.M. (1992). Confidence in expectations: A test of the triangle hypothesis. *European Journal of Personality, 6,* 371-379.

Van Lange, P.A.M., Liebrand, W.B.G., Messick, D.M., & Wilke, H.A.M. (1992). Introduction and literature review. In W.B.G. Liebrand, D.M. Messick, & H.A.M. Wilke (Eds.), *Social dilemmas: theoretical issues and research findings*. Oxford: Pergamom Press.

Acknowledgement

This research was supported by a grant from the Netherlands Ministry of Transport, Public Works and Water Management. The contribution of the third author was made possible by a grant from the Netherlands Organization for Scientific Research. Correspondence concerning this chapter should be addressed to Mark Van Vugt, University of Limburg, Department of Health Education, P. Debyeplein 1, 6200 MD Maastricht, The Netherlands.

Evolution of norms without metanorms

Toshio Yamagishi[1] and Nobuyuki Takahashi[1]

Abstract

A social dilemma can be resolved if group members sanction each other's choices to defect. However, the provision of mutual sanctioning involves another social dilemma (*i.e.*, a second-order dilemma), in which non-sanctioning is the dominant choice. Based on a series of computer simulations, Axelrod (1986) concluded that this second-order social dilemma can be resolved by metanorms (i.e., sanctioning the non-sanctioners). An alternative interpretation of Axelrod's simulation results is proposed and tested through a series of computer simulations. Specifically, it is shown that the evolution of norms (which entail mutual sanctioning) does not require metanorms (i.e., sanctioning the non-sanctioners) insofar as the decisions to cooperate and the decisions to sanction are linked (*i.e.*, cooperators punish defectors, and defectors do not punish other defectors). Furthermore, the linkage between these two types of decisions itself is shown to emerge through an "evolutionary" process.

Mutual sanctions and the second-order social dilemma

The administration of "selective incentives" is considered the standard economic approach to solving the free riding problem (*e.g.*, Olson, 1965). Selective incentives is the term used by economists to refer to positive and negative sanctions applied to cooperators and/or defectors. Some selective incentives are monetary or material rewards, such as the program guides provided to public TV subscribers. Some are social or psychological, such as the prestige and praise given to cooperators. The administration of such selective incentives helps resolve the social dilemma by altering the underlying incentive structure. It is rational for each actor to cooperate if the extra cost or benefit associated with the selective incentive (or sanction) exceeds the cost of cooperation.

Many social dilemmas exist in the absence of an agency that is responsible for administering selective incentives. Without a central authority, however, people may voluntarily monitor and sanction each other to solve the social dilemma. The question addressed in this paper concerns the possibility of mutual sanctioning as a solution to social dilemma. More specifically: can the necessary selective incentives be provided voluntarily by egoistic group members without a central authority? The answer to this question depends on how we deal with the problem of the second-order dilemma.

Suppose that people begin cooperating after they have started monitoring and sanctioning each other. This is typical in small traditional communities. Most people in a village know what the others are doing, and will pressure deviants to conform. In many other situations, however, people may not voluntarily monitor and sanction each other, especially since such activities often involve substantial costs. If you remind a colleague of yours who is always late for meetings that he should not be late, you might become disliked by this colleague. In this case, the cost is relatively minor. However, if this colleague was your boss, the cost of such sanctioning might rise dramatically.

Now, we face a second-order social dilemma concerning the provision of mutual monitoring and sanctioning. If many people facing a social dilemma (*i.e.*, a first-order social dilemma) monitor and sanction their neighbors, the majority will cooperate and, as a result, everyone will benefit. In other words, the first-order social dilemma will be resolved with the provision of mutual sanctioning among group members. But the fruit of mutual monitoring and sanctioning can also be enjoyed by those who do not participate in such activities. The increase in the overall cooperation level due to mutual monitoring and sanctioning is thus a public good in and of itself. People can free ride on others' efforts to monitor and sanction any defectors.

The second-order dilemma discussed above has stimulated a considerable amount of interest among sociologists and political scientists. The reason is that the notion of mutual sanctioning is conceptually very close to the notion of social norms. Among the three types of definitions of norms--those based on expectations, values, and behavior--discussed by Axelrod (1986), the existence of mutual sanctioning is most central to the behavioral definition of norms. According to Axelrod (1986: 1097), a norm is said to "exist in a given social setting to the extent that individuals usually act in a certain way and are often punished when seen not to be acting in this way."

Axelrod's (1986) solution to second-order social dilemmas

To find a solution to the second-order social dilemma discussed above, Axelrod (1986) conducted a series of computer simulations of the *emergence of norms without a central authority*. An iterated social dilemma among twenty actors was used in his simulation. Each actor was programmed to have a certain level of "boldness," which was used as the basis for the actor's decision in each trial period. The higher the level of boldness, the lower was the probability that the actor would cooperate. As the simulation progressed, poor performers "imitated" better performers' boldness levels. That is, the "offspring" of the actors with little earnings accumulated over four trials (called a "generation") adopted, in the next generation, the boldness levels of the ones who made large cumulative earnings. The result of this simulation is easy to guess. Those with high levels of boldness earned better scores than those with low levels of boldness and, as a result, all actors in the group gradually became bolder. After many generations (100 generations in Axelrod's simulation), the boldness levels of all actors approached the maximum value of seven and hardly anyone cooperated at all toward the end of the 100 generations. This result clearly shows the existence of the first-order social dilemma problem in which defection is the dominant choice. The result of the above simulation demonstrates the dismal logic of social dilemmas without mutual sanctioning. Will the result be different when actors monitor and sanction each other? The next simulation examined this question. In this new simulation, each actor decided not only whether or not to cooperate, but at the same time, whether or not to punish the defectors. Each actor was endowed with a "vengefulness" level as well as a "boldness" level. How likely an actor would be to punish a defector, when the actor found one, was based on the level of the actor's vengefulness. The results of this simulation were straightforward. The overall vengefulness level eventually approached zero, the overall boldness level approached the maximum value, and hardly anyone ever cooperated. The result of this simulation thus indicated the clear existence of a second-order social dilemma.

Metanorms. Do the above results of Axelrod's simulation imply that voluntarily provided mutual sanctioning, which Axelrod (1986) termed social norms, cannot be produced through an "evolutionary" (or "learning") process? Not necessarily, according to Axelrod. He argued further that the sanctioning of non-sanctioners would be the only ingredient needed for a social norm of cooperation to develop. So, in his next simulation, Axelrod let "vengeful members" punish non-punishers (*i.e.*, the ones who did not punish defectors) as well as the defectors. The vengefulness level was kept high and the boldness level remained low. The cooperation level was high over repeated generations in the results of this simulation. The general implication was that social norms would develop and be maintained when the norms include sanctions against apathy (which Axelrod terms "metanorms") as well as sanctions against non-cooperative behavior.

Linkage as an alternative solution

The solution proposed by Axelrod consists of two components: (1) those who do not punish the non-cooperators can be punished, and (2) the two types of punishments are linked (*i.e.*, the same "vengefulness" level was used to determine whether or not to punish defectors and whether or not to punish non-punishers. The generalizability of the solution proposed by Axelrod, however, seems dubious. If his solution is widely applicable, punishing those who do not punish the defectors (metanorms) should be as common as punishing those who punish the defectors (norms). Of course, we can find such examples; the United States threatened to punish Japan for not cooperating enough with the coalition to punish Iraq during the Gulf War. On the other hand, examples of such second-order punishment are not very common in everyday life. You may complain to your neighbor about being too noisy, but you may not complain to another neighbor of yours for not complaining to the noisy neighbor. Or, if someone is late for a meeting you may grumble at him, but you would seldom grumble at your colleagues for not complaining to the late comer. What would happen if you, for example, say to your colleague: "Joe is always late for committee meetings and we have to wait for him. I often complain to him about that. I know you don't, why don't you? You should." If you do, you will be considered too presumptuous and your anger will be viewed as misdirected.

The reason why second-order sanctioning (*i.e.*, punishment of the non-punishers) is not as common as predicted by Axelrod's solution, we hypothesized, is because there is a simpler, more straightforward solution to the second-order dilemma. The alternative solution we have introduced in our simulation study requires only the punishment of defectors (norms); that is, it does not require second-order punishment or the punishment of non-punishers (metanorms). But we already know, in the simulation we have just described, that the punishment of defectors alone is not sufficient to maintain a high level of cooperation. So, we borrowed from Axelrod the notion of "linkage." That is, in Axelrod's solution, the punishment of defectors was linked with the punishment of non-punishers, such that actors punished non-punishers with the same probability (represented by their vengefulness level) as they punished defectors. Instead of this particular linkage between the two kinds of punishment, however, we introduced another kind of linkage, this time, between actions in the first-order dilemma and those in the second-order dilemma. In our simulation, those who cooperated in the original social dilemma also cooperated, with the same probability, in the second-order dilemma involving the provision of sanctioning. Actors in our simulation used the boldness level to make the punishment decision as well as the cooperation decision.

The results of our simulation (using the same algorithm and the same set of parameters as in Axelrod's simulation) show that this option works as well as Axelrod's solution. After replicating the major findings of Axelrod's (1986) simulation study, we conducted a simulation of the norm game with the added feature of the linkage between actions in the first- and the second-order dilemmas.[2] Actors in this simulation punished the defectors, when they were detected, with a probability corresponding to their levels of boldness. The average boldness level during the last 10 generations (of the total of 200 generations) in this simulation (with 10 replications) was extremely low (0.04). The results clearly demonstrate that metanorms are not needed for the "evolution" of norms insofar as actions in the first-order dilemma and those in the second-order dilemma are linked or consistent. In order to examine the robustness of these findings, we conducted another series of simulations in which the cost of punishment was increased from 2 (the value used in the Axelrod's simulation) to 3, 4, 5, and finally to 6. The final average boldness levels in these simulations were 0.03, 0.03, 0.03, and 0.04 with costs of 3, 4, 5, and 6, respectively. The effectiveness of the linkage of actions in each dilemma was thus demonstrated to be fairly robust.

Linkage as a means of matrix-transformation

The success of linkage in this simulation can be interpreted in terms of its ability to **transform** the incentive structure of the group from an N-person PD to an N-person *Assurance* game. Let us use the following social dilemma situation to illustrate this. In this n-person social dilemma, *the cost of contribution for each actor is set at one* (to make the following discussion simple), and each actor's contribution produces x amount of benefit to each of the n members of the group (including the actor him or herself). The net benefits for a cooperator, C, or a defector D, when the proportion of the cooperators in the group is c, is:

$$C = cnx - 1$$
$$D = cnx$$

In this social dilemma, each actor can punish a defector with a cost of y. When punished, a defector suffers a loss of z. Let us use CN, CP, DN, and DP to represent the net benefits of a cooperator-nonpunisher, cooperator-punisher, defector-nonpunisher, and defector-punisher, respectively. For simplicity, it is assumed in the following argument that a punisher always punishes all the defectors (including self). The proportion of punishers in the group is given by p. Then,

$$\text{CN} = cnx - 1 \tag{1}$$
$$\text{CP} = nx - 1 - (1 - c)ny \tag{2}$$
$$\text{DN} = nx - pnz \tag{3}$$
$$\text{DP} = cnx - pnz - (1 - c)ny \tag{4}$$

In this situation, CN > CP and DN > DP. That is, N (non-punishment) is dominant over P (punishment). If all actors take this dominant choice the situation is reduced to the original dilemma in which C is dominant over D. The result will be unanimous defection ($c = 0$), in which each actor's outcome is zero. On the other hand, when even a relatively small proportion of the actors punish defectors ($p > 1/nz$), C becomes dominant over D in the first-order dilemma:

$$CN - DN = CP - DP = pnz - 1 > 0 \text{ when } p > 1/nz$$

With a relatively small proportion ($p > 1/nz$) of punishers, unanimous cooperation ($c = 1$) will result, and each actor will receive $nx - 1$ which is greater than 0 in any social dilemma (where the overall benefit generated by each actor's cooperation, nx, exceeds the cost of cooperation, 1). This indicates the existence of a second-order social dilemma; N (non-punishment) is dominant over P (punishment), but if all actors choose N each will receive 0, which is less than the benefit of $nx - 1$ that is expected when all chose P.

What will happen if the two types of choices C-D and N-P are completely linked, such that the remaining choice is only between CP and DN? DN is no longer a dominant choice. Since $p = c$,

$$CP > DN \text{ when } cz > 1/n + (1 - c)y \tag{5}$$

In a large group in which $1/n$ is very small (*i.e.*, $1/n$ is almost 0), CP is a better choice than DN when the effectiveness of punishment z/y is greater than the ratio of the defectors to cooperators $(1 - c)/c$. This is an N-person Assurance situation since whether the outcome of cooperation, CP, is better than the outcome of defection, DN, depends on the overall cooperation rate. When many others cooperate (*i.e.*, c is large, so that $(1 - c)/c$ is small), even relatively weak punishment can make the outcome of cooperation-punishment better than the outcome of defection- nonpunishment. On the other hand, the outcome of defection-nonpunishment is better than the outcome of cooperation-punishment when the overall cooperation rate is low. The linkage between C-D and P-N choices thus transforms the original N-person PD incentive structure to that of an N-person Assurance game.

The level of the critical cooperation rate at which the reversal between CP and DN occurs in the transformed Assurance structure can be obtained from Inequality 5. That is, the critical cooperation rate is:

$$(1 + ny)/\{(y + z)n\}.$$

In the replication of Axelrod's simulation reported above, n was 20, y was 0.5, and z was 2.25, so the critical cooperation rate was 0.20.[3] Even when the cost of punishment was increased to 6, the critical cooperation rate was only 0.41. These low values for the critical cooperation rate explain the success of this type of linkage in producing high levels of cooperation in the above simulations in which the initial average cooperation rate was around 0.5.

Evolution of the linkage strategy

The success of the linkage between actions in the first and second-order dilemmas can be attributed to the fact that the incentive structure was transformed to an N-person Assurance structure. Depending on the initial distribution of the CP and DN choices and the location of the critical cooperation rate where the reversal in the incentive structure occurs (which is determined by the nature of the social dilemma incentive structure and the cost and size of the punishment), CP can be the final outcome.

A question still remains. This linkage transforms the dilemma, and thus helps to resolve the social dilemma, especially the second-order dilemma. However, *where does the linkage come from?* The linkage in our simulation as well as in Axelrod's (1986) simulation was externally imposed. This practice may be justified if the linkage exists among human beings as an innate behavioral tendency, or at least if it is strongly ingrained in our culture. Until either of these possibilities are proven, this type of linkage as a solution to social dilemma remains one of many external solutions such as a central authority capable of administering selective incentives. In other words, the "evolutionary solution" to social dilemma proposed by Axelrod (1986) eventually depends on this externally imposed assumption of the linkage.

This limitation to the evolutionary approach can be removed if we can demonstrate that the linkage itself spreads among group members through an "evolutionary" process. Then, the evolutionary would approach provides an internal or intrinsic solution to the social dilemma, a solution that is based on the internal dynamics of the social dilemma situation. In the next simulation, we examine this possibility.

In the final series of simulations designed to answer the above question, we investigated whether or not linkage spreads among group members through the same "evolutionary" mechanisms used in the previous simulations. To answer this question, we introduced an additional "gene" responsible for the linkage. Each actor in this final simulation was programmed to have not only the "genes" for boldness and vengefulness but also a "gene" to link the two. Yamagishi's simulation program instead of Morita's program (see Footnote 1 for the differences between the two) was used in this simulation. Boldness and vengefulness levels took a real value between 0 (never defect or never punish) and 1 (always defect or always punish). The linkage level, on the other hand, took an integer value 0 or 1. An actor with the linkage level of 0 always made the C-D and P-N decisions independently. An actor with the linkage level of 1 always linked these two kinds of decisions. That is, when the linkage level was 1, the simulated actor punished a defector with the probability of (1 - the boldness level).

We first conducted a simulation in which all actors independently made C-D decisions and P-N decisions, replicating the results of the previous simulations (100 replications with 500 generations). The results were consistent with the previous simulation using Morita's and Axelrod's programs. Then we replicated the simulation in which all the actors linked these two types of decisions. Again, the results of this simulation were consistent with the previous results. Finally, we conducted a simulation including the linkage "gene." When the initial levels of all three "genes" (boldness, vengefulness, and linkage) were randomly distributed (100 replications with 500 generations), the average cooperation rate during the last 10 generations reached 0.72. The final cooperation rate (during the last 10 generations) was higher than 0.60 in 79 of the 100 replications. Even in another simulation in which the initial linkage level was set to zero for all actors, the final cooperation rate was not much different. Table 1 reports results of this simulation with different sets of initial levels of the three parameters, boldness, vengefulness, and linkage. Whatever the initial combination of the three parameters, the final result was similar.

T. Yamagishi and N. Takahashi

Table 1

Results of the emergence of the linkage simulation during the last 10 generations.

Initial Values			Frequency Distribution of Cooperation Rates					Average			
B[1]	V[2]	L[3]	0-.2	.2-.4	.4-.6	.6-.8	.8- 1	C[4]	B[1]	V[2]	L[3]
R[5]	R	R	13	2	6	21	58	0.72	0.28	0.52	0.46
R	R	0.0	11	5	6	18	60	0.72	0.28	0.52	0.47
0.0	0.0	0.0	12	3	3	24	58	0.73	0.27	0.55	0.47
1.0	0.0	0.0	22	1	6	19	52	0.64	0.36	0.47	0.49
0.0	1.0	0.0	5	2	5	22	66	0.79	0.21	0.59	0.47
1.0	1.0	0.0	9	2	7	21	61	0.74	0.51	0.57	0.47

(1) The average level of boldness.
(2) The average level of vengefulness.
(3) The average level of linkage.
(4) The average level of cooperation.
(5) Uniform random distribution between 0 and 1.

The average linkage level during the last 10 generations in these simulations are also shown in Table 1. It is interesting that the average final linkage level did not depend on the distribution of the initial levels of boldness, vengefulness and linkage. About 40 to 50 percent of the actors came to possess the linkage strategy in all settings. The relatively high levels of cooperation observed in this set of simulations were supported by about a half of the group members who came to possess the linkage strategy through the "evolutionary" process.

The results of this simulation suggest the possibility that the linkage strategy itself can be produced through dynamic processes involved in these social dilemmas. It is important to note especially that the linkage strategy spread to about half the group members even when no one initially possessed the linkage strategy. This implies that there must have been a situation in which actors possessing the linkage strategy performed better than actors without it. Thus, the next question that needs to be answered is: when do actors with this linkage strategy perform better than actors without it?.

Comparison of the expected outcomes of linkage actors and non-linkage actors

This last question can be answered by comparing the expected outcomes for the actors with the linkage strategy (the "linkage actors") with those of the actors without the linkage strategy (the "non-linkage actors"). In this analysis, the range of boldness and vengefulness is 0 to 1. The average cooperativeness (*1 minus boldness*) in the group is b, and the average vengefulness in the group is v. The linkage ratio (the ratio of linkage actors) in the group is assumed (for the sake of convenience) to be independent of b or v. With this assumption, the expected ratio of CP and DN actors among the linkage actors are b and $1 - b$, respectively. Then, the expected outcome for the linkage actors, R, in this group is:

$$R = b\text{CP} + (1 - b)\text{DN} \tag{6}$$

The expected ratio of CN, CP, DN, and DP choices among non-linkage actors are $b(1 - v)$, bv, $(1 - b)(1 - v)$, and $(1 - b)v$, respectively. The expected outcome for non-linkage actors, I, in this group is:

$$I = b(1 - v)\text{CN} + bv\text{CP} + (1 - b)(1 - v)\text{DN} + (1 - b)v\text{DP} \tag{7}$$

From Equations 6 and 7,

$$R - I = b(1 - v)(CP - CN) - (1 - b)v(DN - DP) \tag{8}$$

From Equations 1, 2, 3 and 4,

$$CN - CP = DN - DP = (1 - c)ny \tag{9}$$

From Equations 8 and 9,

$$R - I = (1 - c)ny\{-b(1 - v) + (1 - b)v\} = (1 - c)ny(v - b) \tag{10}$$

Since $(1 - c)$, n, y are all positive,

$$R > I \text{ when } v > b \tag{11}$$

Inequality 11 indicates that, if we can assume that the linkage ratio in the group is independent of b or v, the expected outcome for the linkage actors is greater than the expected outcome for the non-linkage actors when the average vengefulness level in the group exceeds the average level of cooperativeness (1 minus boldness). In other words, *the expected outcome for the linkage actor is greater than the expected outcome for the non-linkage actor when the sum of the average boldness and the average vengefulness exceeds one*. The linkage strategy can proliferate in such a situation.

    This explains why the linkage ratio (the proportion of linkage actors in the group) did not take extreme values in our simulation. The linkage ratio will increase when both the average boldness and the average vengefulness are high; it will decrease when both are low. Either of these extreme situations will be rare. Without linkage, equilibrium is the situation in which the average boldness level is high and the average vengefulness level is low, as discussed earlier. In such a situation, the sum of these two averages will be around one (because the former is close to one and the latter to zero), and linkage is neither advantaged or disadvantaged to non-linkage actors. Only random fluctuations due to mutation will govern the linkage ratio. The linkage actors emerging via mutation in such a situation will have a random chance of survival, and in many generations they will gradually increase. This gradual increase in the linkage actors will, at least partly, transform the incentive structure an N-person Assurance structure. Boldness levels among the linkage actors may then be lowered in case the average cooperation level in the group exceeds the critical cooperation ratio. If this happens, the boldness level among non-linkage actors will also decrease. This is because a few cooperative linkage actors, who also punish defectors, make C a better choice than D (remember that only a few punishers can transform the structure). As a result, nearly unanimous cooperation will result. The linkage ratio in this situation will be around 50 percent since the sum of the average boldness and vengefulness levels in such a situation is around one. Whether this nearly unanimous cooperation results or not depends on whether the average initial boldness level among the linkage actors exceeds the critical cooperation rate. If the average boldness level among linkage-actors is extremely high, nearly unanimous defection will result.

Discussion

Some researchers (*e.g.*, Heckathorn, 1988, 1989) think that people can voluntarily provide mutual sanctions if their individual regulatory interest exceeds the individual cost of sanctioning. Regulatory interest is the benefit derived from making other people more cooperative through sanctioning. It is rational for one to sanction others if the extra benefit gained by the improved cooperation of others exceeds the costs of sanctioning. This situation will be rare, however, in relatively large groups in which one actor's sanctioning activities has very little effect on the general cooperation level in the group. In these situations, the cost of sanctioning usually exceeds the regulatory interest, and as a result of this second-order dilemma, rational actors will not voluntarily engage in sanctioning activities. One way to avoid this second-order dilemma is to impose collective sanctions (Heckathorn, 1988). If a group, rather than individual defectors, is sanctioned for harboring defectors in the group, members will have a strong regulatory interest in sanctioning. In such a situation, rational actors will voluntarily sanction each other. Another situation where voluntary mutual sanctioning is likely to emerge is the N-person Assurance situation (Yamagishi, 1991). Except for these special occasions, mutual sanctions are not likely to be provided by rational actors due to the second-order dilemma. The rational choice approach to explaining social norms (as voluntarily supported mutual sanctioning) is thus very limited in scope, if not altogether impossible.

An alternative approach to the second-order dilemma and an "intrinsic" explanation of social norms was presented by Axelrod (1986) in his study of the "evolution" of norms without central authority. He concluded that the emergence of norms without a central authority only requires metanorms. The series of computer simulations reported earlier in this paper, however, demonstrated that metanorms were not the necessary condition for the "evolution" of norms. What was critical for the success of metanorms in Axelrod's (1986) simulation was actually the linkage between the punishment of the defectors and the punishment of the non-punishers, not the metanorm (punishment of non-punishers) *per se*. And when a linkage was provided between C-D decisions and P(punishment)-N(non-punishment) decisions, almost unanimous cooperation emerged.

Although the simulations reported here (as well as Axelrod's simulation) were based on the algorithm that represents "evolutionary" processes, the results can be interpreted from a rational choice perspective. As clearly demonstrated in the analysis of the incentive structure, the linkage strategy can produce unanimous cooperation because it transforms an N-person PD into an N-person Assurance game in which cooperation is individually a better choice than defection once the overall cooperation rate in the group exceeds the critical rate. Furthermore, analysis of the incentive structure shows that there is a situation in which the linkage strategy is individually a better choice than the non-linkage strategy; being consistent is sometimes a good policy for one's own benefit.

Footnotes

1   Hokkaido University, Department of Behavioral Sciences, Japan

2   The computer program used in our simulation was written in Turbo C by Atsuko Morita as a part of her Bachelor's Thesis project. The initial values of boldness and vengefulness were randomly determined between 0 and 7. In addition, another simulation program, written by Toshio Yamagishi in Quick Basic (and by Nobuyuki Takahashi in C), was used to confirm the results. The social dilemma situation used in Yamagishi's simulation program was different from Axelrod's and Morita's; each of the twenty actors decided whether or not to contribute one point to the group, which was multiplied by a factor of 5 (this factor

was the same as in Axelrod's simulation) and was evenly allocated among the 20 actors. Furthermore, the actors in Yamagishi's simulation program monitored one randomly determined actor's decisions, and punished the actor when it defected with the cost of one point. The punished defector received -4.5 points (this cost-punishment ratio was again the same as in Axelrod's simulation). Finally, the boldness level and the vengefulness level in Yamagishi's simulation program were given by a real number between 0 and 1. Despite these differences in the programs, results of Yamagishi's simulations were consistent with those of Morita's simulation.

3   The cost of cooperation in Axelrod's simulation was 4 (3 plus 1 from own cooperation), cost of punishment was 2, and the size of punishment was 9.

References

Axelrod, R. (1984). *The evolution of cooperation*. New York: Basic Books.

Heckathorn, D.D. (1988). Collective sanctions and the creation of prisoner's dilemma norms. *American Journal of Sociology, 94*, 535-562.

Heckathorn, D.D. (1989). Collective action and the second order free rider problem. *Rationality and Society, 1*, 78-100.

Olson, M. (1965). *The logic of collective action*. Cambridge, Mass.: Harvard University Press.

Yamagishi, T. (1986). The structural goal/expectation theory of cooperation in social dilemmas. In E.J. Lawler (Ed.), *Advances in group processes, Vol. III* (pp.51-87). Greenwich, Connecticut: JAI Press.

Yamagishi, T. (1991). Social exchange and social dilemmas. In K. Seiyama & M. Umino (Eds.), *The problem of social order and social dilemmas* (pp.227-257). Tokyo: Harvest Press. (In Japanese)

Acknowledgement

The research reported in this chapter was supported by a Ministry of Education Scientific Grant to Toshio Yamagishi and Hiromi Shinotsuka. We would like to thank Atsuko Morita for her help in conducting computer simulations.

Computer simulations of the relation between individual heuristics and global cooperation in prisoner's dilemmas

David M. Messick[1] and Wim B.G. Liebrand[2]

Abstract

In this paper we explore the aggregate consequences of three simple individual choice rules in a simulated society in which the interaction between pairs of actors is constituted as a Prisoner's Dilemma (PDG). After several simulations under different conditions, the most important conclusion is that in highly competitive PDG settings, using a competitive type of social comparison for performance evalution, cooperative behavior is maintained in large groups. There remain however several findings which need further study before we better understand the relation between individual heuristics and their global consequences.

The problem that we address in this paper is to describe the global consequences of heuristic choice strategies in the social situation embodied by the Prisoners' Dilemma (PDG). In particular, we will examine what happens in large groups of individuals all of whom use a well-defined decision heuristic for evaluating and making choices in the PDG. Our approach resembles that of Axelrod (1984) who also used the PDG as a model situation for self-sacrificial cooperation, but it differs in a number of important ways. We need to make the differences clear at the outset because our goal is very different from his. First, Axelrod's tournament investigated the efficiency of various strategies for playing the PDG in an environment consisting of all the other strategies that had been submitted for the tournament. This was a maximally heterogeneous environment. Our interest is in the fate of cooperation in environments in which all persons use the same strategy. The environment for any strategy is simply a population of individuals using exactly the same strategy.

Thus our goal is not to determine which of several strategies will perform better than others but to ask whether cooperation is sustainable in a population when all of its members make decisions in the same way.

A second important difference is that in Axelrod's work, each strategy played a PDG for 200 trials with each other strategy providing each interaction with a relatively long history. In our work, each individual will play the PDG with another only once on any occasion. Moreover, each individual will play only with neighbors and will not interact at all with more remote others. Thus our work assumes a "geography" that allows us to talk about neighborhoods and interactions among neighbors. Last, even among neighbors, those with whom one will play on any given trial will be determined randomly. Axelrod's procedures create a factorial environment in which the relative success of different strategies can be scientifically assessed. Our procedures bear a closer resemblance to a real social environment in which people interact most often with those close to them and not at all with remote persons. Moreover, each interaction is relatively brief.

The simulation environment that was used for this research is the Warsaw Simulation System (WSS) developed in the Department of Psychology and the Computing Center of The University of Warsaw. This system has been described by Gasik (1990). The system allows the user to define a rectangular group of up to 400 individuals and to specify the form of the interaction that will occur among them. The simulation then executes the specified processes and records prespecified dependent variables to describe the consequences of the simulation.

Our use of the WSS involves the following general processes. From a population of a specified size, one individual, the subject, is randomly selected. One of the subject's neighbors is then randomly selected. In our studies, a neighbor will be one of the eight individuals (in the three by three grid) surrounding the selected individual. (Other definitions of "neighbor" are also possible and some of them will be explored in future papers.) The subject and neighbor "play" a two person PDG in which mutual cooperation yields two points each, mutual defection yields one point each, and mixed choices provide three points to the defector and one point to the cooperator. Each individual in the population is randomly assigned an initial response, either cooperate (C) or defect (D), and this assignment determines the choice that the individuals make on the first encounter. The payoff to the subject from the interaction is recorded. The subject then employs a choice heuristic that determines what the subject's next choice will be. The heuristic will be one of the three described below. This terminates one play. Another individual is then randomly selected and the process repeats itself. One "generation" is completed when a sample the size of the population has been selected to play. Sampling is done with replacement, however, so some individuals in the population will have played more than once and some will not have played at all. The simulation can be run for a fixed number of generations, or until some specified condition is met. One such condition is that the population becomes either homogeneously cooperative or homogeneously defecting.

The choice that characterizes each individual is the choice that the individual will use when the individual next plays, regardless of whether the play is as subject or neighbor. However, only subjects recalculate the choice after an interaction; neighbors do not. (We have run some simulations in which this condition was changed and we observed no qualitative differences.) Unless otherwise specified, our simulations assumed that each subject had eight neighbors meaning that there were no edges or corners on the rectangle that defined the population. Thus a subject on the right-hand edge had a corresponding point on the left-hand edge as a neighbor, and subjects on the lower edge had corresponding points on the upper edge as neighbors, and vice versa.

Our simulations used three decision heuristics which are discussed here.

Tit-for-tat. Of the three decision heuristics that we will explore, TFT is the best know and the simplest. Using TFT, the subject will simply mimic the neighbor's choice on subject's subsequent play. It is important to note the difference between TFT as it is applied in this study and the way it has been used previously. In most previous studies, TFT has been shown to be effective in maintaining high levels of cooperation when the interaction was between the same two individuals. In our simulation, this is not the case. When the subject becomes cooperative after having interacted with a cooperative neighbor, the individual will be cooperative, if selected as a neighbor, regardless of which neighbor is the subject. Moreover, when again selected as subject, the cooperator will cooperate with any neighbor selected, not just the one that was previously cooperative.

Reciprocity in this case is not a direct one-to-one reciprocity but a generalized reciprocity in which the cooperator will cooperate with any individual with whom it interacts so long as it is in the cooperative state. The same is true with non-cooperation. The reciprocation is broadcast to the entire neighborhood.

Also, unlike the TFT strategy submitted by Anatol Rapoport to Axelrod's (1984) tournament, our version of TFT did not always begin with a cooperative choice. Half the population began with C and half began with D as their initial choice. Ours was not a "nice" TFT.

Clearly, if a population becomes homogeneously cooperative or homogeneously defecting with TFT it will stay that way indefinitely. Most simply, TFT is simple mimicry. It cannot change what it is imitating.

Win-Stay, Lose-Change (WSLC). A WSLC process is one that has two components. The first is an evaluative component that determines what is a win and what is a loss; the second is the action component the dictates what should be done contingent on the output of the first component. In this abstract sense, elementary reinforcement mechanisms are WSLC processes. Such mechanisms differentiate positive from negative reinforcers and postulate that perseveration of behavior (stay) will tend to follow positive reinforcers while extinction (change) will follow negative reinforcers. Thus the WSLC process might be taken to be a primitive adaptation mechanism that steers the organism toward positive outcomes (approach) and away from aversive ones (avoidance).

In our simulations, we want to embrace the realism that derives from assuming that outcomes are socially evaluated. As a result, we define "win" and "lose" socially in terms of the payoffs of the neighbors. Specifically, "win" results when the payoff to the subject is equal to or greater than the average of the payoffs of the subject's eight neighbors. After the subject and its neighbor play the game, the payoff to the subject is compared to a reference point that is calculated as follows: The payoff to the neighbor from that play is averaged together with the other seven neighbors' payoffs from the last time they were subjects. If subject's payoff is at least as large as this average, the subject "wins". When the subject's payoff is smaller than this local average, the subject "loses". Following a win, subject repeats its choice; following a loss, subject changes to the other choice.

Win-Cooperate, Lose-Defect (WCLD). The previous rule, WSLC, is content-free in the sense that it is blind to the consequences of its choices. C and D are interchangeable and the WSLC does not discriminate between them. WCLD is different in that it follows a win with a cooperative choice and a loss with defection. WCLD is a reciprocity rule whose justification comes from the matching of positive outcomes with positive outcomes. The C choice always provides a better payoff to the other but at a cost to the chooser. It is precisely this quality that has allowed the PDG to be used as a model of altruism. By paying attention to the content of the choices, WCLD becomes an affective version of TFT rather than a mere mimic. The rule responds to the positive outcome of winning by cooperating and giving a positive outcome (at some cost), and to the negative outcome of losing by defecting, making the dominating choice. Win and loss are defined, of course, as in WSLC. WCLD is a kind of reciprocation rule. Later we will discuss its relationship to TFT.

There is evidence in the social psychological literature to support the principles on which this rule is based. It is known, for example, that positive moods enhance prosocial tendencies (Krebs & Miller, 1985), and that these tendencies are not restricted to the person or persons responsible for the positive mood. Being the beneficiary of a generous act by one person enhances the likelihood of behaving generously to another unrelated person. On the negative side, the tendency to punish one's spouse for the frustrations experienced in the work-place is common-place. Reciprocity is affective, not imitative, and it may be directed to parties other than the instigator.

As with WSLC, there are some immediate consequences of this rule. The DC and CD outcomes will always be coded as wins and losses, respectively, because the DC outcome (3) is the maximum possible and the CD outcome (0) is the smallest possible. The DC combination, which always gives a win, will lead to C as the next choice with this rule and the CD combination will always lead to D as the next choice.

The implications of the three rules are outlined in Table 1. In this table, we specify, if possible, what the payoff and choice consequences are for each combination of subject and neighbor choices. It is impossible to say what the next choice of the WSLC and WCLD will be following CC and DD choices since it depends on the neighbors' average payoff. All rules follow the CD choice with a D. The CC combination is more likely than the DD to be coded as a win since the payoff is 2 rather than 1. Both WSLC and WCLD will chose C if it is a win and D if not. Thus these two rules are identical in their response to the consequences of their own C choice. However, they are exactly opposite in their responses to the consequences of their D choices. WSLC and WCLD respond to the coding of the DD outcome in opposite ways--WSLC repeats D to a win and changes to C after a loss, while WCLD does the reverse. The two reciprocal rules, TFT and

WCLD, follow the win of DC with a cooperative choice, while the WSLC repeats D. In fact, the two reciprocal rules have identical responses to the DC and CD plays, and if the neighbors' means were always between 1 and 2, these two rules would be identical. We will return to this point later.

Table 1

Payoff and next choice consequences for each pair of subject and neighbor choices for the three rules.

CHOICE PAIR (S,N)	C,C		C,D	D,C	D,D	
PAYOFF TO SUBJECT	2		0	3	1	
NEXT CHOICE BY RULE	WIN	LOSE			WIN	LOSE
TFT	C		D	C	D	
WSLC	C	D	D	D	D	C
WCLD	C	D	D	C	C	D

Certain default initializations characterize all our simulations unless we state otherwise. We begin all runs by randomly assigning cooperative and defecting strategies with equal probability. We begin with an initial payoff of 1.5, the average of the four numbers in the payoff matrix, to each individual.

In this article, there is only space to summarize several of our most interesting discoveries. A more complete account of our findings will appear elsewhere.

Small groups versus large groups. We take a group (population) of size nine to be the smallest group with which we will be concerned. In this case the population coincides with the neighborhood. This choice is based on the symmetry that, in a group of nine, each individual has eight neighbors and each individual is neighbor to every other individual. We have found important differences between groups of size nine and larger groups. The major finding with groups of nine is that such groups always become permanently homogeneous, either with cooperation or defection. For a group to become permanently homogeneous, it must be that once the group is in the state it will never leave, and there must be a positive probability that the group can enter the state. With the TFT strategy, the probability is one half that the group will become all cooperative and one half that it will become all defecting. Since this strategy is purely imitative, there are no forces that favor either cooperation or defection. Our experiments, which have now involved thousands of runs of TFT, confirm that the all-cooperate and all-defect outcomes occur equally often. It is important to understand that once a population using TFT has become homogeneous it will remain so forever. In fact, TFT with a nine person group can be summarized as a ten-state Markov chain (states are defined by the number of cooperators) with stationary transition probabilities and two absorbing states, all-cooperate or all-defect.

What is less obvious is that with nine person groups, both WSLC and WCLD also become permanently homogeneous. WSLC becomes all-defect and WCLD becomes all-cooperate. With the latter, one can see that if the group entered the state in which all members were C so that they exchanged 2 points per play, they would receive outcomes that are coded as wins since they are equal to the outcomes of their neighbors, and they would continue to cooperate.

The properties of WSLC are somewhat more subtle. First, it is not possible to go into an all-C state. The all-C state must be preceded by a eight-C and one-D state in which the D individual is subject. The D subject will always receive 3 points interacting with any neighbor and the three points will always be a win, causing the D to stay. It is possible for the group to become all-D, on the other hand. In an eight-D, one-C group, when the C is subject, the C will receive zero points which will always be coded as a loss, causing the cooperator to change to defection. However, the new all-D group will only be stable if the mean of the payoffs is one or less causing the payoff for mutual defection (1 unit) to be coded a win.

The discussion above suggests that the processes by means of which small groups become homogeneous are different for the three different heuristics. One manifestation of these differences is in the speed with which the groups become homogeneous. In a series of simulations, we estimated that TFT is the fastest, requiring an average of 5.42 generations to enter an absorbing state. WCLD is next, requiring an average of 15.04 generations and by far the slowest is WSLC which took an average of 65.3 generations to converge. These means are clearly significantly different, and in this, as in other cases where differences are obvious, we will not report statistical tests or significance levels.

Cooperation in large groups. In this section we will summarize the results of several of the simulations that we conducted. We first outline some basic findings regarding the global consequences of WSLC and WCLD, rules that do not become homogeneous in populations of 100, which will be our basic size. Thereafter we will describe an experiment to study the effects of changes in the payoff structure, following which we will describe some studies investigating variations in the evaluation processes, the way in which wins and losses are framed.

We can summarize our basic findings by describing an experiment in which we manipulated the size of the population and the heuristic rule, either WSLC or WCLD, used to generate choices. In this experiment, we varied the population from 36 (62), 64 (82), 100 (102), 144 (122), to 196 (142). For each population size, each rule, following a random 50-50 initial assignment of cooperation and defection, was run for 50 generations. The status of the population at the end of the 50 generations was measured. Each rule was replicated 50 times for each population size yielding a total of 500 simulations each of which was 50 generations long. This experiment allows us to investigate the joint effects of population size and rule on the prevalence of cooperation.

In this as in the other experiments, we will not list values of F-ratios nor present significance levels for most of the results we describe. We will discuss only effects that are large and significant. Our statistical tests are all extremely powerful because the noise levels are moderate at worst and because the experiments usually have a minimum of five hundred degrees of freedom for the error terms.

The only factor influencing the prevalence of cooperation was the rule. WSLC generated an average of 40.2% cooperation, while WCLD led to 55.4% cooperation. These levels have been replicated in hundreds of further simulations. As with most of our simulations, population size does not influence the frequency of cooperation.

The data from our basic experiment provide a baseline against which a variety of changes can be compared. It is to these other questions that we will now turn our attention. One important issue that is not addressed by the first study is the speed with which the population changes from its initial configuration. In one experiment we varied the number of generations that the simulations ran before stopping. We varied the stopping time from 2 generations to 30. In all cases the simulations began with random 50-50 distributions of the 100 cooperators and defectors. The results of this experiment are displayed in Figure 1. What is clear from this figure is that the proportion of cooperators rapidly settles in on the asymptotic values of about 40% for WSLC and 55% for WCLD. There is little change following trial number six.

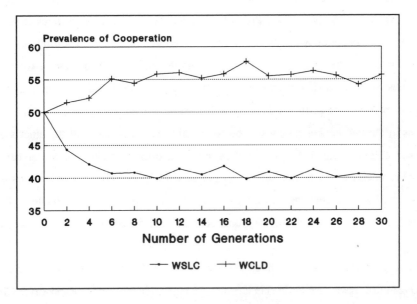

Figure 1: Mean prevalence of cooperation for WSLC and WCLD as a function of generations. Each mean is based on 50 simulations.

The prevalence of cooperation is stable over initial distributions of cooperators and defectors. In one experiment, we varied the initial relative density of cooperators from .10% to 90% in populations of 100 and we stopped the simulation after 25 generations. We ran 50 replications of each condition. While the initial distributions had a significant effect on the prevalence of cooperation, especially for the WCLD rule, the magnitude of the effect was very small. The range of final rates of cooperation for WCLD was from about 54% to 59% and that for WSLC was from 40% to about 42%. Other experiments have given similar results, indicating that the initial distribution has little or no effect on the prevalence of cooperation after as few as 15 generations. However, some of the experiments give suggestive evidence that the system may have a slight "memory" for its starting distribution. This problem is one that deserves further investigation, but for the present purpose it is sufficient to observe that the distribution of cooperation we observed in our basic experiment is not an artifact resulting from our use of 50-50 initial distributions of cooperators and defectors.

One of the most commonly studied features of the PDG is the payoff structure itself (Liebrand, Messick & Wilke, 1992; Pruitt & Kimmel, 1977). How do changes in the payoffs influence the levels of cooperation? We are naturally interested in the same question, but we remind the reader that our simulations are very different from the traditional two-person experiments that have been reported in the experimental social psychological literature. These latter studies typically involved two persons interacting exclusively with each other over a long series of trials. Outcome evaluations in the two person setting will be restricted to comparisons with the other's outcomes (see Messick & Thorngate, 1967, for evidence of the importance of this type of comparison) and this type of comparison will be different from comparison with all neighbors. Also our simulations are not intended to represent the dynamics of cooperation in one-on-one encounters. The whole point of our simulations is to investigate global consequences for cooperation under very different conditions.

There are many ways in which the payoff structure of a PDG can be manipulated. Cooperative indices have been defined in terms of the payoffs in the matrix (Rapoport & Chammah, 1965), concepts of fear and greed have been defined as functions of the matrix (Coombs, 1973), and Messick & McClintock (1968) showed how additive matrices, like the one used here, can be decomposed into additive components.

We will describe the results of only one experiment involving manipulations of the payoff matrix. In this study, we systematically varied the so-called "temptation" parameter (T), the payoff received by a defector when the other person cooperates. This payoff will always be the largest in a PDG matrix and the goal of the study we conducted was to assess the impact of increasing the temptation parameter from its canonical value of three. In this experiment, we let T vary from 3 to 19 in steps of 4. We simultaneously varied the population size through three levels, 49, 100, and 225. (Even though our basic experiments had shown no effects for population size, we occasionally included it as a factor to check for the possibility that size might interact with some of the other factors we examined.) Of course, we also varied the heuristic choice rule. Each replication ran for 50 generations and there were 50 replications of each combination of rule, population size, and T level.

The main findings of this experiment with regard to the prevalence of cooperation are displayed in Figure 2 where we have plotted the prevalence of cooperation for both rules against the temptation parameter. (An analysis of variance reveals that both main effects, for rule and T, as well as their interaction are highly statistically significant). Cooperation decreases as T increases, as we would expect, but the impact of changing T is much greater for WCLD than it is for WSLC, which proves relatively insensitive to variations in T. WCLD, on the other hand, is most sensitive to changes in T when T is small. Cooperation drops from the basic rate of about 56% at T=3 to about 33% when T is increased to 7 and the rate of cooperation falls only marginally thereafter (to about 30%). Future experiments will attempt to determine why WCLD is so sensitive to changes in T around T = 3.

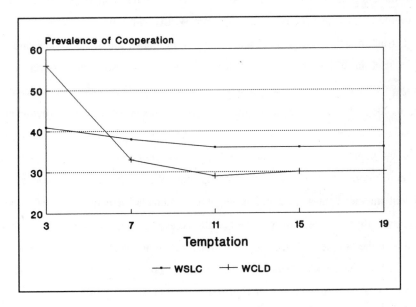

Figure 2:   Mean prevalence of cooperation for WSLC and WCLD as a function of the temptation parameter. Each mean is based on 50 simulations.

The outcome evaluation process is the psychological heart of our simulations. It is here where we make assumptions about the intra-individual psychological processes the lead to cooperative or non-cooperative choices. Therefore, it is important to investigate the extent to which changes in our assumptions lead to changes in the prevalence of cooperation in groups.

The first question we address is what difference does it make that the reference point is a local, dynamic, socially defined reference point rather than a fixed, non-social one. Assume, for instance, that the relevant reference point is the average of the four scores that are available in the payoff matrix (namely, 1.5) so that a win is an outcome that is above 1.5 and a loss is one that falls below. This definition makes the outcomes "two" and "three" wins and "zero" and "one" losses. With this classification, the WCLD rule simply becomes TFT because one wins when the neighbor chooses cooperatively and loses when the neighbor defects. Thus the solitary feature that differentiates TFT from WCLD is the use of a local social reference point for WCLD and the use of a fixed one in TFT. The large group implications of this difference are, as we have seen, immense. The changes in the dynamics are qualitative, not quantitative. With WSLC, using a fixed reference point that falls between one and two produces a different type of process as well. In this case it is simple to show that the rule resulting from WSLC with a fixed reference is to cooperate following a trial in which the subject and the neighbor make the same choice and to defect following a trial in which they make different choices. This rule could never lead to the homogeneous defection we observed in small groups with WSLC because mutual defection leads the subject to cooperate. Since mutual cooperation leads to cooperation, if the group ever reached a homogeneously cooperative state, it would remain there. However, under the rules of our simulations, the population can never become homogeneously cooperative. To see why this is so, imagine a population that is all cooperators except one. When the single defector is selected as subject it will interact with a cooperative neighbor, leading to defection the next time around. Under slightly different simulation procedures all-cooperate would be a feasible outcome. For example, if both the sampled subject *and* the sampled neighbor changed their choices according to this rule, then homogeneous cooperation would result. Again, changing from a social to a fixed reference point changes the dynamics of cooperation qualitatively.

Many experiments have shown that the global distribution of cooperation depends delicately on the nature of the evaluation process. Whether the dimension of evaluation is the last payoff or the accumulated payoffs makes a difference, for instance. An even more important difference can be shown to be the extent of bias in the evaluation. When the difference between one's outcome and the local average must equal or exceed only -.25, for instance, rather than zero, in order to code the outcome as a win, the prevalence of cooperation leaps to nearly 100% with the WCLD heuristic, and it drops to essentially zero with WSLC. These dramatic effects on global cooperation of small changes in the location of the comparison criterion, an intrapersonal psychological parameter, illustrate the intimate connection between the global level of cooperation and the details of the assumed psychological process that govern individual decision making.

Summary and conclusions

Our research investigates the relationship between individual choice heuristics in the Prisoner's Dilemma Game and the prevalence of cooperation in large populations. We found that small groups, groups with nine simulated members, become either homogeneously cooperative or homogeneously competitive, depending on the heuristic. Larger groups using the WSLC and WCLD rules reach an intermediate level of cooperation. We have found that the prevalence of cooperation in the population depends of the parameters of the payoff matrix, but in ways that are not transparent. Finally, we found that the dynamics of cooperation in large groups depend on the details of the individual choice process. The nature and location of the reference point that is used to code wins and losses has an immense impact on spread of cooperation within the group. The results that we have described cry for interpretation. We have been able to provide a theoretical account for a few, but only a few, of our results. Our research, like social dilemmas generally, challenge us to expand the frontier of our understanding of the relationship between individual level decision processes and their global surround.

Footnotes

1   Northwestern University, Evanston, USA

2   University of Groningen, Groningen, The Netherlands

References

Axelrod, R. (1984). *The evolution of cooperation*. New York: Basic Books.

Coombs, C.H. (1973). A Re-parameterization of the Prisoners'Dilemma Game. *Behavioral Science, 18*, 424-428.

Gasik, S. (1990). *Definition of the Warsaw Simulation Language*. Unpublished manuscript, Warsaw University.

Krebs, D.L., & Miller, D.T. (1985). Altruism and aggression. In G. Lindzey & E. Aronson (Eds.), *The Handbook of Social Psychology*, Vol. 1. Hillsdale, New Jersey: Erlbaum.

Liebrand, W.B.G., Messick, D.M., & Wilke, H.A.M. (1992). *Social Dilemmas, theoretical issues and research findings*. London: Pergamon Press.

Messick, D.M., & McClintock, C.G. (1968). Motivational bases of choice in experimental games. *Journal of Experimental Social Psychology, 4*, 1-25.

Messick, D.M., & Thorngate, W. (1967). Relative gain maximization in experimental games. *Journal of Experimental Social Psychology, 3*, 85-101.

Pruitt, D.G., & Kimmel, M.J. (1977). Twenty years of experimental gaming: Critique, synthesis, and suggestions for the future. *Annual Review of Psychology, 28*, 363-392.

Rapoport, A., & Chammah, A.M. (1965). *Prisoner's Dilemma: A study in conflict and cooperation*. Ann Arbor: University of Michigan Press.

Acknowledgement

This research described in this paper was performed while the first author was a visitor at the Institute for Social Science Information Technology (SWI) at the University of Groningen, The Netherlands. The preparation of this chapter was supported by a grant from the Dispute Resolution Research Center of the J. L. Kellogg Graduate School of Management, Northwestern University. This article was published earlier in the Fall 1993 issue of "Social Science Computer Review".

What risk should a selfish partner take in order to save the life of a non-relative, selfish friend? A stochastic game approach to the prisoner's dilemma

Ilan Eshel[1], Daphna Weinshall[2], and Emilia Sansone[3]

Abstract

A model of cooperation versus defection in a sequence of games is analyzed under the assumptions that the rules of the games are randomly changed from one encounter to another, that the decisions are to be made at each situation anew, according to the specific rules of the specific local game, and that the outcome of each such game affects the ability of a player to participate and, thus, cooperate (if in its own interest) in the next game. Players wish to maximise their total payment at the entire supergame. Under plausible assumptions it is shown that all Evolutionarily Stable Strategy (ESS) of the supergame determine cooperation over a non-degenerate range of situations determining encounters of the P.D. type - A moderately altruistic cooperation is selected because it enables the survival of a potential partner for future cooperation. The model also explains the evolution of gratitude, rather than the assumption thereof, and predicts a qualitative difference between partnership altruism and kin altruism.

Introduction

It seems that an appropriate question to begin the present article with may be "Why should a selfish partner take *any* risk in order to save the life of a non-relative selfish friend?" (instead of what risk he should take, as mentioned in the title of this paper). An established fact, though, is that non-relatives who have a history of cooperation (in this context "friends") do tend to take limited risks in order to help each other. It is precisely this fact that raises the question that we now refer to as the paradox of the prisoner's dilemma.

In the last three decades, many answers were given to this apparent paradox. Most, if not virutally all of them, were based on the simple idea (e.g. Rapoport, 1967) that human beings (and, most likely, other social animals) are bound to play again (at least with high probability) with the same player they are now encountering. It is beyond the scope of this article to summarize the bulk of literature, devoted to the analysis of the repeated game of the prisoner's dilemma type, or to list the difficulties which still face this model. (For a general survey and references, see Axelrod, 1980).

It seems to us, however, that most of these difficulties stem from one unrealistic assumption, common both to the bulk of theoretical models and laboratory experiments, namely that individuals are assumed to play the *same* game repeatedly under exactly the same conditions. It seems, on the other hand, that all natural examples of cooperation involve a rather multidimensional situation in which two (or more) individuals meet each other repeatedly, being faced with a somewhat different situation each time. In such natural cases, a natural question may not be whether or not to cooperate in the next encounter. More likey, an individual has to decide under what condition or in what situation to cooperate.

Repeated encounters under a varied situation

Let us start by imagining an encounter of two shepherds with a lion. Sticking together, the two shepherds have the best chance to survive, yet each of them may drastically increase his chance by escaping and letting the other die. An observer who is familiar with the repeated game model is likely to be aware of the fact that encounters with lions occurred repeatedly in the past and are likely to repeat in the future and to explain their behavior on this basis. Yet such encounters may be too rare and the immediate advantage of escaping may be too big as to account for the cooperative behavior of the partner.

The dilemma may partly be resolved if the observer is aware of a much more frequent situation in which the same two shepherds must cooperate in rescuing their herd from frequent attacks of, say, jackals. Indeed, cooperating against an invading jackal involves no serious risk and thus represents no theoretical difficulty. Hence, it is likely to escape the eye of the kin-minded, theoretically oriented observer. But as cooperation in defining the herd against jackals becomes a key factor in the shepherds' lives, the death of one of them presents the other with a serious problem in the very near future. This is not because the deserted, now dead, partner will "remember" and desert the deflector in the future, say a year from now, when perhaps the next encounter with a lion takes place, but because he will not be there to help even if it is in his best interest to, and he will certainly not be there to help the following day in the daily fight against jackals. Hence, it may be in his partner's best interest to help him now, taking a big risk against a lion, or it may not, depending on the parameters. But it becomes more likely if, in addition to the risk of attacks by jackals and lions, we also take into consideration other risks, say attacks by wolves.

The incentive of saving your partner's life in order that he will be there to help you against jackals the next day, may not be enough to take as big a risk as fighting a lion. But it is sufficient to make it worthwhile to take the smaller risk of cooperating against a wolf. However, if encounters with wolves are sufficiently common (perhaps not as common as encounters with jackals), the life and welfare of one partner becomes crucially important to the other, since a wolf, unlike a jackal, may be quite dangerous when faced alone. It may be sufficiently important as to risk one's life cooperating in a struggle against a lion, or perhaps in the case of a not-too-frightening lion, but then we come back to the more realistic question of under what circumstances to cooperate rather than whether to cooperate.

We believe that the evolution of cooperation must have started in the simplest and most natural way in a limited (and, one has to admit, theoretically uninteresting) range of situations wherein cooperation is of a direct advantage to both participants. Thus, the appropriate supergame-strategy for this initial stage is "cooperate at any future encounter in which you cannot gain by exclusive defection". However, once such a strategy is established in a population, the very survival (and, maybe, well-doing) of your present time partner until the next possible encounter becomes important to your *long-term* survival (see, for comparison, Eshel & Cohen, 1976, Eshel & Motro, 1981; Motro, 1988). Indeed, his death throughout the present encounter will surely prevent him from any future cooperation even under those situations wherein he will have all the incentives to cooperate.

It can, therefore, be shown that an individual can increase his long-term success by a slight increase of the range of situations under which he is willing to cooperate. More specifically, it is in his best interest to cooperate in such situations in which, by paying a sufficiently small price, he can substantially increase the success of his partner, so as to enable him to cooperate in the future (at least under situations wherein cooperation will be advantageous to both parties). Yet as anyone in the population increases his own range of cooperation, the higher the probability becomes that a present-encounter-partner, if he survives, will cooperate in the future and, thus, the higher the incentive to overcome the temptation of short term gain through defection.

In the present work we suggest a model for a natural process in which individual selection operates to increase the range of cooperation in a continuous way from selfish cooperation to an evolutionary stable range of cooperation which includes some or all possible encounters of the prisoner's dilemma type. For this, neither kinship nor ability to reciprocate are required (though we do believe that these are likely to be enhancing factors in real situations).

We start by describing in the next section, a closely related, previously published model developed under a somewhat restrictive assumption of independence between death events of the two players. For detailed mathematical proofs, the reader is referred to Eshel and Weinshall (1988). We then summarize some new results, stemming from the relaxation of this assumption. Detailed mathematical analysis of this case will be published elsewhere.

Repeated game with a random encounter rule - The case of independent death events

Assume that two players encounter each other, repeatedly, a random number of times so that at the end of each encounter there is a probability p > 0 for having another one. Assume a general matrix of a symmetric two-person encounter inw hich each of the players can either cooperate or defect:

	cooperate	defect
cooperate	X_1, X_2	X_3, X_2
defect	X_2, X_3	X_4, X_4

where the parameters $X = (X_1, \ldots, X_4)$ are random variables, drawn from a four dimensional distribution, F, independently of the past. By choosing the term "cooperation" for the first strategy, however, we mean that

$$X1 > X3 \text{ and } X2 > X4 \qquad (3.1)$$

(i.e., by cooperating, a player always helps his partner),

$$\qquad (3.2)$$

(i.e., mutual cooperation is always in the Pareto's optimum of the encounter), and

$$X2 > X3 \qquad (3.3)$$

(i.e., if only one player defects, then his reward will be higher than that of his cooperating partner).

We assume a positive probability for encounters of the prisoner's dilemma type, i.e.,

$$p(D) > 0 \text{ where } D = \{X \,|\, X_2 > X_1 > X_4 > X_3\} \qquad (3.4)$$

We also assume, however, a positive probability for encounters in which cooperation is of immediate self reward, i.e.,

$$p(R) > 0 \text{ where } R = \{X \,|\, X_1 \geq X_2; \ X_3 \geq X_4\} \qquad (3.5)$$

We assume, moreover, that F has positive density f over a convex set of parameters, Ω, including at least part of the boundary $\{X \,|\, X_1 = X_2 > X_3 = X_4\}$ between R and D.

At each stage of the supergame each player possesses full knowledge of the present situation (i.e., about the realization of X). However, we assume no memory so that a pure strategy is a measurable set G of situations (game-matrices) over which the player is willing to cooperate. A mixed strategy is a measurable function $\Gamma: \Omega \to [0,1]$, determining the probability $\Gamma(a)$ that a player will cooperate in situation $a \in \Omega$, where Ω is the space of all payoff matrices.

If player i (i = 1,2) chooses the strategy Γ, then the survival probability of player 1 during a single encounter is

$$s_1(\Gamma_1,\Gamma_2) = \iint_{\Omega} \{\Gamma_1(a)\Gamma_2(a)\alpha_1 + \Gamma_1(a)(1-\Gamma_2(a))\alpha_3$$

$$+(1-\Gamma_1(a))\Gamma_2(a)\alpha_2+(1-\Gamma_1(a))(1-\Gamma_2(a))\alpha_4\}\,dF(a) \qquad (3.6)$$

The survival probability of player 2 is, by symmetry:

$$s_2(\Gamma_1,\Gamma_2) = s_1(\Gamma_2,\Gamma_1) \qquad (3.7)$$

Finally, we assume that the survival probability of any player at an "encounter situation" in which his partner is missing is

$$s_1(\Gamma_1,-) = \iint_{\Omega} \alpha_4 dF = EX_4 = \lambda \qquad (3.8)$$

independently of the player strategy.

Assuming now that, given the probabilities $s_i = s_i\,(\Gamma_1,\Gamma_2)$, the survival of player 1 and player 2 at a given encounter are independent random variables, the probability that both players survive a single encounter is, then, s_1s_2 and the probability that they both survive the entire sequence of games is, therefore:

$$\sum_{k=0}^{\infty} p^k q(s_1s_2)^k = \frac{q}{1-ps_1s_2} \qquad (3.9)$$

where p, as we recall, is the chance of a new encounter, $q = 1-p$. (Note that $p^k q$ is the probability that the sequence of encounters will be of length k) In the same way, the probability that only player 1 will survive a single encounter is $s_1(1-s_2)$. Hence, if both players do not survive until the end of the sequence, then, using the Bayes formula, we know that there is probability

$$\frac{s_1(1-s_2)}{1-s_1s_2}$$

that at any single encounter, player 1 survives and player 2 dies. Employing the stationary property of the sequence of games, we know that the survival probability of player 1 until the end of the sequence, conditioned on this opponent's death at one stage of the supergame is

$$\sum_{k=0}^{\infty} p^k q \lambda^k = \frac{q}{1 - p\lambda} \tag{3.10}$$

The unconditioned survival probability of player 1 to the end of the sequence is, therefore,

$$V(\Gamma_1, \Gamma_2) = \frac{q}{1 - ps_1s_2} + \left[1 - \frac{q}{1 - ps_1s_2}\right] \frac{s_1(1 - s_2)}{1 - s_1s_2} \frac{q}{1 - p\lambda}$$

where s_1s_2 and λ are given by (3.6)-(3.8). By simple algebraic manipulation one readily gets

$$V(\Gamma_1, \Gamma_2) = \frac{q}{1 - p\lambda} (1 + p\psi) \tag{3.11}$$

where

$$\psi = \psi(\Gamma_1, \Gamma_2) = \Phi(s_1, s_2) = \frac{s_1 - \lambda}{1 - ps_1s_2} \tag{3.12}$$

Hence, the game is determined by the attempt of player 1 to choose a strategy Γ_1 that will maximize $\psi(\Gamma_1, \Gamma_2)$ against Γ_2 and of player 2 to choose a strategy Γ_2 that will maximize $\psi(\Gamma_2, \Gamma_1)$ against Γ_1.

From (3.12) it immediately follows that indeed

$$\frac{\partial \psi(s_1, s_2)}{\partial s_2} > 0 \tag{3.13}$$

i.e., at each encounter each player will gain by increasing his own survival probability, but as long as $s_1 > \lambda$ (which is true for any reasonable strategy-choice since player 1 can guarantee the survival probability $s_1 = \lambda$ by the apparently non-optimal strategy of never cooperating) also

$$\frac{\partial \psi (s_1, s_2)}{\partial s_2} > 0 \tag{3.14}$$

which means that it is in the interest of each player to increase the survival probability of his partner. Note, however, that since both s_1 and s_2 are functions of Γ_1 and Γ_2 and since player 1 can only change Γ_1, he cannot, in general, simultaneously increase both s_1 and s_2. Thus, if by a small change of his own strategy, player 1 adds a small value θ_1 (either positive or negative) to his own survival probability during an encounter and θ_2 (positive or negative) to his companion's, then this change will be for his long-term advantage if and only if

$$\theta_1 \frac{\partial \varphi}{\partial s_1} + \theta_2 \frac{\partial \varphi}{\partial s_2} > 0 \tag{3.15}$$

Thus, a pure strategy Γ (say, a measurable set Γ, over which the individual is willing to cooperate) is a strict ESS if when both players choose Γ, the reverse of (3.15) holds with respect to any small change made by player 1, either in the direction of more cooperation, less cooperation, or cooperation at different situations.

The analysis of the exact set of all possible strict ESSs is complicated since it involves problems of measure and integration. It can be shown, though (Eshel & Weinshall, 1988), that an infinite set of strict ESSs exists, each determining cooperation on a wider set of situations. But even the minimal Ess always determines cooperation on a non-degenerate set of encounters of the prisoner's dilemma type.

Repeated game with a random encounter rule -
The general case of dependence between death events

In the general case, death of one player at a given encounter is not independent of the death of the other. Thus, full information about the survival probabilities of the two players in a given encounter is given by the 2 x 2 matrix of quadruplets $(X_{11}^{ij}, X_{10}^{ij}, X_{01}^{ij}, X_{00}^{ij})$ $i,j = 1,2$ where

X_{11}^{ij} is the probability that both survives

X_{10}^{ij} is the probability that only the first one survives

X_{01}^{ij} is the probability that only the second one survives

X_{00}^{ij} is the probability that none survive

all under the assumption that the first player takes the i-th and the second takes the j-th alternative decision of cooperate non-cooperate.

Denote by s_{11}, s_{10}, s_{01} and s_{00}, the appropriate one encounter survival probabilities, and let $s_1 = s_{11} + s_{10}$, $s_2 = s_{11} + s_{01}$ (the survival probabilities of the first player and the second player, respectively, in a single encounter). These values are calculated as functions of Γ_1 and Γ_2 very much in the same way as shown in (3.6) and survival until the end of the supergame is easily shown (very much as in (3.9)-(3.12) to be

$$V(\Gamma_1, \Gamma_2) = \sum_{k=0}^{\infty} p^k q s_{11}^k = \left[1 - \sum_{k=0}^{\infty} p^k q s_{11}^k\right] \frac{s_{10}}{1 - s_{11}} \sum_{k=0}^{\infty} p^k q \lambda^k$$

$$= \frac{q}{1 - ps_{11}} + \left[1 - \frac{q}{1 - ps_{11}}\right] \frac{s_{10}}{1 - s_{11}} \frac{q}{1 - \lambda q} \qquad (4.1)$$

$$= \frac{q}{1 - \lambda} \left[1 + p \frac{s_{11} + s_{10}\lambda}{1 - ps_{11}}\right]$$

$$= \frac{q}{1 - \lambda}\left(1 + p\varphi(s_{11}, s_{10})\right)$$

where

$$\varphi(s_1, s_{10}) = \frac{s_1 - \lambda}{1 - ps_{11}} = \frac{s_1 - \lambda}{1 - ps_1 - ps_{10}} = \psi(\Gamma_1, \Gamma_2) \qquad (4.2)$$

and we assume that player 1, by changing Γ_1, is seeking to increase this function. As before, Γ is a strict ESS if, when chosen by both players, player 1, by exclusively changing his own strategy, can change s_1 and s_{11} (or s_1 and s_{10}) only in such a way that the value $\varphi(s_1, s_{10})$ will decrease.

Analysis of the entire set of possible ESSs is similar to that done for the case of independent death events and, except for the case $s_{11} = 0$ (in which at each encounter, only one of the two players can survive), there is always a non-degenerate set of encounters of the prisoner's dilemma type (i.e., a set with a positive probability) on which there is full cooperation under any of the ESS strategies.

However, it can be shown that as the correlation between death events increases, the range of cooperation increases. In the extreme case of negative correlation, on the other hand, where $s_{11} = 0$, and hence $s_1 = s_2 = s_{01}$, (4.2) becomes

$$\varphi(s_1, s_{10}) = s_1 - \lambda \qquad (4.3)$$

independently on s_{10} or s_{11}, hence, in this case, player 1 is absolutely indifferent to the fate of player 2, and no cooperation can evolve.

Discussion: Partnership altruism versus reciprocal altruism and kinship altruism

Partnership altruism (help your partner now in order that he will be *able* to help you in the future, when worthwhile to him) is to be distinguished from *reciprocal altruism* (help your partner in order that he will *remember* and return in kind for kindness; Trivers, 1971). In this work we suggest a basic model for partnership altruism based on physical survival. The same model can be applied to survival in a wider sense, say staying in business, avoiding bankruptcy, keeping academic position, etc., and the idea of partnership altruism can easily be extended beyond that of preventing full destruction of the partner. In many cases it is in one's own interest to keep one's partner rich, healthy, or powerful in order that he will be *more efficient* in providing help in the future.

Unlike reciprocal altruism, partnership altruism does not assume gratefulness, a rather problematic component in the attempt to explain the evolution of altruism on the basis of reciprocity. Indeed, being ungrateful, when in your own interest, may be as tempting as defecting in encounters of the prisoner's dilemma type. In fact, we see that the evolution of partnership altruism does not even require memory, and the model suggested may thus be applicable to the evolution of apparently altruistic cooperation among non-relatives, observed in some populations of very primitive organisms (e.g., see Eshel & Cohen, 1976). Yet, as we see in this discussion, memory can be useful in enabling the partners to switch from one ESS level of cooperation to a higher one for the benefit of both. The existence of infinitely many such ESSs has been demonstrated in the analysis of the model and it is not very surprising intuitively. Indeed, as a higher level of cooperation is established between two partners, each becomes more valuable for the other from the point of view of future perspective help and this in turn can perpetuate the new, high level of cooperation (up to some upper limit). (See for comparison Eshel & Motro, 1981).

This possibility makes it advantageous for any partner to let his altruistic action be known to the other (a factor which, unlike in reciprocal altruism, is not a necessary prerequisite for help). At the same time, it is as advantageous for the recipient of the altruistic help to notice and remember the *level* of altruistic cooperation of his partner as to adjust himself to the appropriate ESS level and to stick to the highest level obtained, to his own benefit.

But is such an *adjustment* to the partner's level of altruistic behavior not equivalent, from a behavioral point of view, to gratefulness? Indeed, a rational partner may calculate the future advantage of adjusting his behavior to that of his partner, but more likely, as the *same* behavior can result from a sincere feeling of gratefulness, natural selection will favor the evolution of a tendency to feel grateful and act accordingly up to some level. The model of partnership altruism, thus, does not mean to replace that of reciprocal altruism but, instead, to provide a complementary explanation to its evolution. Yet factors of partnership altruism can be distinguished in practice from those of pure reciprocity by the possible tendency of a participant to help (or in most real cases, not to harm too much when in one's immediate advantage) another participant even when that action (or inaction) is certain not to be known to the other.

Finally, developing a model for partnership and reciprocity, we do not suggest here that these are the only or even the m ain factors in the evolution of human (and animal) altruism. Early human population structure seems likely to be most favorable for the evolution of altruism due to kin selection (Hamilton, 1964) or weak group selection, say neighbor-effect (Eshel, 1972). Moreover, as it has been shown (Axelrod & Hamilton, 1981), a tendency toards altruistic cooperation, originally evolving on the basis of kin selection, may be only a first step towards the establishment of stable altruistic cooperation (in this case, tit-for-tat) among non-relatives.

However, as indicated by the result of this work, partnership altruism can have crucial aspects that make it *qualitatively* different from kinship altruism. These aspects can be revealed (in daily life or, suggestedly, in laboratory experiments) only if we observe the individual's behavior under different types of encounters.

The qualitative difference between partnership and kinship altruism stems from the fact that in the case of partnership, one is interested in the survival of one's companion (or in improving his status) only as long as the partnership can be continued, first of all, as l ong as he himself is alive, or have a substantial chance to remain alive, together with his partner. Pure kinship altruism, on the other hand, is aimed to benefit the relative as potential carrier of one's own genes (Hamilton, 1964) and as such, is likely to be endowed (e.g. in terms of life insurance, last will, etc.) even after death. (For the fact that any kinship altruism must include a factor of partnership altruism, though; see Eshel & Motro, 1981. Indeed, if a relative is supposed to help you because he is a relative, then once he is dead you are bound to lose more than his genes. You lose a potential helper as well as perhaps a competitor, a factor that must affect kinship.)

To illustrate the difference between kinship and partnership altruism, let us return to the imaginary example of two companions encountering a lion. Each of them may either stay and fight or escape. Assuming the following symmetric matrix of individual survival

	Fight	Escape
Fight	(0.5:0.5)	(0:0.7)
Escape	(0.7:0)	(0.2:0.2)

First, assume the case of a one-shot encounter between relatives. Indeed, by sticking to one's companion (as an alternative to exclusive escape), one decreases one's chance of survival by 0.2 while increasing his relative's chance by 0.5. Thus, the inclusive fitness, accrued by this action, is 0.5r-0.2, where r is the coefficient of relatedness between them. Cooperation is stable if and only if r > 0.4. Thus, in the case of kinship altruism, the only information needed for the decision whether to cooperate or to defect is given by the matrix of individual survival probabilities.

Suppose, on the other hand, that the two companions are non-relatives, but they know they still have to find their way out of the forest, and the chance of each of them surviving alone (after escaping the lion) is θ times smaller than in the presence of his companion. Does the matrix of individual survival (together with the value of θ) give us sufficient information to make a rational decision in this case? The answer is no. One must resort to additional information about the correlation between the death events of the two companions. To illustrate this, assume the two extreme situations, both fitting well to the information given above in the matrix of individual survival.

Case I. Fighting together, the partners have a 0.5 chance to chase the lion away. If not, they both die.

In this case, sticking to your partner and fighting together, you have a 0.5p chance to escape safely from the forest (p being the chance of escaping the forest with a partner). Escaping the lion you have a chance of $0.7\theta p$, hence cooperation is beneficial if and only if $\theta < \dfrac{5}{7}$

Case II. Fighting together, the lion will kill just one of the two.

This still agrees with the figure of 0.5 individual chance of survival given by the matrix. But whatever θ may be, escaping the lion is always advantageous because, in this case, if you survive, you remain alone anyhow, and by escaping you at least increase your first survival probability.

In the same way it might be shown, more generally, that if the correlation between the death events in fighting the lions is $-1 < R < 1$, then cooperation is advantageous in the long run if and only if

$$\frac{1 + R}{4} + \frac{1 - R}{4}\theta > 0.70 \quad \text{or} \quad \theta < \frac{1 - R}{1.8 - R}$$

and correlation between the partner's survival events becomes a crucial factor in partnership altruism while it does not affect kinship altruism.

Keeping this in mind, the notorious saying "after me, the deluge" may not necessarily reflect utmost selfishness. Instead, it may reflect a change of attitude from a paternal approach of a king as a "father of the nation" (fitting the model of Axelrod & Hamilton, 1981), to a more modern approach towards a political leader as a senior partner whose best interest may (though, unfortunately as we know, may not) lie in the welfare of his disciples, as long as he remains in power and indeed stays alive, but not after his death.

Footnotes

1   Tel Aviv University, Dept. of Statistics, School of Mathematics, Tel Aviv, Israel

2   The Hebrew University, Dept. of Computer Science, Jerusalem, Israel

3   University of Naples, Dept. of Mathematics and its Applications, Italy

References

Axelrod, R. (1980). Effective choice in the prisoner's dilemma. *Journal of Conflict Resolution, 24*, 3-25.

Axelrod, R., & Hamilton, W.D. (1981). The evolution of cooperation. *Science, 211*, 1390-1396.

Eshel, I. (1972). On the neighbor effect and the evolution of altruistic behavior traits. *Theor. Pop. Biol., 3(3)*, 258-277.

Eshel, I., & Cohen, D. (1976). Altruism, competition and kin selection in populations. In S. Karlin & E. Nevo (Eds.), *Population genetics and ecology.*

Eshel, I., & Motro, U. (1981). Kin selection and strong evolutionary stability of mutual help. *Theor. Pop. Biol., 19*, 420-433.

Eshel, I., & Weinshall, D. (1988). Cooperation in a repeated game with random payment function. *J. Appl. Prob.*, *25*, 478-491.

Hamilton, W.D. (1964). The genetical evolution of social behavior I-II. *J. Theor. Biol.*, *7*, 1-52.

Motro, U. (1988). Evolutionary stable strategies of mutual help between relatives having unequal fertilities. *J. Theor. Biol.*, *135*, 31-39.

Rapoport, A. (1967). Escape from paradox. *Scientific American*, *217*, 50-56.

Trivers, R.L. (1971). The evolution of reciprocal altruism. *Quart. Rev. Biol.*, *46*, 35-57.

Learning models for the prisoner's dilemma game: A review

Hans Christoph Micko[1]

Abstract

The paper provides a review of mathematical learning models for gaming behavior in sequences of prisoner's dilemma games. The introductory part of the paper gives some basic information about the mathematics of traditional learning models. Three types of models are explained: Linear operator models, choice models and Markov-models. In the first part classical learning models for overt gaming behavior are presented. They were developed by Anatol Rapoport and his co-workers. Results for two Markov-models and a linear operator model are discussed. Van der Sanden developed a Markov-model with two latent value states and a transitional intermediate state. This model is based on earlier work of Meeker. Micko, Brückner und Ratzke developed a linear operator model with two latent dimensions called "cooperative inclination" and "trust". The basic ideas of this model are very similar to Pruitt and Kimmel's goal-expectation theory. Schulz and co-workers developed a series of learning models which account for players' expectations and separate social value parameters and information processing parameters. In the most recent model of this type goals, expectations, and choices are overt variables. This model allows empirical tests of the goal expectation theory.

Three types of learning models have been applied to players' behavior in series of prisoner's dilemma games. They are characterized by recursive equations which give the probability of a choice made in the n+1-th game, cooperative or defective, as a function of its probability in the n-th game:

1. Linear operator models: $p_{n+1} = (1-a) \cdot p_n + a \cdot l$

with $0 \leq a \leq 1$ as learning rate parameter and l as measure of the effect of the outcome, CC, CD, DC, DD, of the n-th game, i.e. $l = 1$ (or at least $p_n \leq l \leq 1$) in the case of a satisfactory outcome and $l = 0$ (or at least $0 \leq l \leq p_n$) in the case of an unsatisfactory outcome. Thus, linear operator models represent p_{n+1} as weighted mean of p_n, the probability resulting from the outcomes up to the n-1-th game, and l, the effect of the outcome of the n-th game (Bush & Mosteller, 1955).

2. Choice models: $$\frac{p_{n+1}}{(1 - p_{n+1})} = b \cdot \frac{p_n}{(1 - p_n)} \quad ,$$

with p_n as before and b as learning rate parameter, $b > 1$ in the case of a satisfactory and $b < 1$ in the case of an unsatisfactory outcome. Whether the outcome of a game results in an increase or decrease of the choice probability of the response that brought about the outcome need not be assumed beforehand in Luce's (1959) choice model but is a result of the estimation procedure, i.e. it is indicated by the size of b. The recursive equation for choice models was derived from the idea that the strength v of the response exhibited in the n-th game is modified by the multiplicative, outcome dependent operator b, i.e. $v_{n+1} = b \cdot v_n$, and that the probability of some response i is

given by $p_i = \dfrac{v_i}{\sum\limits_{i=1}^{k} v_j}$ the sum taken over the response strengths of all (mutually exclusive)

alternative responses. That idea, in turn, was derived from more fundamental assumptions of choice theory.

3. Markov-models: $p_{j,\,n+1} = \sum\limits_{i=1}^{k} p_{i,\,n} \cdot p_{ij}$

with $p_{i,n}$, $p_{j,n}$ as the probability of choosing the i-th resp. j-th response alternative in the n-th game and p_{ij} as a parameter representing the probability of a transition from the i-th to the j-th response alternative in any two successive games (see e.g. Wickens, 1982).

The above models have been applied to overt behavior, i.e. to the choice probabilities of the cooperative or defective behavior alternative, as well as to the probabilities of other observed or latent variables or states, e.g. cooperation mindedness, expectation of cooperation etc. Latent variables or states, of course, have been related by some rule to overt behavior.

If not arbitrary responses but only two relevant (classes of) responses are considered, e.g. correct - incorrect, cooperative - defective etc., or if only two latent states are considered or a single latent variable p, then the learning rate parameters of the three models can be made dependent on the values of the response probability in the preceding game, i.e. $a,b,p_{ij} = f(p)$, without violating the combined classes condition (see Bush & Mosteller, 1955, sec. 1.8), e.g. for the linear operator model

state proportionality of change (snowball effect):

$$a = \begin{cases} p, & l > p \\ 1\text{-}p, & l < p; \end{cases}$$

negative state proportionality of change (surprise effect):

$$a = \begin{cases} 1\text{-}p, & l > p \\ p, & l < p; \end{cases}$$

error proportionality of change (indifference effect):

$$a = p \cdot (1\text{-}p).$$

As can be seen, the snowball effect refers to situations in which the relative increase/decrease of a probability is the greater, the larger/smaller the probability already is, e.g. situations in which experts learn faster than novices or early extinction is retarded because of previous intermittent reinforcement. The surprise effect, on the contrary, refers to situations in which the relative increase/decrease of a probability is the smaller, the larger/smaller the probability already is, e.g. in the revision of expectations on the basis of forthcoming evidence. The indifference effect represents situations in which relative probability shifts are large for probabilities close to .5 and smaller as they approach the extreme values 0 or 1, e.g. opinion changes which are known to be easier for neutral as compared with extreme opinions. Expectation of cooperation is likely to be governed by a surprise effect, cooperative inclination perhaps by a snowball or rather by an indifference effect.

These parameter free learning models can be relaxed by introducing an exponential parameter, $0 \leq r \leq \infty$, and/or a multiplicative parameter, $0 \leq s \leq .5, 1, 4$ (the upper limits depending on the case considered and properties required), for speed of learning and, thus, assuming only state or error monotony instead of state or error proportionality, e.g. $a = p^r$,

$$a = (1 - p)^r, \quad a = s \cdot p \cdot (1 - p), \quad a = s^{r_1} \cdot (1 - p)^{r_2} \quad \text{etc..}$$

Similar dependencies of rate of change on state can be explored for choice models, e.g. $b =$

$f\left(\dfrac{p}{(1 - p)}\right)$ or equivalently $b = f(v)$, and Markov models $p_{ij} = f(p_i, p_j)$. In the choice model

a snowball effect for the acquisition of a successful response may be modelled e.g. by applying the

operator $\quad b = 1 + \dfrac{p}{(1 - p)} \quad$ to the odds of the response. In order to obtain a surprise effect

for successful responses the operator $\quad b = 1 + \dfrac{(1 - p)}{p} \quad$ may be applied, and an indifference

effect is obtained by letting $\quad b = 1 + \dfrac{p \cdot (1 - p)}{(1 - p \cdot (1 - p))} \quad$. In order to model the extinction of unsuccessful responses the respective operators $b = 1 + \dfrac{(1 - p)}{p}$, $b = 1 + \dfrac{p}{(1 - p)}$

and $b = 1 + \dfrac{p \cdot (1 - p)}{(1 - p \cdot (1 - p))}$ would have to be applied to the odds, $\dfrac{(1 - p)}{p}$,

against the response in question. These parameter-free models, too, may be relaxed by introducing multiplicative constants or exponents as parameters that accelerate or decelerate the probability

shifts, i.e. $b = s \cdot \left(1 + \dfrac{p}{1 - p}\right)^{r}$.

In Markov-models a snowball effect for the acquisition of successful responses is obtained e.g. by setting $p_{ii} = p_i + (1-p_i)p_i$, $p_{ij} = (1-p_i)p_j$, a surprise effect by setting $p_{ii} = p_i + (1-p_i)(1-p_i)$, $p_{ij} = p_ip_j$ and an indifference effect by setting $p_{ii} = p_i + (1-p_i)\cdot p_i\cdot(1-p_i)$, $p_{ij} = (1-p_i\cdot(1-p_i))\cdot p_j$. A snowball effect for the extinction of unsuccessful responses is obtained by

setting $p_{ii} = p_i^2$, $p_{ij} = (1+p_i)p_j$, a surprise effect by setting $p_{ii} = p_i(1-p_i)$, $p_{ij} = \dfrac{1 - p_i(1 - p_i)}{(1 - p_i)} \cdot p_j$

and an indifference effect by $p_{ii} = p_i\cdot(1-p_i\cdot(1-p_i))$, $p_{ij} = (1 + p_i^2)p_j$. Again, these parameter-free models can be relaxed by introducing parameters that increase or decrease the rates of

change, e.g. $p_{ii} = p_i + (1 - p_i) \cdot s \cdot p_i^{r_1} \cdot (1 - p_i)^{r_2}$, $p_{ij} = (1 - s \cdot p_i^{r_1} \cdot (1 - p_i)^{r_2}) \cdot p_j$

for acquisition and

$$p_{ii} = p_i \cdot (1 - s \cdot p_i^{r_1} \cdot (1 - p_i)^{r_2}) ,$$

$$p_{ij} = (1 - p_i \cdot (1 - s \cdot p_i^{r_1} \cdot (1 - p_i)^{r_2})) \cdot \dfrac{p_j}{(1 - p_i)} \quad \text{for extinction.}$$

This review does not cover cognitive models designed to take account of behavior in more complicated social dilemmas which e.g. require players to acquire knowledge about the availability of ressources to be shared as well as about the competences and intentions of the co-players (see e.g. Spada & Ernst, 1992). Likewise, the learning of overall-strategies, like all C, all D, tit for tat, fixed interval or fixed ratio benevolent tit for tat etc., as opposed to the learning of simple choices, will not be covered in this review. Most of the conclusions of the research elicited by Axelrod's (1984) work on the prisoner's dilemma game in the context of evolution theory can be reformulated in terms of learning theory.

Classical learning models pertaining to overt gaming behavior

Rapoport and Chammah (1965) and Rapoport and Dale (1966) explored a number of Markov- and linear operator models to take account of the course of cooperation-frequency and of the frequency of the outcomes CC, CD, DC, DD in series of prisoner's dilemma games.

First, a Markov-model was advanced with the above mentioned four outcomes as states, equiprobable in the beginning. Transition probabilities were computed as products of the two players' conditional probabilities of a cooperative choice given a particular outcome, CC, CD, DC or DD, of the preceding game. The four probabilities were estimated from experimental data. The model was discarded because, irrespective of the adopted estimates, the model predicted a much faster attainment of an asymptotic behavior than was observed in experiments. Its predictive value could not be improved, either, by estimating the values of the conditional probabilities for each player separately as compared with the estimation of values common to all players.

A better agreement of predictions and data was obtained by a four state Markov-model with absorbing states. The authors postulated players to be either in a permanently cooperative state, a transient cooperative state, a transient defective state or a permanently defective state. The first and fourth state, of course, are absorbing states. It was assumed that each state can be reached in one step from a neighbouring state only. As long as the players are not permanently locked in an CC- or DD-run, the occurence of a C- or D-choice is a definite indication of the respective transient state of the player. That is not true for the choices made in the, short or long, final CC- or DD-runs, because each player may have shifted at any time during the run, or even not at all before the end of the finite game series, from the respective transient to the respective permanent state. Thus, the two absorbing states are latent states which are not isomorphically related to the respective choices. As a consequence, this is true for the transient states as well, at least during the final CC- or DD-runs. In fact, the probabilities of transition from one transient state to another were not estimated directly from the available data. Rather, they were adjusted freely so as to fit optimally the average course of cooperation frequency as the game series progressed. So were the probabilities of entering the permanent states during the final CC- or DD-runs. In the most typical ("pure matrix") condition intermediate values of the transition probabilities, i.e. .3 - .6 depending on the preceding outcome, were obtained for shifts between the transient states and small values, .018 and .0024, for the probabilities of entering the permanent cooperative and defective state respectively. The latter probabilities indicate that players remain responsive to their co-players' behavior for most of the time. The data fit of the four state Markov-model was somewhat improved by assuming the probability of a cooperative choice after mutual cooperation CC to grow as the game series progressed.

The best agreement with experimental data was obtained with a linear operator model applied to players' probabilities of a cooperative choice. Cooperation probability was assumed to be .5 at the beginning of the game series. The learning parameters, a and l, were made dependent on the outcome of the preceding play. Cooperation probability was assumed to increase after mutual cooperation, i.e. $l_{CC} = 1$, it was assumed to decrease after active or passive exploitation, i.e. $l_{CD} = l_{DC} = 0$. The effect l_{DD} of a mutual obstruction DD as well as the four learning rates were estimated from the data in the same way as the parameters of previous models so as to yield the best agreement between the average courses of cooperation frequency obtained in simulations and experiments. Values of .4 and .5 were obtained in different studies for l_{DD}, indicating that after mutual obstruction cooperation probability tends towards intermediate values. The rates of change showed intermediate values $.26 \leq a \leq .6$, varying between outcomes, between experiments, and between the sexes of the players. They tend to be slightly smaller for increases, a_{CC}, than for decreases, a_{CD} and a_{DC}, of cooperation probability.

Herniter, Williams and Wolpert (1967) modified the linear operator model of Rapoport and co-workers (1965, 1966) by making the reasonable assumptions that cooperation probability always increases after mutual obstruction, i.e. $l_{DD} = 1$, and that the learning rates, a_{CC}, a_{CD}, a_{DC}, a_{DD}, are proportional to the absolute values of the pay-offs (gains or losses) associated with the four outcomes. That leaves one free parameter to be estimated in order to adjust the arbitrary unit of measurement of the (0,oo)-scale for pay-offs to the (0,1)-scale of learning rates. Unfortunately, that ambitious model did not fit satisfactorily the data of Rapoport and Chammah (1965).

Learning models with latent states or latent variables

Meeker (1971) proposed a Markov model to take account of the behavior in series of prisoner's dilemma games against a 100% cooperative co-player. The model aimed at testing predictions derived from the theories of balance and cognitive dissonance (Festinger, 1957; Heider, 1958) rather than predictions about behavior in repeated partial conflicts of interest. Two latent states were postulated, a reciprocating and a rational state or, in more familiar terms, a state of cooperation mindedness and a state of defection mindedness. They are latent value states because the occurence of inconsistent behavior was explicitly assumed. Its probability of occurrence was estimated from the data of three experiments as about .1 for the state of cooperation mindedness and about .1 - .3, depending on experimental condition, for that of defection mindedness. In the case of inconsistent choices, subjects were assumed to shift from the behavior inconsistent to the behavior consistent value state with some probability, estimated from the same data at intermediate values .3 - .7, depending on state and experimental condition. Thus, the model has four parameters, i.e. one probability of inconsistent behavior and one transition probability for each of the two latent states. Obviously, subjects appear quite likely to change their value state because of occasionally occuring attitude-behavior inconsistencies, as would be predicted from balance and dissonance theory. In view of the very special situation considered, namely that of a perfectly cooperative co-player, no provision was made for taking account of changes of value state or behavior in response to co-players' behavior as in the models of Rapoport and co-workers reported above. In a model test excellent predictions were obtained for three observed relative frequencies per experiment which were not used in the estimation procedure.

Van der Sanden (1979) explored Meeker's (1971) model further. He showed that the transition probabilities, as opposed to the probabilities of a value inconsistent choice, depend on the pay-offs structure of the prisoner's dilemma game. The results of his estimation procedures supported the following interpretation: The larger the difference between player's pay-offs in the cases of mutual cooperation and exploitation by the co-player, i.e. the more a player gains from the perfect cooperation of his co-player, the larger, assumedly, the strain induced by cognitive dissonance between the cooperative value state and an occasional inconsistent defective choice, and consequently the larger the probability of transition from the state of cooperation to the state of defection mindedness. Similarly, the larger the difference between player's pay-offs in the cases of active exploitation and mutual cooperation the stronger, assumedly, the strain induced by cognitive dissonance between the defection mindedness state and an occasional inconsistent cooperative choice, and consequently the larger the probability of transition from that state to that of cooperation mindedness. The latter effect, however, is offset if the co-player's pay-off difference between active exploitation and mutual cooperation is large. Apparently, it can be compensated by the player's observation that the 100% cooperative co-player, too, renounces a large possible pay-off which he could obtain by exploiting players' (inconsistent) cooperation.

Van der Sanden (1979) also varied the cooperation rate of the co-player from 60 to 90 per cent, retaining the property that the cooperative choices of the co-player are random, i.e. noncontingent on player's own choices. Again, he showed that the probabilities of an inconsistant choice is not affected by the co-player's degree of cooperation; neither are the very small probabilities of transition from one value state to the other after a choice consistent with the existing value state. The transition probabilities after an inconsistant choice, however, are affected. They are clearly non-zero, their values depending in a somewhat complicated and not always obvious manner on the overall cooperation rate and the actual choice of the co-player.

Motivated by Howard's (1966, 1971, 1976) theory of metagames, van der Sanden (1979) also proposed a Markov-model for natural series of prisoner's dilemma games in which both players must be supposed to make their choices in response to previous choices of their co-player and expect him to do the same. It is a three transient state Markov-model with a cooperative state in which the player expects and makes exclusively cooperative choices, a state of defection mindedmess in which the player expects and makes exclusively defective choices and a transitional state in which the player does not know what to expect and cooperates with some probability, $0 < p < 1$, to be estimated from the data. All three states are latent states because cooperative choices can result from the cooperative as well as from the transitional state and defective choices from the transitional as well as from the defection state. Transition probabilities from the cooperation state to the defection state and vice versa were assumed to be zero, i.e. the extreme states can be reached from each other only via the transient state. According to the model, the cooperation state can be reached from the transitional state only after mutual cooperation CC. The respective transition probability, a, is to be estimated from data, as are the probabilities b,c,d introduced below. The reverse transition from the cooperative to the transitional state is supposed to occur with probability b only after the player has been exploited, CD. The defection state can be reached from the transitional state with probability d after mutual obstruction DD only, and the reverse transition is assumed to occur with probability c after active exploitation DC only. All subjects were assumed to start in the transitional state. In an applica-tion of the model to the data of Rapoport and Dale (1966) the parameters were estimated as $p = .5$, b and $c > .9$, a and $d < .1$. These parameter values suggest that players rarely leave and quickly return to the transitional state. The fit of the model was moderate for data obtained from men and acceptable for those of women.

Brückner (1976) and Micko, Brückner and Ratzke (1977) proposed a two factor theory of behavior in series of prisoner's dilemma games. Their latent variables "insight" and "trust" were more or less equivalent to those of "goal" and "expectancy" of Pruitt and Kimmel (1977) who were not aware of that model in their review of experimental gaming research. In terms of the present review the latent variables may be renamed "cooperative inclination" and "trust", since the term "cooperation mindedness" was used already to denote a state. Both variables are measured on $(0,1)$-scales and might be interpreted as player's subjective probability of cooperation being more successful in the long run than defection and his subjective probability of the co-player cooperating in the subsequent game. The initial assumption that cooperation probability at any time equals the smaller of the two measures of cooperative inclination and trust prevented a satisfactory fit of the model to the data of Rapoport and Chammah (1965). Therefore, it had to be discarded as too pessimistic. Instead, cooperation probability was assumed to equal a weighted mean of the measures of cooperative inclination and trust, the measure of cooperative inclination and its complement serving also as weights for the measures of trust and cooperative inclination respectively. Thus, cooperation probability was assumed to be determined mainly by cooperative inclination in the case of low cooperative inclination and mainly by trust in the case of high cooperative inclination. Markov-models and, more successfully, linear operator models were assumed to account for the courses of the two latent variables during a game series with starting values of .5. Cooperative inclination was assumed to increase (slowly) as a result of the fairly satisfactory pay-off in the case of mutual cooperation CC and the fairly unsatisfactory pay-off in the case of mutual obstruction DD ($l_{CC} = l_{DC} = 1$). A common rate of increase $a_{CC} = a_{DD} = .19$ was estimated. Cooperative inclination was supposed to decrease (faster) because of the highly satisfactory pay-off in the case of active exploitation and the highly unsatisfactory pay-off in the case of passive exploitation ($l_{CD} = l_{DC} = 0$) with rate of decrease estimated as $a_{CD} = a_{DC} = .43$. Trust was supposed to increase after observing cooperation on the part of the co-player ($l_{CC} = l_{DC} = 1$) and to decrease after observation of defection on the part of the co-player ($l_{CD} = l_{DD} = 0$). A single value for rate of change of trust, $a = .5$ applying to both directions, was estimated from the data. The model which has only three parameters to be estimated fitted the data of Rapoport and Chammah (1965) better than any other model so far explored but failed to predict the behavior of German subjects who played against a number of fixed interval benevolent tit for tat strategies. Contrary to fact, it suggested such strategies to be the more cooperation inducing, the more frequently a series of mutual obstructions DD is interrupted by an offer of cooperation. The theory is presently under revision: The weights of the weighted mean must be exchanged in the computation of cooperation probability, social orientations (see e.g. Schulz, 1991) must be taken into account, rates of change of cooperative inclination ought to be made dependent on the pay-offs of the preceding outcome, snowball, surprise and indifference effects are considered, and the effect of active exploitation DC on trust must be reconsidered in view of an argument given in the subsequent paragraph.

Learning models that account for players' expectations as well as choices

Schulz and Hesse (1978) and Schulz (1979) not only observed players' choices in series of prisoner's dilemma games but also asked them before each game which choice on the part of their co-player they expected. They proposed a three factor model to take account of their data. Two of their latent variables equalled those of the previous model of Micko et al. (1977) and their courses were supposed to be governed by the same linear operator model - with one noteworthy exception. Trust was not supposed to increase after active exploitation DC. Indeed, the trust increasing effect of observing co-player's cooperation in the preceding trial is likely to be compensated by the trust decreasing effect of fear of co-player's retaliation in the subsequent game. Moreover, this latent variable, although formally almost identical with that of cooperative inclination in the previous model, was conceived in this model rather as a tendency to reciprocate co-player's choices in the sense of Meeker (1971). Accordingly, a third latent variable, competitive inclination, was postulated, i.e. a sort of negative cooperative inclination. It was supposed to be governed by a linear operator model as well, but to follow a course at least partly independent from that of reciprocatory inclination. It was assumed to increase after active exploitation DC only and to decrease after mutual cooperation CC only. All three variables, of course, were measured on $(0,1)$-scales. For increases $l = 1$ was assumed, for decreases $l = 0$. The median learning rates, a, were estimated separately for increases and decreases of the variables. They rarely exceeded the value .1, i.e. they were much smaller than those obtained by Rapoport et al. (1965, 1966) and Micko et al. (1977). The joint probabilities of action and expectation were predicted in the following way: The probability of a cooperative choice, while expecting cooperation on the part of the co-player, was assumed to equal the product of the measures of reciprocatory inclination and trust. The probability of cooperation while expecting defection on the part of the co-player was assumed to equal the product of the complements of the measures of reciprocatory inclination and competitive inclination. Thus, gambit-type offers of cooperation were supposed to occur most likely in the absence of reciprocatory as well as competitive inclination. The probability of defection while expecting defection of the co-player was assumed to equal the product of the measure of reciprocatory inclination and the complement of the measure of trust. Thus, competitive inclination is not assumed to be involved in the defence against exploitation. It is involved, however, in active exploitation since the probability of defection while expecting co-player's cooperation is assumed to equal the product of the measure of competitive inclination and the complement of the measure of reciprocatory inclination. The parameters of the model were adjusted, and the fit of the model was tested, for each pair of players separately yielding satisfactory results in most cases.

Schulz and Jonas (1982) fitted a linear operator model to the courses of their subjects' stated expectations of cooperation resp. defection on the part of the co-player in a series of 40 prisoner's dilemma games. Trust was supposed to increase, $l = 1$, after co-player's cooperation, CC and DC, and to decrease, $l = 0$, after co-player's defection CD and DD. Thus, the assumptions of Micko et al. (1977) were adopted again and the more sophisticated assumption of Schulz and Hesse (1978) and Schulz (1979) for the outcome DC was discarded. The two rates of change, a, for increases and decreases of trust respectively, estimated for each player separately, varied widely between subjects. Their medians were not related to players' habitual social orientations, cooperative or egoistic, which were determined before the gaming experiment from players' preferences for particular types of games and outcomes. Social orientation influenced the median probability of expected cooperation in the first game only, yielding values of about .95 for cooperative and about .75 for egoistic subjects. The gaming behavior itself was predicted from two conditional probabilities which were assumed to be constant over the whole game series and were also estimated from the data of each player separately. They were the probabilities of a cooperative choice given the expectations of co-player's cooperation and defection respectively. As would be predicted, the median estimates of the former were large in both social orientation groups, $\geq .94$, those of the latter small, $\leq .22$. The model had to be rejected for 3 out of 27 pairs of subjects only.

May (1983) revised the model of Schulz and Jonas (1982). He replaced their linear operator model by a choice model to account for the courses of players' trust. One parameter, b, was estimated for each of the four outcomes of the game and separately for each of the players. In somewhat more than 50% of the cases expectation of cooperation increased, $b > 1$, after co-player's cooperation, CC and DC, and decreased, $b < 1$, after the player was exploited, CD. After mutual obstruction, DD, the expectation of cooperation more often increased if that outcome resulted in a negative pay-off for both players and more often decreased if it resulted in a small positive pay-off. (The parameters were estimated from data of subjects playing one of two pay-off matrices differing in the DD-pay-off). As in the previous model, choices were predicted from the two conditional probabilities given the expectation of cooperation and defection on the part of the co-player respectively. They were assumed to be constant over the whole game series. Again, the median probability of a cooperative choice was high $(> .69)$ if cooperation on the part of the co-player was expected and low $(\leq .24)$ if his defection was expected. Players of cooperative social orientation were more likely to make a cooperative choice than players of egoistic social orientation, particularly if they expected cooperation on the part of the co-player. In addition, they were more likely to expect a cooperative choice on the part of the co-player in the first game. The model had to be rejected for six out of 36 pairs of subjects only.

Schulz and May (1983) asked players before each game not only for their expectations about co-players' choices but also for their confidence in these expectations. Thus, they worked with a scale of four ordered categories of expectations: cooperation sure, cooperation unsure, defection unsure, defection sure. A modified choice model was assumed to account for the revisions of confirmed and disconfirmed expectations respectively. Instead of Luce's operator $v_{n+1} = b.v_n$ which revises a response strength, $0 < v < \infty$ by multiplication with a positive constant, the transformation $p_{n+1} = b.p_{n1/b}$, $0 < b < \infty$, was applied to the probability p_n of the category of expectation to be modified. After a confirmed expectation the probability of the respective certain expectation (cooperation sure or defection sure) was modified, after a disconfirmed expectation the probability of the respective uncertain expectation (cooperation unsure or defection unsure). The probabilities of the other categories were revised in proportion so as to add up to $1-p_{n+1}$. Four learning parameters, b, one for each category of expectation and confidence, were estimated from the data protocols of each player separately. Their values varied considerably between players, each of the parameters indicating a probability increase of the respective category for some players and a decrease for others - with no apparent lawfulness to be discernible. Perhaps, more pairs of players have to be run in future experiments in order to obtain a more informative result. The gaming behavior of the players was predicted again by computing four time invariant conditional probabilities of a cooperative choice given one of the four expectation/confidence categories. They were estimated from the goaled data of all subjects playing some pay-off matrix. If cooperation on the part of the co-player was expected, player's cooperation probability was high, $> .64$, if defection was expected, cooperation probability was low, $< .20$, both probabilities varying as a function of the pay-off matrix played. The degree of confidence of a player's expectation, however, had little influence on his cooperation probability. The fit of the model was tested for each pair of players separately with satisfactory results in most cases.

Finally, Schulz (1991) made observable both latent variables which were assumed to account for players' behavior in series of prisoner's dilemma games, namely cooperative inclination and trust (Micko et al., 1977) or goal and expectancy (Pruitt & Kimmel, 1977). Both variables were conceived as two-valued, cooperative inclination comprising goal states cooperation mindedness and defection mindedness and trust comprising the states expectation of cooperation and expectation of defection on the part of the co-player. Accordingly, players were asked before each game whether or not they wanted to cooperate and whether or not they expected co-players to cooperate in the subsequent game. Choice models were assumed to govern the courses of the probabilities of players reporting to be in the states of cooperation mindedness and expectance of cooperation respectively. Four operators were estimated for cooperative inclination, b_{CC}, b_{CD}, b_{DC}, b_{DD}, one for each outcome of the preceding game, and two operators for trust, $b_{CC} = b_{DC}$ and $b_{CD} = b_{DD}$, one for each choice of the co-player observed in the preceding game. Common parameters, b, were estimated from the pooled reports of intention and expectation of all players in each of the following classes of social orientation which were determined beforehand in the same way as in the above study of Schulz and Jonas (1982): prosocial (i.e. maximizing sum of pay-offs for both players), egoistic (i.e. maximizing own pay-off), and competitive (i.e. maximizing difference between own and other's pay-off). Egoists were subclassified into more or less friendly egoists according to their stated intentions to cooperate or defect in the first game. The choice models were fitted to the sequence of reports of intention and expectation of each player separately, mostly with success. The estimated values of the learning parameters, b, suggest that cooperative inclination decreased after players suffered an exploitation, CD, except for prosocial players. An increase of cooperative inclination was found only for, apparently remorseful, prosocial players and friendly egoists after active exploitation DC. Otherwise the parameters suggest only minor changes in one or another direction of cooperative inclination. In all social orientation groups the learning parameters for expectation of cooperation showed slight increases after co-player's cooperation in the preceding game and slight decreases after his defection. Players' choices were predicted from four invariant conditional probabilities of a cooperative choice given one of the combinations of the two states of cooperative inclination and the two states of trust. In all social groups, the probability of a cooperative choice was high, $p \geq .89$, if the player was cooperation minded and expected cooperation on the part of the co-player. It was low, $p \leq .28$, if the player expected co-player's defection and particularly low, $p \leq .12$, if he was defection minded as well. If defection mindedness occured in combination with expectation of cooperation, the probability of a cooperative choice increased with the friendlyness of the player from $p = .12$ for the competitive group up to $p = .68$ for the prosocial group. Moreover, the social orientation of players seems to influence cooperative inclination and trust in the first game. The more friendly groups show somewhat larger probabilities of cooperation mindedness, $p \geq .82$, and perhaps more expectation of cooperation, $p \geq .6$, than the less friendly groups for which the respective probabilities $p \leq$ .46 and $p \leq .53$ were obtained. The agreement of the predictions of the model with experimental choice behavior was determined by simulations and found to be satisfactory except for the first 2 - 4 games the data of which, accordingly, were dropped from the estimation procedure.

As a rule, models that predict gaming behavior from learning models which operate on the latent variables cooperative inclination and trust, or goal and expectation equivalently, seem to account fairly well for players' intentions, expectations and choices in series of prisoner's dilemma games, except for one or another detail that still requires refinements of the models.

Schulz (1991) gives a more comprehensive review in German language of experiments on the prisoner's dilemma game and of learning models to account for their data. It served as a main source of this review.

Footnote

1   TU Braunschweig, Department of Psychology, Braunschweig, Germany

References

Axelrod, R.M. (1984). *The evolution of cooperation*. New York: Basic Books.

Brückner, G. (1976). Vorhersage und Erzeugung von kooperativem Verhalten in einem Nicht-Nullsummenspiel (Prediction and induction of cooperative behavior in a non-zero game), Unpublished diploma thesis, Technische Universität Braunschweig.

Busch, R.R., & Mosteller, F. (1955). *Stochastic models for learning*. New York: Wiley.

Festinger, L. (1957). *A theory of cognitive dissonance*. Stanford, CA: Stanford University Press.

Heider, F. (1958). *The psychology of interpersonal relationships*. New York: Wiley.

Hermiter, J., Williams, A., & Wolpert, J. (1967). Learning to cooperate. *Peace Research Society*, Vol. VII, Papers. Chicago, Conference.

Howard, N. (1966). The theory of metagames. *General Systems, 11*, 156-200.

Howard, N. (1971). *Paradoxes of rationality: The theory of metagames and political behavior.* Cambridge: MIT Press.

Howard, N. (1974). "General" metagames: An extension of the metagames concept. In A. Rapoport (Ed.), *Game theory as a theory of conflict resolution* (pp. 258-280). Dordrecht: Reidel.

Howard, N. (1976). Prisoner's Dilemma: The solution by general metagames. *Behavioral Science, 21*, 524-531.

Luce, R.D. (1959). *Individual choice behavior.* New York: Wiley.

May, T.W. (1983). *Individuelles Entscheiden in sequentiellen Konfliktspielen* (Individual decision making in sequential conflict games). Frankfurt a.M.: Lang.

Meeker, B.F. (1971). Value conflict in social exchange A Markov model. *Journal of Mathematical Psychology, 8*, 389-403.

Micko, H.C., Brückner, G., & Ratzke, H. (1977). Theories and strategies for Prisoner's Dilemma. In W.F. Kempf, & B.H. Repp (Eds.), *Mathematical models for social psychology*. Bern: Huber.

Pruitt, D.G., & Kimmel, M.J. (1977). Twenty years of experimental gaming: Critique, Synthesis, and suggestions for the future. *Annual Review of Psychology, 28*, 363-392.

Rapoport, A., & Chammah, A.M. (1965). *Prisoner's Dilemma.* Ann Arbor: University of Michigan Press.

Rapoport, A., & Dale, P. (1966). Models for Prisoner's Dilemma. *Journal of Mathematical Psychology, 3*, 269-286.

Schulz, U. (1979). Ein mathematisches Modell für das Verhalten in Sequenzen von Prisoner's-Dilemma-Spielen unter Berücksichtigung von Erwartungen. (A mathematical model for the behavior in sequences of prisoner's dilemma games in consideration of expectations). In W. Albers, G. Bamberg, & R. Selten (Eds.), *Entscheidung in kleinen Gruppen.* (Decision in small groups.) *Mathematical Systems in Economics, 45*, 107-123, Meisenheim: Hain.

Schulz, U. (1991). *Verhalten in Konfliktspielen: Modelle für Entscheidungsverhalten und Informationsverarbeitung in Sequenzen von einfachen Konfliktspielen mit zwei Personen* (Behavior in conflict games: Models for decision behavior and information processing in sequences of simple two person conflict games). Frankfurt a.M.: Lang.

Schulz, U., & May, T.W. (1983a). The dependence of cognition and behavior in 2x2 matrice games. In R.W. Scholz (Ed.), *Decision making under uncertainty* (pp. 253-270). North Holland: Elsevier Science Publishers B.V.

Schulz, U., & May, T.W. (1983b). Ein Modell für das Verhalten in Sequenzen von Konfliktspielen unter Berücksichtigung von Antizipationen und subjektiven Sicherheiten. (A model for the behavior in sequences of conflict games in consideration of anticipations and subjective confidence). *Zeitschrift für Sozialpsychologie, 14,* 322-340.

Spada, H., & Ernst, A.M. (1992). Wissen, Ziele und Verhalten in einem ökologisch-sozialen Dilemma. (Knowledge, goals and behavior in an ecological-social dilemma), In K. Pawlik, & K.-H. Stapf (Eds.), *Umwelt und Verhalten* (Environment and behavior) (pp. 83-106). Bern: Huber.

van der Sanden, A.M.L. (1979). *Value states and dynamic decision making in the Prisoner's Dilemma Game.* Nijmegen, Stichting Studentenpres.

Wickens, T.D. (1982). *Models for behavior: Stochastic processes in psychology.* San Francisco: W.H. Freeman & Co.

Social capital and cooperation:
Communication, bounded rationality, and behavioral heuristics

Roy Gardner, Elinor Ostrom, and James Walker[1]

Abstract

Common-pool resources are natural or man made resources used in common by multiple users, where yield is subtractable (rival) and exclusion is nontrivial (but not necessarily impossible). The role of face-to-face communication in CPR situations, where individuals must repeatedly decide on the number of resource units to withdraw from a common-pool, is open to considerable theoretical and policy debate. In this paper, we summarize the findings from a series of experiments in which we operationalize face-to-face communication (without the presence of external enforcement). In an attempt to understand the high degree of cooperation observed in the laboratory, we turn to a bounded rationality explanation as a starting point for understanding how cooperative behavior can be supported in decision environments where game theory suggests it will not.

Introduction: The communication mechanism

Common-pool resources (CPRs) are natural or man made resources used in common by multiple users, where yield is subtractable (rival) and exclusion is nontrivial (but not necessarily impossible). Examples of CPR situations include fisheries, commonly held forrest areas, and university computing systems. Individuals using such resources are generally assumed to face a social dilemma, where over use and possible destruction is a predicted outcome. The ameliorative role of face-to-face communication in common-pool resource situations, where individuals must repeatedly decide on the number of resource units to withdraw from a common-pool, is open to considerable theoretical and policy debate. Words alone are viewed by many as frail constraints when individuals make private, repetitive decisions between short-term, profit maximizing strategies and strategies negotiated by a verbal agreement. On the other hand, the "shadow of the future" may reduce the temptation to break promises so as to avoid the "unraveling" of a mutually productive verbal agreement (see Keohane, 1986).

Game-theoretical models do not always yield unique answers to how individuals will (or ought to) behave in repeated, social dilemma situations. Such games can have multiple equilibria, even if the one-shot game has a unique equilibrium. The number of equilibria grows with the number of repetitions. When there are finitely many repetitions, no equilibrium can sustain an optimal solution although it may be possible to come close (Benoit & Krishna, 1985). When there are infinitely many repetitions, some equilibria can sustain an optimal solution (Friedman, 1990). In all cases, the worst possible one-shot equilibrium, repeated as often as possible, remains an equilibrium outcome. The players thus face a plethora of equilibria. Without a mechanism for selection among these equilibria, the players can easily be overwhelmed by complexity and confusion.

There is also a debate within the literature about the necessity of external enforcement. Some theorists presume that stable and efficient equilibria can be achieved by participants in repetitive situations without the necessity of external enforcers (Schotter, 1980; Runge, 1984). This argument is based primarily on the efficacy of trigger strategies. On the other hand, many assume that individuals in repetitive CPR situations will not reach jointly efficient outcomes unless external agents monitor and enforce agreements. Even if individuals promise to adopt strategies that generate the highest joint outcome, promises are considered worthless when individuals face a series of private decisions without individual monitoring and enforcement. Why should a person keep a general promise made to a group when the short-term payoff from breaking that promise is substantially better, especially if no one knows the identity of those who break their promise? A deeper examination of the role of communication in facilitating the selection of efficient strategies is of considerable theoretical (as well as policy) interest.[2] The demarcation line between cooperative and noncooperative game theory is based on the presumption that communication alone does not affect players' decisions unless there is external enforcement or some other form of making agreements binding.

In prior laboratory investigations, communication has been shown to be an affective mechanism for increasing the frequency with which players choose joint income maximizing strategies, even when individual incentives conflict with the cooperative strategies (Caldwell, 1976; Dawes, McTavish, & Shaklee, 1977; Edney & Harper, 1978; van de Kragt et al. 1986; Isaac & Walker, 1988a, 1991; Jerdee & Rosen, 1974; Orbell, van de Kragt, & Dawes, 1991; E. Ostrom & Walker, 1991; E. Ostrom, Walker, & Gardner, 1992; Hackett, Schlager, & Walker, 1992). Hypotheses forwarded to explain why communication increases the selection of cooperative strategies identify a process that communication is posited to facilitate (1) offering and extracting promises, (2) changing the expectations of others' behavior, (3) changing payoff structure, (4) the reenforcement of prior normative orientations, and (5) the development of a group identity.

In this paper, we summarize the findings from a series of experiments in which we operationalize face-to-face communication (without the presence of external enforcement) in an experimental CPR appropriation environment.[3] The role of communication and its success in fostering outcomes more in line with social optimality is investigated in settings in which (1) the communication mechanism is provided as a costless one-shot opportunity and (2) the communication mechanism is provided as a costless opportunity and on a repeated basis. After summarizing the experimental findings, we turn to a bounded rationality explanation as a starting point for understanding how cooperative behavior can be supported in decision environments where game theory suggests it will not. Specifically, we examine a notion of measure-for-measure behavior where subjects adhere to verbal commitments when others do, and react to defections in a measured response that allows for cooperation to be potentially sustained, even when some subjects are noncooperative. We first turn to a summary of the CPR decision environment in which our subjects participate.

The CPR decision situation

The decision task faced by our subjects can be summarized as follows:

Subjects faced a series of decision rounds in which they were endowed with a specified number of tokens, which they invested between two markets. Market 1 was described as an investment opportunity in which each token yielded a fixed (constant) rate of output and that each unit of output yielded a fixed (constant) return. Market 2 (the CPR) was described as a market which yielded a rate of output per token dependent upon the total number of tokens invested by the entire group. Subjects were informed that they would receive a level of output from Market 2 that was equivalent to the percentage of total group tokens they invested. Further, subjects knew that each unit of output from Market 2 yielded a fixed (constant) rate of return.

The experiments used subjects drawn from the undergraduate population at Indiana University. Students were volunteers recruited primarily from principles of economics classes. Prior to recruitment, potential volunteers were given a brief explanation in which they were told only that they would be making decisions in an "economic choice situation" and that the money they earned would be dependent upon their own investment decisions and those of the others in their experimental group. All experiments were conducted on the NovaNET computer system at IU. The computer facilitates the accounting procedures involved in the experiment, enhances across experimental/subject control, and allows for minimal experimenter involvement.

At the beginning of each experimental session, subjects were told that (1) they would make a series of investment decisions, (2) all individual investment decisions were anonymous to the group, and (3) they would be paid their individual earnings (privately and in cash) at the end of the experiment. Subjects then proceeded at their own pace through a set of instructions that described the decisions.[4] Subjects knew with certainty the total number of decision makers in the group, total group tokens, and that endowments were identical. After each round, subjects were shown a display that recorded: (a) their profits in each market for that round, (b) total group investment in Market 2, and (c) a tally of their cumulative profits for the experiment. During the experiment, subjects could request, through the computer, this information for all previous rounds. They knew that the experiment would not last more than two hours. They did not know the exact number of investment decision rounds. All subjects were *experienced*, i.e., had participated in at least one experiment using this form of decision situation.[5]

The theoretical specification of our CPR environment can be summarized as follows. Assume a fixed number n of appropriators with access to the CPR. Each appropriator i has an endowment of resources e which can be invested in the CPR or invested in a safe, outside activity. The marginal payoff of the outside activity is normalized equal to w. The payoff to an individual appropriator from investing in the CPR depends on aggregate group investment in the CPR, and on the appropriator investment as a percentage of the aggregate. Let x_i denote appropriator i's investment in the CPR, where $0 \leq x_i \leq e$. The group return to investment in the CPR is given by the production function $F(\Sigma x_i)$, where F is a concave function, with $F(0) = 0$, $F'(0) > w$, and $F'(ne) < 0$. Initially, investment in the CPR pays better than the opportunity cost of the foregone safe investment [$F'(0) > w$], but if the appropriators invest a sufficiently large number of resources ($\hat{q}$) in the CPR the outcome is counterproductive [$F'(\hat{q}) < 0$]. The yield from the CPR reaches a *maximum net level* when individuals invest some but not all of their endowments in the CPR.[6]

Let $x = (x_1,...,x_n)$ be a vector of individual appropriators' investments in the CPR. The payoff to an appropriator, $u_i(x)$, is given by:

$$u_i(x) = \quad we \qquad\qquad \text{if } x_i = 0 \qquad (1)$$
$$w(e-x_i) + (x_i/\Sigma x_i)F(\Sigma x_i) \quad \text{if } x_i > 0.$$

Equation (1) reflects the fact that if appropriators invest all their endowments in the outside alternative, they get a sure payoff (we), whereas if they invest some of their endowments in the CPR, they get a sure payoff $w(e-x_i)$ plus a payoff from the CPR, which depends on the total investment in that resource $F(\Sigma x_i)$ multiplied by their share in the group investment $(x_i/\Sigma x_i)$.

Let the payoffs (1) be the payoff functions in a symmetric, noncooperative game. Since our experimental design is symmetric, there is a symmetric Nash equilibrium, with each player investing x_i^* in the CPR, where:

$$-w + (1/n)F'(nx_i^*) + F(nx_i^*)((n-1)/x_i^* n^2) = 0. \qquad (2)$$

At the symmetric Nash equilibrium, group investment in the CPR is greater than optimal so group yield is less than optimal, but not all yield from the CPR is wasted.[7]

Compare this deficient equilibrium to the optimal solution. Summing across individual payoffs $u_i(x)$ for all appropriators i, one has the group payoff function $u(x)$,

$$u(x) = nwe - w\Sigma x_i + F(\Sigma x_i) \qquad (3)$$

which is to be maximized subject to the constraints $0 \leq \Sigma x_i \leq ne$. Given the above productivity conditions on F, the group maximization problem has a unique solution characterized by the condition:

$$-w + F'(\Sigma x_i) = 0. \qquad (4)$$

According to (4), the marginal return from a CPR should equal the opportunity cost of the outside alternative for the last unit invested in the CPR. The group payoff from using the marginal revenue (MR) = marginal cost (MC) rule (4) represents the maximal yield that can be extracted from the resource in a single period.

In our experimental investigation we have operationalized this CPR situation with eight appropriators (n = 8) and quadratic production functions $F(\Sigma x_i)$, where:

$$F(\Sigma x_i) = a\Sigma x_i - b(\Sigma x_i)^2 \qquad (5)$$

with $F'(0) = a > w$ and $F'(ne) = a - 2bne < 0$.

In particular, we focus on experiments utilizing the parameters shown in Table 1. Subjects are endowed each round with either 10 tokens or 25 tokens depending upon design conditions. With the payoff parameters displayed in Table 1, a group investment of 36 tokens yields the optimal level of investment. This symmetric game has a unique Nash equilibrium with each subject investing 8 tokens in Market 2. Note that this Nash equilibrium is independent of whether individuals are endowed with 10 or 25 tokens.

Much of our discussion of experimental results will focus on what we term "Maximum Net Yield" from the CPR. This measure captures the degree of optimal yield earned from the CPR. Specifically, net yield is the return from Market 2 minus the opportunity costs of tokens invested in Market 2 divided by the return from Market 2 at MR=MC minus the opportunity costs of tokens invested in Market 2. In our decision situation, opportunity costs equal the potential return that could have been earned by investing the tokens in Market 1. Note, as with the symmetric Nash equilibrium, net yield is invariant to the level of subjects' endowments in our two designs.[8] Thus, even though the range for subject investment decisions is increased with an increase in subjects endowments, the equilibrium and optimal levels of investment are not altered. At the Nash equilibrium, subjects earn approximately 39% of maximum net yield from the CPR.

Table 1

Experimental Design Baseline: Parameters for a Given Decision Round

Experiment Type:	LOW ENDOWMENT	HIGH ENDOWMENT
Number of Subjects	8	8
Individual Token Endowment	10	25
Production Function: Mkt.2*	$23(\Sigma x_i)-.25(\Sigma x_i)^2$	$23(\Sigma x_i)-.25(\Sigma x_i)^2$
Market 2 Return/unit of output	$.01	$.01
Market 1 Return/unit of output	$.05	$.05
Earnings/Subject at Group Max.**	$.91	$.83
Earnings/Subject at Nash Equil.	$.66	$.70
Earnings/Subject at Zero Rent	$.50	$.63

* Σx_i = the total number of tokens invested by the group in Market 2. The production function shows the number of units of output produced in Market 2 for each level of tokens invested in Market 2.

** In the high-endowment design, subjects were paid in cash one-half of their "computer" earnings. Amounts shown are potential cash payoffs.

Summary experimental results

Repeated communication

Our first communication design involves repeated communication with both 10 token and 25 token endowments. At the outset, the CPR game was repeated for 10 rounds. After round 10, the players read an announcement, informing them they would have an opportunity for discussion after *each* subsequent round. The instructions are given below.

> Sometimes in previous experiments, participants have found it useful, when the opportunity arose, to communicate with one another. We are going to allow you this opportunity between rounds. There will be some restrictions: 1) you are not allowed to discuss side payments, 2) you are not allowed to make physical threats, 3) you are not allowed to see the private information on anyone's monitor. Since there are still some restrictions on communication with one another, we will monitor your discussions between rounds.

The experimenter informed the subject that they would have up to 10 minutes for their first discussion session. Each subsequent discussion session would be no longer than 3 minutes. After the experimenter publicly reviewed this announcement, the players left their terminals and sat facing one another.[9] Define x to be a single play of the CPR game and c as the opportunity to communicate. Using this notation, our repeated communication design is xxx..cxcx...cx.

The summary data for our experiments is reported as the average *percentage of maximum net yield* actually earned by subject groups. The summary data from the low-endowment 10 token series is reported in Table 2.[10] These repeated communication experiments provide strong evidence for the power of face-to-face communication. Players successfully used the opportunity to (a) calculate coordinated yield-improving strategies, (b) devise verbal agreements to implement these strategies, and (c) deal with nonconforming players through verbal statements. Net yield averaged over 98% of optimum following the introduction of the opportunity to communicate. This high degree of yield from the CPR is in contrast to an average of only 30% in pre-communication rounds. For analytical purposes we define a defection as a Market 2 investment larger than agreed upon. In the low-endowment environment, we identified only 19 defections from agreements out of 368 total decisions (a 5% defection rate).

Table 2

Repeated Communication after Round 10 -- 10-Token Design

Summary Results: Average Net Yield as a Percentage of Maximum -- Design xxx..cxcx...cx

	Round				
Exp. #	1-5	6-10	11-15	16-20	21-25
1	26	26	96	100	100
2	35	21	100	97	100
3	33	24	99	99	--
4	37	39	94	98	100
Means	33	27	97	98	100

The high-endowment (25 token) CPR game is a more challenging decision environment. While the equilibrium prediction for 10- and 25-token endowment games is identical, the disequilibrium implications of the 25-token game change considerably. With 25 tokens, as few as three subjects investing all of their tokens can essentially ruin the CPR (bring returns below w), while with 10 tokens it takes seven out of eight subjects to accomplish this much damage. In this sense, the 25-token environment is more *fragile* than the 10-token environment.

We were interested in exploring whether subjects could cope with this more delicate situation through communication alone. In the field, this type of fragility is manifest in fisheries (small boats versus trawlers) and in forestry (individuals with chain saws versus bulldozers). Further, we were interested whether varying the information players received about past actions of all players and joint outcomes affected patterns of behavior. In the first three experiments of this design, subjects received only aggregate information on actions and outcomes between rounds. This level of information was identical to that of the 10-token repeated information discussed above. In last three experiments, subjects also received information on individual Market 2 investments. This information was by subject numbers only. Unless the subjects successfully used the discussion rounds to ascertain actual subject identity, this information treatment left subject identity anonymous.

Table 3 summarizes the data for the 25-token repeated communication experiments under both information conditions. In all six experiments, joint yield increased dramatically over that achieved in the first 10 rounds, averaging 71% of optimum in contrast to -2% in pre-communication rounds. Experiments 1, 3 and 5, however, demonstrate the fragile nature of nonbinding agreements in this high-endowment environment. In the high-endowment environment, we identified 100 defections from agreements out of 624 total decisions (a 16% defection rate).

Table 3

Repeated Communication after Round 10 -- 25-Token Design

Summary Results: Average Net Yield as a Percentage of Maximum -- Design xxx..xcxcxcx

			Round		
Exp. #	1-5	6-10	11-15	16-20	21+
1	35	-43	76	75	54
2	60	8	85	82	85
3	4	-8	61	68	68
4	-60	13	80	93	99
5	-24	-3	40	67	-15
6	36	-41	84	86	80
Means	8	-13	71	79	62

One-shot communication

In this design, we turn to examining the robustness of the communication mechanism. Following 10 decision rounds without communication, subjects were given a one time opportunity (10 minutes) to communicate followed by a series of repeated (up to 22) independent decisions. Thus, this design is xx..cxx...x. This environment allows for several insights into the role of communication. Subjects have a one time opportunity to discuss the decision problem. They can work at determining a joint income maximizing strategy and agreeing to such a strategy. They have a one time opportunity to impress on each other the importance of cooperation. But since the communication mechanism is not repeated, they have no opportunity to react jointly to ex post behavior. As with a subset of the 25-token repeated communication experiments, following each decision round these subjects received information on aggregate and individual investments.

The transcripts of the discussion during the single communication round reveal that subjects perceived their problem as involving two tasks: (1) determining the maximal yield available and (2) agreeing upon a strategy to achieve that yield. Results from our three one-shot communication experiments are summarized in Table 4. The results are mixed. In experiment 1, the group achieved over 82% of maximum net yield in all but 2 of 22 rounds following communication. In experiment 2, communication had little efficiency-improving effects. Finally, in experiment 3, the group improved net yield significantly following communication, but could not sustain such behavior. Interestingly, the rate of defection on agreements in these 3 experiments jumps to 25% (132 defections out of 528 decisions).

Table 4

One-Shot Communication after Round 10 -- 25-Token Design

Summary Results: Average Net Yield as a Percentage of Maximum -- Design xx..cxx...x

Round

Exp. #	1-5	6-10	11-15	16-20	21-25	26+
1	-48	-20	89	89	85	83
2	-73	-16	45	-0	12	32
3	-2	-2	88	48	31	61
Mean	-41	-13	74	45	43	59

Why so much cooperation in the lab?

We are not the first to observe high levels of cooperation in experimental social dilemmas. The theory of infinitely repeated games is one explanation offered for this finding.[11] In infinitely repeated games, one of the many possible equilibria is that of full cooperation based on the use of a trigger strategy (Friedman, 1990). A trigger strategy consists of two parts: a recommendation to play a better strategy for all concerned, and a punishment (playing an inefficient equilibrium) in the event that anyone deviates from the recommendation. The punishment is triggered by deviation. A *grim* trigger strategy is one where the punishment lasts forever. Players using the grim trigger strategy in an infinitely repeated CPR dilemma game can sustain cooperation as a subgame perfect equilibrium.

There are several reasons why we find unsatisfactory an explanation of cooperation in the laboratory CPRs that relies on the predictions from the theory of an infinitely repeated game in which grim trigger strategies are used to support the optimal solution. First, the situation individuals confront in the lab is explicitly finite.[12] More worrisome is that the most important behavior consistent with this explanation of cooperation are not observed. Specifically, if subjects were behaving as if the game were infinite and using grim strategies, we should observe:

(1)   no deviations from agreements (or, at most a very small number),

(2)   all participants investing substantially more than their agreement in the CPR for the rest of the experiment, if (by error or some other problem) deviations did occur.

Our observations are not consistent with either prediction. As shown in Table 5, the defection rate in our experiments ranged from 1% to 42%. The defection rate was systematically related to the extent of communication. When subjects discussed strategies during communication rounds, they explicitly rejected anything like a grim trigger. "We'd only be screwing ourselves" was the usual reaction to such a proposal. We never observed grim trigger strategies played in the laboratory on any of the many occasions when subjects had the opportunity to use them. A small amount of chiseling on agreements rarely meant the rapid end of generally cooperative behavior. In those situations where individuals could discuss the problems of small defections, they were usually able to surmount this problem. Even when they could not discuss the problem, they often sustained close to optimal outcomes even though some individuals made investments at a somewhat higher level than that agreed upon. On both theoretical and empirical grounds, assuming that our experimental setting approximated an infinite game solved by the use of grim trigger strategies does not provide an answer to why there was so much cooperation.

Table 5

Aggregate Results all Designs[*]

Experimental Design	Average % Net Yield CPR	Defection Rate
Baseline 10TK[**]	34	—
Baseline 25TK	21	—
One-Shot Communication 25TK	55	25
Repeated Communication 10TK	99	5
Repeated Communication 25TK	73	13

[*]   All computations are for rounds in which the treatment was in effect. Nash equilibrium for all designs is 39% net CPR yield. Not applicable is represented with a — .
[**]   TK corresponds to tokens per subject.

It is not inconceivable that the subjects perceive this finite game as if it were infinite, but do not use grim triggers. For example, suppose the players approach the game as if it were repeated, but with only a vague notion of how many repetitions. Assuming a very low termination probability, they may realize there is more than one sensible way of playing the game and that there are group gains to some of these possibilities. That is, not knowing exactly when it ends, they form their own continuation probability and act as though the game might last forever. In this case, there are many other equilibria available to them besides those associated with grim triggers. Some of these have efficiencies higher than that implied by the one shot Nash equilibrium being played repeatedly, but less than 100%. Our data are not inconsistent with such an interpretation. Indeed, almost any observed play could be consistent with some equilibrium. Given the plethora of equilibria available to the players (if they perceive the game as infinite), the players face an insuperable problem of equilibrium selection.

In the face of these complications, two principles suggest themselves. The first principle is that agents use communication to address their equilibrium selection problem.[13] The second principle is that agents will find and adopt a simple equilibrium strategy rather than a complicated one. In a communication session our subjects tend to do two things: (1) focus on a simple symmetric solution approximating the group maximum and (2) formulate a simple symmetric plan of play for the repeated game. The principle of simplicity in the one shot case carries over to the repeated case. Interestingly enough, these two principles are also consistent with arguments of bounded rationality.[14]

Game theory based on complete rationality requires that players have a strategy--a complete plan of play for every contingency. Selten, Mitzkewitz, and Uhlich (1988) argue that players are basically reactive in nature. Suppose that players in a communication phase have reached agreement on how play should proceed. As long as play proceeds according to the agreement, there is no need to react. Reaction is only called for when something unexpected happens, in particular, a defection from the agreement. The first principle, that subjects use communication for equilibrium selection, gives the subjects a reference point, their agreement, for reactions. The second principle, simplicity, reinforces the agreement as a reference point and suggests the form that reactions may take to deviations from the agreement. One possible type of "simple" reaction is a *measured reaction*.[15] There are other possible reactions, some of which we briefly discuss below.

Measured reactions

In a measured reaction, a player reacts mildly (if at all) to a small deviation from an agreement. The larger the deviation from an agreement, the larger the reaction. Thus, a measured reaction is already different from a grim trigger strategy. The intuition behind measured reactions is that, by keeping play near the agreement, it is easier to restore the agreement. Further, the risk of a complete unraveling toward the one-shot game equilibrium is reduced when players do not overreact to deviations. Since the payoff achieved from an agreement (or, play close to the agreement) dominates the one-shot game equilibrium, measured reactions represents a useful response to the problem of equilibrium selection.

Consider our designs with one-shot or repeated communication, where agents have agreed to contribute 6 tokens each to the CPR (this is the agreement reached in several of our experiments). Then a typical measured reaction would look as shown in the top panel of Figure 1. The reaction shown in this figure has on the x-axis the average decision of all other players in the previous round (t-1), and on the y-axis the decision of a given player in the current round (t). The measured reaction passes through the agreement: if all others kept to the agreement in t-1, then this player keeps to it in round (t). Moreover, if others invest less than the agreed amount, this player sticks to the agreement. Finally, if others invest more than the agreement calls for, this player responds in a measured fashion by investing somewhat more or by sticking to the agreement in the hopes of getting others to return to the agreement. Measured reactions continue until the one-shot equilibrium is reached. At this point, no further reactions are called for. Play has now reached the one-shot equilibrium, and any further deviations reduce a player's payoff. If investments were to exceed the Nash equilibrium, eventually a player would do best to leave the CPR entirely and invest all tokens in the safe alternative.

The linear reaction shown in the top panel of Figure 1 is simple, but ignores the restriction that decisions have to be integer valued. We call any reaction function passing through the agreement point and the one-shot equilibrium a measured reaction. The lower panel of Figure 1 graphically presents the measured reaction box, which shows the limits within which all such reactions must be found. Note that the lower left and upper right corners of this box are defined by the agreement reached in an experiment, AGREEMENT, and the one-shot Nash equilibrium point (8, 8), NASH. All integer-valued step functions lie within this box.

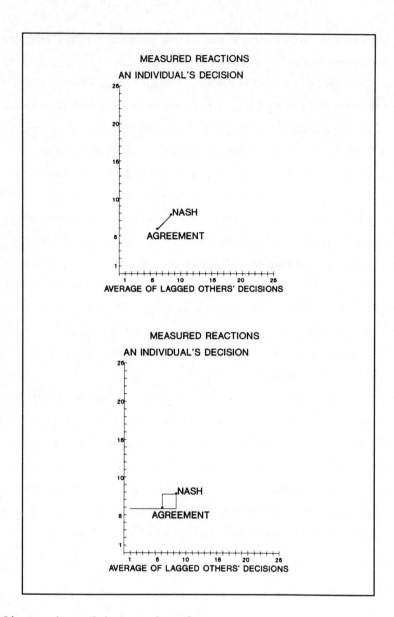

Figure 1: Linear and extended measured reactions

Table 6

Measured Reactions in Communication Experiments

Type of Communication Experimental Design	Agreement	Extended Agreement	In the Box	Total Measured Reactions	Large Reactions	Average % of Yield
One-Shot						
1**	53	7	82	89	0	88
2**	0	3	31	34	15	23
3**	0	10	41	51	10	57
Repeated 10 Token*						
1	100	0	100	100	0	99
2	88	0	97	97	3	99
3	99	0	99	99	0	99
4	95	0	97	97	2	97
Repeated 25 Token						
1	0	0	93	93	0	70
2	99	0	99	99	0	84
3	97	0	99	99	1	65
4**	100	0	100	100	0	89
5**	57	0	75	75	3	37
6**	82.	0	96	96	0	84

*   In the 10 token design, subjects were constrained to make a large deviation of 15 tokens. For these experiments, a bounded investment decision of 10 tokens is considered as a large deviation.

**   Subjects received information on Market 2 decisions for each individual subject--by anonymous identification number.

Besides measured reactions, there are many alternative reactions subjects might exhibit in our decision situation. At one extreme, they may make the same decision under all circumstances, "constant play." We have observed behavior consistent with other possibilities as well. For instance, a subject who invests at a maximal rate while other subjects hold back there investment level to an agreed upon level, is playing "never give a sucker an even break." A variation on this strategy is observed when a subject convinces the others to invest at low levels, and then proceeds to invest at a maximal level themselves. This could be called "sand-bagging the suckers."

Measured reactions appear to have improved cooperation in our communication experiments. As summarized above, we report 13 experiments where subjects had at least one opportunity to communicate. A summary analysis of the responses made by subjects in these experiments is reported in Table 6 and discussed below.

High-endowment experiments with one-shot communication

In Experiment 1 (Table 4), the subjects stressed that they wanted to obtain a fair outcome where everyone received the same payoff. The subjects agreed upon a strategy of investing 6 tokens each in the CPR. While the agreement was not at the optimum, if all participants followed this agreement, they earned 89% of the optimum yield. The experiment lasted 22 rounds after the single communication round, leaving 21 rounds x 8 decisions to seek evidence of measured reactions. Figure 2 shows how the reactions appear in reaction space. In 53% of all decisions (89/168) a subject invested at the agreement in round t in response to an average investment equal to the agreement in t-1. This can be interpreted to mean: the individual knows that on average the others kept to the agreement in t-1, and so the individual keeps to the agreement in t. This 53% is represented in Figure 2 in parentheses next to the word "AGREEMENT." Besides the 53% of all reactions at the agreement point, there were an additional 29% inside the measured reaction box. This is depicted in Figure 2 by the number 82% within the measured reaction box which includes the reactions at the agreement point, the Nash point, and interior to the box. There were no observations of one-shot Nash. This is represented by the 0% in parentheses next to NASH on the figure. Measured reactions are only defined between the AGREEMENT and one-shot NASH. In this experiment, and, as we shall see in most one-shot communication experiments, a noticeable percentage of players stick to the agreement when the group average is less than the amount agreed upon. In this experiment, for example, 7% of all responses were of the form where "i's reaction is 6 in round t, when the other's average in t-1 was less than 6." This is represented by the number 7% above the line extending leftward from the agreement point.

There are two other types of reactions worth emphasizing. One is the optimum. The second is what we refer to as a *large* reaction. In this experiment, we observed no reactions where the individual invested at the optimum in response to an investment in the previous round that averaged at the optimum. We define a *large* reaction as any reaction greater than or equal to the one-shot best response to the agreement. For instance, the one-shot best response to the agreement at 6 tokens is 15 tokens by the player breaking the agreement. In this experiment, there is only 1 large deviation (rounded to 1%), displayed next to LARGE DEVIATIONS. In this experiment, the measured reaction is very much in evidence.

In Experiment 2 (Table 4), the participants again had only one communication session. After a short discussion, they agreed to invest 5 tokens each. They saw on their screens that one player had invested 25 tokens in each of the first ten rounds. Only one player speculated about the payoffs that the "all 25" player had obtained and mused that this player "could be coming up with real money if everyone else is pulling back." Unfortunately for the others, this player could make twice the money the others made by persisting in his behavior and was perfectly willing to exploit the reaction.[16] He had actively promoted the decision to select 5 rather than 6 tokens as their agreement. As his parting shot at the end of the round, he told the others, "So we all need to stick to it." This player did not follow the same heuristic as the others. He adopted something closer to "never give a sucker an even break." With no further communication, the other seven players could see on their screens round after round that the same player invested 25 tokens. As shown in Figure 3, 31% of the responses were in the measured reaction box while 15% were large reactions--most of which were the actions of this one player.

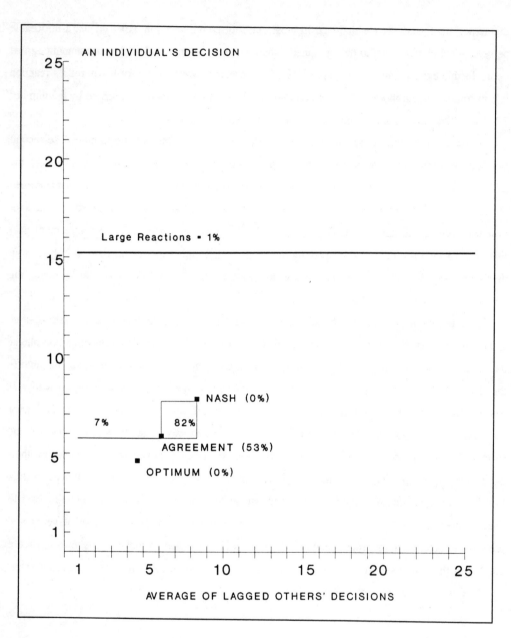

Figure 2: Measured Reactions - Experiment 1 - One Shot Communication

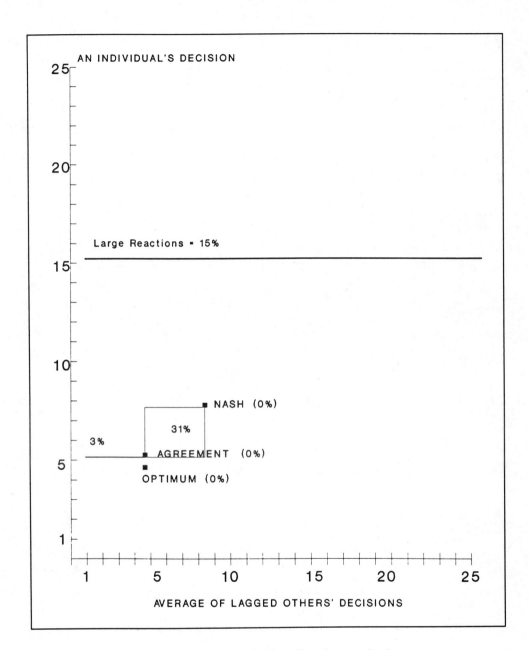

Figure 3: Measured Reactions - Experiment 2 - One Shot Communication

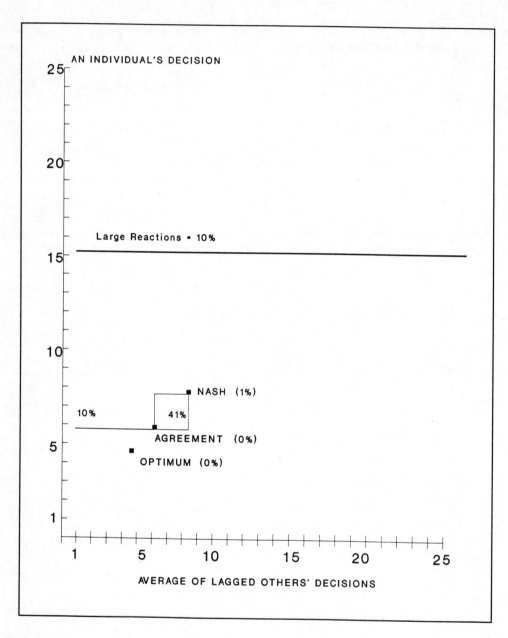

Figure 4: Measured Reactions - Experiment 3 - One Shot Communication

In Experiment 3 (Table 4), the subjects disagreed on what the optimal investment was. They finally decided to invest 3 tokens each in round 11, 4 tokens each in round 12, 5 tokens each in round 13, and 6 tokens each in round 14 and then to pick the best (independently). During this trial phase, there were 2 large reactions, as well as 1 reaction out of sequence. Once the trial phase was completed, the modal subject choice from then on was 6 tokens. From this we infer that an implicit agreement at 6 had been reached. Since the group never had another chance to communicate, there is no way to check this inference. Clearly, the lack of a clear agreement point at the end of the communication session jeopardized the performance of any heuristic, such as measured reactions. As shown in Figure 4, 41% of the responses were in the measured reaction box, while 10% were large reactions.

Repeated communication

In all four of the repeated 10-token communication experiments (reported in Table 2), subjects followed their agreements with a high level of fidelity and responded to the few deviations in such a manner that one could safely argue that the subjects used measured reactions. The response diagrams for these four experiments all have higher than 97% of the responses in the measured reaction box, and almost all of these are at the agreement point. For this reason, we have not reproduced these response diagrams here.

As discussed earlier, the 25-token design is behaviorally a far more difficult situation than the 10-token design. We conducted 6 experiments with high endowments and repeated opportunities to communicate (reported in Table 3). In all 6 experiments, subjects reacted consistently with measured reactions, with at least 75% of all reactions in the box. We now consider each experiment in some detail.

In Experiment 1, subjects agreed to invest 6 tokens each. Thus, the agreement point in reaction strategy space is the point (6,6). The big difference between this experiment and the low-endowment experiments is that a single reaction of the form (6,6) was never observed. This group was literally never at the agreed-upon point. Nevertheless, the group did achieve a reasonable net vicinity of the agreement. In the 12 rounds where reactions could be observed following the initial

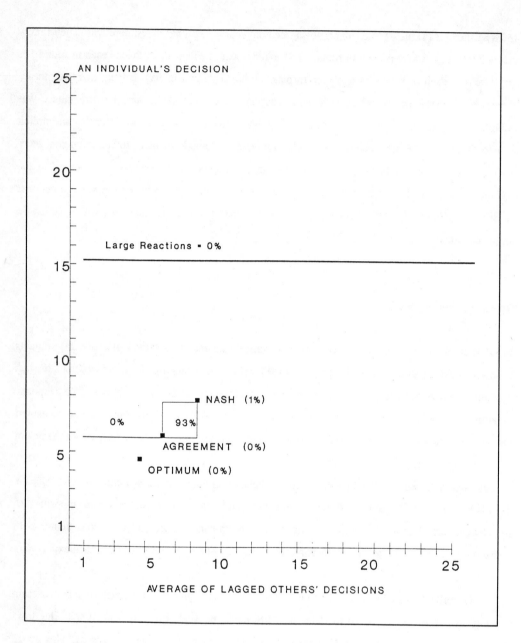

Figure 5: Measured Reactions - Experiment 1 - Repeated 25 Token

yield (70%), and stayed in thecommunication round, 93% (89/96) of the reactions lay within the measured reaction box, as shown in Figure 5. There were only 7 reactions lying outside the box, and none of these were large. This is especially impressive given that there are no observations at (6,6).

The transcript of this experiment provides evidence about the expressed thoughts of the subjects as they coped with the continuing problem of defecting members. In the first rounds, seven subjects invested at the agreement and the eighth subject (Player C) invested two tokens over the agreement. After considerable discussion about what to do, they finally agreed that "staying with 6 is the best." The last two comments made before they returned to their terminals were:

Player B: Let's not get greedy. We've just got to start trusting.

Player H: Let's everyone do 6.

In the next Round, the 12th, Player C increased investments in the CPR from 8 tokens invested in Round 11, to 19 tokens. This constituted a real challenge to their agreement and an affront to the other players. Player A invested 7 rather than 6 tokens (consistent with measured reaction). All the others stayed with the agreement and invested 6 tokens. After this round, the discussion opened with:

Player B: This should be our last meeting--if we can't get some trust, we might as well go back and screw each other over. We could all make more money if we could stick together, but if some are going to do the others in, then, we just should go. Does *everyone* agree to do the same thing?

Player D: If there is any objection to this, can we just plain hear why not?

Player H: Well, it is obvious that someone is making a little more money.

Player B: Well, they know that they are going to make more money, they could probably make all of two bucks, but still, I mean, if we go back to the way we were, none of us will make as much.

Player E: Let's try it one more time.

Player H: No, let's go back to the way we were doing it.

Player D: If you do, you sure lose!

Player G: If you don't work together, you lose.

Player E: That person will do it, whatever we agree to.

Player H: Does anyone want to confess?

Player D: Let's try one more time.

Player G: If this doesn't work, then forget all about it.

Player H: Want to try to invest 6? Let's try it.

Player B: Let's go for 6. [Player B then looks at each and every one of the other 7, points
             to each one, and looks at each one directly in the eye.] It shouldn't take very
             long for anyone to put in 6 in Market 2!

After this dramatic close, Player C dropped back to the agreed-upon 6 tokens in Round 13,
but Player A invested 8. In the discussion following Round 13, the players were so glad to be close
to their agreement that they simply congratulated themselves on getting closer and asked to return
to their terminals early. They had similarly short discussions from then on. After the 15th round,
for example, they had the following exchange:

Player H: Not everyone is investing 6.

Player B: Evidently not.

Player C: Unless everyone keeps to it, it starts to get away from us.

Player H: Let's say we invest 6 again. Obviously somebody is cheating, but what can we
             do? But the rest of us can just continue to invest 6.

At a still later point, Player E suggested that they dump whatever they wanted into Market 2.
Player H disagreed and pointed out that "we screw ourselves too." The transcript reflects a group
of subjects' trying to grapple with a situation on the brink of disaster. Instead of going over the
brink, their measured reactions to the provocation sustained behavior close to their agreement, even
though they never achieved perfect compliance.

In Experiment 2, the participants miscalculated the optimum at 50 tokens (instead of 36) and
devised a rotation scheme whereby 6 individuals invested 6 tokens and 2 individuals invested 7
tokens. They had perfect compliance to their rotation system through Round 20, when one subject
invested 11 rather than 6 tokens. Given past experience in experiments with 20 rounds, this may
have been an "end effect." The discussion after Round 20, reproduced earlier in this paper, reflects
individuals who are puzzled why someone would break their agreement. They resolved to return
to their rotation scheme. They did return to their terminals and continued with perfect compliance

from there on. They achieved 84% of the potential yield, rather than a higher percentage, because they had miscalculated the optimum and not because they had difficulty keeping to their agreement.

In Experiment 3, the players again overestimated the number of tokens that was optimal and agreed to invest 50 each round for four rounds (with a rotation system) and then 49 tokens each round. They faced only 3 defections during the course of their experiment. In the discussion following these defections, the players stressed the importance of not "messing it up" by small deviations and never discussed the possibility of punishing those who deviated. The central focus was on keeping the agreement going still further.

In Experiment 4, the subjects initially miscalculated the optimal investment level, but used their discussion to improve their agreement. By the last five rounds, they obtained 99% of the yield. Since they never faced a defection throughout the experiment, they never discussed a response for coping with this problem.

Experiment 5 was unique in one crucial respect. These subjects agreed to invest 1 token each in the CPR. This represents by far the worst agreement ever reached, with a potential group yield of only 40%. This agreement at the point (1,1) further creates the largest measured reaction box, with corners at (1,1) and (8,8). A large box is really easy to hit; indeed, 75% of all reactions in the 13 rounds following the agreement landed in the box (see Figure 6). Despite this deficient agreement, subjects held to it for 7 rounds. Then the *same* player who had suggested the agreement in the first place made the largest possible reaction, 25 tokens.[17] A lively discussion ensued, as reported earlier in this paper. In the last 5 rounds of the experiment, there were 17 double-digit reactions, and the agreement clearly unraveled. The combination of deficient agreement and unraveling meant an overall average yield of only 37%, by far the lowest of the set of repeated communication, 25-token experiments.

Experiment 6 also helps illuminate how individuals who have measured reactions avoid the complete deterioration of an agreement when presented with small infractions by one or two individuals. In this experiment, the group agreed to invest 6 tokens each. While they did achieve some rounds of perfect compliance, they frequently faced rounds in which one or two persons invested 7 or 8 tokens rather than the agreed-upon 6. The participants discussed the possibility of trigger strategies at several points in their discussions and always rejected the idea. Here is one exchange:

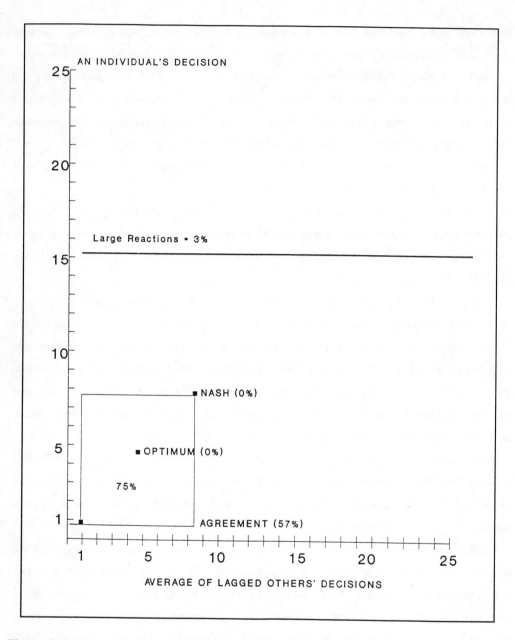

Figure 6: Measured Reactions - Experiment 5 - Repeated 25 Token

Player D   What can we do to lose the most?

Player A   Lose the most?

Player D   Yeah, to get back at her--point at E (who was suspected of having overinvested).

Player A   But that hurts us all as well.

Player D   We probably don't have that many rounds left to really worry about this stuff of putting one more penny than we have agreed on. Let's just keep on putting in those 6's--and let them have the benefits of their stupid penny.

At a later juncture, one player commented that the set of reliable players is even smaller (while only two people had defected, one of those individuals had never defected before). This was followed with:

Player E   What are we going to do, are we going to go for a free-for-all?

Player B   Go for a free-for-all? Shucks no, we all lose.

Player D   No, we all lose.

The discussion rounds in this experiment were quite heated, but by stressing the fact that they would all lose if they moved too far away from the agreement point, the group was able to gain 84% of net yield even when facing the problem of repeated but small defections.

Summarizing, from the results of the 6 repeated communication, 25-token experiments, we find high rates of measured reactions, at least 75% in all cases and at least 93% in five cases. We find very low rates of large reactions, never higher than 3%, with no large reactions whatsoever in four cases. In the five experiments where the initial agreement promised a high average yield (at least 90%), measured reactions enabled groups to obtain on average 78% yield in a very challenging situation. Of course, measured reactions cannot salvage a very deficient agreement.

Conclusions: Communication, bounded rationality, and behavioral heuristics

The above discussion of measured reactions provides part of an explanation of "Why so much cooperation in communication experiments?," but only part. Communication allows individuals to agree on a joint strategy and to begin a process of building trust in others to abide by that agreement. When sanctioning is not available, trust has to be built through communication and consequent changes in patterns of behavior. When behavior is relatively close to the agreed-upon level, most individuals respond to deviations in a measured fashion. When most individuals use a measured reaction, even in challenging situations, they are able to gain joint returns close to the level agreed upon. Their closeness to optimality depends both on the yield potential of their agreement and on their rate of compliance. Individuals who exhibit measured reactions are able to sustain cooperation for an extended period and reap the benefits of doing so.

On the other hand, when one or a few individuals do *not* respond consistently with measured reactions and are able to deviate in an extreme manner from an agreement (by having sufficient resources to be very disruptive to attempts by others to form near optimal agreements), measured reactions are not very effective. Dealing with extreme deviations is especially problematic when players communicate only once. To prevent agreements from unravelling, the ability to chastise offenders verbally on a repeated basis is essential in laboratory experiments without sanctions.

Even if measured reactions work, this still leaves unanswered why some groups exhibit them and others do not. Where do such reactions come from? One answer to this question starts with Selten's dictum that complete rationality is the limiting case of bounded or incomplete rationality (see Selten, 1975: 35). From this perspective, a behavioral response like measured reactions are heuristics used by individuals as problem-solving tools when complete analysis is difficult and short-term self-interest dictates unsatisfactory long-term outcomes, such as the case where the cognitive task is beyond the immediate scope of the individual, or game equilibria lead to suboptimal outcomes. Individuals learn to use a repertoire of heuristics depending upon their experience and their perception of the situation in which they find themselves, including the likely behavior of others.

In simple situations where short-term self-interest leads to a near optimal outcome, individuals may very well exhibit behavior that closely parallels that predicted by a model of complete rationality. In simple situations where short-term self-interest leads to a highly suboptimal outcome, individuals may learn from experience or be taught by mentors that use of a heuristic may lead to better outcomes, as long as others follow similar behavior. In complex situations individuals may adopt heuristics as a first approach to learning about the decision situation. Many terms are used for the concept of a heuristic including "rule of thumb," "standard operating procedure," and "standard of behavior."[18]

In a situation without communication and with more than two individuals, it is extremely difficult to initiate a process by which individuals learn a measured type heuristic. Similarly, if groups only communicate once, and if some individuals adopt less cooperative strategies than measured reactions, it is harder to sustain cooperation over time than when groups are able to discuss their joint behavior and outcomes continuously. As we see in our experiments, the same individuals who use a measured reaction when communication is possible, may not use it when communication is impossible.

But once individuals communicate (and, especially if they can communicate with one another repeatedly), they can build up trust through their discussions and by achieving better outcomes through their behavior. If individuals come to these situations with a willingness to devise sharing rules and to follow a measured reaction, then communication facilitates agreement selection and the measured reaction facilitates agreement retention. The measured reaction heuristic prevents the full unraveling of an agreement when minor deviations first start to occur, but is not effective when major deviations occur. In the latter event, no response other than a sanction directed at a large reaction is likely to be effective.

In situations as complex as these CPR experiments, the evidence suggests that individuals may perceive the world differently from the rational players of noncooperative game theory. Individuals may come to these situations armed with an array of previously-learned heuristics. With communication, these individuals have a chance to discover the approaches others are using to the game. Without communication, they do not know what to do in the situation they face and adopt strategies that vary tremendously.

The adoption of a measured reaction heuristic enables individuals to start on a productive path toward higher joint outcomes without outside enforcers. So long as the population of individuals sampled for laboratory experiments has a sufficient proportion of individuals who know and use a measured reaction heuristic, individuals can use this shared knowledge or social capital as a resource for gaining substantially better outcomes than they would otherwise have gained. Even when groups discover individuals within their midst playing entirely different strategies, the restraint shown by the remaining individuals keeps their joint returns higher than they were when pursuing completely independent strategies.

Footnotes

1   Indiana University, Department of Economics, Bloomington, USA.

2   See Banks and Calvert (1992a, 1992b) for an important discussion of the theoretical significance of communication in incomplete information games.

3   See E. Ostrom and Walker (1991) for a more detailed discussion of the role of communication and the experimental evidence summarized here.

4   A complete set of instructions is available from the authors upon request.

5   Subjects were randomly recruited from initial runs to ensure that no group was brought back in tact. The number of rounds in the initial experiments varied from 10 to 20.

6   Investment in the CPR beyond the maximum net level is termed "rent dissipation" in the literature of resource economics. This is conceptually akin to, but not to be confused with, the term "rent seeking," which plays an important role in political economy and public choice. For the latter, see Tullock (1967) and Krueger (1974).

7   See Walker, Gardner, and E. Ostrom (1991) for details of this derivation.

8   An alternative measurement of performance would be to calculate overall experimental efficiency (actual earnings as a percentage of maximum possible earnings for the group). In this decision situation, this measurement has the undesirable property that for any given level investments in the CPR, overall efficiency is different according to the number of tokens remaining to invest in Market 1. Further, our use of net yield gives a more accurate measure of the effect of behavior on the CPR, our primary interest.

9   Each person was identified with a badge that was unrelated to their player number. This facilitated player identification in our transcripts. If unanimous, players could forego discussion.

10 These low-endowment communication experiments were conducted very early in our research and used a modified 10 token payoff function for Market 2 $(15(\Sigma x_i)-.15(\Sigma x_i)^2)$. Yield as a percentage of maximum from experiments without communication using this payoff function closely parallel the yields observed in our 10 token low-endowment baseline design. Across 20 decision rounds, the difference in mean yields between experiments using these two alternative payoff functions for Market 2 was only 6.4%, slightly higher in the low-endowment baseline design presented in the text.

11 If a game were to be repeated infinitely, there would be no last round and the logic of backward induction no long applies.

12 As mentioned in Chapter 5, subjects are told that the experiment will last about one and a half hour and have already experienced training experiments that lasted no more than 20 rounds. In a similar set of public good experiments, where the end round was specifically announced, similar behavioral outcomes were observed (see Isaac & Walker, 1988a, 1988b). For finitely repeated games with a unique equilibrium, one can still invoke grim trigger strategies, but they will necessarily involve incredible threats and promises, whose incredibility will come due in a finite amount of time.

13 This point is made forcefully by Banks and Calvert (1992a, 1992b).

14 Colleagues working with Reinhard Selten in the Department of Economics at the University of Bonn have developed and tested a series of behavioral strategies related to various types of games. See Rockenbach and Uhlich (1989) on two-person characteristic function games; Mitzkewitz and Nagel (1991) on ultimatum games with incomplete information.

15 Our use of this term was inspired by the concept of "measure-for-measure" introduced by Selten, Mitzkewitz, and Uhlich (1988). However, there are important differences is our application relative to theirs. Namely, their subjects do not have a communication phase, and they model their subjects using Selten's three-stage theory of bounded rationality. Our

application makes use of only one of these three stages and substitutes communication for another stage.

16 When the other players contributed 5 tokens each, someone contributing 25 tokens could make 8 "experimental cents" on each token in the CPR and only 5 "cents" on the same tokens in the alternative investment. That meant that the individual investing 25 tokens made a total of 200 "cents" on any round when the others invested no more than 35 tokens in total. The others made 140 "cents." If everyone had followed the agreement, all would have made 185 "cents." Subjects were paid one half of the "experimental cents" they earned in the 25-token experiment.

17 The heuristic this player may have been playing could be described as: "Set the suckers up for a preemptive strike."

18 See Groner, Groner, and Bischof (1983) for a general discuss of heuristics.

References

Banks, J.S., & Calvert, R.L. (1992a). A battle-of-the-sexes game with incomplete information. *Games and Economic Behavior, 4*, 1-26.

Banks, J.S., & Calvert, R.L. (1992b). Communication and efficiency in coordination games. Working Paper. Rochester, N.Y.: University of Rochester, Department of Economics and Department of Political Science.

Benoit, J., & Krishna, V. (1985). Finitely repeated games. *Econometrica, 53*, 905-922.

Caldwell, M.D. (1976). Communication and sex effects in a five-person prisoners' dilemma game. *Journal of Personality and Social Psychology, 33*(3), 273-280.

Dawes, R.M., McTavish, J., & Shaklee, H. (1977). Behavior, communication, and assumptions about other people's behavior in a commons dilemma situation. *Journal of Personality and Social Psychology, 35*(1), 1-11.

Edney, J.J., & Harper, C.S. (1978). The commons dilemma: A review of contributions from psychology. *Environmental Management, 2*(6), 491-507.

El-Gamal, M., McKelvey, R.D., & Palfrey, T.R. (1991). A Bayesian sequential experimental study of learning in games. Social Science Working Paper no. 757. Pasadena: California Institute of Technology.

Friedman, J.W. (1990). *Game theory with applications to economics* (2nd ed.). New York: Oxford University Press.

Groner, R., Groner, M., Bischof, W.F. (1983). *Methods of heuristics*. Hillsdale, N.J.: Lawrence Erlbaum Associates.

Hackett, S., Schlager, E., & Walker, J.M. (1992). The role of communication in resolving commons dilemmas: Experimental evidence with heterogeneous appropriators. Working Paper. Bloomington: Indiana University, Workshop in Political Theory and Policy Analysis.

Isaac, R.M., & Walker, J.M. (1988a). Communication and free-riding behavior: The voluntary contribution mechanism. *Economic Inquiry, 24*(4), 585-608.

Isaac, R.M., & Walker, J.M. (1988b). Group size effects in public goods provision: The voluntary contributions mechanism. *Quarterly Journal of Economics, 103*, 179-199.

Isaac, R.M., & Walker, J.M. (1991). Costly communication: An experiment in a nested public goods problem. In T.R. Palfrey (Ed.), *Laboratory research in political economy* (pp. 269-286). Ann Arbor: University of Michigan Press.

Jerdee, T.H., & Rosen, B. (1974). Effects of opportunity to communicate and visibility of individual decisions on behavior in the common interest. *Journal of Applied Psychology, 59*(6), 712-716.

Keohane, R.O. (1986). Reciprocity in international relations. *International Organization, 40*, 1-27.

Krueger, A.O. (1974). The political economy of the rent-seeking society. *American Economic Review, 64*, 291-303.

Mitzkewitz, M., & Nagel, R. (1991). Envy, greed, and anticipation in ultimatum games with incomplete information: An experimental study. Discussion Paper B-181. Bonn: University of Bonn, Sonderforschungsbereich 303.

Orbell, J.M., van de Kragt, A.J.M., & Dawes, R.M. (1991). Covenants without the sword: The role of promises in social dilemma circumstances. In K.J. Kofford & J.B. Miller (Eds.), *Social norms and economic institutions* (pp. 117-134). Ann Arbor: University of Michigan Press.

Ostrom, E., & Walker, J.M. (1991). Communication in a commons: Cooperation without external enforcement. In T.R. Palfrey (Ed.), *Laboratory research in political economy* (pp. 287-322). Ann Arbor: University of Michigan Press.

Ostrom, E., Walker, J., & Gardner, R. (1992). Covenants with and without a sword: Self-governance is possible. *American Political Science Review, 86*(2), 404-417.

Rockenbach, B., & Uhlich, G.R. (1989). The negotiation agreement area: An experimental analysis of two-person characteristic function games. Discussion Paper B-126. Bonn: University of Bonn, Sonderforschungsbereich 303.

Runge, C.F. (1984). Institutions and the free rider: The assurance problem in collective action. *Journal of Politics, 46*(1), 154-181.

Schotter, A. (1980). *The economic theory of social institutions.* Cambridge: Cambridge University Press.

Selten, R. (1975). Reexamination of the perfectness concept for equilibrium points in extensive games. *International Journal of Game Theory, 4*, 25-55.

Selten, R., Mitzkewitz, M., & Uhlich, G.R. (1988). Duopoly strategies programmed by experienced players. Discussion Paper B-172. Bonn: University of Bonn Special Research Project 303.

Tullock, G. (1967). The welfare costs of tariff monopolies and theft. *Western Economic Journal, 5*, 224-232.

van de Kragt, A., Dawes, R.M., Orbell, J.M., Braver, S.R., & Wilson, L.A. (1986). Doing well and doing good as ways of resolving social dilemmas. In H. Wilke, D. Messick, & C. Rutte (Eds.), *Experimental social dilemmas* (pp. 177-204). Frankfurt am Main, FRG: Verlag Peter Lang.

Walker, J.M., Gardner, R., & Ostrom, E. (1991). Rent dissipation and balanced deviation disequilibrium in common pool resources: Experimental evidence. In R. Selten (Ed.), *Game equilibrium models II: Methods, morals, and markets* (pp. 337-367). Berlin: Springer-Verlag.

Acknowledgement

Financial support from the National Science Foundation (Grant Nos. SES-8619498 & SES-4843901) and USDA Cooperative Agreement #43-3AEM1-80078 is gratefully acknowledged. We thank Rick Wilson and our colleagues at the Workshop in Political Theory and Policy Analysis for their comments. All data are stored on permanent NovaNET disk files.

Send inquiries to James M. Walker, Department of Economics, Ballantine 901, Indiana University, Bloomington, Indiana, U.S.A. 47405.

Cooperation in an asymmetric volunteer's dilemma game
Theory and experimental evidence

Andreas Diekmann[1]

Abstract

The symmetric Volunteer's dilemma game (VOD) models a situation in which each of N actors faces the decision of either producing a step-level collective good (action "C") or freeriding ("D"). One player's cooperative action suffices for producing the collective good. Unilateral cooperation yields a payoff U for D-players and U - K for the cooperative player(s). However, if all actors decide for "freeriding", each player's payoff is zero (U > K > 0). In this article, an essential modification is discussed. In an asymmetric VOD, the interest in the collective good and/or the production costs (i.e. work) may vary between actors. The generalized asymmetric VOD is similar to market entry games. Alternative hypotheses abaout the behavior of subjects are derived from a game-theoretical analysis. They are investigated in an experimental setting. The application of the mixed Nash-equilibrium concept yields a rather counter-intuitive prediction which apparently contradicts the empirical data. The predictions of the Harsanyi-Selten-theory and Schelling's "focal point theory" are in better accordance with the data. However, they do not account for the "diffusion-of-responsibility-effect" also observable in the context of an asymmetric VOD game.

Introduction

In a N-person non-cooperative matrix game called "volunteer's dilemma" (Diekmann 1985), each actor has the choice between a favorite alternative D with payoff U and a less favorite alternative C with payoff U - K (U > K > 0). However, while C-players, irrespective of other actors' choices, obtain the maximin payoff U - K, D-players receive payoff U only if there is at least one other player choosing C. Otherwise D-players' payoff is zero.

The game describes a collective good problem with a step production function. Cooperative actors pay K units of utility for the production of the collective good, while cooperators as well as defectors gain U. However, if all actors decide on freeriding, the worst payoff is obtained.

There are several applications of a volunteer's dilemma in economics, sociology, political science, and biology. Examples are the market entry decision of two firms (Sherman and Willett 1967), voting behavior (Brennan and Lomasky 1984), the sanctioning dilemma of N actors facing a norm violation, the investment decision of two or more privileged actors in a "privileged group" (Olson 1965), bystander intervention in emergencies as analyzed by Darley and Latané (1968) in social psychology, and "vigilance games" in biology.

Obviously, there are N asymmetric equilibria in pure strategies, which are usually not attainable without coordination. In addition, a symmetric mixed Nash-equilibrium exists with the probability of

defection $q^{*} = \sqrt[N-1]{K/U}$ (Diekmann 1985). Since only one mixed Nash-equilibrium with symmetric

payoff-vector exists, theories of equilibrium selection, which require that solutions are invariable concerning the renumbering of players, will clearly select the mixed strategy equilibrium (e.g. Harsanyi and Selten 1988). This solution implies that the probability of freeriding will increase with group-size N, which corresponds very well to the "diffusion of responsibility"-effect observed by Darley and Latané in situations of helping behavior. Experimental evidence confirms the negative correlation of group-size and freeriding in experiments on helping behavior (Darley and Latané 1968) as well as experimental gaming (Diekmann 1986) although the mixed equilibrium solution systematically underestimates the percentage of cooperation.

Volunteer's dilemma assumes a symmetric decision situation for all players. An interesting question arises if this assumption is discarded. What are the consequences for the game theoretic solution if there is, for instance, a "strong" player with the ability to produce the collective good at a lower cost than his or her co-players? In this article, an asymmetric volunteer's dilemma game will be explored allowing for an unequal distribution of costs K_i and interests U_i among $i = 1, 2, ..., N$ actors. It will be shown that the mixed Nash-equilibrium yields highly counterintuitive results unlikely to be observed in actual behavior.

Game theoretical analysis

Consider the binary decision N-Person matrix game with actor i's $(i = 1, 2, ..., N)$ decision alternatives C_i and D_i respectively. With $U_i > K_i > 0$ the payoff structure is as follows:

(i)   Strategy C_i yields $U_i - K_i$,

(ii)   while, for D_i U_i is obtained if there is at least one other actor choosing C,

          0   otherwise.

Obviously, the game has N efficient and strict equilibria with exactly one "volunteer" and N-1 "freeriders". Moreover, an additional equilibrium point in mixed strategies may exist.

If D_i is chosen with probability q_i, actor i's expected utility E_i is

$$E_i = q_i U_i \left(1 - \prod_{j \neq i} \right) + (1 - q_i)(U_i - K_i) \qquad (1)$$

Partially differentiating with respect to q_i yields

$$\frac{\partial E_i}{\partial q_i} = -U_i \prod_{j \neq i} q_i + K_i \tag{2}$$

The following system of N equations results if the derivatives are set equal to zero:

$$\prod_{j \neq i}^{N} q_j = \frac{K_i}{U_i} \quad i = 1, 2, \ldots, N \tag{3}$$

The solution of (3) is

$$q_i^* = \frac{U_i}{K_i} \left[\prod_{j=1}^{N} \frac{K_j}{U_j} \right]^{\left(\frac{1}{N-1}\right)} \tag{4}$$

This is a (weak) mixed Nash-equlibrium if $0 < q_i^* < 1$ for $i = 1, 2, \ldots, N$. For the special case $N = 2$ it follows from (4) that a mixed equilibrium does always exist. Also, for $U_i = U$ and $K_i = K$ there is always a solution under the restriction $0 < q_i^* < 1$, which is the mixed equilibrium of the symmetric game: $q_i^* = \sqrt[N-1]{K/U}$ (Diekmann 1985).

Substitution of q_i in (1) by q_i^* yields the payoff-vector of the mixed equlibrium strategy. Payoffs are $U_i - K_i$, which is identical to the payoff of the pure maximin-strategy.[2]

This can be seen more easily by substitution of the product term in equation (1) by formula (3). It also becomes apparent that the expected value in the equilibrium E_i^* does not depend on q_i, i.e. the mixed Nash-equilibrium is weak.

$1 - q_i^*$ is the probability that actor i will decide on cooperation under the mixed equilibrium strategy. From (3) and (4), we obtain the probability that the collective good will be produced:

$$P = 1 - \prod_{i=1}^{N} q_i^* = 1 - \left[\prod_{i=1}^{N} \frac{K_i}{U_i} \right]^{\left(\frac{1}{N-1}\right)} \tag{5}$$

P(N) is not necessarily a decreasing function of N. In a symmetric game, however, the likelihood of collective good production decreases with group-size.

Now, consider solution (4). The Nash-equilibrium strategy implies that actor i's defection probability will increase with decreasing production costs K_i or increasing interest in the collective good U_i. This is a very paradoxical result which hardly will be in line with observed behavior of individual decision makers.[3] An explanation in formal terms is that the mixed equilibrium strategy yields the maximin payoff, which is higher for "strong" players with either greater interest U_i or lower costs K_i. In order to achieve at least the maximin payoff, a "stronger" actor's defection probability has to be greater than the defection probability of co-players with a lower maximin payoff.

Referring to empirical behavior, however, the paradox does not vanish. Imagine, for example, a price cartel with one firm violating the price level agreed upon by the member firms of the cartel. If identification and individual sanctioning of that firm is possible, a sanctioning dilemma arises. Assume that all firms have the same interest in the collective good U_i (conservation of the cartel price), that sanctioning is costly (K_i), and that one firm k has the lowest sanctioning costs K_k (figure 1). Then the mixed equilibrium solution implies that firm k has the lowest probability of sanctioning the norm-violator despite its highest sanctioning power in the group. As another example, consider three bystanders observing a victim in danger of being drowned in a lake. If only one of the observers is able to swim $(K_k < K_i)$, it is not the swimmer but the non-swimmers who are expected to jump in the water and save the victim.[4]

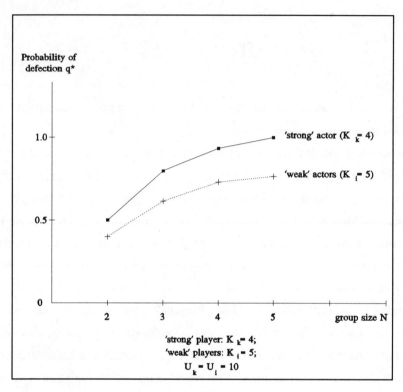

Figure 1:   Mixed equilibrium strategy for asymmetric volunteer's dilemma with one "strong" player and N-1 "weak" players

The opposite predicted by Schelling's (1960) concept of a "prominent solution" is probably much more realistic. As mentioned above, there are N pareto-efficient equilibria. The asymmetric game, however, contains a clue pointing to the single "eligible" equilibrium. It is the strongest player who is expected to take action, thereby yielding a pareto-efficient equilibrium.

In the special case of an asymmetric volunteer's dilemma with one "strong" and N-1 "weak" players investigated in the experiment described below, the conclusion following from "prominence theory" can be drawn from the Harsanyi-Selten theory of equilibrium selection. Consider first the subclass of games with constant interest ($U_i = U$ = constant; $i = 1, 2, \ldots, N$) and strictly increasing costs, i.e. $K_1 < K_2 < ... < K_N$; $0 < K_i < U_i$; $i = 1, 2, ... , N$. This subset of asymmetric volunteer's dilemma games belongs to the class of "regular market entry games" discussed in Selten and Güth (1982).[5] By application of the Harsanyi-Selten theory, Selten and Güth derive the theorem that "the solution of the game is that equilibrium point where the firms with the lowest entry costs enter the market," whereby "market entry" corresponds to the "cooperative" choice (C) in the asymmetric volunteer's dilemma game. It follows from the theorem that the strict equilibrium point is selected as the solution of the game where the player with the lowest costs (the "strong" player) acts cooperatively, while the "weaker" co-players defect. However, due to the assumption of the strict order of costs, the theorem does not cover the situation of one strong and N-1 co-players with equal degree of weakness and $N > 2$. For the strong player / weak co-players asymmetric volunteer's dilemma (i.e. $K_1 < K_2 = K_3 = ... = K_N$; $N > 2$), the theorem has to be generalized. It can be shown that the Harsanyi-Selten theory selects the equilibrium point where player 1 employs the cooperative strategy ("market entry") and players 2, 3, ..., N "defect".[6] This is the single strict and efficient equilibrium point in pure strategies with symmetric payoffs for players in a symmetric position.

In the strong-player-weak-co-players asymmetric situation, the mixed Nash-equilibrium predicts a higher probability of defection for the strong player who receives a payoff bonus compared to his weak co-players. The opposite conclusion follows from Schelling's "prominent" solution and the Harsanyi-Selten theory. While the former theory values "strength", the latter theories imply the "strength of weakness". By these theories, defective choices of weak players result in higher payoffs than the strong player's gain if players meet the mutual expectation of tacit coordination. Strong players are, so to speak, exploited by their weak co-players. However, if strong actors do not comply with their role as "rational hero", all freeriding actors might loose. The interesting question arises: How do real subjects behave in an asymmetric volunteer's dilemma? In the following, the opposing predictions are confronted in an "experimentum crucis".

Experimental test

An experimental test was arranged in order to find out which of the opposing predictions from, on the one hand, mixed Nash-equilibrium and, on the other hand, Schelling's theory of tacit coordination as well as the Harsanyi-Selten theory would better match the actual behaviour of decision makers. The experimental factor of main interest is the "weak player / strong co-players" versus "strong player / weak co-players" condition. In addition, the degree of weakness and strength and the group-size ($N = 2$ versus $N = 5$) were varied (see table 1).

328 students of various disciplines at the University of Mannheim, West Germany, participated in the experiment. Subjects were randomly distributed over ten experimental groups. They were asked to fill out a questionnaire containing the volunteer's dilemma and three versions of the prisoner's dilemma.[7] Volunteer's dilemma was presented first in this sequence of games. Thus, sequence effects probably did not influence the subjects' decision behaviour in volunteer's dilemma. The game was presented in matrix form, with subjects' payoffs and co-players' payoffs displayed in separate matrices (table 1). In addition, the game was described verbally and subjects were asked to give their own choice, the expected choice of co-players, and resulting payoffs. Subjects had plenty of time to think over the decision problems carefully and were motivated by relatively high monetary gains. It was announced that achieved points would be converted to money according to an exchange rate of 0.10 DM per point. The monetary payoff for a defective choice matched by co-player(s)' cooperative choice, consequently, amounts to DM 10.- , approximately US$ 6 (In fact, participants received an amount of 5.- to 15.- DM, depending on the experimental conditions to which they were randomly assigned).

Results are based on those subjects who correctly answered the question of expected payoffs, given the supposed choice of co-player(s). Hence, only the subset of 301 subjects who passed this "test of understanding" of the game structure was included in the analysis.[8]

For the 2*2-games, all three experimental tests clearly contradict the mixed Nash-equilibrium hypothesis. While this hypothesis predicts that increasing strength of the co-player will decrease the probability of player's defection, experimental data show a significant trend in the opposite direction (figure 2a). Moreover, player's strength is inversely related to defection proportions (figure 2b). Again, the differences are highly significant and contradict the mixed Nash-equilibrium implications. Finally, there is an extreme and highly significant difference in defection rates in the third test-situation (figure 2c), which directly contradicts the mixed Nash-equilibrium hypothesis.

Of course, we do not know whether actors really have employed mixed strategies. Besides various possible interpretations of the meaning of mixed strategies on the individual level (e.g. Harsanyi and Selten, 1980, 14pp.), the experimental test allows for potential falsification on the group level. Whether or not subjects employ mixed strategies on the individual level, aggregate results on the group level clearly falsify the mixed Nash-equilibrium hypothesis. The implication of this hypothesis is that proportions of defection should vary in accordance with formula (4), which apparently is not true.

On the other hand, the experimental data are much more in accordance with Schelling's "prominence theory" and the Harsanyi-Selten theory. Although the behaviour of subjects does not coincide with the prediction of the strict deterministic version of the Harsanyi-Selten theory of equilibrium selection, the data at least approximate the theoretical expectations. The more extreme the payoff-differences between weak and strong actors, the better the theory is approximated.

In the symmetric conditions A and H (table 1), the prediction of the Harsanyi-Selten theory is identical to the mixed Nash-equilibrium. In both conditions, however, the empirical defection proportions are overestimated by the theory. These findings are perfectly in accordance with three earlier experiments of the symmetric volunteer's dilemma (e.g. Diekmann 1986).

A. Diekmann

Table 1

Experimental design

Experimental condition	Group size	Type of game:	Cost benefit structure	Subject's Matrix **	Matrix of co-player(s) *	Predicted probability of defection by mixed Nash-equilibrium	Proportion of "defection" in experiment
A	2	symmetric:	K = 50, U = 100	50 50 / 100 0	50 50 / 100 0	0.50	0.39
B	2	weak player; strong co-player:	K = 50, U = 100 / K = 40, U = 100	50 50 / 100 0	60 60 / 100 0	0.40	0.55
C	2	weak player; extremely strong co-player:	K = 50, U = 100 / K = 10, U = 100	50 50 / 100 0	90 90 / 100 0	0.10	0.81
D	2	strong player; weak co-player:	K = 40, U = 100 / K = 50, U = 100	60 60 / 100 0	50 50 / 100 0	0.50	0.33
E	2	extremely strong player; weak co-player:	K = 10, U = 100 / K = 50, U = 100	90 90 / 100 0	50 50 / 100 0	0.50	0.05
F	2	very weak player; very strong co-player:	K = 80, U = 100 / K = 20, U = 100	20 20 / 100 0	80 80 / 100 0	0.20	0.93
G	2	very strong player; very weak co-player:	K = 20, U = 100 / K = 80, U = 100	80 80 / 100 0	20 20 / 100 0	0.80	0.16
H	5	symmetric:	K = 50, U = 100	50 50 50 50 / 0 100 100 100	50 50 50 50 / 0 100 100 100	0.84	0.72
I	5	weak player, three co-players; one strong co-player:	K = 50, U = 100 / K = 40, U = 100	50 50 50 50 / 0 100 100 100	60 60 60 60 / 0 100 100 100	0.80	0.44
J	5	strong player; four weak co-players:	K = 40, U = 100 / K = 50, U = 100	60 60 60 60 / 0 100 100 100	50 50 50 50 / 0 100 100 100	0.99	0.70

* First line refers to subject's payoffs.

** Subject's matrix and matrix of co-player(s) as displayed to subject in the questionnaire. Upper row = cooperative choice, lower row = defective choice, left column = other player's cooperative choice, right column = other player's defective choice. For group size 5, columns from left to right = number of other players choosing the cooperative alternative. In condition I, subjects were instructed that player's decision matrix was also presented to three of the four co-players.

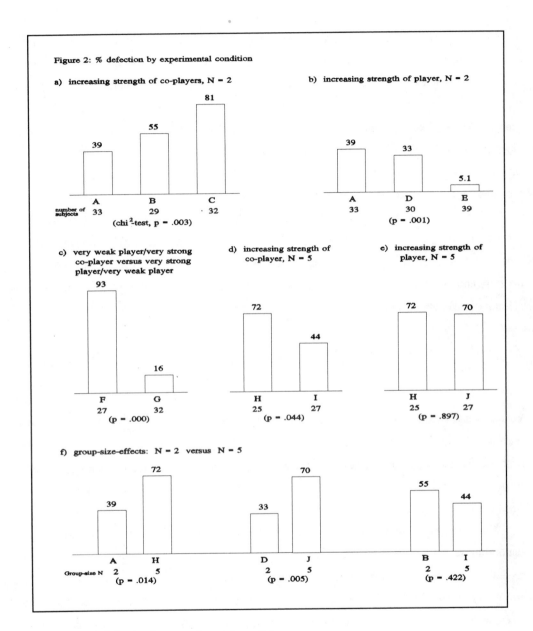

Figure 2: % defection by experimental condition

a) increasing strength of co-players, N = 2

b) increasing strength of player, N = 2

c) very weak player/very strong co-player versus very strong player/very weak player

d) increasing strength of co-player, N = 5

e) increasing strength of player, N = 5

f) group-size-effects: N = 2 versus N = 5

Figure 2: % defection by experimental condition

For group-size 5, subjects' behaviour shows a much less clear pattern. In the case of co-player's increasing strength, the sign of the significant difference is in the direction of the mixed equilibrium hypothesis, although the degree of defective behaviour in condition I is much less than predicted by formula (4) (figure 2d). On the other hand, no significant effect of player's increasing strength could be detected (figure 2e). It may be the case that the extraordinarily low level of defection in group I is an "outlier-effect".[9] In three earlier experiments with (symmetric) volunteer's dilemma, such a low level of defection was never observed. Whether this might be the case can only be answered by a replication of the experiment.

Group-size-effects as expected by the mixed Nash-equilibrium hypothesis could be observed in two out of three test situations (figure 2g). This "diffusion of responsibility" mechanism is well supported by a great variety of experiments (e.g. Darley and Latané 1968, Diekmann 1986). Again, the difference is reversed for conditions B and I because of the extraordinary low proportion of defectors in the latter group.

Conclusions

Volunteer's dilemma is a game with some interesting properties paradigmatic for a variety of social situations. In the symmetric game, theories of equilibrium selection yield the solution of the mixed Nash-equilibrium which is, however, weak and non-efficient. The solution implies a decline of cooperation with increasing group-size. This mechanism is well known in social psychology as the effect of "diffusion of responsibility," which is confirmed by a large bulk of experimental data.

In the generalized, asymmetric version of the game the strict equilibria are also candidates for equilibrium selection. The mixed equilibrium solution, on the other hand, yields the counter-intuitive result that the "strongest" actor capable of producing the collective good on lowest costs has the highest probability of freeriding. In the special case of one "strong" and N-1 "weak" actors investigated in this article with experimental data, the Harsanyi-Selten theory as well as Schelling's "prominence theory" predict the opposite result (i.e., the strongest player will choose the cooperative strategy). The experimental results are ambiguous for group-size N = 5. In the experimental conditions with 2*2-games the data clearly support the latter theories if these are interpreted in a probabilistic sense. In other words, the findings show that the higher the payoff-difference between strong and weak players, the more likely the strong player and the less likely actors in the role of weak players will opt for cooperation. Note however, that the Harsanyi-Selten theory underestimates the level of cooperation in the symmetric game and does not imply the "diffusion-of-responsibility" effect in the asymmetric game. The reason is that the selection of a strict equilibrium point in the asymmetric game is independent of group-size. In contrast to rationality theory, this psychological effect seems to be present in asymmetric dilemmas as well.

Footnotes

1   University of Berne, Institute of Sociology, Berne, Switzerland

2   Hence, the mixed equilibrium strategy is "unprofitable". For 2*2-games this is always true (Holler 1990). However, it does not necessarily hold true in N-person games.

3   See, also, Wittman (1985) for a critique of the counter-intuitive implications of mixed equilibrium strategies in 2*2 games.

4   See Weesie (1993) for an analysis of this example and the problem of "rational timing" in a "volunteer's timing dilemma".

5   Another requirement is: $K_i + K_j \,] \, K_k + K_l$ for i, j, k, 1 = 1, ..., N pairwise different. An asymmetric volunteer's dilemma subject to these restrictions satisfies assumptions (1) to (6) in Selten and Güth (1982). It is, moreover, a "regular market entry game" because dominated strategies are excluded by the defining properties of a volunteer's dilemma game. Note that

"market entry" corresponds here to "cooperation". In other market entry games, which under certain conditions are structurally equivalent with volunteer's dilemma, "market entry" is the "defective" choice. For example, this is the case in the game of Sherman and Willet (1967), which is a symmetric volunteer's dilemma for $N = 2$.

6   I owe a sketch of the proof for this assertion to Reinhard Selten (personal communication): "The primitive formations are those generated by the strict equilibrium point. These equilibrium points form the first candidate set. The restricted games for the risk dominance comparisons between any two elements of this set are 2*2-games. If player 1 is stronger than the players $2,...,N$, then the equilibrium point where player 1 cooperates risk dominates all other candidates and therefore emerges as the solution (there are no payoff dominance relationships among the candidates). Assume that player 1 is weaker than players $2,...,N$. Then the equilibrium point where player 1 cooperates is risk dominated by all other candidates. For reasons of symmetry these other candidates do not risk dominate each other. Therefore the equilibrium point where player 1 cooperates is eliminated. The second candidate set is formed by the other strict equilibrium points. A substitution step becomes necessary (see Harsanyi and Selten 1988, p. 228). The application of the tracing procedure to the centroid of the second candidate set must yield a symmetric equilibrium point. This can be either the strict equilibrium point where player 1 cooperates or the mixed equilibrium point. Obviously, in the first case the assertion holds. In the second case, the third candidate set consists of the mixed equilibrium point and the strict equilibrium point where player 1 cooperates. It can be seen without difficulty that this strict equilibrium point risk dominates the mixed equilibrium point. Obviously the mixed equilibrium point does not payoff dominate this strict equilibrium point. It follows that, in this case too, the strict equilibrium point where player 1 cooperates is the solution of the game."

7   Participants were recruited in the university cafeteria during lunch time. Students who agreed to participate were asked to come to a separate room in the cafeteria building where the

experiment was arranged. In order to avoid sequence effects, we did not choose a design where the different versions of the dilemma game were presented to the same subjects. Rather, we decided for the more "expensive" design of a random assignment to the various experimental conditions. Hence, each participant was confronted with one decision problem of volunteer's dilemma type. Subjects did not know their co-players and were, in fact, not matched to co-players.

8   27 subjects or 8.2% did not pass the test for the volunteer's dilemma. Not surprisingly, there are more errors in the asymmetric game compared to the symmetric versions. In the latter conditions (A and H in table 1), no inconsistencies were detected at all. With this exception, no systematic variations of "failure rates" over experimental conditions were found. The distribution of excluded cases is as follows: A 0, B 0, C 4, D 3, E 3, F 5, G 5, H 0, I 5, J 2.

9   However, no "outlier effect" was observed in condition I for the decision behaviour in three prisoner's dilemma situations. Also, it is unlikely that presentation effects may have caused the ambiguous results for group-size $N = 5$. Under both conditions ($N = 2$ and $N = 5$) the game was described verbally and presented in matrix form as depicted in table 1.

References

Brennan, G., & Lomasky, L. (1984). Inefficient unanimity. *Journal of Applied Philosophy, 1*, 151-163.

Darley, J.M., & Latané, B. (1968). Bystander intervention in emergencies. Diffusion of responsibility. *Journal of Personality and Social Psychology, 8*, 377-383.

Dawkins, R. (1976). *The selfish gene*. New York: Oxford University Press.

Diekmann, A. (1985). Volunteer's dilemma. *Journal of Conflict Resolution, 29*, 605-610.

Diekmann, A. (1986). Volunteer's dilemma. A 'social trap' without dominant strategy and some experimental results. In A. Diekmann & P. Mitter (Eds.), *Paradoxical effects of social behaviour. Essays in honor of Anatol Rapoport.* Heidelberg, Wien: Physica.

Harsanyi, J.C., & Selten, R. (1988). *A general theory of equilibrium selection in games.* Cambridge, Mass: M.I.T. Press.

Holler, M. (1990). The unprofitability of mixed strategy equilibrium in two-person games. A second folk-theorem. *Economic Letters, 32,* 319-323.

Olson, M. (1965). *The logic of collective action.* Cambridge, Mass.: Harvard University Press.

Selten, R., & Güth, W. (1982). Equilibrium point selection in a class of market entry games. In M. Deistler, E. Fürst, & G. Schwödiauer (Eds.), *Games, economic dynamics, and time series analysis - A symposium in memoriam of Oskar Morgenstern* (pp. 101-116). Würzburg, Wien: Physica.

Schelling, Th.C. (1960). *The strategy of conflict.* Cambridge, Mass.: Harvard University Press

Sherman, R., & Willet, Th.D. (1967). Potential entrants discourage entry. *Journal of Political Economy, 75,* 400-403.

Wittman, D. (1985). Counter-intuitive results in game theory. *European Journal of Political Economy, 1,* 77-85.

Acknowledgement

I am indebted to Wulf Albers, Norman Braun, Werner Güth, Norbert L. Kerr, Reinhard Selten, and the participants of the "V[th] International Social Dilemma Conference" in Bielefeld for critical and helpful comments. I am grateful to Axel Franzen who organized the experiment at the University of Mannheim. This work was supported by a grant of the "Deutsche Forschungsgemeinschaft" (DFG).

Ten rules of bargaining sequences
A boundedly rational model of coalition bargaining
in characteristic function games

Wulf Albers[1]

Abstract

The paper presents a first outline of a model of the bargaining process in characteristic function games. It is based on the conclusions from more than 1000 experimental games with free communication with 3, 4, 5 and sometimes more players. The essence of this approach is, that the bargaining process can be modeled as a sequence of states or proposals, each of which dominates the preceding one. And, that there are certain laws or rules of boundedly rational behavior, according to which players behave when they change coalitions. These rules are presented.

The concept is based on the following behavioral aspects:
- structure of sequences of proposals (Rule 1)
- phenomena of prominence (Rules 2, 3)
- the phenomenon of reciprocal loyalty (Rules 4, 5)
- conclusions from actions of others (attributed demands, Rule 6)

These phenomena restrict possible schemes of arguing to chains of proposals of which each dominates the preceding one. The space of all these chains is ordered by the natural inclusion of chains. It is a tree–shaped, finite set. On this space strategic considerations of the players are modeled by
- the recursive definition of stable states (Rule 7),
- the opportunity to break a coalition, and thereby force the game back to a former state of the process (Rule 8),
- principles of fairness, when forming the coalition of all players, and the stability of this coalition (Rules 9, 10).

Examples illustrate and motivate the conditions, and show phenomena that cannot be explained by traditional solution concepts.

A remark concerning the relation to experimental data

The process of detection of these rules from experimental data was not easy. A big knot of interacting rules had to be solved by improving the model stepwise, finding its respective weak points, and performing clarifying experiments. The model here seems to explain all phenomena we found and seems to be a good basis for further research.

The aim of this approach was to deduce a concept from the observed behavior which captures those boundedly rational rules according to which experienced players behave. The model tries to describe the behavior of idealized experienced players, when experience becomes high, when errors in strategic behavior are excluded, and when personal specificities of the players can be neglected.

One of the main difficulties of the bargaining sequence approach is that players apply foresight. Long chains which go through all steps of possible future moves of bargaining as predicted by the model here, will in reality not be observed: experienced players will usually stop bargaining sequences in states which are favorable and stable for them, and will not enter states, which are better, but only intermediate steps. The character of their foresight is part of the model here. The predicted analytical sequences can only be observed in experiments when the players are unexperienced, and therefore make mistakes (one of which is that they do not stop the sequence early enough). On the other hand, experienced players stop the sequences early (frequently in the first state), and it is necessary to reconstruct their views of possible future moves, and the character of their arguments from the obtained results by using the patterns observed in the long sequences of unexperienced players.

Some examples of games and experimental results are given which motivate and support the model. It was not the intention to support the model by experimental data in detail, but rather to give an impression that the model is in fact related to experimental observations. Detailed experimental analysis will be done in other papers.

Anyway, it is our opinion that the quality of a solution concept cannot be given by its average success over all games that have been played (or that might be played). We think that the quality is given by its minimal success taken over all games the solution concept is intended to serve for. From this point of view, it is (only) important to find that game, where the concept works worst. Finding these exceptions, and accordingly refine the concept, was the aim of our research for more than 15 years. Still the model is not complete, the process of refining goes on. But we think that the model in its present state is meanwhile ripe enough to be presented to others.

The approach seems to model bargaining processes of 1–step characteristic function games with not too many (may be below 7) players adequately. It is formulated for (and addresses questions of) more complicated characteristic function games as well. But there is not much experimental evidence for more general games. For instance we do not know anything about principles of simplification of games with many or very many players.

A The ten rules of bargaining

A.0 Introduction

Before we introduce the concept, we give a short overview of the different aspects that the model refers to. The first aspects characterize the space of bargaining chains (Rules 1–6). Stable states of this space are defined (Rule 7). Breaking of coalitions as a strategic act is introduced and serves to implement criteria of fairness (Rule 8). The last two rules address fairness criteria when the grand coalition is formed, and the stability of the grand coalition (Rules 9 and 10).

Proposals and bargaining chains (Rule 1). Empirical observations show that coalition bargaining in experimental characteristic function games is performed in chains of proposals. We distinguish essential and inessential proposals. Essential proposals are those, to which later proposals refer, and the final result. Nearly all empirical chains of proposals made in processes of coalition bargaining are such that every essential proposal refers to the respective last essential proposal made, and dominates it. So it seems sufficient to restrict bargaining chains to sequences of proposals of which each dominates the preceding one.

Conclusions from the theory of prominence (Rules 2, 3). When they solve a problem, persons structure the space of alternatives in a way that is sufficiently easy that they can handle the problem. For one–dimensional numerical problems the restriction of alternatives is given by the theory of prominence and the prominence selection rule which predicts the degree of exactness of analysis. This principle can be transferred to the multidimensional and multiscenario case of negotiations related to characteristic function games. In a first (simplified) step of analysis we assume that the degree of exactness only depends on the game and the conditions of communication (as face to face contact, communication via terminals,etc.), and can be predicted endogenously as a constant. This parameter restricts the numerical shape of proposals (in fact reduces the set of reasonable proposals to a finite set), and gives a lower bound of the payoff improvement of a player who actively changes a coalition.

The phenomenon of reciprocal loyalty (Rules 4, 5). "Reciprocal Loyalty" is the phenomenon, that players, who are in symmetric positions with respect to the given game and their present (sub–)coalition spontaneously feel sympathy with one another. Specificly they prefer to enter maximal groups with this property ("loyal groups") when the respective payoffs are the same. They do not leave a loyal group except for essentially higher additional payoffs than in ordinary changes (the necessary improvement is two or three units of prominence, while ordinary improvements are usually one unit). Moreover, players enter loyal groups even in cases where they do not increase their payoff.

Attributed demands (Rule 6). During a bargaining process, by switching from one coalition with payoff x to another with payoff $y > x$ a player indicates that he is incontent with his old payoff and wants to get more. The others will conclude from his action, that he will not be content with the amount x also in other coalitions. They will therefore not enter a coalition with him unless he receives more than x. I.e. the others' attribute a demand greater than x to this player.

Stable states (Rule 7). States of the bargaining process are sequences of proposals that fulfill Rules 1–6. – The space of states is ordered by the natural "follower" relation: a state $(p_0, p_1, .., p_t, p_{t+1})$ follows the state $(p_0, p_1, .., p_t)$, etc.. This way a tree–shaped structure of the state space is obtained. The problem in a state $(p_0, p_1, .., p_t)$ is, which of the possible next states will be entered, i.e., which next proposal p_{t+1} will be selected. – By Rules 2, 3 and 4 the space of all possible states is finite. This permits a roll back analysis on the space of states. – The central component of this roll–back analysis is the stability of states which is defined recursively.

Breaking coalitions (Rule 8). The general rule of the structure above, that a player can reach a next state from a preceding state only by dominance, is too restrictive for some situations. (In fact forming new coalitions via dominances from preceding states can give inadequately high power to certain formed subcoalitions.) In these situations players can prefer to cancel their membership to a coalition without forming a new coalition. Experimental data show that players do so, when the "minimal expected payoff" of the subgame entered by breaking the coalition is higher than their present payoff in the current proposal p_t. By this principle no player has to accept a payoff that is lower than that he can expect to get, when he stops cooperation in a group. From this point of view, the possibility of breaking coalitions permits to keep actual payoffs within certain "boundaries of fairness".

Fairness criteria and stability of the grand coalition (Rules 9, 10). When coalitions of players unite to form a larger coalition, there are two extreme cases to distribute the additional joint payoff: 1. they can give the same amount to every player, or 2. they can give the same amount to each of the subcoalitions that united. Empirical payoff distributions are usually between these extremes. This principle is formulated for the case that the grand coalition is formed. – A final rule states that the grand coalition is always stable.

A.1 Basic definitions and notations

A **characteristic function game** is a finite set of players $N = \{1, 2,..., n\}$, and a value function $v: P(N) \to \mathbb{R}_+$ with $v(\emptyset) = 0$, which assigns a value $v(S)$ to any subset S of N. The problem of such a game is, which coalition S is formed, and how the members of the coalition split their joint payoff $v(S)$.

A characteristic function game is a **1–step game**, if for all $S \subseteq N$ either $v(S) = \Sigma_{i \in S} v(i)$, or there is no $T \supseteq S$ such that $v(T) > v(S)$.

For general characteristic function games the process of stepwise coalition formation can generate coalition structures:

Notation. A **coalition structure** $\mathscr{S}$ on N is a set of subsets of N with

(1) $S, T \in \mathscr{S} \Rightarrow S \subseteq T$ or $T \subseteq S$ or $S \cap T = \emptyset$

(2) $\{i\} \in \mathscr{S}$ (for all $i \in N$)

In the games considered here, coalition structures result from a process of stepwise coalition formation.

For a coalition structure $\mathscr{S}$, and $S \in \mathscr{S}$ we will sometimes use the notations

$\mathscr{S}_{\subset S} := \{T \in \mathscr{S} \mid T \subset S\}^2$, and

$\mathscr{S}_{\subset_1 S} := \{T \in \mathscr{S} \mid T \subset S, \text{ and there is no } R \in \mathscr{S} \text{ with } T \subset R \subset S\}$

Notation. A **proposal** $(x, \mathscr{S})$ is a payoff vector $x \in \mathbb{R}^n$, and a coalition structure $\mathscr{S}$ on N, such that

(1) $x(S) \geq v(S)$ (for all $S \in \mathscr{S}$)[3]

(2) $x(S) = v(S)$ (for all S, S maximal in $\mathscr{S}$)

By condition (1) it is assured that no coalition $S \in \mathscr{S}$ can object to the distribution x by claiming that the players of S can get more, if they form a coalition by themselves. – Condition (2) states that the payoffs of the players have to be verified as coalition payoffs in the maximal formed coalitions. (These coalitions form a partition of N, so that every player is in just one of them.)

Bargaining is modeled by a sequence of proposals of which each "dominates" the preceding one:

Notation. A proposal $(y, \mathscr{T})$ **dominates** a proposal $(x, \mathscr{S})$ via a coalition $T \in \mathscr{T}$ (in symbols: $(x, \mathscr{S}) \rightarrow_T (y, \mathscr{T})$), iff

(1) $y_i > x_i$ (for all $i \in T$)

(2) $\mathscr{T} = \{ S \in \mathscr{S} \mid S \subseteq T \text{ or } S \cap T = \emptyset \} \cup \{ T \}$

(3) if there is a loyal group $L \subseteq T$, then also $L \in \mathscr{T}$.

T is the coalition formed in this bargaining step. All players of T improve their payoff (condition (1)). (What happens with the payoffs of the players outside T will be defined in the definition of bargaining chains, below.) All coalitions that are subsets of T remain formed and become subcoalitions of T; coalitions outside T are not touched by the formation of T; coalitions that intersect both, T and its complement $N \backslash T$ are "broken", and not contained in the new coalition structure (condition (2)). Condition (3) models the case that there is a certain type of "symmetric subgroup" L of T that players spontaneously identify as a subcoalition. This is included in T. (For details see section A.4.)

Notation. A Player i **changed his coalition** in $(x, \mathscr{S}) \rightarrow_T (y, \mathscr{T})$, iff

(1) $i \in T$, and   (2) there is $S \in \mathscr{S} \backslash \mathscr{T}$ such that $i \in S$.

So in $(x, \mathscr{S}) \rightarrow_T (y, \mathscr{T})$ a player changed the coalition iff he is a member of the new coalition T, and "broke" at least one coalition of $\mathscr{S}$.

Notation. A **bargaining chain** is a sequence $((x_0, \mathscr{S}_0) \rightarrow_{T_1} (x_1, \mathscr{S}_1) \rightarrow_{T_2} \cdots \rightarrow_{T_t} (x_t, \mathscr{S}_t)$ of proposals, such that

(1) $(x_0, \mathscr{S}_0) = ((v(1), v(2), .., v(n)); \{1\}, \{2\}, .., \{n\})$,

(2) every proposal dominates the preceding one, and

(3) for every dominance $(x_r, \mathscr{S}_r) \rightarrow_{T_r} (x_{r+1}, \mathscr{S}_{r+1})$ holds
     if $i \notin T_{r+1}$ then the payoff $(x_{r+1})_i$ is as follows:

let $(S_{r+1})_i$ that set of the partition of $(\mathscr{S}_{r+1})_{C_iS}$ that contains i, and
let $(x_k, \mathscr{S}_k)$ the last proposal before $(x_r, \mathscr{S}_r)$, in which $(S_{r+1})_i$ is maximal
then $(x_t)_i = (x_k)_i$.

By convention the chain starts with the "null–proposal" $(x_0, \mathscr{S}_0)$, where no coalition is formed. If a coalition is broken in step $r+1$ (i.e. it is in $\mathscr{S}_r$ but not in $\mathscr{S}_{r+1}$) then the remaining players that do not enter the new coalition keep those subcoalitions that do not intersect with the dominating coalition T_{r+1}. Their payoff is given according to the distribution arranged in the state, where the largest remaining coalition was formed that contains the respective remaining player.

A.2 Bargaining processes as sequences of essential proposals

On a natural level of abstraction the bargaining process related to the process of coalition formation and payoff distribution in a characteristic function game can be modeled by the proposals of the players.

For the analysis of the sequence of given proposals it is helpful to distinguish essential and inessential proposals.

Notation. A proposal is called **essential,** if it is the final result, or if a next proposal refers to it. Otherwise it is called inessential.

An interesting experimental result is that the proposals of an unrestricted bargaining process with free communication meet the

General principle. Every proposal refers to the last essential proposal that has been made, and dominates it.

In experimental data there are only a few cases of deviations from this principle, where the bargaining process jumps back to a previous essential state (see Albers, 1986). It seems that these cases are exceptions resulting from mistakes, made during the bargaining process.

The principle suggests to restrict the analysis to essential proposals, omitting inessential proposals as ideas which have just been mentioned but did not influence the bargaining process essentially. It seems reasonable and is confirmed by experimental results that the sequence of essential proposals covers the essence of the bargaining process.

Accordingly we get

Rule 1 *("Bargaining chains")*

Every bargaining process can be modelled as a sequence of (essential) proposals, of which each dominates the preceding one, and that also fulfills the other conditions of a bargaining chain.

A.3 Exactness of bargaining

The exactness of bargaining is determined by the exactness of perception by the individuals. The relation is given by the theory of prominence:

Notation. The **prominent numbers (of the decimal system)** are

$$P = \{b \cdot 10^z \mid b \in \{1, 2, 5\}, z \text{ integer}\} = \{...,.1,.2,.5, 1, 2, 5, 10, 20, 50,...\}[4]$$

Every real number x can be presented by means of the prominent numbers as
$x = \Sigma_{p \in P} \, a_p \cdot p$, with all coefficients $a_p \in \{-1, 0, +1\}$.

Notation. A sum $\Sigma_{p \in P} \, a_p \cdot p$ is called a **presentation of x** , if

(1) $x = \Sigma_{p \in P} \, a_p \cdot p$

(2) $a_p \in \{-1, 0, +1\}$ for all p, and

(3) the sequence $(a_p \mid p \in P, a_p \in \{-1,+1\})$ (ordered according to the amount of p) does not contain three subsequent numbers with the same sign.

It may be remarked that the presentation of a number is not unique. In the following examples we selected the respective "shortest" presentations.

Examples (presentation of numbers). $1=1$ $2=2$ $3=5-2=2+1$ $4=5-1$ $5=5$ $6=5+1$ $7=5+2$ $8=10-2$ $9=10-1$ $10=10$ $11=10+1$ $12=10+2$ $13=10+5-2$ $14=10+5-1$ $15=10+5=20-5$ $16=20-5+1$ $17=20-5+2$ $18=20-2$ $19=20-1$ $20=20$ $21=20+1$ ... $23=20+5-2$ $24=20+5-1$ $25=20+5$ $26=50-20-5+1$ ...

Notations. The **exactness of a presentation** $\Sigma \, a_p \cdot p$ is the minimal prominent number $p \in P$ with $a_p \neq 0$. The **exactness e(x) of a number** x is the maximal exactness of all presentations of x.

A Number x has prominence p $(p \in P)$, iff its exactness is $e(x) \geq p$.

Empirical data of different experiments support the

Prominence selection rule (for 1–dimensional problems)

Version 1: The numerical response x selected by a person to characterize a diffuse numerical stimulus has that prominence p∈P, that is **minimal** subject to the condition that there are **at most five numbers with prominence p** in the "range of reasonable alternatives" of the signal.

Version 2: The numerical response x selected by a person to characterize a diffuse numerical stimulus has that prominence p∈P, that is **maximal** subject to the condition that there are **at least three numbers with prominence p** in the "range of reasonable alternatives" of the signal.

In most cases, both versions lead to the same levels of prominence. In empirical situations subjects are not able to specify the range of "reasonable alternatives" precisely. So it may be that it is not possible to decide between the two versions by experiments. – From a theoretical point of view, version 1 addresses the fact that in certain decision situations some kind of "short term memory" gets an overflow, when more than about five alternatives are involved, version 2 addresses the idea that at least three values are necessary to identify a maximum.

(1) When the diffuse signal can be characterized by a density function, then the range of reasonable alternatives is the 80 %–interval obtained by omitting the 10 %–tails on both ends.

(2) There are cases where an upper or lower bound of the range of reasonable alternatives is given by theoretical considerations or social norms. (In this case there are no tails that have to be omitted.)

The general impetus of a person to restrict possible alternatives is to reduce a given decision problem to a manageable one. It seems that some kind of "short term memory" gets an overflow, when it has to govern more than five alternatives at the same time. This is excluded by the first formulation of the prominence selection rule.

This key–argument permits to transfer the prominence selection rule to the more complicated problem of analyzing (or deciding among) reasonable proposals for characteristic function games. The main difference is that for these games payoff alternatives have to be considered for several different types of coalitions. It seems that the "short term memory" can analyze each coalition (or coalition structure) separately, so that the following rule is obtained:

Prominence selection rule (for payoffs in proposals)

The numerical response selected by a person to characterize reasonable payoff distributions of a characteristic function game has a prominence p, which is **minimal** subject to the condition that **for every coalition structure there are at most five alternatives with prominence p** in the "range of reasonable alternatives".

Example (Apex game with payoff 100, n=5 players). Let $N = \{1,...,n\}$ and $v(S) = 100$ if $1 \in S$ or $S = N-\{1\}$, $v(S) = 0$ otherwise. Empirical data of outcomes in the two–person coalition $\{1, i\}$ ($i \in \{2, 3, 4, 5\}$) are $0 \times (50, 50)$, $0 \times (55, 45)$, $5 \times (60, 40)$, $7 \times (65, 35)$, $4 \times (70, 30)$, $2 \times (75, 25)$. These are 18 data. The 80% – interval ranges from $(60, 40)$ to $(75, 25)$. To obtain at most 5 numbers with prominence p in this interval, p cannot be smaller than 5. So 5 is the prominence. – Theoretical considerations suggest that in $\{1, i\}$ Player 1 should get more than Player i, i.e. $x_1 > 50$. On the other hand $x_1 \leq 75$, since otherwise Player i would prefer to enter a coalition $\{2, 3, 4, 5\}$ with equal shares. This gives a range $50 < x_1 \leq 75$, which again requires a prominence of 5 by (both versions of) the prominence selection rule.

When coalition structures are formed (with n–tuples of payoffs), then – in addition to the considered decimal prominence – elements of structural prominence can determine the outcome. A payoff has equality prominence, if it is obtained by giving equal shares to certain subgroups.

Example (equality prominence). An example of an outcome with equality prominence is $(—, 33 \frac{1}{3}, 33 \frac{1}{3}, 33 \frac{1}{3})$ in a 4–person Apex game with payoff 100.

Moreover, when a coalition value $v(S)$ does not have prominence p, and the payoffs of all but one member of the coalition S have prominence p, then the last member of S gets the remainder, which may not have prominence p. Nevertheless we want to define this payoff distribution to have prominence p, since all decisions that determined the payoff are on this level of prominence.

Example (remainder prominence). Let $v(N) = 91$ in a 3–person game. Then the payoff distribution $(30, 30, 31)$ gives Player 3 the remainder $x_3 = v(N) - x_1 - x_2$. Since x_1 and x_2 have prominence 10, also $(30, 30, 31)$ has prominence 10.

The following definition of prominence is not easy, since for all coalitions formed during the negotiation process all marginal payoffs received by forming the coalition have to be distributed among the different formed subcoalitions. Each single agreement of this type is enacted according to the theory of prominence, where different types of prominence can arise.

Definition   (Prominence of a proposal)

A **proposal** $(x, \mathscr{S})$ **has prominence p** $(p \in P)$, iff there are

(1) a coalition structure $\mathscr{S}'$ (with the property that $\mathscr{S} \cup \mathscr{S}'$ is a coalition structure);
for any $S \in \mathscr{S}$ let $C(S): = (T \in \mathscr{S}'/ \ T \leq S)$, and

(2) a mapping $a: \mathscr{S} \times \mathscr{S} \to R^n$ that assigns to every $S \in \mathscr{S}$ and every $C \in C(S)$ a
vector $a^s_C \in R^n$ in a way that $\Sigma \, (a^s_C(C)| \ C \in C(S)) = m(S) :=$
$v(S) - \Sigma(v(T)| \ T \in \mathscr{S}_{C,S})$ and $a^s_C(i) = 0$ for all $i \notin C$.
such that
for all $S \in \mathscr{S}$ and all $B, C \in C(S)$, $B \leq C$:

$a^s_C(Q) = a^s_C(R)$ for all $Q, R \in C(S)_{C_1B}$ (equality prominence), or

$a^s_C(R)$ or $a^s_C(R) + \Sigma(a^p_D(R)| \ P \in \mathscr{S}_{C,S}, D \in C(P))$ has prominence p for all (or all
but one) $R \in C(S)_{C_1B}$ (normal or remainder prominence).

The mappings C and a are closely related. For any coalition S, the mapping C
informs about the set of those subcoalitions of S, that get a share from the additional payoff
m(S) obtained by forming S from its subcoalitions in $\mathscr{S}$. Mapping a informs, how the
additional payoff is distributed among the different subcoalitions of C(S), and moreover,
how these subcoalitions distribute their shares among their members. All these
distributional decisions have to fulfill the theory of prominence for the distribution of every
additional payoff, where different ways of argumentation can lead to different forms of
prominence.

We do not yet have experience with complicated coalition structures with several
inclusions. Up to now, our experiments only involved structures where threefold inclusions
as $R \subset S \subset T$ did not occur.

The definition of prominence of a proposal permits to formulate the next two rules of
bargaining sequences:

Rule 2   *("Prominence of a proposal")*

For every proposal $(x, \mathscr{S})$ the payoff distribution x has prominence p with respect to
$\mathscr{S}$, where p is the level of prominence on which the game is analyzed.

Presently we do not have a complete theory that predicts the level of prominence
from other data. We therefore decided to introduce the level of prominence as an exogenous
variable of the model.

Rule 3 ("Minimal improvement")

A dominance $(x, \mathscr{S}) \rightarrow_T (y, \mathscr{T})$ is only performed, if $y_i \geq x_i + p$ for all $i \in T$, where p is the level of prominence under which the game is analyzed.

Example (5–person Apex game with payoff 120). If $v(S) = 120$ instead of 100 for the winning coalitions, then the interval of predicted payoffs of Player 1 in $\{1, i\}$ is $60 < x_1 \leq 90$. Accordingly 10 becomes the prominence of this stimulus– situation, and 10 is the minimal improvement, if $\{1, i\}$ is entered. (Note that the interval of Player i is $30 \leq x_i < 60$ (by subtracting the values above from 120.) So the analysis of the payoff of Player i leads to the same level of prominence.)

An interesting experimental observation is, that not only the payoffs are selected according to the prominence structure, but also the incentive of a possible payoff improvement x_i to y_i by a dominance $(x, \mathscr{S}) \rightarrow (y, \mathscr{T})$ is proportional to the number of steps of prominence between x_i and y_i. (This contradicts the axiom of strategic equivalence, which (implicitly) states that multiplying all payoffs $v(S)$ of a game with the same constant, does not change the result of the bargaining process.)

Example. In the 5–person Apex game, the incentive of a Player i $(i \neq 1)$ to deviate from an equal share distribution in coalition $\{2, 3, 4, 5\}$ (giving $v(N)/4$ to Players 2, 3, 4, 5) into coalition $\{1, i\}$ (where Player i can get at most an equal share, i.e. $v(N)/2$) is given by the steps $30-40-50-60$ if the payoff is $v(N) = 120$, and by the steps $25-30-35-40-45-50$ if the payoff is $v(N) = 100$. These are 3 steps of improvement in the first, and 5 steps of improvement in the second case. This gives an essentially higher incentive to deviate from $\{2, 3, 4, 5\}$ in the game with $v(N) = 100$. Accordingly, there were essentially less coalitions of type $\{2, 3, 4, 5\}$ for $v(N) = 100$. (For more details see Albers & Albers (1983).)

A.4 Loyal groups and sympathy

One aim of the boundedly rational behavior of players in experimental games is the reduction of complexity. A helpful tool in this context is to recognize symmetries and assume similar or identical behavior of players in symmetric positions. The main phenomenon is that "symmetric players", who enter a coalition in a symmetric way, have a higher than the usual incentive to keep the coalition with the other symmetric players.

This phenomenon may be explained by the fact, that players – by applying arguments of symmetry – conclude from expectations concerning the own behavior to expectations concerning the behavior of the other players being symmetric to them. Since the own behavior is to a certain extent influenced by social norms of fairness, they transfer these incentives to the others in symmetric positions.

On the other hand, it is a well known phenomenon that persons in symmetric positions spontaneously feel sympathy with one another and accordingly interact with them in a more friendly way. (In some social psychologic experiments sympathy is manipulated by introducing the feeling of symmetry, as for instance by informing subjects that they filled out a questionnaire in a (nearly) identical way.)

In the context of the experiments here symmetry seems to create a feeling of solidarity. The consequence is that players in symmetric positions either want to show that they do not, or simply do not break coalitions with symmetric partners as easily as they break ordinary coalitions. This is shown, when they break coalitions only, if either all symmetric partners enter the new coalition too, or if they get a clearly higher payoff improvement than in ordinary coalition changes.

This raises two questions:
1. What is the precise definition of "players in symmetric positions"?
2. What is a "clearly higher than the ordinary payoff improvement"?

The answer to question 1 is given by the next definition. The answer to question 2 will be addressed later, by Rule 5.

Definition (Loyal group)

Let $(x, \mathscr{S}) \to_T (y, \mathscr{T})$.

$L \subseteq T$ is a loyal group, iff the following three conditions hold:

(1) (the game is "symmetric" with respect to I and J)
Let I, J two elements of $\mathscr{T}$ that are contained in L and maximal with this property. Then $v(S \cup I) = v(S \cup J)$ for any $S \subseteq N$ with $I \cap S = \emptyset$ and $J \cap S = \emptyset$.

(2) (the new payoff is "symmetric" with respect to I and J)
Let I, J two elements of $\mathscr{T}$ that are contained in L and maximal with this property. Then $y(I) = y(J)$.

(3) (maximality) If $(x, \mathscr{S}) \to_{T'} (y', \mathscr{T'})$, and $L' \subseteq T'$ fulfills (1) and (2) with respect to this dominance, then $L' \subseteq L$.

Loyal groups seem to be easily and immediately recognized by the players. They are automatically part of the coalition structure of the corresponding state.

Refinement of the definition of dominance. Every loyal group L contained in a dominating coalition T is in the coalition structure $\mathcal{T}$ of the new state.

Based on their similarity players of a loyal group spontaneously feel sympathy and some kind of solidarity. They therefore prefer to enter a domination into a loyal group to other alternatives that give the same payoff:

Rule 4 ("Sympathy")

If a proposal $(x, \mathcal{S})$ permits different dominances $(x, \mathcal{S}) \rightarrow_T (y, \mathcal{T})$ and $(x, \mathcal{S}) \rightarrow_U (z, \mathcal{U})$, then a Player $i \in T \cap U$ prefers the dominance via T, if

(1) $y_i = z_i$, and

(2) there is a loyal group $L \subseteq T$ with $i \in L$, and there is no such loyal group $K \subseteq U$.

Example (5–person Apex game with payoff 100). In the beginning of the game the small players (2, 3, 4, 5) prefer to enter $(-, 25, 25, 25, 25)$ instead of a coalition with Player 1 with payoff 75 for Player 1, 25 for the small player.

We now address the answer to question 2: The other consequence of feeling solidarity is that players within a loyal group do not leave the group as easily as ordinary coalitions. It seems that they want to make the others notice that they do not betray symmetric partners for a peanut. Accordingly they only leave a loyal group, when their payoff improvement is clearly higher than the usual improvement in an ordinary dominance.

Rule 5 ("Reciprocal loyalty")

Players within a loyal group L enter a coalition S with $S \cap L \neq L$ only, if they receive at least $p + \ell \cdot p$ more (where $\ell = 0, 1,$ or 2 is the degree of reciprocal loyalty, given as an exogenous parameter of the game). The amount $\ell \cdot p$ is denoted as the reciprocal loyalty.

Experimental data indicate that the degree of reciprocal loyalty does neither depend on the type of game nor on the type of loyal group. It seems that reciprocal loyalty only depends on the conditions of communication. It seems that

– face to face contact gives $\ell = 1,$ or 2

– anonymous communication via terminals gives $\ell = 0$.

Only some special research has been done addressing the degree of reciprocal loyalty as a function of different conditions of communication. One paper in this context is the dissertation of Havenith (1991).

Example (5–person Apex game with payoff 100 with face to face communication). After (—, 25, 25, 25, 25) Player 1 needs to offer a substantial additional amount, to "bribe" one of the Players 2, 3, 4, 5 to enter a coalition with him. (70, 30) is not sufficient. Experimental data show that a successful offer is (65, 35).

Traditional utility theory would model that players in a loyal group have an additional payoff $\angle$ p . It seems, however, that that this "additional payoff" is only applied as a numerical argument, when players break the loyal group. When entering loyal groups, the additional "utility" only seems to have a second order quality, namely that for identical payoffs, players prefer to enter a loyal group. Accordingly we get

Refinement of Rule 3 *("Dominance into a loyal group")*

A dominance $(x, \mathscr{S}) \to_T (y, \mathscr{T})$ is permitted with $y_i = x_i$ (for a Player i), if i is in a loyal group in $\mathscr{T}$, and was not in a loyal group in $\mathscr{S}$.

Example (3–person game with quotas (80, 80, 40)). $v(1, 2) = 160$, $v(1, 3) = 120$, $v(2, 3) = 120$, $v(S) = 0$ otherwise. In this game the following dominance with zero–improvement is permitted by the given refinement:

—	80	40
80	80	—

A.5 Attributed demands

The next rule models the conclusions that players draw from coalition changes of others: They assume that a player was incontent with his payoff in the preceding state. Accordingly they will enter a coalition with this player only, when he gets more than in the state he left. This means that players "guess" others' demands, and are so careful to enter new coalitions with them only, when their guesses of others' demands are met by the others' payoffs ("attributed demands"). According with experimental observations the concept implies, that it is not possible that players revise the demands they once attributed to others.

As we will see, attributed demands are the central element guiding the foresight of players.

An important observation is that attributed demands depend on the coalition structure of the situation where they are implemented, more precisely, they depend on the partition $M(\mathscr{T})$ of players in the moment before the coalition structure $\mathscr{T}$, was formed:

Notation. Let $(x, \mathscr{S}) \rightarrow_T (y, \mathscr{T})$. If T is a loyal group of $(y, \mathscr{T})$ then $\mathbf{M(\mathscr{T}/T)}$ is the set of all coalitions which are maximal in $\mathscr{T}$, otherwise $M(\mathscr{T}/T)$ is the set of maximal coalitions of $\mathscr{T} \setminus \{T\}$.

The following Rule 6 consists of three parts. Part (1) says, that attributed demands (as minimal suggested payoffs) are induced by a dominance for all dominating players for the two partitions given by the state before and after leaving the coalition. Part (2) considers the case, that in a later state a loyal group is formed. In this case it is assumed that players are content with lower payoffs. Part (3) states that players, who signalled twice, that they want to get a certain amount (or more) in a certain partition, will not be trusted to be content with less than that amount in that partition afterwards.

Rule 6 ("Attributed demands")

(1) Assume within a bargaining chain there are the dominances

$\rightarrow_A (a, \mathscr{A}) \rightarrow_B (b, \mathscr{B})$ and later $\rightarrow_S (x, \mathscr{S}) \rightarrow_T (y, \mathscr{T})$, such that

(a) there is a Player i with $i \in B$, $i \in T$,

(b) $M(\mathscr{T}/T) = M(\mathscr{A}/A)$ (case a) or $M(\mathscr{T}/T) = M(\mathscr{B}/B)$ (case b)

then (*) $y_i > a_i$ and $y_i \geq b_i - p$.

(2) If (in addition to the assumptions of (1)) $T \in M(\mathscr{T}/T)$ and:

$A \notin M(\mathscr{A}/A)$ (in case a) or $B \notin M(\mathscr{B}/B)$ (in case b),

then (instead of (*)) it is sufficient that $y_i \geq a_i$

(3) If (in addition to the assumptions of (1)) a dominance

$\rightarrow_C (c, \mathscr{C}) \rightarrow_D (d, \mathscr{D})$ happened before $\rightarrow_S (x, \mathscr{S}) \rightarrow_T (y, \mathscr{T})$ with

(a) $i \in D$,

(b) $M(\mathscr{D}/D)$ equals $M(\mathscr{A}/A)$ or $M(\mathscr{B}/B)$,

(c) $M(\mathscr{C}/C)$ equals $M(\mathscr{A}/A)$ or $M(\mathscr{B}/B)$), and

(d) $d_i \geq b_i$

then (instead of (*)) $y_i \geq b_i$.

By Rule 6, Rule 2 (prominence structure), and Rule 3 (minimal improvement), every bargaining chain has finite length.

Example (3–person game with quotas (120, 80, 40), prominence 10). $v(1, 2) = 200$, $v(1, 3) = 160$, $v(2, 3) = 120$, $v(S) = \emptyset$ otherwise. For this game the following bargaining chain has maximal length by Rule 6

120	80	—	
130	—	30	
—	80	40	(maximal)

(Further domination is not possible, since Player 1 has a demand greater than 120.)

The following example shows that conditioning attributed demands on coalition structures permits to extend coalitions and form nested coalitions. Players who did not succeed to find coalition partners in a first step of coalition formation may reduce their demands after others formed a coalition. In the next step of coalition formation they can be content with essentially lower shares of the remaining cake.

Example (3–person game with quotas (120, 80, 40) and $v(N) = 200$, prominence 10). $v(1, 2) = 200$, $v(1, 3) = 160$,, $v(2, 3) = 120$, $v(S) = 0$ otherwise. For this game the following sequence fulfills the rules:

120	80	—	(partition 1, 2, 3)
130	—	30	(partition 1, 2, 3)
—	80	40	(partition 1, 2, 3)
40	100	60	(partition 1, {2, 3})

(In the new partition 1, {2, 3} (which is the result of the first step of coalition formation) Player 1 can have a different (lower) demand than before. (The table gives the respective partitions before coalition formation.))

The next example shows, that the formation of coalition structures, and the fact that attributed demands depend on coalition structures can be important even for 1–step games. (In this context see also Albers (1978) on bloc forming tendencies.)

Example (5–person Apex game with 100, prominence 5, reciprocal loyalty 10). The following sequence fulfills the rules and is maximal:

—	25	25	25	25	(partition 1, {2, 3, 4, 5})
60	40	—	—	—	(partition 1, 2, 3, 4, 5)
65	—	—	—	35	(partition 1, 2, 3, 4, 5)
—	20	20	20	40	(partition 1, {2, 3, 4}, 5)
65	—	35	—	—	(partition 1, 2, 3, 4, 5)
70	—	—	30	—	(partition 1, 2, 3, 4, 5)
—	21	21	35	21	(partition 1, {2, 3, 5}, 4)

In step 4 the subcoalition {2, 3, 4} is formed. Player 2's attributed demand of more than 25 is not valid for the new partition. In the following step the subcoalition breaks, and the old attributed demands are valid again.

A.6 Stable states

As mentioned above, from Rules 2, 3 concerning the prominence structure of payoffs, and Rule 6 of attributed demands follows, that every bargaining chain ends after finitely many steps. This makes it possible to analyze bargaining chains in a roll–back manner.

Experimental results indicate that the main part of this analysis is done by evaluating the "stability" of states. This type of analysis is very reasonable for 1–step games. It is based on the idea that in any state of the process, a player asking himself which next move to select, will decide for a certain move only, when he feels sure, that after this next move it will not happen that a next move follows, where he is worse off than in the beginning.

(The assumption is, that in this analysis a player does not evaluate a state by possible payoffs in reasonable next moves, but just checks, whether he can be sure that the next proposal is (sufficiently) stable.)

Before a corresponding definition is given, it has to be clarified, on which state space this roll back analysis is done: does it depend on the history of all preceding moves, which move is made next, or does the next move only depend on the last proposal (i.e. payoff distribution and formed coalition/coalition structure) and the attributed demands following from the preceding sequence of (dominating) proposals. We assume that next moves can depend on the whole chain. This leads to the following model of the state space:

The central elements of the negotiation process are the states. A **state** $s_t = (p_0, p_1, .., p_t)$ is a sequence of proposals. The state space is ordered in a natural way by the "follower"–relation:

Notation. A state $s_{t+1} = (p_0, p_1, .., p_t, p_{t+1})$ **follows after** $q_t = (q_0, q_1, .., q_t)$, if $p_i = q_i$ for $i = 1, ..., t$.

We can now define stable states:

Recursive definition (**Stability of a state for a player i**)
1. (initiation)   A state is stable for all players, if no dominating next proposal is possible.

2. (recursion)   A state $s_t = (p_0, p_1, .., p_t)$ is stable for a Player i, if
for any proposal p_{t+1} that dominates the last proposal p_t via a coalition that does not include Player i,
there is a proposal p_{t+2} dominating p_{t+1}, that is stable for the dominating players, and in which at least one of the players who performed the dominance to p_{t+1} has a lower payoff than in p_t.

Using this definition we get

Rule 7   ("Stable states")

In a state $s_t = (p_0, p_1, .., p_t)$ a Player i performs a dominance to a next proposal p_{t+1} iff the new state $s_{t+1} = (p_0, p_1, .., p_t, p_{t+1})$ is stable for him.

A weaker formulation would be:

A player performs a dominance to a next state, when it is stable for him. He leaves a stable state only, when the next state is stable for him.

The latter condition permits several dominances before the first stable state is reached. However, in the games we considered in our experiments, the first formulation seems to apply. Experienced players try to enter a stable state by the first coalition they enter.

Some examples are presented, that may explain the idea behind the concept of stable states. We restrict the presentation to the chain of that proposals that are selected (or might be selected) on the main path of the bargaining process. (It is left to the reader, to add possible decisions for the other parts of the decision tree.) This type of analysis typically involves "stable" and "unstable" states alternatingly.

Example (3–person quota game with quotas (120, 80, 40), prominence 10). For this game the sequence

120	80	—
130	—	30
—	80	40	(stable)

ends with a stable state. Since this state is stable, Player 3 supports the dominance $(130, —, 30) \rightarrow (—, 80, 40)$. Therefore Player 1 does not support $(130, —, 30)$. – In the same way any domination $(120, 80, —) \rightarrow (120+\Delta, —, 40-\Delta)$ is dominated by $(—, 80, 40)$ in the following step, and $(—, 80, 40)$ is then stable. So $(120, 80, —)$ is stable for Player 2. – It can be shown in a similar way that $(120, 80, —)$ is stable for Player 1. So $(120, 80, —)$ is stable. – Analogously the other quota – outcomes $(120, —, 40)$ and $(—, 80, 40)$ are stable.

The following sequence shows by example that there are no other stable initial states:
If one player receives more than his quota, for instance Player 1 in coalition $\{1, 2\}$, then this
state is not stable:

130	70	—
—	80	40	(stable for 2)
110	—	50
120	80	—	(stable)

---

or more generally

$120 + \Delta$	$80 - \Delta$	—
—	80	40	(stable for 2)
$120 - \Delta$	—	$40 + \Delta$
120	80	—	(stable)

These principles also explain another interesting experimental result:

Example (Sympathy paradox). 3–person game with quotas (80, 80, 40), prominence
5, reciprocal loyalty 0.

80	80	—
85	—	35	(stable for 1)
—	80	40
80	80	—	(stable)

(80 for 1 permitted by Rule 6)
(80 for 2 permitted by refinement of Rule 3)

This sequence explains the surprising experimental result that the quota – distribution
(80, 80, —) is **not** stable for this game, although it is socially desired. In fact it is just its
high social desirability which permits to form (80, 80,—) in state 4 and thereby destabilizes
(80, 80, —) as an initial state. ("sympathy paradox")

A.7 Breaking coalitions

There are situations where subjects do not enter a new coalition but, nevertheless, break the
preceding one. This makes sense when the expected outcome thereafter is higher than in all

states that can be reached when the coalition is not just broken but changed by dominance.

Notation. Breaking a coalition T in a state $(x, \mathscr{S})$ creates the new coalition structure $\mathscr{S} \backslash \backslash T := \{S \in \mathscr{S} \mid (S \subset T \text{ and } S \neq T) \text{ or } S \cap T = \emptyset\}$.

The main problem of modelling breaks of coalitions is in which way the expected payoffs determine the decision. In the preceding part of the model we assumed that players do only perform an action, when the actual payoff in the new state is better than in the present state. We will now leave this principle.

When a player recognizes that the general principle of stepwise dominance is disadvantageous for him, and he breaks his coalition, he thereby leaves the common ground of agreement given by the structure of bargaining chains. All attributed demands that have been built up in the part of the game between the state to which the game drops back and the present state, are cancelled.

Empirical observations indicate, that players evaluate the new state reached by breaking the coalition (which is usually worse than the present state), by the "worst average payoff", they can reach in the next stable states thereafter.
Accordingly we formulate

Rule 8   *("Breaking coalitions")*
If a player breaks a coalition T, then the next state s is
(1) the coalition structure is obtained from the coalition structure of the last proposal by breaking the coalition T, and
(2) for every player the payoff in the new state is given by his minimal reasonable average payoff of the subgame following the new state, where
– the average is taken over all states that are reached from the new state, and that are stable for all players in the dominating coalition (enacting this state) "minimal average outcome" of the subgame following the new state,
– and the minimum is taken over all "reasonable measures" on the space of dominating states.

We do not want to define in detail, what the "reasonable measures" on the set of next states are. The experiments, where this rule was applied, involved only simple cases, where every next state had the same weight.

It should be mentioned, that Rule 8 also implements some principles of fairness: in no state of the game no player, who is needed to support that state gets less than he would get, when he cancels his support.

The following interesting example shows that breaking a coalition can be in fact reasonable:

Example ("three of four" game). Any 3 of 4 players {1, 2, 3, 4} receive 120, all four receive 120, smaller coalitions receive zero. It is assumed that the prominence is 5, and the reciprocal loyalty is 10.

40	40	40	—	({1, 2, 3,} is no loyal group, since 4 is not in {1, 2, 3})
45	45	—	30	
50	50	20	—	
		x		(3 breaks the coalition)
30	30	30	30	(average outcome, by symmetry of the game)

After (50, 50, 20, —) Player 3 breaks the coalition. The new game starts with no coalition structure and is identical to the given game. By symmetry the average payoff over the next stable states is the same for all players under every reasonable measure on the space of next states.

Accordingly Players 1, 2 would have done better, not to agree to (50, 50, 20, —). So the game will stop in (45, 45, —, 30), where no player gets less than his expected outcome of the game.

It may be interesting that the stability of (45, 45, —, 30) (for Player 2 or 1) is supported by the following argument:

40	40	40	—	
45	45	—	30	(partition {1, 2} 3, 4)
50	—	35	35	
—	40	40	40	(partition 1, 2, {3, 4})

The last state is stable by the revealed demand 50 of Player 1 in 1, 2, {3, 4} . This stabilizes (45, 45, —, 30) by foresight.

A.8 The grand coalition

As mentioned, Rule 8 (also) ensures that players do not get less than the "minimal fair share" they would get when they leave the coalition. Since we did not specify the set of measures on the set of "reasonable next moves", this principle remains unprecise. – For the special case that the grand coalition is formed, fairness is implemented by the fact, that every player can immediately break the grand coalition. For this case we give the set of fair distributions:

Rule 9 *("Fair payoff distributions in the grand coalition")*

Let the grand coalition N be formed in a state $(x, \mathscr{S})$.

For any $S \in \mathscr{S}$ let $m(\mathscr{S}, S)$ the maximal elements of the set $\{T \in \mathscr{S} \mid T \subset S\}$ (If $S \in \mathscr{S}$ this is a partition of S.)

Then the additional payoff $a(N) := v(N) - \Sigma(v(S) \mid S \in m(\mathscr{S}, N))$ obtained by forming the grand coalition can be distributed among the players according to the following recursive procedure:

For any coalition $S \in \mathscr{S}$ let us assume that $a(S)$ is assigned to S by recursion (the start is of the recursion is $S = N$)). There are two extreme principles of distributing $a(S)$ among the members of $m(\mathscr{S}, S)$:

(1) every $T \in m(\mathscr{S}, S)$ receives $a(S) \cdot \#T/\#S$ (per capita distribution)

(2) every $T \in m(\mathscr{S}, S)$ receives $a(S) \cdot 1/\#m(\mathscr{S}, S)$ (per coalition distribution).

(R) Applying rules (1) or (2) recursively (it may be allowed to use different distribution principles for different coalitions $S \in \mathscr{S}$), a specific distribution of the amount $a(N)$ among the players is obtained.

The payoff distribution verified when the grand coalition is formed is in the convex hull of all payoff distributions that can be obtained via (R).

(Principles (1) and (2) can also be found in Thrall and Lucas (1963), or Maschler (1963).)

Example (3–person game with quotas (120, 80, 40) and $v(N) = 240$). $v(1, 2) = 200$, $v(1, 3) = 160,$, $v(2, 3) = 120$, $v(S) = 0$ otherwise. Assume that in the first step coalition (2, 3) is formed:

$$— \quad 80 \quad 40 \quad \text{(partition 1, 2, 3)}$$

In the next step this coalition shall be extended to the grand coalition. Then the following two extreme cases are possible by Rule 10:

(1)   40   120   80   (per capita distribution)

(2)   60   110   70   (per coalition distribution)

The payoff the players may agree to is in the convex hull of these two alternatives.

It may be remarked, that the grand coalition has been the result of several games, even of 1–step games, where the subjects so to say neglected the competitive structure of the game and preferred to form a grand coalition, although there could be additional payoffs verified in several subcoalitions. The interesting result is, that the grand coalition (despite of the high incentives of additional payoffs, if smaller coalitions were formed) did not break in any case. This seems to be a general rule:

Rule 10 *("Stability of the grand coalition")*

A state $(x, \mathscr{S})$, where the grand coalition is formed (i.e. with $N \in \mathscr{S}$), is stable.

B   "Solutions" of the model

B.1 Solution states and relation to demand equilibrium

Rule 7 only permits bargaining chains, where a stable state is reached in each step. Assuming, that bargaining processes start with the null–proposal p_0 , where no coalition is formed, we get the following set of solution states:

Definition. A state $s_t = (p_0,...,p_t)$ is a **solution state**, iff its preceding states $s_r = (p_0,...,p_r)$ are stable for $r = 1,...,t$.

A solution state consists of a sequence of states that describe the stepwise extension of a coalition. For one–step games the solution states consist of two proposals, namely the null–proposal, and the proposal describing the formed coalition.

This definition is not unproblematic. The question arises, if there are games, for which $s_0 = (p_0)$ is a solution state, i.e. that no coalition is formed. This makes sense for inessential games, where $v(S) = \Sigma (v(i)| \ i \in S)$ for all $S \in N$. However, for other games it seems unreasonable to assume that players do not enter any state, because they must be afraid, that this state is not stable. Up to now we do not know such games (but we did not invest high efforts in finding them). If such games are found, we expect that addditional rules of bargaining will be found too, that enable to solve these games.

It may be remarked, that for many one–step games the set of solution states (or, more precisely, the set of last proposals of solution states) coincides with the predictions made by the quota concept of v. Neumann & Morgenstern (1944), if it exists, or as predicted by the demand equilibrium concept of Albers (see 1974, 1979, or 1991).

Presently it seems that severe deviations from the demand–concept do only occur in the following cases:

- in experimental situations with reciprocal loyalty (an example is the Apex Game, for which reciprocal loyalty is the **only** reason for these deviations), and
- for games as the "three of four" game, where groups of players can form subcoalitions, and play the others off against each other,

Nevertheless, generally, the approach here can be seen as an approach to a behavioral implementation of the demand concept, which, however, does not always lead to the same results, and in these cases explains why deviating experimental results occur. – Moreover, in addition to the demand equilibrium, the approach here does not only model the first, but also the following steps of coalition formation.

B.2 Relation to empirical results

According to the theoretical predictions, for most experimental games that have been played by us and other experimenters, experienced players tend to stop the game after the first move.

The only game that we played where experienced players did not select the "one move solution" was the "three of four" game, where the theory does not predict the symmetric coalition of three players, with which the subjects started the process.

Unexperienced subjects play bargaining chains with more than one move. This is not surprising, since the subjects must first learn to analyze the game. It cannot be expected that they "know" the ten rules in advance, and apply them. In fact it is an interesting question of research, how the subjects learn these rules during one, or several bargaining processes. It may be that the rules are transferred from a general pool of rules that govern decision behavior.

A problem of experimental research is, that bargaining chains can be only observed for unexperienced subjects who make mistakes (if they would not make mistakes, they would stop the chain earlier), while experienced players stop the sequences immediately, and thereby permit conclusions on the model only in an indirect way.

We feel quite sure that the theory captures the essence of the boundedly rational part of the subjects' motives. Some comments concerning the relation of our results to those of other authors may be helpful:

1. All results we refer to, are observed in experiments, where subjects participated for at least 5 hours (face to face communication), and for several days (about 25 hours, communication via terminals). (Under the face to face condition no player was matched with another player more than once. This reduces the number of games that can be played by one group essentially. Under face to face condition, our subjects played at most 5–6 5–person games, or 4–5 4–person games.)

2. When the type of game was changed, subjects had enough time to accommodate to the new situation. – Some experiments of other authors are such that a high number of different games is played, and the type of game is changed in every round. In this setup, players cannot develop a detailed analytical pattern. They structure the space of reasonable alternatives much more rigorously. Results tend more into the direction of equal share analysis (see Selten (1972) or (1982)).

3. In experiments via terminals we repeatedly observed different behavior in the first hours, when players still learn. Therefore we include data of the first hours only, when we have checked that the observed phenomena are still valid after several hours of experience. In the case of communication via terminals, we frequently do not use the data produced in the first 3–5 hours. – Many experiments of other authors do not generate experienced subjects. Frequently subjects participate only for 2–4 hours.

4. Strategic behavior is learned much quicker, when players' communication is not restricted, so that they can reflect consequences of strategic behavior in communication. Certain strategic acts or threats need that complex information can be exchanged. It is very difficult for subjects to learn nonverbal "languages of threats". The reduction of communication can reduce the deepness of strategic thinking essentially. We therefore decided to perform all our games with free communication, in order to avoid that only limited forms of strategic reflection are applied. (Experiments of this type frequently need about one hour per game.)

5. We give quite essential marginal incentives. (For instance 1.00 DM, i.e. about 70 Cents per point in the Apex game with payoff 100.)

6. After the experiments, we arrange discussions among the participants for 15–20 hours. Aim of the discussion is, that they describe and try to model the process of individual, and group decision making in which they were involved. These sessions are an

explorative instrument, which permits to get insight into the subjects' perception of the situation, and into details of their decision processes. – These sessions produce a pool of experiences concerning how reasonable models may look like, how much models differ among individuals, and which parts of models may be easily verified in further experiments.

C Comments concerning possible modifications

The concept here presents the state of model building that we have reached. There is no question that additional experiments will give additional insights that suggest to refine or extend the model. However, the model should not be perceived as an arbitrary one. From our point of view, it seems to be the best we can do, to explain our experimental observations. Moreover, all experiments we selected did address open questions of the respective latest state of the model. This is the reason why we feel that by now a state is reached, where the model can be presented to others, who may help to refine or extend it.

In the following paragraphs we give some comments concerning possible different approaches and additional rules (including some rules that on the first view sound reasonable, but are not applied by subjects).

C.1 A comment concerning consistency of players' behavior

The aim of a bargaining process (as modeled by the bargaining sequence) is, to get information about the intentions of the other players, accordingly adjust the own behavior, and try to enter a stable state.

The intentions of the other players can only be deduced from their preceding behavior assuming consistency of action. These conclusions from the consistency requirement essentially depend on the type of model:

Example (a negotiation chain of the 5–person Apex Game with payoff 100, prominence 5, reciprocal loyalty 10).

65	35	—	—	—
70	—	—	—	30
—	20	20	20	40
65	—	35	—	—

Does consistency mean, that Player 1 will again switch from (65, 35, —, —, —) to (70, —, —, —, 30)? Or will he select another partner, whom he gives 30, for instance Player 4? Or did he learn from the history that after (70, 30) follows (40, 20, 20, 20) and therefore will not enter (70, 30) a second time. The answer of this question is important for player 3 when he decides, whether to enter (65, —, 35, —, —) or not. In the model here, this situation is ruled by attributed demands. It is assumed that by his initial switch from (65, 35, —, —, —) to (70, —, —, —, 30) Player 1 revealed to be incontent with 65, and it is assumed that the others imply from that that he will never again be content with 65 (except for cases with different coalition structures). All other types of arguments that may be applied to cut the chain of possibly circular arguments seem to be less stringent.

C.2 Two rules that may be and may be not applied

The following two refinements of Rule 6 (attributed demands) may be addressed by further research. Presently we are not sure, if they are applied as general rules, or not. Both rules are quite reasonable and simplify reasoning essentially. On the other hand, by introducing these additional rules the system of rules becomes more complicated.

Is it really structural simplicity, that "brain looks for", or is it easy decidability? Other observations of decision processes suggest that brain permits structural complexity as long the problem is "handable in a reasonable way". This could mean that certain rules that help to simplify the problem may be applied in complex, and not applied in less complex situations. Our present state of insight into "human brain's behavior" supports this assumption. Our phantasy suggests that there might be an ordered set of possible rules of which in any specific case the first r are applied, where r is selected according to the specific problem in such a way that the created system reaches "reasonable complexity" which permits "solvability in a reasonable time". (The latter idea may be interpreted as a generalization of the exactness selection rule of the theory of prominence (section A.3).)

Attributed demands of first moves

The first refinement of Rule 6 applies to games, where it can happen, that a player can decide between different offers of other players, and this selection determines the first move of the game. (This type of situation is not covered by the strategic model of next state's selection given in section A.6, it needs a more extensive way of modeling.)

Refinement of Rule 6 *("Attributed demands of first moves")*
If in the first move of a game entering the proposal $(y, \mathscr{S})$ a player could select between several alternatives, and thereby decided the first move of the game, then his attributed demand in $M(\mathscr{S})$ is y_i.

Example (5–person Apex game with payoff 100). Under free communication it frequently happens that Players 2, 3, 4, 5 do not want to form a joint coalition, but prefer to coalesce with player 1. Then player 1 can select one of them as a partner, and can determine the payoff distribution in this coalition. When this is known to all players (and this is the case for experimental Apex games after the experience of one game), then the initial payoff in his first coalition settles Player 1's attributed demand.

Attributed demands of players in symmetric positions

As mentioned above, in their analysis of a game subjects use given symmetries. On a formal level (and this seems to be generally applied, as long as there are no players who show unexpected, strange behavior) players who are in symmetric positions are expected to have identical (attributed) demands. By this assumption, experiences with one player are transferred to other players of the same symmetry type.

To make this model precise, we have to define symmetry of players with respect to a given game.

Notation. Two players i, j are of the **same symmetry type,** if there is a bijection b on the set N of players, such that
1. b maps i to j, and j to i
2. for any subset S of N the members are mapped in such a way that $v(S) = v(b(S))$.

By this definition we can extend the condition of attributed demands:

Refinement of Rule 6 *("Attributed Demands of Symmetric Players")*
A set of players of the same symmetry type have identical attributed demands. If the attributed demand of one of them is raised, then the same is done with the attributed demands of all players of the same symmetry type.

It may be that this refinement does not apply when one player of a symmetric group received an attributed demand, but only when two players received attributed demands.

The demand attributed to the other players of the group are then the minimum of the attributed demands of the first two.

C.3 Three reasonable rules that are not applied

The following rules (which look quite reasonable on the first view) do not seem to guide the bargaining process:

Rule A (*"Initial demands"*)
The initial demand settles a revealed demand for the player who made the proposal.

This rule seems not to be necessary to explain experimental data. It is not needed for theoretical predictions, since anyway the theoretical approach predicts that players immediately enter a stable state.

Rule B (*"No coalition with a traitor"*)
If a player once left a coalition with you, than never again coalesce with him.

If this rule were true, then in the 3–person game with quotas (80, 80, 40) and $v(1, 2, 3) = 0$ the following sequence would lead to a stable state

80	80	—
85	—	35
—	80	40	(stable by Rule B)

From this follows that (80, 80, —) is stable. However, experimental results show that this is not true. – Another example may be given by the 3–person game with quotas (120, 80, 40), $v(1, 2, 3) = 0$:

115	—	45
120	80	—
—	85	35
120	—	40	(would be excluded by Rule B)

In this sequence the last state would be excluded by rule B, and it would follow that the first state is stable. In the same way **every** payoff distribution (which gives more than $v(i)$ to the individual players) would be stable. This is obviously wrong. Rule B is not supported by experimental data.

Rule C   *("Condition own demands on demands of others")*

A Player i announces that he will reduce his demand level, if another player (or other players) show higher demands than Player i assumes. These levels of others are given by Player i.

I cannot remember any experiment where such a tricky approach has ben tried.

D   Solutions of four selected games

In this section we give the theoretical solutions of four games that we played in several of our experiments. For games 1, 3, and 4 there are phenomena of experimental bargaining explained by this approach which are not (or not that precisely) explained by traditional theories. (The bargaining chains given, may help to get an idea, why the respective states are stable. Proofs would need a more extended reasoning.)

D.1   The 5–person Apex game with payoff 100

$(N = \{1, 2, 3, 4, 5\}$, $v(S) = 100$ if $(1 \in S)$ or $(S = \{2, 3, 4, 5\}$, $v(S) = 0)$ otherwise, prominence 5, reciprocal loyalty 10 (communication face to face))

If the game is played with free communication then the prominence unit is $p = 5$, and the reciprocal loyalty is 5 or 10.

If the reciprocal loyalty is 10 then the theoretical result is, that $(65, 35, —, —, —)$ is stable. The reasoning can be explained by the following two sequences

65	35	—	—	—	(stable for 2)
70	—	30	—	—	↑
—	20	40	20	20	(stable)

This sequence has reached a stable state since Player 1 needs more than 65 (by revealed demands) and Players 2, 4, 5 need at least 35 (by reciprocal loyalty and dominance). So Player 3 performs the change from step 2 to step 3. From that follows that Player 1 remains in state 1.

65	35	—	—	—	(stable for 1)
—	40	20	20	20	(3, 4, 5 form a loyal group)
65	—	35	—	—	(stable for 3)
70	—	—	30	—	↑
—	20	20	40	20	(stable)

Here no further domination is possible since the revealed demand of Player 1 is 65 (i. e. 1 needs more than 65) and by reciprocal loyalty and dominance 2, 3, or 5 need 35 for a dominance. Accordingly the change to step 5 will be performed, and the change to step 4 not. So step 3 is stable for Player 3, and the change to step 3 will be performed. Therefore the change from step 1 to step 2 will not be performed, and Player 2 does not leave state 1.

Note that for a reciprocal loyalty of 10 the state (60, 40, —, —, —) is not stable. The domination to (65, —, 35, —, —) will be performed, since Player 3 will not leave this state (this follows in the same way as above.)

It can also be shown that (—, 25, 25, 25, 25) is stable, since by reciprocal loyalty a player needs at least 40 to leave this coalition:

—	25	25	25	25	(stable for 2, 3, 4, 5)
60	40	—	—	—	↑
65	—	35	—	—	(stable for 1 , as above)
	etc.				

Similar to the considerations above, it can be shown that (65, —, 35, —, —) is not left by Player 3. So the change to step 3 will be performed and the change to step 2 will not be performed. Since both cases are cases with minimal improvement of the dominating player, it follows that step 1 is stable.

It may be remarked that, for even for a reciprocal loyalty of 10, cautious subjects in position of Player 1 may select (60, 40, —, —, —). This state will also not be left by Player 2 (but can be left by Player 1). This may be illustrated by

60	_40_	—	—	—	(not left by Player 2)
—	50	16^6	16^6	16^6	↑
_65_	—	35	—	—	(not left by Player 1)
70	—	—	30	—	↑
—	20	20	40	20	(stable)

$((\text{—}, 50, 16^6, 16^6, 16^6)$ may be replaced by $(\text{—}, 45, 18^3, 18^3, 18^3))$

Experimental outcomes of this game are $(\text{—}, 25, 25, 25, 25)$, two person coalitions with payoffs around $(65, 35)$, and sometimes results of type $(\text{—}, 40, 20, 20, 20)$. The latter results are obtained by experienced players after mistakes of Player 1. The results can be explained by disevaluations of the amount of reciprocal loyalty by Player 1, which permits to go through sequences as

65	35	—	—	—
70	—	30	—	—
—	20	40	20	20

and reach their final states.

The results different from $(65, 35)$ in the two–person coalition of Player 1 with another player can be explained by different values of reciprocal loyalty. In this context it should be noticed that for instance $(75, 25)$ remains stable, when b=1, and the reciprocal loyalty is zero,

75	25	—	—	—
—	28	24	24	24
75	—	25	—	—

might happen.

D.2 The 3–person game with quotas (80, 80, 40)

$(v(1, 2) = 160,\ v(1, 3) = v(2, 3) = 120,\ v(S) = 0$ otherwise, prominence 1, reciprocal loyalty 0 (communication via terminals)).

The experimental results were $(81, \text{—}, 39)$ and $(\text{—}, 81, 39)$ nearly exclusively. This indicates that the analysis was done with an exactness of 1. The 10 rules explain this result:

$(81, \text{—}, 39)$ is stable for Player 1:

81	—	39	(stable for 1)
—	80	40	(3 has attributed demand > 39)
80	80	—	(stable, permitted since 1, 2 form a loyal group)
			(no domination possible where 3 receives > 39)

$(81, —, 39)$ is stable for Player 3:

81	—	39	
82	78	—	(1 has attributed demand > 81)
—	80	40	(stable)
——————————			(no domination possible where 1 receives > 81)

Player 1 cannot get more (at prominence 1):

82	—	38	
—	81	39	(stable, see above)
	etc.		

Player 3 cannot get more (at prominence 1):

80	—	40	
80	80	—	(stable for 1)
—	81	39	(2 has attributed demand > 80)
80	—	40	(stable)
——————————			

(Since $(80, —, 40)$ is stable after the preceding steps, $(80, 80, —)$ is stable for Player 1. Therefore $(80, —, 40)$ is unstable.)

D.3 The 3–person game with quotas (120, 80, 40)

$(v(1, 2) = 200, v(1, 3) = 160, v(2, 3) = 120, v(S) = 0$ otherwise, prominence 1, reciprocal loyalty 0 (communication via terminals))

The experimental results were $(120, 80, —), (120, —, 40), (—, 80, 40)$. The 10 rules explain this result. (Considerations are restricted to $(120, 80, —)$, but are similar for the other two proposals.):

$(120, 80, —)$ is stable for Player 1:

120	80	—	(stable for 1)
—	81	39	(2 has attributed demand > 80)
120	—	40	(stable)
——————————			

$(120, 80, —)$ is stable for Player 2 (shown in similar way)

Player 1 cannot get more in {1, 2}:

121	79	—	
—	80	40	(stable for 2)
119	—	41	(3 has attributed demand > 40)
120	80	—	(stable)

(Since step 4 is stable, step 2 is not dominated via Player 3. So Player 1 will support the change from step 1 to step 2 and step 1 is unstable.)

Similarly it can be shown that Player 2 cannot get more in {1, 2}.

D.4 The "three of four" game

(N = {1, 2, 3, 4}, v(S) = 120 if S has at least 3 players, v(S) = 0 otherwise, prominence 5)

The experimental results are 3–person coalitions with (45, 45, 30), exactness 5. This can be explained as follows:

(45,45,30) is stable for Player 2 (we consider several cases of dominations excluding Player 2):

case 1:	45	45	30	—	
	50	—	35	35	(most stable alternative)
	—	30	45	45	(3 will not leave this state)
	35	35	50	—	↑
	40	40	—	40	(stable)

It can be shown that all other dominances from step 3 (—, 30, 45, 45) are also unstable So (—, 30, 45, 45) is stable for Player 4. By symmetry it is also stable for Player 3. So step 2 is unstable. Therefore step 1 is stable for Player 2 (and for Player 1 by symmetry).

We now show that asymmetric distributions among {3, 4} dominating the first state are not stable:

case 2:	45	45	30	—	
	50	—	40	30	
	—	30	45	45	(stable)

case 3:

45	45	30	—
50	—	45	25
—	25	50	45	(stable)

(45, 45, 30) is stable for Player 1 (by symmetry).

(45, 45, 30) is stable for Player 3:

45	45	30	—	
47^5	47^5	—	25	
			x	(4 breaks the coalition)
30	30	30	30	("expected payoff")

Since (30, 30, 30, 30) modeled as final, (47.5, 47.5, —, 25) is unstable. So (45, 45, —, 25) is stable for Player 3. (Asymmetric distributions among 1, 2 do not create stable states in step 2.)

D.5 Which rules are applied in which games?

The following table shows which of the Rules of Part A are used in the examples D.1 to D.4.

		D.1	D.2	D.3	D.4
	example no.				
Rule 1	"Bargaining chains"	x	x	x	x
Rule 2	"Prominence of proposals"	x	x	x	x
Rule 3	"Minimal improvement"	x	x	x	x
Rule 4	"Sympathy"	–	–	–	–
Rule 5	"Reciprocal loyalty"	x	–	–	–
Rule 6	"Attributed demands"	x	x	x	x
Rule 7	"Stable states"	x	x	x	x
Rule 8	"Breaking coalitions"	–	–	–	x
Rule 9	"Fairness in the grand coalition"	–	–	–	–
Rule 10	"Stability of the grand coalition"	–	–	–	–

The result may again confirm that Rules 1–3, and 5–8 are really needed for the model. Rules

4, and 9 have been motivated by examples, when they were introduced, and do clearly have empirical relevance as well. Rule 10 was true in all cases where the grand coalition was formed in our experiments.

Footnotes

1   Institute of Mathematical Economics, University of Bielefeld, Bielefeld, Germany

2   We use the symbol $\subset$ to denote the strict inclusion. Otherwise we use $\subseteq$.

3    $x(S)$ denotes $\Sigma_{i \in S} x_i$

4   In Albers and Albers (1974) we also permitted $b = 2{,}5$. This addresses the fact, that data as12.5 can result as compromises between 10 and 15 by selecting the midpoint when the general level of exactness of analysis is 5. We know that this midpoint selection can arise in conflict situations, but it seams not typical for general n–person games. (Nevertheless, the problem needs further research.)

References

Albers, W. (1974).   Zwei Lösungskonzepte für kooperative Mehrpersonenspiele, die auf Anspruchsniveaus der Spieler basieren. *Operations Research Verfahren XXI* (pp. 1–13). Meisenheim.

Albers, W. (1978). Bloc forming tendencies as characteristics of the bargaining behavior in different versions of apex games. In H. Sauermann (Ed.), *Contributions to experimental economics VIII, Coalition forming behavior* (pp. 172–206). Tübingen.

Albers, W. (1979). Core– and kernel–variants based on imputations and demand profiles. In   O. Moeschlin, & D. Pallaschke (Eds.), *Game theory and related topics* (pp. 3–16). Amsterdam, New York, Oxford.

Albers, W. (1981). Some solution concepts based on power potentials. In O. Moeschlin & D. Pallaschke (Eds.), *Game theory and mathematical economics* (pp. 3–13). Amsterdam, New York, Oxford.

Albers, W. (1986). Reciprocal potentials in apex games. In R.W. Scholz (Ed.), *Current issues of west german decision research* (pp. 157–171). Frankfurt, New York.

Albers, W. (1988a). Aspirations and aspiration adjustment in location games. *Working Paper No 159*. Institute of Mathematical Economics, Bielefeld.

Albers, W. (1988b). Revealed aspirations and reciprocal loyalty in apex games. In R. Tietz, W. Albers, & R. Selten (Eds.), *Bounded rational behavior in experimental games and markets* (pp. 333– 350). Berlin, Heidelberg, New York, Tokyo.

Albers, W., & Albers, G. (1984). On the prominence structure of the decimal system. In R.W. Scholz (Ed.), *Decision making under uncertainty* (pp. 271–287). Amsterdam.

Albers, W., & Laing, J. D. (1991). Prominence, competition, learning and the generation of offers in computer aided experimental spatial games. In R. Selten (Ed.), *Game equilibrium models III, Strategic bargaining* (pp. 141–185). Berlin, Heidelberg, New York, Tokyo.

Albers, W., & Laing, J. D. (1991). Implementing demand equilibria as stable states in a revealed demand approach, *Working Paper No 199*. Institute of Mathematical Economics, Bielefeld.

Bennet, E. (1983). The aspiration approach to predicting coalition formation and payoff distribution in sidepayment games. *International Journal of Game Theory*, 12, 1–28.

Bennet, E. (1990). Folk theorems for the proposal–making model. In R. Selten (Ed.), *Game equilibrium models III, Strategic bargaining* (pp. 70–79). Berlin.

Binmore, K. (1985). Bargaining and coalitions. In A.E. Roth (Ed.), *Game theoretic models of bargaining*. Cambridge 1985.

Chatterjee, K., & Dutta, D., & Ray, D., & Sengupta, D. (1987). *A non–cooperative theory of coalitional bargaining*. mimeo, 1987.

Havenith, W. (1991). *Phänomene des Verhandlungsverhaltens im 5–Personen Apex–Spiel*. Frankfurt/Main.

Maschler, M. (1963). The power of a coalition, *Management Science, 10* (pp. 8–29).

v. Neumann, J., & Morgenstern, O. (1944). *Theory of games and economic behavior*. Princeton, N.J.

Ostmann, A. (this volume). Aspiration processing in multilateral bargaining: Experiment, theory and simulation.

Schelling, T. C. (1960). *The strategy of conflict.* Cambridge.

Selten, R. (1972). Equal share analysis of characteristic function bargaining. In H. Sauermann (Ed.), *Contributions to experimental economics, Vol. III* (pp. 130–165). Tübingen.

Selten, R. (1981). A noncooperative model of characteristic function bargaining. In V. Boehm & H. Nachtkamp (Eds.), *Essays in game theory and mathematical economics in honor of Oskar Morgenstern* (pp. 131–151). Mannheim, Wien, Zürich.

Selten, R. (1982). Equal division payoff bounds for 3–person characteristic function experiments. In R. Tietz (Ed.), *Aspiration levels in bargaining and economic decision making* (pp. 265–275). Berlin.

Selten, R. (1985). Equity and coalition bargaining in experimental 3–person games. In R. Tietz, W. Albers, & R. Selten (Eds.), *Bounded rational behavior in experimental games and markets.* Berlin.

Thrall, R. M., & Lucas, W. F. (1963). N–person games in partition function form, *Naval Research Logistics Quarterly, Vol 10*, 281–298.

Vogt, B. & Albers, W. (1992). Zur Prominenzstruktur von Zahlenangaben bei diffuser numerischer Information – Ein Experiment mit kontrolliertem Grad der Diffusität. *Working Paper No 214*, Institute of Mathematical Economics, Bielefeld.

Aspiration processing in multilateral bargaining: Experiment, theory and simulation

Axel Ostmann[1]

Abstract

A growing tradition in analysing bargaining behaviour uses an experimental setup to provide tools for controlling parameters of the underlying conflict. Game theory is used to provide a model of the conflict, to analyse the possible actions of the agents and the arguments that might be used within the bargaining process and to understand the results of the bargaining. In face–to–face bargaining, we usually find a great variety of actions that are not explainable and sometimes not even compatible with the usual rationality–assumptions on the agents. It is widely accepted that bounded rationality approaches are more adequate especially for the face–to–face settings. But it has not been really examined what concepts should be used in the corresponding models, and what tools are adequate for testing them. After a previous report on the use of the concept "social field" (Ostmann, 1992a), and another on a first attempt to explain bargaining results by aspirations and the social field (Ostmann, 1992b), this paper deals with aspiration processing in a more detailed way. We shall be exploring the limits of the concept "aspiration" with respect to explaining or predicting face–to–face bargaining processes.

Experimental bargaining

Imagine an experimental face–to–face bargaining situation. Imagine a sample of different people. What are the individual differences that are essential for the bargaining task? One can imagine that it is the specific configuration that influences the communication process. One can think of emotional and cognitive processes that determine the acts of communication. It is a drastic simplification to represent an individual only by his or her aspirations and some rules of aspiration processing. Nevertheless, in the following I shall try to concentrate on aspirations and ask how far we can get with such an approach, and where we shall reach the limits.

Individual aspirations are formed in the context of the situation or, in our specific case, in the context of the bargaining task. The bargaining task is based on a conflict structure induced by experimental game–playing. The game used is a specific simple game. Some coalitions of partners can win and distribute a fixed sum of money, and others cannot. There are five minimal winning coalitions; all of them get the same joint payoff. Any larger coalition also wins and can distribute the payoff.

If we instruct the subjects to bargain (directly and verbally) in order to reach an agreement according to the rules of the game, we hope that the subjects will take on the given rôles (i.e. formally: the characteristics of the players of the game), and will try to bargain in such a way that they can expect to gain the best possible outcome with respect to their rôles. To make the formally given preference–structure of a player a valid one in the experimental situation, we additionally set an individual incentive for the subjects by paying each one according to the final outcome of the game.

For behavioural sciences the use of game–theoretical conceptions and models offers the specific advantage of making it possible to determine, classify and describe in precise language the important structural characteristics of a conflict situation (such as situational type, number and kind of resources, description of the action space of an agent, and strength of the formal rôle of an agent.). A conceptual system is thereby given to the experimental researcher which helps him or her to determine the interesting variables and structural characteristics of the conflict situation which is to be constructed and given to the subjects. Moreover, what subjects really do can be compared to game–theoretical solutions and measures or other game–theoretical relations or concepts.

A general hypothesis in Ostmann (1992a) was that the way persons perceive and estimate one another influences in an important way how these persons deal with one another and with the demands presented by the conflict situation. The guiding idea was to assume a two–stage classification decision which differentiates first between friend and enemy and then between the strategically next relevant criteria. If the other is my friend it is important for me to know if I can rely on his or her efficiency; if the other one is my enemy it is important for me to know if he or she will attack me. In order to measure those strategically relevant decisions we used Bales' SYMLOG theory as a theory of the social field (Bales, 1970) and Orlik's work on the corresponding judgement–clusters (with the clusters withdrawal, fight, sympathy and accomplishment (Orlik, 1987). Judgement data came from a questionnaire of the type: "During the last group meeting, did you see an act of your partner x that can be characterized by the following adjective?" One result given in Ostmann (1992a) and of importance for this paper was that membership in the final coalition could be seen as strongly influenced by extreme social field positions. For example, subjects with extremly high fight–scores were usually excluded and subjects with extremely low withdrawal–scores were nearly always members of the final coalition. This result was confirmed in a second series of experiments (cf. Ostmann, 1992c).

The game

Let us represent the bargainers by the following symbols: S, P, B, W, Z, F. These simple letters used as names are abbreviations of theoretical characteristics of the corresponding players. In the following we will learn that we can characterize:

S to be strong, P to be a protector of a dependent follower F, B to have a "bourgeois middle–class" position and, finally, W and Z to be weak and symmetric.

The game was first designed for experiments by Kravitz (1987), and can be represented by listing its five minimal–winning coalitions:

Tab.1: Minimal–winning coalitions

coalition	players					
	S	P	B	W	Z	F
a	x	x	–	–	–	–
b	x	–	x	x	–	–
c	x	–	x	–	x	–
d	–	x	x	–	–	x
e	–	x	–	x	x	x

x: member, –: not member

It is evident that the players W and Z are symmetric. In a short substitution analysis (for determining the so–called desirability relation of that simple game) we can find out that S and P are stronger than any of the other players because on the one hand, a substitution for either one by one of the others retains the set of winning coalitions and, on the other hand, a substitution for another player by S or P can enter that set and will never leave it.

If we denote "x is stronger than y determined by substitution" with x>y, and if we know that the relation is transitive, we can represent that relation of strength with the following shorthand:

S,P > B,F and B > W,Z;   W ~ Z

The following pairs are cannot be related by > : S and P, F and B, F and W, F and Z. If we relate the membership of P and F in the five minimal winning coalitions, we can see that F is dependent on P in so far as each of the minimal winning coalitions F is a member in requires the membership of P too, while P has an alternative coalition without F being member of it. In the game given here, no other pair of players is related in such a way.

According to the relations of strength and dependance, the rôles of the players can be characterized by the following names: the **strong** S, the **protector** P, the **bourgeois** B, the **weak–symmetric** W/Z and the **follower** F.

A sample of intentions

Before the bargaining started, subjects were asked to fill in a questionnaire for judging the situation, developing plans, and giving strategies and reasons for them. Moreover, subjects were asked for different kinds of aspirations. In the following we will use two of them:

– a variable called "start", that is their planned initial demand, and
– a variable called "min", that is their planned lower limit for acceptance.

Reporting their knowledge on the situation and on their partners, subjects usually do not separate emotional and cognitive influences upon their perception. For example, one can judge another to be a preferred partner for both emotional and strategic reasons without further analysis. Analytically, we assume that the actions of the subjects will be prepared by routines and that we can distinguish cognitive routines like analyzing, inferencing, evaluating the actions of others, updating, and rationalizing one's own actions from routines that are emotionally motivated. The following rules are examples that are socio–emotionally motivated:

– Do not cooperate with somebody that has treated you in an unfriendly manner.
– Look for a friendly partner that can be trusted and is powerful.
– Try to isolate "fighters" except if they can punish you.
– Do not contradict the strong.

If we look at the data from the questionnaires, we can recognize a similar mixture of cognitive and emotional sources of judgement, decisions, and plans even before the bargaining started. We can say the participants are dealing with more intuitive knowledge. Sometimes they try to imagine more clearly what the bargaining will look like; sometimes they even make alternative plans in case their primary plan proves to be untenable. Subjects imagine unfavourable possible events or actions they have to prevent their partners from performing.

Intentions have a cognitive, an emotional and a socio–emotional background. Even the pure aspiration data is influenced by both social perceptions and the structure of the game. The following table gives one sample set of primary goals, reasons, plans and aspirations. The sample is taken from Experiment 12.

Tab.2: Intentions

agent	some intentions
S	60% in b (W seems to be friendly and both seem to cooperate) bind B; else a, but not c start: 59 min: 49
P	a, eventually 50:50 (S will demand much, too); neither d nor e start: 50 min: 10
B	d or b; I prefer D as a partner, and like to avoid a partnership with P; start: 24 min: 14
W	b or e; danger of a,50:50; we have to give more to the strong start: 59 min: 49
Z	c; but I see no chance for a realization; the strong cannot get 50% from us; not e start: 11 min: 11
F	d or e; mainly becoming a member; but if it happens that S runs out, I will be strong start: 28 min: 0

Given the initial demands only coalition c is possible. But member W of c is never a planned partner. Will W succeed in changing his or her image? Or will W's partner finally adapt to the power structure and neglect the more personal considerations?

For the above set of minimal aspirations, nearly all coalitions are admissible. What can be our predictions on what will happen, on what cooperation will be established, on the result? On what type of information should we base our predictions? Notice there are different types of aspiration flexibility. The extreme types are bargainer F (min=0) and Z (not flexible at all).

Aggregate data for the face–to–face experiments

Before going into details, let me summarize some data on aspirations and results from the two series of face–to–face experiments mentioned above (and reported in Ostmann 1992a, 1992b and 1992c; all experiments are based on the same game, given above). In each of the two sets of 13 negotiation experiments under free communication, 16x6 subjects took part. Every subject took part only once. There was only one (one–shot) game per group. Time used for instructions, pre–negotiation group work and filling in questionnaires was about one hour. Time used for the negotiation itself was between half an hour and one and a half hours. Not in all cases was the conflict successfully induced. In nine cases the group decided to equally distribute the payoff in the grand coalition without discussing conflictual issues. Let us call the 17 remaining negotiations with conflict "regular". In these 17 cases of the 2x13=26 single experiments, the criteria for "conflict successfully induced" were fulfilled. Data reported in the following refer to these seventeen regular single experiments.

Tab.3: means of 17 face–to–face experiments (in %)

		rôle			
	S	P	B	W/Z	F
start	53	41	35	25	27
min	30	22	22	13	14
members' payoff	46	45	28	15	19
membership	71	71	53	38	35

All minimal–winning coalitions formed (a, b, c, d, e) were observed 5, 1, 2, 3 or 2 times, respectively. Sometimes we observe oversized coalitions: a+F and the grand coalition once each, and coalition b∪c twice. Both members' payoffs and membership were strongly related to strength in the game. But note: the dependent follower is rather successful (game–theoretical solution concepts assign a zero–gain to him).

   One can ask if the aspiration data from the questionnaires can be assumed to be valid for the whole (following) bargaining process. Only six actions against the stated minimum were observed. Three of them were due to an oversized coalition. In the other three cases a further reduction of 3 to 6% was accepted. My interpretation of these facts is as follows:

   In most cases the aspiration data can be assumed to be valid for the whole process. If at a given point in the negotiation people can feel that the situation has essentially changed, the planned minimum aspirations can be revised or can lose their importance for determining an acceptance. If oversized coalitions are formed some partners are no longer important for the validation of the contract: even if they withdrew, the new coalition would still win (for a theoretical motivation of oversized coalitions see Peleg 1980, 1981). Some people react to such a finding by verbal protest, but most people accept the unavoidable fate. Another possible and observed reaction on an oversized coalition and also in general is to redefine the situation as "having a social component". At some point at the bargaining process, this issue was introduced and accepted. As a consequence, some or all partners accept a "reasonable amount of social cost". They notice that they can gain in reputation and like to feel others' gratitude. Another occasion to revise aspirations is the emergence of the view that the situation has changed into a mere contest of who is a member. Sometimes such a revision can be seen as a panic reaction caused by a need to ensure membership at any price. To guarantee membership and to maximize payoff can be seen as two different competing goals. One can speculate about a trade–off between the probability of being member and the final aspiration. In the example case given below (Experiment 12), it can be assumed that P learned (probably falsely) that the only chance for him to come back was to offer a substantial bribe to S, lowering the own aspiration. In this case the final aspiration was not less than P's planned minimum min, but this case illustrates that there can be strategic revisions of the minimum.

The aspiration variables are strongly related to rôles and results. Some points of relation between aspirations and rôles are given in Table 3. The corresponding variances are below 0.01 except start for P (0.019) and for B (0.021) and min for S (0.017). Let us define the free share $F(S,x)$ for coalition S at payoff–vector x, usually named excess of S at x:

$$F(S,x) = 1-\Sigma(x_i; i \text{ member of S})$$

For a given agreement (S,x) let us define a vector mix=mix(S,x) with the following components: for a member i of coalition S agreeing on x take the corresponding share x_i and

for a nonmember take her/his minimum aspiration planned. Coalitions such that $F(S,mix)$ is positive would have been better off accepting the actual aspirations and adding some distribution of the surplus. A part of the surplus can be used to bribe one or more members of the last coalition.

If we consider means of start, mix of the result and min, we get the following free shares for the minimal winning coalitions:

Tab.4: free shares for aspiration means (in %)

	coalition					sum
	a	b	c	d	e	
start	06	−14	−13	−02	−18	−41
mix	19	20	21	21	19	101
min	48	36	36	43	39	200

Let us interpret the sum of the free shares at x over all minimal winning coalitions to be a measure of how easy it is to find new acceptable proposals at x. We have the following values for this measure: −0.41 at start, 1.01 at mix and finally 2.00 at min.

We can assume for the bargaining process that initially aspirations are too high to find acceptable proposals. Usually the planned minimum admits an agreement, but at an inefficient level (large free shares). Thus, subjects face the task of stopping negotiations before concessions are too large to be effective. They have to stop the process even if there are attractive bribing proposals. If their concession expectations were rational, the free share aggregate at min would be 0, and the stopping problem would be removed. The more their aspirations are and become realistic the nearer to zero the value of the free share aggregate at mix is to be expected. Only in one case was the maximal bribe rather small: 1.4% of the payoff. In all other cases for all other minimal winning coalitions there was a substantial potential surplus of more than 18%. This raises the question by which mechanisms those inefficient results became stable. A part of one possible answer assumes some foresight (that after being bribed to join a new proposal, that proposal too would be unstable; for a theoretical model see Albers in this volume). Another more sociopsychological explanation refers to preferences for special partners; moreover, some bargaining partners can be seen to be leading group–members that are not easily excluded, while some other individual can be isolated. A third complex of explanations refers to the fact that with time, subjects become tired of renegotiation and tired of any change, and the desire to stop becomes more influential than any possible gains from renegotiation.

The binary variable membership is positively correlated with both start (0.24, sign.l. 0.014) and min (0.16, sign.l. 0.099). Too low aspirations seem to be combined with high scores of withdrawal and with lack of initiative during the bargaining process. Such behaviour can favour non–membership. Considering only members of the final coalitions, we get a correlation of 0.57 for payoff and start and a value of 0.61 for payoff and min (both significant; $a<0.0001$).

Subjects are of different types with respect to their planned flexibility. Let us define the quotient of min and start as resistance. Then the following distribution (median = 0.56) was observed:

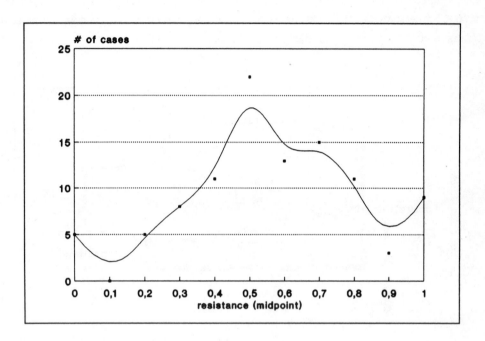

Figure 1: Resistance

In contrast to min and start, resistance seems to be uncorrelated to rôle and result. Only for the rôle B were slightly larger values observed (testing the difference by the Kolmogorov–Smirnow statistic yields DN=0.27 and alpha=0.25: far from significance). Correlations between payoffs and resistance are also far from significance (0.05, and considering members only –0.23, alpha=0.11). Comparing resistance of members and nonmembers results in an average rank of 50.76 (n=50) for members and an average rank of 52.21 (n=52) for nonmembers (even without test, a far from significant difference). To summarise: counter to expectations, the data shows no influence of the resistance on the results. Moreover, no influence of the rôle on resistance can be detected.

Simulation of aspiration processing

Let us design some simple rules to generate proposals and acceptances or rejections. Taking the aspiration data (start and min) of the questionnaires, we can hope to improve our understanding of the aspiration dynamics by comparing face–to–face data to simulation data. The decision for the rules to be used and the simulation program is discussed in Ostmann (1992b). Here I would like to give a short sketch of the program.

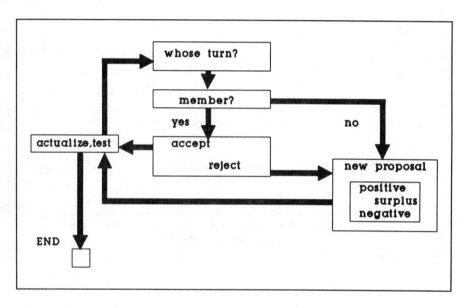

Figure 2: Sketch of the simulation program

The simulated bargaining process is sequenced by chance. If a name is drawn, it is asked if the person is a member of the coalition corresponding to the last proposal. If a member, the person is asked for acceptance. If the person's share is greater or equal to his or her actual aspiration, the person accepts; otherwise, s/he rejects. If the person is not a member or has rejected the proposal, s/he tries to make a new proposal. It is assumed that the aspirations of the others are known and accepted as given. In case of a non–negative surplus with respect to the given aspirations, the coalition with the largest surplus is taken (if there are more than one one of them is drawn by chance) and surplus is divided equally.

In case of a negative surplus, one's own aspiration is lowered just as needed, including a bribe of 1% for one partner of the last coalition. The new coalition is determined by this procedure and perhaps by chance if there is more than one candidate. The partner to get the bribe is drawn by chance out of those that are members of both the former and the new coalition. If the minimum aspiration excludes making the proposal constructed, no proposal is made. In the updating, the aspirations just revealed are set and the aspirations of the others are set to the maximum of shares in the proposals not yet rejected by one of their members. If there are enough contractors the process will end. In the interactive version of the program, one subject is confronted with five simulated partners.

A rational expectation solution for the simulation process

Before discussing results of the simulation and of the interactive simulation experiment, we shall consider the simulation process more closely. Note that the procedure can be used for any monotone superadditive simple game. Let n be the number of players and m be the number of minimal winning coalitions of the game. After it is randomly determined whose turn it is (equally likely with respect to those $n-1$ players who had not made the actual proposal) the one chosen can either agree to or reject the actual proposal. In case of rejection, s/he can make a new proposal. In case of agreement, s/he becomes a member of the built-up coalition for the actual proposal. If this coalition is winning, the process stops. In all other cases the next period starts by determining the next player in turn as above.

In Ostmann (1992b), it is argued that after some starting phase a boundedly rational agent would know the aspirations of the others and would make proposals that could be agreed upon by the members of the respective coalition. Moreover, if duration was long enough, the process would lead to a vector of aspiration levels that would allow for a subset of minimal winning coalitions that covered all players. In the following (as in Ostmann, 1991), let us assume a bit more: the aspirations should be rational expectations in the following sense. Actual aspirations $a=(a_1,...,a_n)$ are assumed to fulfill

$$| \Sigma(a_i; i \epsilon S) - 1 | < k$$

for some small k (but k suffiently large to enable the switch from any minimal winning coalition to any other minimal winning coalition by bribing) and all minimal winning coalitions a. According to these aspirations, every player can use every minimal winning coalition s/he is member of. Let us define the incidence matrix M of the game as the mxn–matrix, having as rows the characteristic vectors 1_S of the m minimal winning coalitions S. Then in the limit the above formula can be substituted by Ma=1. If we interpret a coalition S fulfilling $1_S a=1$ to be effective, then the above assumption can be verbally described as all minimal winning coalitions being effective.

Now let us assume we are dealing with an actual proposal x. What can we find out about the **period of life of a new proposal**? Let us assume the actual proposal refers to coalition S. Let s be the number of members of S. We would like to determine the probability p(S final | S actual) of S becoming final under the condition that the new proposal stays actual. Let $f_{s,k}$ be the probability of leaving the actual proposal, under the condition that k–asked players have already accepted. In Appendix C, the probability $g_S = f_{s,s-1}$ of leaving the actual proposal is determined to be equal to (n is the number of players)

$$f_{s,s-1} = 1 - \begin{bmatrix} n-1 \\ s-1 \end{bmatrix}^{-1} \tag{6}$$

In a second step, Appendix C deals with possible sequences of proposals. Since it can be assumed that an agent i choses all minimal winning coalitions s/he is in with equal probability, the probability w_S of chosing coalition S can be determined by evaluating the incidence matrix M of the game (see formulas (11) and (12) in the appendix). In the appendix it is shown that under certain conditions the process of proposals has a limit distribution q that is proportional to $(...,g_S(1-g_S),...)$, with $q=(q_S)$ and q_S being the probability of S being final (or of stopping the process at S).

Let $h_{n,s} = g_S(1-g_S)$; then by formula (6)

$$h_{n,s} = \left[1 - \begin{bmatrix} n-1 \\ s-1 \end{bmatrix}^{-1} \right] \begin{bmatrix} n-1 \\ s-1 \end{bmatrix}^{-1} \tag{16}$$

With the last formula, we can go back to our specific game and can treat it as an example.

In the game under consideration we have n=6 and

$q=(q_a,...,q_e)$ proportional to $(h_{6,2} , h_{6,3} , h_{6,3} , h_{6,3} , h_{6,4})$

We find (see Table 14 in the appendix)

$q = (16,9,9,9,9)/52$

and the vector of the expected memberships to be

$z = (34,34,27,18,18,18)/52$

Comparing results from experiments and simulation

In the following, the above–introduced expected memberships are labeled "theory". Observations based on the simulation are labeled "sim" and observations of the interactive experiment are reported as "is". Procedure and design of the experiment "is" is given in Appendix A.

In order to judge differences between results of face–to–face experiments, simulations and interactive simulations, we build expectations according to the above aspiration processing theory. The possible range is discussed in the appendix. Let us compare the data of the two plausible theoretical inner solutions x_1 and x_2 calculated in the appendix. Let us call Theory i (i=1,2) the expectations according to x_i. For $x_1 = (33, 33, 17, 6, 6, 6)$ all "small" players are weigthed equally. In case of Theory 2, the dependent follower F gets the same weight as the pair of the weak symmetric and we get $x_2 = (37, 28, 15, 5, 5, 10)$. The following table shows that simulation results (with empirical non–equilibrated starting aspirations) fall in that (restricted) range, whereas in the face–to–face setup one can observe some transfer to the weak symmetric. Data for setup "is" refers only to subjects and excludes payoffs/membership of simulated partners.

Tab.5: mean payoff (in%)

setup	rôle					#runs / #subjects
	S	P	B	W/Z	F	
sim	34	30	17	5	8	1300/–
is	32	31	16	5	8	1039/41
ftf	28	27	17	10	11	17/102
theory 1	33	33	17	6	6	
theory 2	37	28	15	5	10	

The values in Table 6 exhibit an astonishing fit between face–to–face experiments, simulations, interactive experiments and theory. From individual data we know that subjects' processing of bargaining events and their planning of (re)actions are far from being guided by such simple rules as assumed in the aspiration model. Moreover, communication,

Tab.6: membership (in%)

setup	rôle				
	S	P	B	W/Z	F
sim	68	64	55	29	36
is	64	61	51	26	36
ftf	71	71	53	38	35
theory	65	65	52	35	35

especially the sequence of proposals and reactions, is far from being a random sequencing of the type assumed in the simulation model. Nevertheless, in the aggregate, subjects behave as if guided by the simple boundedly rational procedures assumed in the model.

At the end of this section let us compare some free share (excess) measures for the different setups. Remember Table 4 and the aggregate measures for start, mix and min. For mix in the ftf–setup, the aggregate value was 1.01. The corresponding aggregate value for mix in the sim–setup is 0.76 and can be seen as indicating the simulation procedure being more effective than face–to–face bargaining. Counting minimal winning coalition with positive free share and those with negative free share reveals only some differences between face–to–face experiments and the simulation.

Tab.7: fractions of neg./pos. free shares for min–win coalitions (in % of all runs)

setup	sign	coalition				#runs
		a	b&c	d	e	
sim	–	0.2	17	8	15	1300
ftf	–	6	6	0	18	17
sim	+	69	68	72	73	1300
ftf	+	71	85	82	71	17

Coalitions with positive free share can be seen as attractive for renegotiation and those of negative free share as out of renegotiation. Conspicuously, the two–person coalition a is almost never out of renegotiation in the simulation setup. The face–to–face setup seems to favour renegotiation based on mix. In the simulation procedure every agent was bound to his or her proposal or agreement until his/her next turn, even if the aspiration had changed in the meantime. This fact may stabilize some proposals inefficient with respect to mix. The question is how the results of the face–to–face experiments could stabilize without such a procedure and with a larger incentive to renegotiate. The answer is open.

The following two tables refer to members' payoffs and are expected to yield values between start and mix.

Tab.8: members' payoffs in different setups compared to final aspirations in the simulation

setup	rôle					#runs / #subjects
	S	P	B	W/Z	F	
sim	50	46	32	18	22	1300/–
is	52	49	31	18	25	1039/41
ftf	46	45	28	15	19	17/102
final	54	47	35	22	25	1300/–

Tab.9: free shares for different setups (in%)

setup	coalitions			
	a	b/c	d	e
sim	4	0	0	− 4
final	− 1	−11	− 7	−16
is	− 1	− 1	− 5	−10
ftf	9	11	8	6

The positive values for the face–to–face setup are partially due to oversized coalitions (remember: 4 out of 17 coalitions were oversized). But it can also be asked if subjects in the face–to–face condition neglect profitable options. Indeed, with other data we can show that this is really the fact; and neglecting profitable options appears not only at the end of the bargaining but also during the whole process. In the next section we will study one exemplaric bargaining session in detail.

An example of a bargaining process

Let us come back to the single case of Experiment 12. Above, we discussed the intentions of the subjects. The bargaining session ended in coalition a with 70% of the payoff for S.

Tab.10: members' payoffs (in%)

setup	rôle						
	S	P	B	W	Z	D	
ex.12	70	30	–	–	–	–	
sim.12	60	47	27	–	14	25	(n=50)

A possible explanation for the contrast between power in game, simulation and intentions on the one side and the result on the other side can be given by social field data. The bargainer S is seen as leading, ascendent and friendly. In the context of this group S seems to be a leader–initiator and is accepted as such by the others. Bargainer B is seen as struggling for power, active, talkative and seeking influence. In the context of this group B seems to be a fighter–initiator, who is rejected or seen as a difficult partner. Whereas the social field may help in explaining and predicting coalitions, it cannot help in explaining the specific payoffs. So let us consider the aspiration data. Let **aspiration revealed** be the last accepted or proposed share. In the following table we find the means of final aspirations of the corresponding simulation runs, and the first and last aspiration revealed in Experiment 12.

Tab.11: aspirations revealed (in %)

aspiration	rôle						
	S	P	B	W	Z	D	
first	56	50	28	>16	20	23	
last	70	30	31	8	8	20	
final	59	48	27	23	15	27	(n=50)

If we calculate the free share for each minimal winning coalition, we find e to be the worst coalition according to the simulation and the best coalition at the end of the face–to–face bargaining. Bargaining stops at a highly unstable point.

Let us break the negotiation into phases (cp. Fisher, 1973). The revelation phase is followed by an emergence phase and a reinforcement phase. The emergence phase can be reentered. Negotiation acts can reveal aspiration directly by proposals or indirectly by accepting or rejecting. The revelation phase is ending if all negotiators have revealed some aspiration. The end of the emergence phase is defined by an agreement: all partners accept

Tab.12: proposals in Experiment 12

number	coalition proposed				
	a	b	bUc	c	d
1	71.5n,71.5				
2	... discussing alliances ... (see Appendix B)				
3		80,x,x			
4				86,29,29	
5		80,40,23n			
6				86,36,21	
7	80,x				
8		81,x,x			
9					70,40,33
10				90,33,20	
11				83,40,20	
12					70,45y,28y

aspirations revealed: 83,70,45,>23,20,28

13					70,40,33
14	x,73				
15					70,30,x
16	x,x				
17					*70,45y,28y
18				70,50,x	
19				72,51,20	
20			72,51,x,x		
21			x,40n,15,15		
22				*72,51,20	
23		x,x,18/19			
24		*77,56,10			
25			*70y,49,12,12y		
26	100,x				

aspirations revealed: 70,43,49,19,12,28

reinforcement phase
final aspirations: 100,43,45,12,12,28

with respect to some proposal. The reinforcement phase comes to an end if a corresponding decision or contract becomes valid or if some partner withdraws and the emergence phase is reentered.

After the proposal of S to split the profit 50/50 as intended, and its rejection by P as intended, both try to build up a strategic alliance with B − without success. During the revelation phase and the emergence phase different options are discussed but never a proposal based on coalition e. The proposal a with 70% for S sets an end to the emergence phase. In the reinforcement phase only old proposals (designated by *) are repeated. These proposals, one for each alternative coalition, seem to be seen as adequate solutions with respect to the corresponding coalition. Table 12 gives a list of all proposals.

In the above table the share of the proposer is underlined, and clear rejections or acceptances are denoted by n respectively by y. The "|" indicates that the corresponding proposal is "alive", that is, not countered by a member. Before discussing the possible intentions and rules determining the given process, let us consider the free shares for the aspirations revealed at three different states.

Tab.13: free shares for aspirations revealed (in%)

end of phase of	coalition				
	a	b	c	d	e
revelation	−10	−8	−5	0	2
emergence	30	5	12	23	41
reinforcement	0	−14	−14	27	48

Numbers in this table indicate that **subjects neglect profitable options**. By considering all the process data, it becomes evident that there are specific preferences for partners and coalitions that can be seen as cognitive and as emotional limits to rationality.

Let us use the above example list of proposals, acceptances and rejections for showing some general observations made by analysing the video–documents. According to the classical use of aspiration concepts, we expect a subject to accept if a proposal assigns to him or her a share larger than the revealed aspiration, and to reject if the share is smaller. Examples show that subjects sometimes accept and reject contrary to this rule. Possible strategic motives for this behaviour are, in case of rejections of a large share, the intention to remain an attractive partner, and in case of acceptance of a too–small share, the desire to come back into play.

With respect to proposals, the observations indicate a broad variety of different objectives like bribing, stabilizing, teaching or "poisoning". The intentions are not easy to identify, and our results give only a first impression and show the need for systematic research in this direction. Consider action 8 of Table 12: we can see a bribe for player S simultanuously with a teaching signal to player B that s/he never will get forty marks. With Action 12, player P seems to intend to stabilize the membership of player B by teaching F to accept a smaller share. Action 16 can be seen as stabilizing against a potential bribe. With action 24, player S teaches W (and indirectly P) that for leaving the cooperation with player Z a substantial bribe is demanded; one can speculate if the share for B is poisoned. Indeed (Action 25) player B does not take the larger share, possibly in assuming that afterwards s/he would no longer be accepted as a partner.

Contrary to the simulation program, the others' aspirations are not accepted under all circumstances. If a demand is not accepted but the corresponding bargainer is an intended partner, the usual goal is to lower the other's aspiration. In some cases subjects tried to substantially increase the aspiration of a specific bargainer, either to make the other dependent on the giver (no other one would pay so much) or to draw that person out of competition, to make him/her unattractive.

Footnote

1   Axel Ostmann, FR Psychologie, University of the Saar, Saarbrücken, Germany

References

Albers, W. (this volume). Ten rules of bargaining sequences.

Bales, R.F. (1950). *Interaction Process Analysis: a Method for the Study of Small Groups.*   Reading, Mass.: Addison–Wesley.

Bales, R.F. (1970). *Personality and Interpersonal Behavior.* New York: Holt, Rinehart and Winston.

Bales, R.F. (1982). *SYMLOG: Ein System für die mehrstufige Beobachtung von Gruppen.* Stuttgart: Klett.

Berresheim, A. (1990). Ein neuer Ansatz zur Erforschung experimenteller 6–Personen–Spiele. Überlegungen zur experimentellen Umsetzung, Durchführung und Auswertung eines komplexen einfachen Spieles. *Arbeiten der FR Psychologie, 148*, Universität des Saarlandes, Saarbrücken.

Berresheim, A., **Ostmann**, A. & **Schmitt**, H. (1991). Verhandeln als sozialer Prozeß – eine Verhaltenstheorie für Verhandlungen. *Arbeiten der FR Psychologie, 153*, Universität des Saarlandes, Saarbrücken.

Chertkoff, J.M. & **Esser**, J.K. (1976). A Review of Experiments in Explicit Bargaining, *J.Experim.Soc.Psy., 12*, 464–86.

Fisher, B.A. (1973). Decision Emergence: Phases in Group Decision–Making. In F.E. Jandt (Ed.), *Conflict Resolution Through Communication*. New York: Harper & Row.

Kahan, J.P. & **Rapoport**, A. (1984). *Theories of Coalition Formation*. Hillsdale: Lawrence Erlbaum.

Kravitz, D.A. (1987). Size of smallest coalition as a source of power in coalition bargaining. *European Journal of Social Psychology, 17*, 1–21.

Komorita, S.S. (1984). Coalition Bargaining, in: L.Berkowitz (ed.): *Advances in Experimental Social Psychology, Vol.18* (pp. 184–245). New York: Academic Press.

McClintock, C.G., **Kramer**, R.M. & **Keil**, L.J. (1984). Equity and Social Exchange in Human Relationships. *Advances in Experimental Social Psychology, 17*, 183–228.

Orlik, P. (1987). Ein semantischer Atlas zur Kodierung alltagssprachlicher Verhaltensbeschreibungen nach dem SYMLOG–Raummodell. *International Journal of Small Group Research, 3*, 88–111.

Ostmann, A. (1990a). Fusionen: Ein einfaches Spiel als Beispiel sowie eine neue Charakterisierung des Banzhafwertes. *IMW Working Paper, 184*, Universität Bielefeld.

Ostmann, A. (1990b). On rationality issues in the bargaining context. *JITE/Zeitschrift für die gesamte Staatswissenschaft, 146*, 673–683.

Ostmann, A. (1991). Aspiration processing and coalition forming by chance. Research Note, FR Psychologie, University of the Saar, Saarbrücken.

Ostmann, A. (1992a). On the relation between formal conflict structure and the social field. *Small Group Research, 23*, 26–48

Ostmann, A. (1992b). The interaction of aspiration levels and the social field in experimental bargaining. *Journal of Economic Psychology, 13*, 233–61.

Ostmann, A. (1992c). Anpassung und Einflußnahme – ein Beitrag aus der

Verhandlungsforschung. *Arbeiten der FR Psychologie, 166*, University of the Saar, Saarbrücken.

Ostmann, A. & **Schmitt**, H. (1990). Einfache Spiele – Theoretische Grundlagen, Kompositionen, Programme. *IMW Working Paper, 196*, Universität Bielefeld.

Peleg, B. (1980). A theory of coalition formation in committees. *Journal of Mathematical Economics, 7*, 115–34.

Peleg, B. (1981). Coalition formation in simple games with dominant players. *International Journal of Game Theory, 10*, 11–33.

Selten, R. (1972). Equal Share Analysis of Characteristic Function Experiments. In H.Sauermann (Ed.), *Beiträge zur experimentellen Wirtschaftsforschung III*. Tübingen: Mohr.

Selten, R. & **Schuster**, K.G. (1968). Psychological Variables and Coalition–Forming Behavior. In K.Borch & J.Mossin (Eds.), *Risk and uncertainty* (pp. 221–240). London: Macmillan.

Selten, R. & **Schuster**, K.G. (1970). Psychologische Faktoren bei Koalitionsverhandlungen. In H.Sauermann (Ed.), *Beiträge zur experimentellen Wirtschaftsforschung, vol.2*, Tübingen: Mohr.

Shubik, M. (1982). *Game Theory in the Social Sciences*. Cambridge, Mass.: MIT Press.

Appendix A: The experiment "is"

Subjects were 41 students of the University of the Saar at Saarbrücken. In one case the student ran out of time and the corresponding session was terminated. The data of this student remained included – it made no obvious difference to other students beside the slow planning and reaction. All sessions were single–subject sessions. A session had an approximate length of two hours. A session consisted of 26 bargaining tasks based on the same game, namely on that one reported in Section Two. Sessions were computerized. For a session, the subject's rôle was first randomly drawn (equal probability for each player). With that rôle, the interactive version of the bargaining procedure described in Section 5 was carried out. Aspiration parameters for the simulated partners were taken from the experimental data of the two series of experiments mentioned in this paper. The session number equals the number of the experiment: 1–13 for the first series, 13–26 for the second.

Subjects were instructed how to use the computer, about the bargaining task, the flow of events (whose turn it was, reaction, proposal, final agreement), about incentives for them and about the experimenters' intention to learn how they would react to those "bargaining partners" that were programmed according to our experience of real face–to–face bargaining sessions. The subjects were motivated by a payment according to the total of the shares they had gained by the agreements. The range of the resulting payments was [17.80, 66.30] Deutsche Marks, mean payment was DM 42.60. Besides the monetary incentive, the task characteristic and presentation was interesting and inviting for most subjects, according to what they reported.

Appendix B: A remark on strategic alliances

In the example negotiation, three strategic alliances were discussed (SB, PB and WZ) but rejected. All these alliances would have been profitable for the mergers if we apply the theory of Section 6.

a. Merging SB leads to the weighted majority game (7; 5 ,2 ,2 , 2 ,1). According to the aspiration rational expectations theory, the mergers will be included with probability 0.75. Staying alone, their probabilities would be 0.65 respectively 0.52. The intended coalition is b, SB can be seen as a precoalition.

b. Merging PB leads to the veto–game (3; 2, 1, 1, 0, 0). Mergers get veto–power. This means sure membership instead of probabilities of 0.65 or 0.52, respectively. Resulting coalition would have been coalition d.

c. Merging WZ leads to the game uo2 (see Ostmann, 1990), a game with a more complicated structure. According to the aspiration equilibrium, the mergers will be included with probability 0.43. Staying alone would yield a value of 0.35. The correspondingly favoured coalition is e.

Appendix C: A random process of coalition forming

As a first step, let us determine the **period of life of an actual proposal**. Let us assume the actual proposal refers to coalition S. Let s be the number of members of S. We would like to determine the probability

$p(S \text{ final} \mid S \text{ actual})$

of S becoming final under the condition that the actual proposal stays actual. Let $f_{s,k}$ be the probability of leaving the actual proposal, under the condition that k–asked players have already accepted. If k of the n–1 members asked have not yet accepted, there is a chance of $(n-s)/(n-1)$ of going directly out because of drawing a non–member, a chance of $(s-k-1)/(n-1)$ of staying in state k and a chance of $k/(n-1)$ of picking up a new member to agree.

Then:

$$f_{s,k} = \frac{n-s}{n-1} \sum_{l=0}^{\infty} \left[\frac{s-k-1}{n-1} \right]^l + \frac{k}{n-1} f_{s,k-1} \sum_{l=0}^{\infty} \left[\frac{s-k-1}{n-1} \right]^l \tag{1}$$

or

$$f_{s,k} = \frac{n-s}{n-s+k} + \frac{k}{n-s+k} f_{s,k-1} \tag{2}$$

Observe $f_{s,0}=0$ and $f_{s,1} = (n-s)/(n-s+1)$. By substitution we find

$$f_{s,s-1} = \sum_{k=1}^{s-1} \frac{(n-s)(s-1)!(n-s+k-1)!}{k!(n-1)!} \tag{3}$$

or

$$f_{s,s-1} = \frac{(s-1)!}{(n-1)!} (n-s) (n-s-1)! \sum_{k=1}^{s-1} \frac{(n-s-1+k)!}{(n-s-1)!k!} \tag{4}$$

and finally

$$f_{s,s-1} = \left[\frac{n-1}{s-1} \right]^{-1} \sum_{k=1}^{s-1} \left[\frac{n-s-1+k}{k} \right] \tag{5}$$

By induction we can show

$$f_{s,s-1} = 1 - \left[\frac{n-1}{s-1} \right]^{-1} \tag{6}$$

or

$$\sum_{k=1}^{s-1} \left[\frac{n-s-1+k}{k} \right] = \left[\frac{n-1}{s-1} \right] - 1 \tag{7}$$

For s=2 both sides of Formula (7) are equal to n–2.

Assume the formula is proven for s. It is to show that

$$\sum_{k=1}^{s} \begin{bmatrix} n-s-2+k \\ k \end{bmatrix} = \begin{bmatrix} n-1 \\ s \end{bmatrix} - 1 \tag{8}$$

The left hand side is equal to

$$\sum_{k=1}^{s-1} \begin{bmatrix} n-s-2+k \\ k \end{bmatrix} + \begin{bmatrix} n-2 \\ s \end{bmatrix} \tag{9}$$

and by means of formula (7)

$$\begin{bmatrix} (n-1)-1 \\ s-1 \end{bmatrix} + \begin{bmatrix} n-2 \\ s \end{bmatrix} - 1 \tag{10}$$

Since this expression in equal to the right hand side of (8), Formula (7) is proven.

In a second step, we shall deal with a sequence of proposals. Let g_S be the probability p(continue | S chosen) and w_S = p(S chosen). Remember $g_S = f_{s,s-1}$ by definition and

$$w_S = \Sigma \ p(\text{player i in turn}) \ p(\text{i choses S | i in turn}) \tag{11}$$

or by using the incidence matrix (respectively an everybody–in matrix M, see Ostmann 1992b) of the game (assume M has m rows)

$$w = (w_S) = (1{:}M1_n)M^T{}_m \tag{12}$$

with 1_k being the vector $(1,1,...,1)$ with k components, and : taken componentwise.

Now consider the following 2m states: m **intermediate states of proposed coalitions** and m **attracting states of coalitions that became final** (i.e. all partners had agreed to the respective proposal).

Let A be the matrix with rows $g_S w$, D=diag(1_m–g) and E a unit matrix.
The process is governed by the following transition matrix

$$Q = \begin{bmatrix} A & D \\ 0 & E \end{bmatrix} \tag{13}$$

The matrix is weakly regular and so the limiting probabilities exist and the limit distribution for the starting value x is given by xQ^{∞}. Since $\lim A^{\nu} = 0$ it is enough to determine $(\Sigma A^{\nu})D$. We have

$$Q^{\infty} = \begin{bmatrix} 0 & (\Sigma A^{\nu}) D \\ 0 & E \end{bmatrix} \tag{14}$$

Let $gw = \Sigma g_S w_S$. *Notice* $xA = (...w_T \Sigma x_S g_S, \ )_T$ and xA is proportional to w. The process exhibits stationary proposals. Moreover, since $A^2 = (gw)A$, we get ΣA^{ν}) $I - (1-gw)^{-1}A$.

Define $q=(q_S)$ by $q_S = p(\text{coalition S will become final})$ and

$\quad z=(z_i)$ by $z_i = p(\text{player i is a member of the final coalition})$.

Because of the stationary proposals let us start the process with w. Then, the resulting final distribution q is proportional to $(\ldots w_S(1-g_S), \ldots)$. According to Formula (12) every player is assumed to be equally likely in proposing next. If we like to replace this assumption by asymmetric probabilities that do not depend on the actually discussed proposal, it may be of failure. Under this assumption we finally get:

$\quad$ q proportional to $(\ldots , g_S(1-g_S) , \ldots)$ $\hfill$ (15)

Let $h_{n,s} = g_S(1-g_S)$; then by Formula (6)

$$h_{n,s} = \left[1 - \begin{bmatrix} n-1 \\ s-1 \end{bmatrix}^{-1} \right] \begin{bmatrix} n-1 \\ s-1 \end{bmatrix}^{-1} \qquad (16)$$

With the last formula we can go back to our specific game and can treat it as an example. Let us start by calculating the numbers $h_{n,s}$. The following table gives those numbers for $n \leq 11$ multiplied by ten thousand:

Tab.14: Weights $h_{n,s}$ for coalitions with s members

n	s				
	2	3	4	5	6
	n–1	n–2	n–3	n–4	n–5
3	2500				
4	2222				
5	1875	1389			
6	1600	900			
7	1389	622	475		
8	1224	454	278		
9	1094	344	175	141	
10	988	270	118	79	
11	900	217	83	47	40

The incidence matrix of the game we are dealing with (see Table 1) is given by

$$M = \begin{bmatrix} 1 & 1 & 0 & 0 & 0 & 0 \\ 1 & 0 & 1 & 1 & 0 & 0 \\ 1 & 0 & 1 & 0 & 1 & 0 \\ 0 & 1 & 1 & 0 & 0 & 1 \\ 0 & 1 & 0 & 1 & 1 & 1 \end{bmatrix}$$

The vector q is proportional to $(h_{6,2} , h_{6,3} , h_{6,3} , h_{6,3} , h_{6,4})$. We find

$\quad q = (16,9,9,9,9)/52$

and the **vector of the expected memberships** to be

$$z = (34,34,27,18,18,18)/52$$

If we consider the range of solutions of $Mx=1$ that are compatible with the desirability relation, i.e. the interval $[(2,3,2,1,1,0)/5 , (5,3,2,1,1,3)/8]$, we get **expected payoffs** in the interval between

$$x_0 = (26,40,21,7,7,0) \text{ and } x_3 = (41,25,13,4,4,13)$$

In case all "small" players are weighted equally, the expected payoffs are

$$x_1 = (33,33,17,6,6,6)$$

In case the dependent follower F gets the same weight as the pair of the weak symmetric, we get

$$x_2 = (37,28,15,5,5,10)$$

Resistance against mass immigration
- An evolutionary explanation -

Werner Güth[1] and Klaus Ritzberger[2]

Abstract

In Europe we face very different living standards in different countries. In former times such discrepancies did not induce mass migration since mobility was restricted, especially between Eastern and Western European countries. But now the relatively richer countries are confronted with mass immigration and also strong resistance against it. We will show that resistance against mass immigration can be explained as being genetically determined. Specifically, we will analyse a very simple game model of immigration with an undetermined preference parameter deciding whether an incumbent engages into opposition against mass immigration or not. It is shown that preference for fighting against mass immigration is the only evolutionarily stable strategy for all possible parameter constellations. In our view this has important political implications regardless whether one wants to argue for a more liberal immigration law or against it.

Introduction

Drastic discrepancies in the living standard of different countries usually induce mass migration if international mobility is not restricted. Europe presently is facing enormous discrepancies in the living conditions of various countries, especially between Eastern and Western European countries. In former times the better living conditions in Western European countries did not induce mass immigration from East to West, since due to the Iron Curtain mobility between East and West Europe was practically non-existing. Fortunately this restriction of international mobility has disappeared. But, of course, one also has to expect mass migration from East to West Europe.

Although nearly all European countries and most of their citizens were very positive and enthusiastic about the dramatic political changes in the formerly communist countries, they often try to limit mass migration. Depending on the country and the political party the justifications for restricting mass immigration vary. In our view, there is, however, a basic and general reason, namely the strong resistance against mass immigration in most of the countries facing it.

Now, resistance against invaders is a typical phenomenon in the animal kingdom where behavior is genetically determined. This fact implies that, at least in the animal kingdom, resistance against invaders seems to provide a greater reproductive success than a more liberal attitude to immigration. Here reproductive success is measured by the expected number of offspring which decide about the future composition of the population. At least in the early stages in the development of mankind, which still determines our present genotype to a large extent, the situation must have been similar: Human genotypes, programmed to fight against invaders, earn a higher reproductive success than the more liberal ones. The main purpose of our paper is to provide a formal model and a methodology to analyse this conjecture more rigorously.

The model will be a simple game model which can be solved by a rather weak rationality requirement, namely repeated elimination of dominated strategies. Depending on the exogeneous parameters there are three generic solutions, called 'the liberal paradise', 'preventive resistance', and 'what we are afraid of'.

The basic methodology is the one of evolutionary stability. Unlike in evolutionary biology, where genotypes directly determine behavior, we rely on a genetically encoded preference parameter which, together with living conditions, decides whether a given behavior is rational or not [see Güth and Yaari, 1992, as well as Güth, 1990, for similar studies]. Thus we can compute the solution for all possible constellation of preference parameters and derive the living conditions which this solution implies. Assuming that reproductive success depends on the living conditions we then can define an evolutionary game the strategies of which, or genotypes, are the possible preference parameters and the payoff function of which measures the reproductive success of the interacting genotypes.

To solve the evolutionary game we apply the concept of evolutionarily stable strategies [Maynard Smith and Price, 1973]. Although this concept is not always in line with dynamic stability of evolutionary processes, our result is unusually strong: The only evolutionarily stable strategy is strictly dominant and, therefore, the only optimal genotype irrespective of how the population is composed. This holds both under the requirement of an evolutionary stable strategy and under the evolutionary dynamics which we will also analyse.

According to our analysis 'the liberal paradise' can only be an episode due to short lived mutants or the absence of migration. Thus one has to expect either 'preventive resistance' or 'what we are afraid of'. We discuss the parameters which influence this result and how they can be influenced politically. A genetically determined preference parameter does not exclude that phenotypical preferences can be influenced by education, personal experiences, and the political climate. To compensate the genetical predisposition one has, however, to exert a continuous opposing influence at least as long as the country is faced with mass migration, since every new generation might oppose to mass migration without this compensating influen ce.

The plan of the paper is as follows: Section II states the simple underlying game model to which in Section III the concept of an evolutionary stable strategy is applied. Section IV considers a fairly general class of dynamic evolutionary processes, reinforcing the results from Section III. Section IV draws conclusions.

The game model

We will model mass migration as an encounter of two individuals, one immigrant and one incumbent, who should be viewed as being members of large populations. The game model is very simple so that it can be solved by very basic, i.e. also non-controversial rationality requirements. Since the model is asymmetric, it will be symmetrised in Section III before we apply the concept of evolutionarily stable strategies.

Let player 1 be the potential immigrant of player 2's, the incumbent's, country or territory. The simple game is graphically illustrated in Figure II.1.

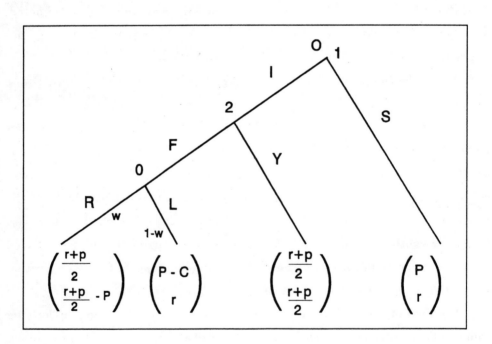

Figure II.1

A play starts at the origine $\mathcal{O}$ (the top decision node) with player 1's choice between I and S where I stands for immigration and S for staying. After S

the game ends immediately since players 1 and 2 do not meet. If, however, 1 enters 2's territory, player 2 can decide whether to engage into opposition against immigration (the move F) or not (the move Y of player 2). In case of Y the game ends with both players living on 2's territory. If 2 has engaged into opposition against immigration, i.e. move F by player 2, it is decided by a chance move (of the chance player 0) whether 1 can become a final resident of 2's territory (the move R with probability w) or not (the move L with the positive complementary portability $1 - w$).

The payoff vectors attached to the terminal nodes, i.e. the bottom nodes in Figure II.1, give the payoff of player 1 above and of player 2 below. Thus 1's choice of S yields the living standard p for player 1 and r for player 2, where we assume $r > p \geq 0$. The play (I, Y) yields the same average living standard $(r + p)/2$ for both players who are living in the same territory. The underlying assumption is, of course, that 2 produces r and 1 only p, regardless of whether he stays in his home country or migrates into 2's territory, and that individuals living in the same country have to share their resources equally.

In case of the play (I, F, L) player 1 finally returns to his home country. Returning after an unsuccessful attempt to migrate may impose a cost $C \geq 0$ on player 1. This cost C may or may not be related to player 1's living conditions. In fact, to determine evolutionarily stable strategies, we will treat C as deductions from the living standard of player 1, while in the dynamic analysis we will also allow for the possibility that C is unrelated to living conditions. Thus after (I, F, L) player 1's resulting living conditions are $p - C$ (or p for the dynamic analysis), while player 2 will enjoy r. Since after the play (I, F, R) player 1 becomes a final resident of 2's territory, he receives the same living standard $(r + p)/2$ as after (I, Y). For player 2 the living standard is also $(r+p)/2$ of which we substract P. Again this cost P may or may not bear directly on living conditions of player 2. For the analysis of evolutionarily stable strategies we will assume that the preference parameter P is purely unrelated to the living standard of player 2 (and, therefore, also to the reproductive success of player 2). For the evolutionary dynamics we will generalize this setup and allow for all possible impacts of P on living conditions. The interpretation of a positive parameter P is obviously that the incumbent hates to live together with somebody, whom he could not make leave. Similarly, a negative parameter P would mean that 2 enjoys 1's company after his unsuccessful attempt to get him out. Here we do not impose any assumption for the parameter P, but try to derive its value in Section III by searching for the evolutionarily stable strategy P [see Güth and Yaari, 1990, and Güth, 1990, who also rely on the idea of genetica lly determined preference parameters], i.e. the parameter P is determined endogeneously, whereas the other parameters p, r, and $w \in (0, 1)$ are exogeneously given. For the evolutionarily stable strategies we will also treat C as exogeneous, while for the evolutionary dynamics C is endogeneous. Before starting our evolutionary analysis we want to derive the optimal behavior for both players for all generic parameter constellations (p, r, C, w, P), $r > p \geq 0$, $C \geq 0$, $1 > w > 0$.

Since the game of Figure II.1 is one with perfect information (the deciding player always knows all previous moves), the solution can be determined by repeated elimination of dominated strategies. Clearly, F is better than Y for player 2, if

$$(II.1) \qquad \frac{(1-w)(r-p)}{2w} > P$$

and Y is better than F if inequality (II.1) is reversed. In case of (II.1) player 1's move I implies an expectation of

$$(II.2) \qquad w\frac{r+p}{2}+(1-w)(p-C)$$

for player 1 which has to be compared with the living standard p implied by 1's choice of S. Thus I is better than S for player 1 if

$$(II.3) \qquad w\frac{(r-p)}{2(1-w)} > C$$

whereas the opposite is true for the reversed inequality.

If inequality (II.1) is reversed, the analogous condition that I is better than S is $r > p$ and therefore always satisfied.

The non-generic parameter constellations (p, r, C, w, P) are those with equality in (II.1) or (II.3). These highly specific constellations are not relevant for our evolutionary analysis and can therefore be neglected.

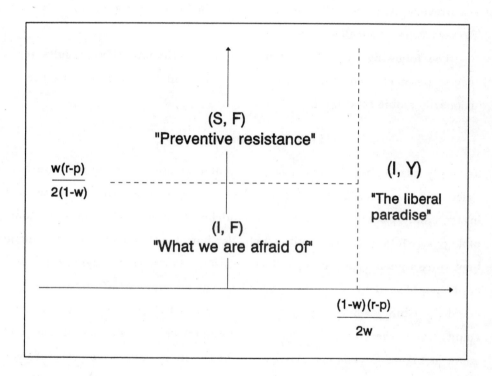

Figure II.2

In Figure II.2 we give a graphical illustration of the three possible generic solutions (I, F), (S, F), and (I, Y) in the (P, C)-plane. Wherever the opposite of inequality (II.1) is true, we are in the region (I, Y), called 'The liberal paradise' since 1 immigrates and 2 does not resist against 1's immigration.

For inequality (II.1) the result depends on whether (II.3) is satisfied or not. If (II.1) and (II.3) are true, we are in the region (I, F) where 1 migrates although he knows 2 will try to keep him out. Because of this unfortunate struggle between the incumbent and the invader we refer to region (I, F) as to 'What we are afraid of'.

The final region (S, F) results from (II.1) and the reverse of inequality (II.3). Here 2 is determined to fight against immigration and induces thereby player 1 to abstain from immigration, i.e. player 2's willingness to fight against immigration is a preventive threat. This explains why the solution region (S, F) is named 'Preventive resistance'.

The following evolutionary analysis will anticipate these results for all generic parameter constellations (p, r, C, w, P) and try to determine the evolutionarily stable strategy P.

Evolutionarily stable strategy

To apply the concept of evolutionarily stable strategies [Maynard Smith and Price, 1973, see also Selten, 1983, and van Damme, 1987] the encounter of an invader and an incumbent has to be modelled symmetrically. In evolutionary biology a genotype has to specify a behavior both for the invader and the incumbent since a phenotype can be in both positions. Furthermore, symmetry can be easily established by introducing an initial chance move which determines with equal probability whether player 1 or player 2 is living in the relatively richer country and, therefore, threatened by immigration of the other pl ayer. The game in Figure III.1 is symmetric, also in the more restrictive sense of evolutionary game theory [Selten, 1983], since every move in the subgame after the left top chance move with probability 1/2 can be identified with a move in the subgame after the right top chance move with probability 1/2. In Figure III.1 this identification is indicated by assigning the same symbol I, S, F, Y, R, or L to both moves.

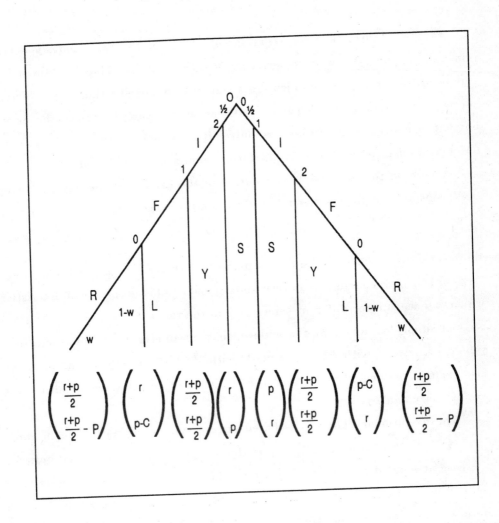

Figure III.1

Similar to Güth and Yaari [1990] and Güth [1990] we assume genotypes which are genetically determined preference parameters. Phenotypes behave rationally according to their preference parameters. This allows us to compute for any possible encounter the resulting payoffs and thereby the reproductive success. We then determine endogeneously the genetically determined preferences by using the concept of evolutionarily stable strategies. The results would, however, also go through, if genetically determined *behavior* would be assumed.

Assume an arbitrary constellation (p, r, C, w) of the exogeneously determined parameters. We want to derive for (p, r, C, w) and all values of P the living conditions for both players which are assumed to determine their reproductive success. The underlying idea is that at least in the early stages in the development of mankind the available resources determined decisively the expected number of offspring and thereby the future composition of the population.

According to Figure II.2 the solution of the game and thereby the living conditions of both players depend on P only in the sense that for P greater than

$$(III.1) \qquad\qquad P^* = \frac{(1 - w)(r - p)}{2 w}$$

the solution is (I, Y), i.e. 'the liberal paradise', whereas for $P < P^*$ it is either (S, F) or (I, F). Of course, P may very well depend on phenotypical characteristics which can account for different values of P in the range $P > P^*$ or $P < P^*$. Here we will simply assume that the endogeneous parameter P can take only two values, namely P^+ with $P^+ > P^*$ and P^- with $P^- < P^*$. By this assumption we also exclude the degenerate case $P = P^*$ which is of no relevance at all for the evolutionary analysis.

The evolutionary analysis is based on the symmetric normal form game $G = (\{P^+, P^-\}; H)$, where $\{P^+, P^-\}$ is the set of strategies or genotypes; for the case at hand it is the set of possible values of the endogeneous preference parameter P. Both players 1 and 2 have the same strategy set since they are both members of the same species. H is the payoff function which determines the reproductive success of both players for all possible strategy combinations (P_1, P_2) with $P_i \in \{P^+, P^-\}$ for $i = 1, 2$. Since the game is symmetric, it is sufficient to specify the reproductive success of player 1 which will be denoted by $H(P_1, P_2)$. For player 2 the reproductive success from the strategy combination (P_1, P_2) is given by $H(P_2, P_1)$.

A strategy $P \in \{P^+, P^-\}$ is called *evolutionarily stable* [Maynard Smith and Price, 1973], if it satisfies the following two conditions:

(i) $$H(P, P) \qquad \geq \qquad H(P_1, P), \quad \forall P_1 \in \{P^+, P^-\}$$

$(ii) \forall P_1 \in \{P^+, P^-\} \setminus \{P\}$ satisfying $H(P, P) = H(P_1, P) \; H(P, P_1) > H(P_1, P_1).$

Condition (i) requires that the genotype P must be optimal in a monomorphic population consisting only of P-genotypes. In other words: In a P-monomorphic population no other genotype can have more offspring than P. Observe that condition (i) does not rule out the case $H(P, P) = H(P_1, P)$ for some alternative strategy P_1. In such a case P must be a better reply against P_1 than P_1 itself, i.e. in a population containing only P_1-genotypes or P_1- and P-genotypes the strategy P has a greater reproductive success than P_1.

The satic concept of evolutionarily stable strategies may not always coincide with dynamic stability of evolutionary processes [see: Weissing, 1991, for a discussion]. For the simple case at hand this, however, cannot occur since the only evolutionarily stable strategy P is *strictly dominant*, i.e. P earns a higher reproductive success than the other strategy for all values of P_2. In this section, where we focus on P; the return-fare of an invader, C, will be deducted from living conditions, while P will be taken to be a pure preference parameter, entirely unrelated to living conditions.

To determine the payoff function H of G for the case at hand we distinguish two cases, namely whether (II.3) is satisfied or whether the converse condition

$(III.2)$
$$\frac{w(r - p)}{2(1 - w)} < C$$

is true.

a. The case (II.3) If the incumbent's strategy is P^+, the solution is (I, Y) according to Figure II.2, i.e. both players receive the reproductive success $(r + p)/2$. For the incumbent's strategy P^-, the solution is (I, F) which yields the reproductive success

$(III.3)$
$$(1-w)(p-C)+w\frac{r+p}{2}$$

for the invader and

$(III.4)$
$$(1-w)r+w\frac{r+p}{2}$$

for the incumbent, since we are in case (**II.3**) and since the payoff parameter P is assumed unrelated to the living conditions and the reproductive success of the incumbent. Our results are summarized by Table III.1 which determines the reproductive success $H(P_1, P_2)$ of player 1 for all four possible strategy combinations (P_1, P_2). Since both players have equal chances for becoming the incumbent, $H(P_1, P_2)$ is determined with probability 1/2 both by P_1 and P_2.

Table III.1

$$P_2$$

		P^+	P^-
P_1	P^+	$\dfrac{r + p}{2}$	$(1 + w)\dfrac{r + p}{4} + (1 - w)\dfrac{p - c}{2}$
	P^-	$(1 + w)\dfrac{r + p}{4} + (1-w)\dfrac{r}{2}$	$(1 - w)\dfrac{r + p - c}{2} + w\dfrac{r + p}{2}$

Due to $1 > w$ and $r > p$ the following two inequalities are true:

(*III.5*)
$$\frac{r+p}{2} < (1+w)\frac{r+p}{4}+(1-w)\frac{r}{2}$$

and

(*III.6*)
$$(1+w)\frac{r+p}{4}+(1-w)\frac{p-C}{2} < (1-w)\frac{r+p-C}{2}+w\frac{r+p}{0}2.$$

Conditions (**III.5**) and (**III.6**) imply that P^- is strictly dominant. Since there can be no alternative best reply in addition to P^-, this proves:

Lemma III.1: If the constellation (p, r, C, w) of exogeneous parameter satisfies condition (II.3), then the strategy P^- is strictly dominant and therefore the only evolutionarily stable strategy of game G.

b. The case (III.2): The only difference results for the incumbent's strategy P^- which implies the solution (S, F) according to Figure II.2. The reproductive sucess implied by (S, F) is r for the incumbent and p for the potential invader. The reproductive sucess for all four possible strategy constellations $(P_1. P_2)$ in game G is illustrated in Table III.2, similarly to Table III.1 for the previous case.

Table III.2

P_2

		p^+	p^-
P_1	p^+	$\dfrac{r + p}{2}$	$\dfrac{r + p}{4} + \dfrac{p}{2}$
	p^-	$\dfrac{r + p}{4} + \dfrac{p}{2}$	$\dfrac{r + p}{2}$

Clearly, due to $r > p$ the strategy P^- is strictly dominant which proves:

Lemma III.2: If the constellation (p, r, C, w) of exogenous parameters satisfies condition (III.2), then the strategy P^- is dominant and, therefore, the only evolutionarily stable strategy of the game G.

Combining the two Lemmas yields:

Theorem 1: In the evolutionary game $G = (\{P^+, P^-\}, H)$, the payoff function H of which is given in Table III.1 for (II.3), respectively in Table III.2 for (III.2), the strategy

P⁻ is the only evolutionarily stable strategy for all constellations (r, p, C, w) of exogenous parameters satisfying $r > p$ and $1 > w$.

The assumption $r > p$ is no restriction at all, since this is the only reason for mass migration within the limited scope of our model. Thus according to the Theorem above we only rule out the highly specific borderline case $w = 1$ meaning that the incumbent cannot make the invader leave at all. Since for $w = 1$ immigration will always imply the same reproductive success $(r + p)/2$ for both players, there can be no evolutionary drive for the endogenous paramter P in the limiting case $w = 1$. Or in other words: For $w = 1$ resistance against mass immigration does not make sense at all. Thus the two conditions, $r > p$ and $1 > w$, are implied by our research problem and no real restrictions to our results. In this sense the Theorem above can be rephrased by saying that $P⁻$ is the only evolutionarily stable strategy regardless of how the exogenous game parameters p, r, C, and w are specified.

Our results assume, of course, that all strategically relevant aspects of the conflict between the incumbent and the invader are captured by our basic game model in Figure IIi: We do not wish to claim that this is an entirely realistic assumption. However, a similar anlysis can be performed for other game models of conflicts between an incumbent and an invader.

Even, if one believes that Figure II.1. is an adequate representation of the conflict, we readily admit that Theorem 1 is only a special result. First of all only the preference parameter P is subjected to genetical evolution. Clearly, the parameter C which measures, how an unsuccessful invader suffers, could also be considered as being subject to genetical evolution. For the evolutionary game of Figure III.1 one could rely on the mutant space (P, C) which contains all possible values of the incumbent's preference parameter P and the invader's cost parameter C.

Furthermore, the assumption that P is entirely unrelated to reproductive success is by no means necessary for our approach. One could easily generalise the analysis by allowing that a certain proportion of P is related to reproductive success, whereas the remaining part is not. Similarly, the more general case of mutants (P, C), described above, can be analysed by requiring that only a certain proportion of P and a possibly different proportion of C are unrelated to reproductive success, where both proportions can range from 0 to 1.

Another restriction of Theorem 1 is that both interacting individuals are certain about the incentive structure of their respective opponent. In a genetically mixed population this implicitely assumes that the opponent's type can be recognized, once the opponent is faced. This need not always be true, since a certain P-type might be able to imitate another P-type, if this is profitable. This shows that the above results implicitely rely on perfect signalling of the respective types. Because of our basic game model it is, however, only necessary that the potential invader is aware of the incumbent's type. The incumbent does not have to know the invader's type, nor, since P^- is strictly dominant, has anyone to know the population composition.

Again, we readily admit that perfect signalling may be highly unrealistic. However, the assumption of perfect signalling is by no means necessary for our fundamental approach. It could easily be generalised to situations, where none of the two encountering individuals is certain about the opponent's type. If signalling is impossible, it seems natural to assume that both individuals know by experience only the distribution of the population, but not the specific type of their actual encounter. In such a scenario the beliefs concerning the other's type are determined by the frequencies of types in the present population.

Here we do not attempt to generalise our analysis along these lines, since we expect similar results. What we will do instead is to generate some support for the result from the static concept of evolutionarily stable strategies by explicitly analysing the dynamics of evolutionary processes. Such processes can des ibe the dynamics of genetical and also of cultural evolution of human populations. There are, however, at least two important differences between genetical and cultural evolution. First, genetical evolution is much slower. Second, cultural evolution does not necessarily require symmetry, as imposed in Figure III.1. We do not wish to exclude the possibility that our dynamic analysis is interpreted as a model of cultural evolution. Therefore, in the sequel we go back to the original game model of Figure II.1, instead of analysing the symmetric encounter in Figure III.1.

Evolutionary dynamics

Let us now turn to an alternative view on how preferences evolve. In Section III we had to symmetrize the game from Section II to apply the concept of an evolutionarily stable strategy. Although this is common in biology, it may not be entirely convincing, when applied to the problems currently facing Europe. Thus in the present section we offer an asymmetric alternative which tries to reflect the dynamics of cultural evolution. In biological terms the model could also be viewed as an evolutionary analysis of the interaction of two different species. Leaving the game from Section II asymmetric as it is, however, forces us to be more explicit on the evolutionary dynamics (as opposed to the static concept of evolutionarily stable strategies). The spirit of the analysis will closely resemble the replicator dynamics as studied by Taylor and Jonker [1978], but will be more general.

Still we will stick to the description of preferences by the two parameters C and P. But now both preference parameters are endogenous: C describes the costs, or rather: perception of costs, of "loosing a battle" to player 1, while P des ibes player 2's perception of the costs associated with loosing a conflict. In particular, imagine that there are two populations, one of potential migrants and one population of incumbents. Both populations are very large and the individuals, of which a given population consists, are identical, except for their

preference parameters concerning their perception of the costs of loosing a fight. These preference parameters may, however, not even influence the living standards of individuals and, therefore, their reproductive success. The extent to which preferences, measured by C for potential migrants and by P for incumbents, impact on living conditions is measured by a parameter δ, $0 \le \delta \le 1$. If $\delta = 0$, then preferences have no impact on the reproductive success of individuals at all, if $\delta = 1$, then C and P are fully deducted from the living standards. Since we make no further assumption on δ, both cases are covered by our analysis. As the interested reader can readily verify, we could even assume different δ's for incumbents and potential immigrants. Since nothing would be changed in our analysis by such an asymmetry of the δ's, we have sa ificed this generalisation for brevity.

Since individuals in a given population are identical except for preferences and their reproductive success depends on living conditions which may be unrelated to preferences, the evolution of the two populations is determined by the success, measured in terms of living standards, of certain preference types in the interaction of the two populations. Given our assumptions, the two populations can be fully described by the joint distribution $\Phi(C, P)$ of preference parameters (suppressing time subs ipts), where C is the parameter relevant for potential migrants and P is the parameter relevant for incumbents. Let $\phi(C, P)$ be the density corresponding to the distribution $\Phi(C, P)$ and define the marginal densities.

$$(IV.1) \qquad f(C) = \int_{-\infty}^{\infty} \phi(C, P)\, dP, \quad g(P) = \int_{-\infty}^{\infty} \phi(C, P)\, dC.$$

We assume that each period pairs of individuals, each pair consisting of one potential migrant and one incumbent, are chosen at random to play essentially the game from Figure IIi: The random matching technology is such that the probability π that a pair, consisting of a potential migrant with cost parameter C and an incumbent with cost parameter P, is matched is given by

$$(IV.2) \qquad \pi(C, P) = f(C) g(P).$$

Thus the matching technology is fair in the sense that it only depends on the marginal densities, such that the conditional probability that a potential migrant (incumbent) with parameter C (P) will meet on incumbent (migrant) with cost parameter P (C) does not depend on C (P), i.e. $\pi(P\,|\,C) = g(P)$ and $\pi(C\,|\,P) = f(C)$. Define

$(IV.3)$
$$
\begin{aligned}
G(y) &= \int_{-\infty}^{y} g(P)\,dP \\
F(x) &= \int_{-\infty}^{x} f(C)\,dC.
\end{aligned}
$$

In contrast to Section II we, however, assume here that the two players matched cannot verify each others type, that is: The potential migrant knows his parameter C, but not the preference parameter of the incumbent with whom he is matched, and the incumbent knows his P, but not the preference parameter of the migrant he confronts. Thus each pair plays the game from Section II under incomplete information about each other's cost parameter.

Still the incumbent's problem does not differ very much from player 2's problem in Section II. If the incumbent's P satisfies

$$
P > P^* = \frac{(1-w)(r-p)}{2\,w},
$$

then he will play Y and obtain a living standards $(r+p)/2$, if the potential migrant immigrates, and living standard r, if the potential migrant plays S. If the inequality is reversed, $P < P^*$, then the incumbent is determined to play F, if the migrant plays I. The potential migrant's problem is slightly more complicated, because he has to take into account both his C and the probability to be in a match with an incumbent, who satisfies $P > P^*$. From (IV.3) the probability to meet an incumbent with $P > P^*$ is given by $1 - G(P^*)$, such that a potential migrant will decide to stay home, if his C satisfies

$$
C > \frac{[1 - (1-w)G(P^*)](r-p)}{2(1-w)G(P^*)}.
$$

Define the function $\gamma\,[0, 1] \to \Re_+ \cup \{\infty\}$ by

$$
\gamma(a) = \frac{[1 - (1-w)a](r-p)}{2(1-w)a}, \qquad \forall a \in (0, 1].
$$

and by $\gamma(0) = +\infty$. With the help of this function which, evaluated at $G(P^*)$, gives the critical value of C, the expected living conditions of a potential migrant with preference parameter C, denoted for given F and G by $u_1(C)$, can be written as

$(IV.4)$
$$u_1(C) = \begin{cases} p, \text{ if } C > \gamma(G(P^*)) \text{ and } G(P^*) > 0, \\ G(P^*)[p + w\frac{r-p}{2} - \delta(1-w)C] + [1 - G(P^*)]\frac{r+p}{2}, \\ \text{otherwise} \end{cases}$$

Recall that δ is the parameter which measures how strongly the preference parameters influence living standards. The expected living conditions of an incumbent with preference parameter P can be written as

$(IV.5)$
$$u_2(P) = \begin{cases} r - w\, F(\gamma(G(P^*)))[\frac{r-p}{2} + \delta P], \text{ if } P \le P^*, \\ r - F(\gamma(G(P^*)))\frac{r-p}{2}, \text{ if } P > P^*. \end{cases}$$

Observe that both $u_1(C)$ and $u_2(P)$ are continuous. The average living conditions in the two populations, given F and G, are denoted by U_1 and U_2,

$$U_1 = \int_{-\infty}^{\infty} u_1(C)\, dF(C), \quad U_2 = \int_{-\infty}^{\infty} u_2(P)\, dG(P).$$

Using the definition of γ, these functions can be written as

$(IV.6.1)$
$$U_1 = \begin{cases} +(1-w)G(P^*)[\gamma(G(P^*))F(\gamma(G(P^*)))- \\ -\delta \int_{-\infty}^{\gamma(G(P^*))} C\, dF(C)], \text{ if } G(P^*) > 0, \\ \frac{r+p}{2}, \text{ if } G(P^*) = 0 \end{cases}$$

and as

$(V.6.2)$
$$U_2 = \begin{cases} r - F(\gamma(GP^*)))[(1 - (1-w)G(P^*))\frac{r-p}{2}+ \\ +\delta w \int_{-\infty}^{P^*} P\, dG(P)], \text{ if } G(P^*) > 0, \\ \frac{r+p}{2}, \text{ if } G(P^*) = 0 \end{cases}$$

with U_1 and U_2 again continuous. Thus both individual as well as average living conditions depend on the two marginal distributions of the preference parameters in the two populations. We now study the evolution of F and G over time.

Let $\mathcal{H}$ be the set of all continuously differentiable distributions on $\Re^2$. Then $\Phi \in \mathcal{H}$ and an evolutionary process can be defined as a mapping $\varphi \mathcal{H} \times \Re_+ \to \mathcal{H}$ or $(\Phi_o, t) \mapsto \Phi_t$. Suppose the distribution of the preference parameters in the two populations at some point in time t is given by $\Phi(C, P)$ with marginal densities $f_t(C)$ and $g_t(C)$. Then the family of evolutionary processes which we will consider is the family of processes which satisfy

(IV.7)
$$\dot{f}_t(C) < 0 \iff f_t(C)[u_1(C) - U_1] < 0$$
$$\dot{g}_t(P) > 0 \iff g_t(P)[u_2(P) - U_2] > 0.$$

This is the family of evolutionary processes such that, if some value of the preference parameter which is still present in the population generates worse living conditions than what obtains on average in the respective population, then the (marginal) frequency of this value of the preference parameter shrinks over time. On the other hand, if some value of the preference parameter results in superior living conditions as compared to the population average, then the (marginal) frequency of this value of the parameter will in ease over time, provided it is still present in the population. A *quasi-stationary* distribution $\Phi \in \mathcal{H}$ is one which satisfies $\dot{f}(C) = \dot{g}(P) = 0$, for all (C, P) in the support of Φ.

Theorem 2: (i) *Whenever $0 < G_0(P^*) < 1$ and $0 < F_0(\gamma(G_0(P^*))) < 1$ holds, then for any $\varepsilon > 0$ there is some $t_\varepsilon > 0$ such that $G_t(P^*) \geq 1 - \varepsilon$ and $F_t(\gamma(1 - \varepsilon)) \geq 1 - \varepsilon$ for all $t \geq t_\varepsilon$.*

(ii) *Any quasi-stationary distribution satisfies either*

$$G(P^*) > 0 = F(\gamma(G(P^*))) \quad \text{or} \quad G(P^*) = 1 = F(\gamma(1)).$$

Proof(i): Assume that for some $t \geq 0$ one has $0 < G_t(P^*) < 1$ and $0 < F_t(\gamma(G_t(P^*))) < 1$.

From $F_t(\gamma(G_t(P^*))) < 1$ it follows that there exists some $C > \gamma(G_t(P^*))$ for which $f_t(C) > 0$. For such a C which satisfies $C > \gamma(G(P^*))$ the payoff $u_1(C)$ is independent of C. Using **(IV.4)** and **(IV.6.1)** one has for this C that

$$u_1(C) - U_1 = (1 - w)G_t(P^*)[\delta \int_{-\infty}^{\gamma(G_t(P^*))} C \, dF_t(C) - \gamma(G_t(P^*))F_t(\gamma(G_t(P^*)))] < 0$$

where the final strict inequality follows from $\Phi_t \in \mathcal{H}$ which implies that F_t cannot have any atoms, such that $F_t(\gamma(G_t(P^*))) > 0$ implies that there is some $C < \gamma(G_t(P^*))$ for which $f_t(C) > 0$. We conclude from **(IV.7)** that $\dot{f}_t(C) < 0$ for all $C > \gamma(G_t(P^*))$ which are still present in the population, $f_t(C) > 0$.

On the other hand $G_t(P^*) < 1$ implies that these exists $P > P^*$ such that $g_t(P) > 0$, and for any such P one obtains from **(IV.5)** and **(IV.6.2)** that (again by the fact that for such a P the payoff $u_2(P)$ is independent of P)

$$
\begin{aligned}
u_2(P) - U_2 &= \delta w\, F_t(\gamma(G_t(P^*))) \int_{-\infty}^{P^*} P\, dG_t(P) - \\
&\quad - (1-w)G_t(P^*)F_t(\gamma(G_t(P^*)))\frac{r-p}{2} = \\
&= w\, F_t(\gamma(G_t(P^*)))[\delta \int_{-\infty}^{P^*} P\, dG_t(P) - P^*\, G_t(P^*)] < 0,
\end{aligned}
$$

where the final strict inequality again follows from $\Phi_t \in \mathcal{H}$, because then G_t cannot have any atoms such that $G_t(P^*) > 0$ implies that there is some $P < P^*$ such that $g_t(P) > 0$. Thus from **(IV.7)** one obtains $\dot{g}_t(P) < 0$ for all $P > P^*$ for which $g_t(P) > 0$.

Under the assumption $0 < G_0(P^*) < 1$ and $0 < F_0(\gamma(G_0(P^*))) < 1$ and for given $\varepsilon > 0$ let t_1 denote the smallest $t \geq 0$ such that $G_t(P^*) \geq 1 - \varepsilon$. By the above argument t_1 ist finite. Also by the above argument there is some finite $t_2 \geq 0$ such that $F_{t_2}(\gamma(G_{t_2}(P^*))) \geq 1 - \varepsilon$. Since γ is decreasing, the latter inequality implies $F_t(\gamma(G_t(P^*))) \geq 1 - \varepsilon$ for all $t \geq \max(t_1, t_2)$. Setting $t_\varepsilon = \max(t_1, t_2)$ thus proves our claim.

(ii) Under quasi-stationarity $F(\gamma(G(P^*))) < 1$ implies $G(P^*) > 0$, because otherwise $G(P^*) = 0$ would imply $\gamma(G(P^*)) = \infty$ which would imply $F(\gamma(G(P^*))) = 1$. Also $F(\gamma(G(P^*))) < 1$ implies from $\Phi \in \mathcal{H}$ that there exists some $C > \gamma(G(P^*))$ such that $f(C) > 0$. For this C one would, under quasi-stationarity, have to have

$$
u_1(C) - U_1 = (1-w)G(P^*)[\delta \int_{-\infty}^{\gamma(G(P^*))} C\, dF(C) - \gamma(G(P^*))F(\gamma(G(P^*)))] = 0.
$$

But the latter can only hold, if $F(\gamma(G(P^*))) = 0$. Thus the first possibility of a quasi-stationary distribution is given by $G(P^*) > 0 = F(\gamma(G(P^*)))$.

If, on the other hand, $F(\gamma(G(P^*))) = 1$, but $G(P^*) < 1$, then there exists some $P > P^*$ for which $g(P) > 0$ such that

$$\delta \int_{-\infty}^{P^*} P\, dG(P) - P^* G(P^*) = 0$$

would have to hold under quasi-stationarity. From $\Phi \in \mathcal{H}$ it follows, however, that the latter inequality cannot be satisfied. Thus $F(\gamma(G(P^*))) = 1$ implies under quasi-stationarity that $G(P^*) = 1$. Thus the second possibility of a quasi-stationary distribution is given by $G(P^*) = 1 = F(\gamma(1))$.

□

What the Theorem says can be rephrased as follows: If the initial distribution of preferences is such that some migration at least will take place, $F_0(\gamma(G_0(P^*))) > 0$, then within finite time any evolutionary process from the family (IV.7) will lead to a distribution of preferences which has alm ost all its mass concentrated on the region "that we are afraid of". Moreover, any distribution Φ, whose marginal densities remain unchanged by evolutionary forces ("quasi-stationarity"), must either be concentrated entirely on the region "that we are afraid of", or must satisfy that virtually no migration at all tak es place, $F(\gamma(G(P^*))) = 0$.

Interpretation and political conclusions

Although $P^- < P^*$ is the only evolutionarily stable strategy of Section III for all reasonable constellations (r, p, C, w) of exogeneous parameters and only $P < P^*$ can be dynamically stable in Section IV the stable genotype is not completely independent of the exogeneous parameters since $P^- < P^*$ and since P^* is determined by these parameters according to equation (III.1).

Now the parameter P des ibes the feelings of the incumbent after an unsuccessful attempt to throw out the invader. Whereas a positive value of P expresses anger, a negative value of P can be interpreted as enjoying a multi-cultural society. Our analysis has shown that it is not the sign of P which matters. Thus a political debate whether a multi-cultural society is good or bad might miss the point. What matters is whether P is larger or smaller than P^*, since, as illustrated Figure II.2, behaviour is ucially different for the case $P > P^*$ for which the 'liberal paradise' results and for $P < P^*$, where the incumbent always threatens to thr ow out the invader.

The positive critical parameter value P^* depends positively on the dis epancy $r - p$ of the prior living standard as well as on the relative probability $(1 - w)/w$ by which an invader will leave, when he faces resistance against immigration. Many political measures currently taken in Western European countries are attempts to reduce the dis epancy in living conditions. The mob, responsible for riots against immigrants in Germany in 1991 and 1992, is definitely trying to in ease the relative probability $(1 - w)/w$.

But, of course, such a discussion assumes that the parameter P is given whereas P^* can still be influenced politically. Our evolutionary analysis shows that the 'liberal paradise', i.e. $P > P^*$, can only be an episode since evolutionary forces in ease the relative frequency of genotypes with $P < P^*$, provided there is indeed any seizable immigration. Depending on whether C is greater or smaller than $\frac{w(r-p)}{2(1-w)}$, the stable situation is therefore either 'preventive resistance' or 'what we are afraid of'. It is interesting to note that the itical value $\frac{w(r-p)}{2(1-w)}$ for C depends on the exogeneous parameters also via $r - p$ and $(1 - w)/w$. But whereas an in ease of $r - p$ enlarges the parameter region for territorial fights, i.e. the solution region (I, F) in Figure II.2, an in ease of $(1 - w)/w$ enlarges the region for 'preventive resistance'.

If resistance against mass immigration cannot be prevented, as suggested by our evolutionary analysis, it becomes an essential political task to determine the relative size of parameter regions, because measures geared at influencing $r - p$ and $(1 - w)/w$, discussed above, can be also viewed as attempts to influence the border line between the two regions 'preemptive resistance' and 'what we are afraid of' in Figure II.2.

According to our approach natural selection has brought about a human genotype with $P < P^*$ where the difference $P^* - P$ should be rather large due to changing environments with different levels of P^*. In particular, P can assume negative values which explains why incumbents sometimes claim that they enjoy other cultures although they resist against mass immigration. Whereas in evolutionary biology genes determine behavior directly, we have assumed genetically determined preference parameters which are influenced by natural selection.

Of course, a genetically determined preference parameter P does not exclude that the phenotypical P can be influenced by education and the political climate. One could, for instance, assume an inborn preference parameter P, whose actual level can change within certain bounds due to phenotypical experiences like education, individual living conditions, exposition to other cultures, etc. Many political campaigns can be considered as attempts to fight against an inborn animosity against immigrants. If, however, there is an inborn animosity against invaders, one has to try continuously to change this attitude, at least as long as the country is facing mass immigration. Since resistance against mass immigration is such a likely phenomenon, one should try to understand those, who really do suffer from mass immigration, and take political actions towards the problem. This certainly may involve measures not captured by our model, like distributional policies among the incumbents.

Our general approach can be applied to other game models than the one of Figure II.1, as long as the dis epancy of living conditions is independent of the play. Certainly, if mass immigration is accompanied by economic integration, equalization of living standards, and finally a Pareto-improvement for the whole world, the process towards the liberal paradise can potentially be achieved. We have selected the game model in Figure II.1 since it captures the essential aspects of the current European problem in the simplest way. The main restrictive assumption of Figure II.1 is probably that only the play (I, F, R) induces feelings concerning multi-cultural societies although another play, namely (I, Y), also results in a multi-cultural society.

If (I, Y) also induces the payoff $\frac{r+p}{2} - P$ for the incumbents, the 'liberal paradise' would disappear, if $w < 1$ and $\frac{r-p}{2} + P > 0$. Consequently, the evolutionary drive for the parameter P towards P^- would become even stronger. Thus Figure II.1 seems to capture the more interesting situation where emotions concerning immigrants are triggered by unsuccessful resistance against mass immigration.

In our view, such an assumption can be defended. Many developed countries have experienced massive immigration movements without serious political debates, especially in situations of high employment. This indicates that emotions concerning immigration become virulent only if one has been strictly opposed to it but unable to prevent it.

If animosity against immigrants or sympathy for a multi-culture society is triggered by unsuccessfull resistance against mass immigration, behavior will depend ucially on the political climate which is not only influenced by the political parties but al so by the mass media. A political debate, like the one in Germany in 1991, might trigger emotions which will seriously endanger the prospects for a peaceful life in a multi-cultural society - as it happened in Germany 1992.

Campaigns aiming at measures against mass immigration may help to win the next election, but may also induce long lasting animosity against immigrants, possibly also against earlier immigrants, who up to now did not encounter any resistance.

If mankind has an inborn tendency to resist against mass immigration, this can be politically exploited, especially by extremely rightist parties. To avoid this, one may want to limit immigration. Actually this is what we observe in all developed countries which partly rely on 'preventive resistance 'and partly experience 'what we are afraid of'. As predicted for the simplistic framework of our model, 'the liberal paradise' does not seem to survive in the real world either.

Of course, one may argue that in case of the 'liberal paradise' the dis epancy $r - p$ in living conditions would vanish, i.e. 'the liberal paradise' could be
responsible for equal living conditions in countries without entry barriers. And
this is perhaps the major lesson concerning the responsibility of economists: To
convince the public that convergence of living standards is the most effective
way to avoid political unrest.

Footnotes

1   Johann Wolfgang Goethe-Universität, FB Wirtschaftswissenschaften,
Frankfurt am Main, Germany

2   Institute for Advanced Studies, Dept. of Economics, Vienna, Austria

References

Güth, W. (January 1990). *Incomplete information about reciprocal incentives - An evolutionary approach to explaining cooperative behavior.* Unpublished manuscript.

Güth, W., & Yaari, M. (1990). *Explaining reciprocal behavior in simple strategic games: An evolutionary approach.* Unpublished manuscript.

Maynard Smith, J., & Price, G.R. (1973). The logic of animal conflict. *Nature, 246,* 15-18.

Selten, R. (1983). Evolutionary stability in extensive 2-person games. *Mathematical Social Sciences, 5,* 269-363.

Taylor, P.D., & Jonker, L.B. (1978). Evolutionarily stable strategies and game dynamics. *Math. Biosc., 40*, 145-156.

van Damme, E. (1987). *Stability and perfection of nash equilibria*. Heidelberg: Springer Verlag.

Weissing, F.J. (1991). Evolutionary stability and dynamic stability in a class of evolutionary normal form games. In R. Selten (Ed.), *Game equilibrium models I: Evolution and game dynamics*. Heidelberg: Springer Verlag.

Authors index

Subject index